Making Public Policy

Making Public Policy

Studies in American Politics

EDITED BY JOHN BRIGHAM
University of Massachusetts, Amherst

D. C. HEATH AND COMPANY
Lexington, Massachusetts   Toronto

Printed in the United States of America.

International Standard Book Number: 0–669–00225–9

Library of Congress Catalog Card Number: 76–20832

Preface

Making Public Policy has been developed as a supplementary reader for introductory courses on American government and politics. It is a source of documentary materials presented in a topical format, and it contains court decisions and related legal material, such as the arguments of counsel; an initiative petition and samples of the debate that surrounded it; a description of a day in the life of a President of the United States; statements from the Federal Reserve Board about what it is trying to do; and materials from committee hearings and from debates on the floor of Congress. The collection thus examines some of the specific tools of the American process of government while suggesting their relationships to actual policy making. This approach has been taken in order to minimize description and analysis in favor of actual source materials.

It is my belief that in their "natural" form the following materials contribute to the substantive debate and procedural developments that comprise the policy making process. Each topic differs as to the amount of introductory and analytical material that has been supplied. In order to provide a collection that complements rather than duplicates the available introductory texts and monographs, the materials maintain their original style. Only where material was unrelated to the issue or political activity being considered was it eliminated.

Policy making, the focus indicated in the title, suggests another complement to the usual approach of introductory courses in government and political science. The title does not imply either a new subfield within political science or a fourth branch of government. It emerges from my belief that most students care about politics or government because it concerns issues that matter to them. Studies that reveal how policy is made are a useful addition to courses whose primary focus is on the institutions of government. My concern with policy formation led to the decision to provide students with a chance to examine original documents that represent the political activity surrounding particularly challenging national issues.

By focusing on policy making, the book raises complexities in politics that add depth to an institutional focus. I have sought to encourage a point of view that integrates process and outcome by emphasizing the materials that are either authoritative or influence the decisions of authorities. Solutions, in the form of policies, emerge from the interaction of interests and ideas with institutions. The following materials — in their style, content, and function in the political process — present both the state of the process and the outcome. There is a message in each of these documents. Each author, whether a governmental official or an active citizen, has some point to make. A citizen might feel that a land-use permit will endanger her property value; a judge may propose that a statute is not consistent with constitutional guarantees. In isolation, that message is generally the reader's primary concern. Within the context of policy formation, however, those messages can be seen as part of a whole. Each individual statement comprises a reaction to certain competing interests and ideas, its form and content structured by the institutions of government and the traditions of politics. The citizen's letter may reveal a commitment to an established "right" and at the same time an interest shared by other citizens. The judge may represent a particular reading of the Constitution, interpretation of a certain statute, or understanding of his role as a judge. The organization of *Making Public Policy* shows how various issues are treated and different policies result from political activity in the United States.

Each chapter takes a situation and divides the material into sections that treat an aspect of American government or the policy making process. The chapter on abortion, for instance, emphasizes public law. It is divided into sections on the constitutional context, the reaction to a Supreme Court decision in Congress and in the state legislatures, and finally the impact on local policy. These sections are meant to constitute units of study. They reflect the chronological development of public policy and a concern that, where possible, traditional subjects of study in the American government curriculum be identified. Only in a few cases are individual documents, such as a decision of the Supreme Court or a statute, presented at enough length to make up a complete section. Rather, the plan of the book has been to provide within the sections materials that encourage discussion of the relationships among the various documents. It was necessary, of course, to choose among a mass of materials. The attempt was to balance variety with coherence of development; many valuable selections could not be included because of the focus on one process and one policy area.

Chapter 1 deals with the subject of abortion. It was developed to show the importance of the legal setting to policy making at all levels of government. Chapter 2 looks at appropriations, the budgetary process, and the subject of military spending. Congress is the focus, but, of necessity, the President and private interests manifest themselves in important ways. Chapter 3 concerns the Presidency and the President — how he works, what he produces, and how his personality may effect public policy. Chapter 4 examines management of the economy and the efforts to develop a coordinated system of national economic planning. Chapter 5 looks at the bureaucratic relationship between the Bureau of Indian Affairs and native Americans. The relationship between this particular institution and its clientele provides an insight into the nature of powerlessness. Chapter 6 focuses on citizen participation, interest groups, and policy making at the state level. It recounts the effort to save the California coastline from overdevelopment.

The particular outcomes shown here will, we hope, be of lasting interest. They present some of the more significant recent "challenges" to the American polity. Yet the topics have been chosen and developed in the belief that their value will be assessed with regard to their contribution to an understanding of the policy making process. Whether these issues continue to reach the headlines, they will doubtless remain controversial in and around the centers of government. In this sense, the original issues have elicited responses that will themselves generate policy making efforts. Familiarity with the process, as well as with the outcome, is essential for a continuing understanding of the dynamics of politics.

Kenneth M. Dolbeare suggested that a collection of readings might show government in operation, not just talk about it. That is what I have tried to present. David Fourney, Michael Semler, and Linda Medcalf each contributed substantially to individual case studies and assisted in working out the conception. Jim Piereson and Larry Preston each made important suggestions that went into the finished collection. Donna Parker, the staff of the Graduate School of Public Affairs of the State University of New York at Albany, and Ellie Perkins provided essential assistance in preparation of the manuscript. Meredith W.

Michaels offers a healthy skepticism concerning the ways of political science and is a nice person to live with. I am fortunate that they have all been in on this.

JOHN BRIGHAM
Amherst, Massachusetts

Contents

PREFACE   v

INTRODUCTION: Toward Understanding

Public Policy Making   xvii

CHAPTER 1   The Supreme Court and the Law: Reform and

Reaction as Abortion Policy   1

JOHN BRIGHAM, EDITOR

Model Penal Code   4

Section A   The Constitutional Framework   7

Challenging the Texas Antiabortion Law   8
  The Texas Abortion Statute   8
  Oral Arguments in Texas   10
All the Way to the Supreme Court   12
  Biographies of the Supreme Court Justices   12
  The Opinion of the United States Supreme Court in *Roe* v. *Wade*   15

*Section B   The Federal and State Responses to the Court's
            Decision*   22

The Federal Response   23

        Constitutional Aspects of the Right to Limit Childbearing: Report
        of the United States Commission on Civil Rights   23

Senate Debate on Antiabortion Amendment to the Social
Security Act   23

The Reaction in the States   34

The Revised Massachusetts Law on Abortion   37

Section C   The Trial of Dr. Edelin   39

The Indictment of Kenneth Edelin   41

Pretrial Maneuvers   42

Hearing on Motions   43

Affidavit in Support of Motion for Grand Jury Testimony   43

Argument in Support of Motion for a "Bill of Particulars"   44

Argument in Support of Motion to Dismiss a Request by the Defense
for Further Specification in the Indictment   46

Query in Motion for a "Bill of Particulars"   47

Reply of District Attorney's Office   47

The Jury   47

A Selection from the Voir Dire   49

"Profile of a Jury," Gary Griffith   51

Postconviction Interviews with the Trial Jurors   53

"The Edelin Jury: Side-Stepping the Reasonable
Doubts," Gary Griffith   54

The Reaction to the Verdict and the Appeal   62

Further Readings   64

CHAPTER 2   Congress and the Budgetary Process: The Politics
of Military Appropriations   65

DAVID FOURNEY, EDITOR

Section A   Realizing Congressional Budgetary Power   68

"The Department of Defense and the New Budget
Process," Burton B. Moyer, Jr.   70

"Congress Report/Alice Rivlin Named Chief of Congressional
Budget Office," Joel Havemann   76

Letter to Dr. Alice Rivlin from Senator Muskie and
Representative Adams 79

Section B   The Military in Congress 80

The President and the Pentagon 83

Remarks by President Ford to a Dinner Meeting of the Conference
Board 83

Statement of Hon. James R. Schlesinger, Secretary of Defense 84

The Military Procurement Bill 88

The Politics of the Budget Process 94

"A Change of Style on House Armed Services," from
the *Congressional Quarterly* 94

"Pentagon Wins Again," John Isaacs 98

Debate on the Conference Report, Defense Authorization
Act of 1976 105

"The Senate Shell Game," Rowland Evans and Robert Novak 110

The Views of the Members 112

Dissenting Views of Hon. Elizabeth Holtzman 113

"Arms Lobbyists Rely on Varied Sources Including Liberals
Seeking to Protect Workers' Jobs," Richard D. Lyons 114

Section C   The B–1 Bomber Controversy 119

The Need for the B–1 Bomber: Remarks of Major General H.M.
Darmstandler to the Commonwealth Club of California 120

Proceedings in the House Appropriations Committee 124

Anti B–1 Bomber Literature 128

Appeal from Clergy and Laity Concerned 129

"The B–1 Bomber: Is It Worth $92 Billion?" *Defense Monitor* 131

Appropriations for the Bomber 136

Department of Defense Appropriation Authorization Act, 1976 136

Further Readings 137

CHAPTER 3 The Presidency: The Policy Agenda, Keeping House, Making Policy 138

JOHN BRIGHAM, EDITOR

Section A   The "Energy Crisis"   139

Energy Becomes an Issue   140

"Motorists Line Up For Gasoline Here," David A. Andelman   141

Energy Policy Options   144

"The Range of Options in Energy Policy," Preliminary Report of the Ford Foundation   145

Making Policy Choices   148

"Attacks on Oil Industry Grow Fiercer," Michael C. Jensen   148

Section B   A President's Day   155

"Tuesday: A Hard-Edged Conservative Voice," John Hersey   159

Section C   The President, the Congress, and Energy Policy   172
Edited by John Brigham and Larry Preston

Economic Analysis of President Ford's Energy Program   180
Further Readings   198

CHAPTER 4   Agency and Advice: The Determinants of National Economic Policy   199

JOHN BRIGHAM AND KENNETH M. DOLBEARE, EDITORS

Section A   Determining Economic Policy   201

The Functions of the Federal Reserve   202
The Federal Reserve Explains Itself   204

Comments by Arthur Burns on the Role of the Federal Reserve System   205

"Monetary Policy as a 'Social Science'," Robert C. Holland   208

The Congress and the Federal Reserve   209

"Burns Tells Congress Fed Hasn't Shifted To Deliberately
Tighter Monetary Policy," *Wall Street Journal*   210

Criticism of the Autonomy of the Federal Reserve Board   212

House Concurrent Resolution 133   213

The Role of Economic Advisers   215

1975 Annual Report of the Council of Economic Advisers   218

Consenting to the Advisers   222

Hearing in the United States Senate on the Nomination of
Alan Greenspan to Become Chairman of the Council of
Economic Advisers   223

The Influence of Advice   229

Economic Report of President Ford   230

Section B   *The Debate and the Strategy of Economic Planning
Legislation*   233

S. 1795, The Balanced Growth and Economic Planning Act of 1975   234

94th Congress, 1st Session: S. 1795   234

The Debate on Planning   245

"The Fear of Planning," *Challenge* Editorial   245

"A Planned Economy in the U.S.?" Jack Friedman   248

"The Empty Promise of the Planner: Private Enterprise
or National Economic Planning?" Thomas A. Murphy   253

"Balanced Growth and Economic Planning Act of 1975,"
Senator Jacob Javits   257

"Who Will Plan the Planned Economy?" James R. Crotty
and Raford Boddy   262

The Educational Process and Legislative Strategy   271

Remarks by Hubert H. Humphrey on Legislative Strategy   271

S. 50: A Summary of the Full Employment and Balanced Growth
Act of 1976   272

Legislation and Education: The Prospects for Economic Planning   275

Further Readings   276

CHAPTER 5   Bureaucracy: Formulating and Implementing

National Indian Policy   277

LINDA MEDCALF, EDITOR

Section A   *History of the Policy Making Process*   280

"Federal Indian Policies: From the Colonial Period Through
the Early 1970's," Bureau of Indian Affairs   281

"Our Brother's Keeper," *The Citizen's Advocate*   304

Section B   *Present Policies and Problems*   305

Good Intentions   307

Nomination of Morris Thompson To Be Commissioner of
the Bureau of Indian Affairs   307

The Perception of Inaction   313

"Colorado River Tribes Charge BIA Delays: Water Rights
Issue," Rupert Costo   313

"BIA now Charged with Foot-Dragging, Indecision by Indian
Regents Council," Jeannette Henry   315

"BIA 'No Help' In Education, Testimony Says," *Wassaja*   316

Bureaucratic Responsibility and Conflicts of Interest   319

Hearings Before the Committee on Interior and Insular
Affairs of the United States Senate on the Nomination
of Thomas S. Kleppe To Become Secretary of the Interior   320

Hearings on the Nomination of Dale Kent Frizzell To Be
Undersecretary of the Department of the Interior   324

Letter from Dale Kent Frizzell to Henry M. Jackson   330

Section C   *Meanwhile — The Individual Client*   334

Reports from Frank's Landing: A Case Study of a Bureaucratic
Relationship   335

"Frank's Landing," Ellen Yaroshefsky   335

"Frank's Landing Flooding Given BIA Priority," Larry Cantil   337

"At Frank's Landing," Larry Cantil   338

"Strange Faces Appear Along the Nisqually," Larry Cantil   341

"Frank's Landing Slipping Away," Larry Cantil and Kai Sylva   342

"Who Is Going To Do Something?" Andy de los Angeles   343

Two Examples of Dependency   344

Hearings Before the Committee on Agriculture, Ninety-First Congress, First Session   345

"Traders on the Navajo Reservation," Southwestern Indian Development, Inc.   350

"Voices from Wounded Knee," *Akwesasne Notes*   354

Further Readings   354

CHAPTER 6   **Interest Groups and the Governmental Process:**

Public Policy for the California Coast   356

JOHN BRIGHAM AND MICHAEL SEMLER, EDITORS

Section A   Interests in Conflict   361

"The New Tide of Coastal Legislation," Norman Sanders   362

Qualifying the Initiative   364

"Coastline Conservationists Switch to Initiative After Senate Unit Kills Bill," Richard Rodda   365

"Stage One — Signature Collection," Janet Adams   366

Initiative Measure To Be Submitted Directly to the Electors   369

The Electoral Process   371

The Campaign for Proposition 20   371

"The New Tide" [continued], Norman Sanders   371

Opponents of Proposition 20   373

"Opponents of Prop. 20, Some from East, Pour Nearly $1–Million into Fight," Gladwin Hill   373

Official Ballot Summary of the Issues Behind Proposition 20   375

Coastal Zone Conservation Act, Initiative   375

Section B *The Commissions and the Final Plan* 385

Putting the Commissions into Operation 386

Staffing the Commissions 386

"The New Tide" [continued], Norman Sanders 386

"The Coastal Zone: Problems, Priorities, and People," Joseph E. Bodovitz 388

The Encina Power Plant Controversy 392

"Statement re Proposed Expansion of the Encina Power Plant," League of Women Voters 394

"Statement to California Coastal Commission," Alan M. Schneider 395

Letter to the Board of Supervisors, County of San Diego, from Lee R. Taylor 396

Minutes of the Meeting of the Board of Supervisors 398

Developing a Final Plan 399

The Preliminary Coastal Plan 399

Selections from the Commissions' Report 399

"Council Samples Voter Attitudes on Environment and Economy," *Environment and the Economy* 408

The Response from the Planning and Conservation League 412

Testimony of the Coastal Plan Task Force, Planning and Conservation League 412

Public Hearing on the Preliminary Plan 414

Summary of Joint Public Hearing on Preliminary Plan, Eureka, California 415

Carrying Out the Plan 419

Selection from the Final Coastal Plan Submitted to the California Legislature, December 1975 420

Further Readings 424

Introduction

Toward Understanding Public Policy Making

Concentration simply on the insights and evidence offered by academics, no matter how sound, is insufficient preparation for political activity or the analysis of politics as it reveals itself in the world. Although knowledge of institutional structures is a necessary background for understanding policy making, as presented in introductory texts such knowledge is difficult to relate to activities outside of the classroom, and the format is too specific to be translated into insight about actual situations. There is a gap that exists between introductory texts and the process itself. The actual sources, by which policy formation is known, are missing. The present collection tries to fill this gap by providing source materials that convey the atmosphere of policy making. For those willing to explore the materials and investigate their relationship, the possibility, indeed the promise, is held out that the actions and events appearing in everyday life, on any number of issues, will be more readily interpreted for their political significance.

Those wishing to affect or merely understand politics must be willing to make the effort of interpretation. The public's information about politics — a report in the press, some commentary, or a political speech — is presented as if each item told the whole story, as if it were the last word. At least the actors usually hope their statements will have that effect. Neither politicians nor commentators want to point out the faults in their position; they seldom present the other side in a credible light. But public policy is full of competing, often contradictory presentations, and the citizen is not free to decide among them if he or she is unable to compare, to look critically at each and to interpret what it may mean. Many insights about the policy making process that may be drawn out of the materials in this collection have not been explicitly

formulated. Here, to a marked degree, are the bits and pieces of political life. Although they have been ordered and briefly commented
upon, they will have to be examined carefully and compared with
formal political analysis. It will be necessary to put the parts together.
Suggestions along these lines have been provided as comments upon
the documents. The material requires active participation by the reader.
It involves more than simply understanding someone else's analysis;
it at least suggests the importance of formulating one's own theory
from the materials available.

It is by confronting the actual materials produced during the process
of making policy decisions that one may develop and refine a capacity
to understand politics. The outputs of agencies and the reports of observers, commentators, and participants challenge the interested citizen
to assess the political process as it is revealed through public, generally
available records. The isolation in which we find the source materials
too often precludes analysis in depth, but once they are assembled,
the interconnections become clearer. It is the way they are interrelated,
the common influences and limitations on thought and action, that enable one to grasp what these diverse sources have to do with one another. A decision of the United States Supreme Court on a woman's
right to an abortion, debate in the Senate over an amendment to a
health care appropriations bill, a transcript from the jury selection in
the trial of a Boston doctor, and a local newspaper account of the trial,
taken together constitute the politics of abortion and suggest some of
the elements of national abortion policy.

People in politics leave signs revealing their activity in the policy
making process. These are traces that provide a record of policy formation. Sometimes the signs are hard to avoid, as with the President's
State of the Union address; in other instances, they must be sought
out, as in the case of committee hearings or reports on the background
of jurors. At times, the material evidence is specifically designated for
public consumption, and in other cases it clearly is not. There is, however, enough in the public record, if one looks around, to establish
what it is that has happened or is happening. Understanding the inter-
relations — the place of each element in the process — gives the material its significance.

This understanding requires that one recognize the unique practices
that constitute the political process. Various actions have their own
forms which are the key to their meaning. Testimony before a Senate

committee takes a different form and has different consequences from testimony before a trial judge. A newspaper editorial differs in form from a directive issued by the Department of Health, Education and Welfare. Understanding their implications requires understanding the unique characteristics of each. They must be recognized before their significance can be examined. A capacity to interpret the nature of these actions is thus a dimension of political insight.

Political skill involves knowing patterns of activity as well as recognizing individual events. To understand the above activities one must be familiar with their use, and their use is influenced by traditions of appropriate activity. One can find the qualities of a bill — its language and form — quite readily in some of the materials that follow. But there are deeper dimensions to the policy making process, such as knowledge of the situations to which a bill can be addressed, what can be included in it, and what its impact is likely to be. Although one finds questions, sometimes answers, and often policy positions at press conferences, some things do not occur, such as the votes that are characteristic of legislative bodies or the cross examination of a criminal trial. For some, these procedures are obvious. Therein lies their power. It is when forms of action are taken for granted that they have the greatest significance. In learning how politics is conducted, it is therefore necessary to uncover the obvious.

Public documents represent meaningful discourse on policy, and no doubt discussion will be generated on the merits of the positions advocated in the following pages. But the debate over the substantive issues is a secondary matter. It is far more important that these materials be viewed as the basis for studying the process of policy formation in a variety of contexts. Students might, for instance, look at the consequences that follow from particular activities. What is the significance of a "letter to the editor"? What is the relationship of such a letter to the outcome of policy making? What can a petition be expected to accomplish? What is the effect of an appellate brief? These are the sort of questions to which the collection is addressed.

In the process of learning from these materials, one should seek to integrate practical experience with critical insight. When a student is immersed in political controversy and encouraged to derive general principles from it, the insight that may result leads to increased ability to handle new situations. Such insight goes beyond comprehension of what has been said to a perspective on the nature of the political process. It takes relatively less effort for the novice political actor to understand the ideas in a bill than it does for him to understand the role of ideas in politics. Critical attention to the supporters of legislation is one way of understanding the process, but comprehension is not complete without knowledge of the ideas and institutional structures as they influence the allocation of political rewards. It is anticipated that the student will be able to derive from the materials contained in this reader both an understanding of what politics looks like and a sense of how it functions.

Although structured around traditional institutions, for the most part, the story of policy making goes beyond the institutions. Institutions are sources of power. The effort is not to convey the formal rules and regulations, but rather to cultivate a capacity to understand how they work in practice. A key to the operating reality is sought. It is necessary to recognize the operational rules, the traditions as they are written down; but it is also essential to recognize that these rules have a contingent character. They depend on acceptance by people involved in politics for their own actual significance. The collection, therefore, looks to the practical influence rather than the rules per se.

The political acts presented here rely on traditional rules of politics. District attorneys can bring indictments; citizens in some states have the option of an initiative; the President formulates a national budget. The significance of the acts depends on changing circumstances. Decisions of the Supreme Court alter the context of politics but settlement of the issues brought before the Court depends on public reactions; citizens may create governing bodies and rather quickly lose control of their operation; and the policies of a President may not be consistent with political realities and, as a result, may fail to be accepted. The way that participants come to understand these activities determines the process of politics. A good deal of important political activity is influenced not so much by rules, but rather by the sorts of things that people understand to have a bearing on the conduct of politics. Through attention to such expectations, the student may learn to recognize the nature of the process in terms not simply of rules but of acceptable activity.

There have been a number of considerations in the selection and editing of these cases that may guide the analysis. Each body of materials has been assembled with attention to three aspects of the policy making process. These are (1) the interests and actors involved; (2)

the substantive beliefs and traditional interpretations through which the political world is understood; and (3) the formal procedures, rules, and institutions that constitute the authoritative structure of government.

In the first place, there are actors in each of these policy areas. They have their own backgrounds, attitudes, and personalities. They represent interests and bring influence to bear on the policy making process. They include citizens, professional politicians, and experts in such matters as law and economics. There is evident here both a personal dimension and a public realm in which the personal operates. The dreams and ideals of a President, as well as his ego, are important in making policy. This is clearly the case with congressmen, district attorneys, jurors, and voters. But influence depends on public recognition, a perception of power or authority, in order for an individual to have an effect on the process. Whether it is a judge, the president of General Motors, or a citizen activist, who these people are and how other people react to their positions determine to a considerable extent what positions they will take.

There is also something like a script that exists in the system of beliefs in each of the policy areas considered. It is usually traditional; there is very little of the avant garde here. And what is new is usually an innovation built on past experiences. Technical as well as general knowledge is represented; knowledge of economic relations, as well as the "intuitive" sense of, say, when a fetus becomes a "person." Such beliefs are cultural and ideological in the sense that, although there are individual variations, they are socially derived phenomena.

A perception of the established bounds of discussion and their effect on policy formation provides the sophistication necessary for a contribution to the debate, but that same perception also constrains political vision. The limits are due to the interests generating the debate as well as to the beliefs generally held about what is acceptable. Citizens with evident needs and desires fought for the California Coastal Initiative; other parties are the clientele for the Federal Reserve Board and they have their view of what is acceptable; similarly, the primary contractors for military materials have an interest in policy that affects them. But traditional beliefs also function independently, without regard to certain particular interests. When energy policy is considered in America, few people raise the issue of nationalization, nor do many speak of total governmental withdrawal from the scene. There is a traditionally acceptable mix of public and private forces that appears as a constraint in a number of other areas. The California Coastal Commission strains this balance in the direction of public control, but the strain is felt with even the most minimal intrusions into values such as property rights. In the field of economic policy, the thrust toward economic planning is dependent on a Keynesian paradigm. As with the forms of political action, innovation and change in our fundamental beliefs do occur.

Finally, policy making has a stage or arena: the Constitution, other laws of the nation, state codes, commission procedures, and local ordinances, as well as the institutions they create. The institutions are important because people accept them as authoritative. In this sense, they are similar in status to the beliefs just mentioned, but since the institutions are physically manifest, the attention they command is clearer than it is with general cultural norms or ideologies. In many cases the arenas examined here are recent creations and thus the interests served are readily noted. For example, in the case of the coastal plan, new values were instituted in spite of opposition from established interests. These values were perpetuated through an institution. With the Presidency, the organization of the office is an aspect of the institution which affects policy positions by determining how decisions will be handled. New modes of operating have also been instituted by Congress, not so much to perpetuate a specific belief, but rather to increase the influence of this branch of government in the formation of the national budget.

Familiarity with the existing forms by which ideas are communicated in making policy is a basis for understanding those skills upon which political decision makers rely. Such things as attorneys' briefs, committee hearings, press conferences, initiative petitions, and staff meetings are tools of the political craft; they are not the only tools, but rather those traditionally employed. Imagination, tempered by experience, will no doubt suggest other tools and new uses for the traditional ones. Learning about politics does not involve simply learning how things are traditionally done. It is of equal or greater value to acquire an understanding of what Americans find appropriate to do in politics, for this is the place to begin to gain a sense of what is possible.

During any period in political history, new forms may enter the political arena. At certain times, old but little used forms may be rejuvenated. Traditional procedures are usually altered as a result of changes in the social and economic environment. The mid-nineteenth century, for instance, introduced war into American domestic politics. The Depression that occurred in the 1930s also led to governmental responses that were novel in form. The existence of multiple agencies, which was a response to those conditions, is now a dominant force in our political life. In the 1960s, the massive demonstration as a tool was rejuvenated by the civil rights and antiwar movements. In the early 1970s, men in government were judged to have abused the power they held, and the abuses were checked by legal action and by the rare threat of impeachment. For the most part, the struggles presented here are not extraordinary in that sense. They rely on continuation of established patterns either in form — the initiative process is an old tool, which has been relied on quite often recently — or in substance — the economic planning bill is a new approach to a commitment three decades old. In some of the cases, however, it is the development and use of new or unique forms of political action that is of greatest interest. Congressional reorganization of the budget process has been mentioned in this regard, because of the new prominence of budget experts in the legislative process.

Understanding the nature of politics and the process of making policy is itself a political resource. In a complex society, where policy is usually made at some distance from the people, most of the decisions affecting our lives are not expected to be understood. Knowing the bases of these decisions allows us to anticipate their effects on our lives. Understanding what they mean is breaking the code — it is getting the message. Knowing what can be done and how to do it is a prerequisite for effective action. The more sophisticated the understanding, the more likely it is that the action based on it will be fruitful.

Understanding is also a source of freedom. Knowing one's place in the political world expands the range of choice. Knowing the significance of public events enlarges the sphere in which one may operate, while ignorance of the factors that determine public policy restricts political opportunity. Understanding may of course be a burden. Some people prefer to remain uninformed, and the political system as it is presently constituted expects that sort of withdrawal on the part of many citizens. To engage in the effort of interpretation is to give testimony to the power of an informed citizenry. It is to take on a burden in order to become free.

Chapter 1 The Supreme Court and the Law

Reform and Reaction as Abortion Policy

JOHN BRIGHAM, EDITOR

Abortion has been legal in the United States for only a few years. Although it became a crime according to state law within the last 100 years, general proscriptions against the operation were widespread by 1970. The movement for repeal of criminal abortion laws began soon after state legislatures approved the laws in the middle of the nineteenth century. Support for repeal was tied closely to technological changes in medicine and birth control, social attitudes, and consciousness of women's rights. The movement reached a peak in the 1960s. In 1973, state efforts to restrict abortion were substantially curtailed, and it became national policy that the operation was legal. Legalization of abortion was the culmination of activity of increasing intensity throughout the preceding decade. The new national posture has engendered a reaction of even greater intensity.

Although national policy on abortion has involved a variety of governmental institutions, the courts have provided the greatest impetus for legalization. Legal abortion became possible primarily due to a decision of the United States Supreme Court. That decision marks a turning point in the formation of national abortion policy. But, a great deal of political activity preceded the decision and laid the foundation for present policy.

The agents for repeal of the criminal statutes can be traced to the struggles against the original statutes, which had been stimulated by Anthony Comstock and the League for the Suppression of Vice. The struggle to change the law on abortion gained momentum slowly. It was not until 1910 that Havelock Ellis, a British psychologist, presented the United States with a view that challenged the prevailing antiabortion ethic. Throughout the first years of this century, the statutes were quite secure, and activity on the issue consisted of sporadic prosecutions of criminal offenders. By the 1930s, popular magazines began carrying articles and commentary calling for more liberal laws on abortion. The medical and clerical communities continued their opposition to such liberalization for another two decades. But, by 1959, the American Law Institute proposed, as part of a model criminal code, that abortion should be legalized in cases of rape or incest, when the pregnancy threatened the physical or mental health of the mother, or when the child was likely to be born with physical or mental defects.

In the 1960s, the issue gained national attention. It became more clearly political and was allied with the goals of family planning and women's movement groups. In the decade prior to the Supreme Court's historic decision, a number of individuals took the heat of national attention and public censure that were to stimulate the drive for repeal of the state laws. In 1962, Dr. W. J. Bryan Henrie was convicted for performing an abortion and became one of the first physicians to take a stand publicly in behalf of liberalizing laws against abortion. Dr. Henrie went to jail. Also in 1962, abortion gained national attention as a result of the case of Sherri Finkbine, one of a number of women who had taken the drug thalidomide while pregnant; the probability of their giving birth to deformed children was discovered to be very high. Mrs. Finkbine attempted to arrange for an abortion in the United States but was refused. She elected to go to Sweden for a legal abortion. Then in 1964 a rubella epidemic occurred in the United States, threatening deformity to as yet unborn children whose mothers had contracted the disease. Few of the mothers were able to acquire abortions given the restrictions in existence at the time. These events, along with changes in public attitudes toward sexual morality and toward governmental involvement in a number of "private" matters, reflect the changing social climate that preceded changes in the law.

As in other areas, the law on abortion depends to a large extent on attitudes, which seem themselves to be influenced by technological and economic considerations.

Originally, state laws against abortion had been justified in terms of maternal health. They were also consistent with the popular desire for large families. Changes in technology in the form of operative and clinical developments had made abortion much safer by the 1960s. Widespread dissemination of the birth control pill made unwanted pregnancy a much less common occurrence than it had been in even the recent past. Economic changes from an agrarian to an industrial and increasingly suburban middle-class society contributed to changes in the relative advantages of large families, which in turn seems to have altered popular perception of the desirability of having a lot of children. A decline in the fertility rate has, in fact, been shown to be related to an increase in the availability of literature on abortion. These changes had been coming for a long period, but, with regard to the issue of abortion, they can be united with a variety of factors to produce a critical mass of supporting evidence to explain the legal changes.

The proposition that the rise in opposition to restrictions on abortion is related to those technical and economic factors is not a claim that certain ideas and established traditions relating particularly to the value of fetal life are not themselves an important influence on developments in the law. Rather, such beliefs have been a powerful, if not the overriding, concern of active groups since the issue became a matter of debate. These beliefs continue to be the primary factor in efforts to alter national policy on abortion. The issue here, however, is not the ideological correctness of the policy but the way in which this particular national policy came about and the responses and reactions that ultimately determine its everyday significance.

The personal choices of individual doctors, as well as the articulated interests of hospitals and organized groups, have always been an important determinant of the actual outcome of abortion policy. Where doctors refuse to perform abortions or where hospitals restrict them, the fact that they are "legal" makes very little difference. With the legalization of the medical procedure, those choices have an even greater importance in assessing the degree to which a national policy has any significant impact among those whom it might be thought to affect. In 1970, the American Medical Association adopted resolutions emphasizing that "the best interests of the patient" should be a prime concern, that "sound clinical judgment" should be used, and, furthermore, that no party to the procedure should be required to violate personally held moral principles.

The decision of the Supreme Court in 1973 followed the trend in a number of states of accepting the model proposed by the American Law Institute. By the time the Supreme Court decided on the constitutionality of abortion, one fourth of the states had accepted the new formulation. The section of the Model Penal Code relevant to the Court's decision on abortion is as follows:

MODEL PENAL CODE

SECTION 230.3   ABORTION

(1) *Unjustified Abortion.* A person who purposely and unjustifiably terminates the pregnancy of another otherwise than by a live birth commits a felony of the third degree or, where the pregnancy has continued beyond the twenty-sixth week, a felony of the second degree.

(2) *Justifiable Abortion.*   A licensed physician is justified in terminating a pregnancy if he believes there is substantial risk that continuance of the pregnancy would gravely impair the physical or mental health of the mother or that the child would be born with grave physical or mental defect, or that the pregnancy resulted from rape, incest, or other felonious intercourse. All illicit intercourse with a girl below the age of 16 shall be deemed felonious for purposes of this subsection. Justifiable abortions shall be performed only in a licensed hospital except in case of emergency when hospital facilities are unavailable. [Additional exceptions from the requirement of hospitalization may be incorporated here to take account of situations in sparsely settled areas where hospitals are not generally accessible.]

(3) *Physicians' Certificates; Presumption from Non-Compliance.* No abortion shall be performed unless two physicians, one of whom may be the person performing the abortion, shall have certified in writing the circumstances which they believe to justify the abortion. Such certificate shall be submitted before the abortion to the hospital where it is to be performed and, in the case of abortion following felonious intercourse, to the prosecuting attorney or the police. Failure to comply with any of the requirements of this Subsection gives rise to a presumption that the abortion was unjustified.

(4) *Self-Abortion.*   A woman whose pregnancy has continued beyond the twenty-sixth week commits a felony of the third degree if she purposely terminates her own pregnancy otherwise than by a live birth, or if she uses instruments, drugs, or violence upon herself for that purpose. Except as justified under Subsection (2), a person who induces or knowingly aids a woman to use instruments, drugs, or violence upon herself for the purpose of terminating her pregnancy otherwise than by a live birth commits a felony of the third degree whether or not the pregnancy has continued beyond the twenty-sixth week.

(5) *Pretended Abortion.*   A person commits a felony of the third degree if, representing that it is his purpose to perform an abortion, he does an act adapted to cause abortion in a pregnant woman although the woman is in fact not pregnant, or the actor does not believe she is. A person charged with unjustified abortion under Subsection (1) or an attempt to commit that offense may be convicted thereof upon proof of conduct prohibited by this Subsection.

(6) *Distribution of Abortifacients.* A person who sells, offers to sell, possesses with intent to sell, advertises, or displays for sale anything specially designed to terminate a pregnancy, or held out by the actor as useful for that purpose, commits a misdemeanor, unless:

(a) the sale, offer, or display is to a physician or druggist or to an intermediary in a chain of distribution to physicians or druggists; or

(b) the sale is made upon prescription or order of a physician; or

(c) the possession is with intent to sell as authorized in paragraphs (a) and (b); or

(d) the advertising is addressed to persons named in paragraph (a) and confined to trade or professional channels not likely to reach the general public.

(7) *Section Inapplicable to Prevention of Pregnancy.* Nothing in this Section shall be deemed applicable to the prescription, administration, or distribution of drugs or other substances for avoiding pregnancy, whether by preventing implantation of a fertilized ovum or by any other method that operates before, at, or immediately after fertilization.

The American Law Institute is a body of prestigious lawyers and legal scholars who have consistently influenced the development of legal reform in the United States. The codes drafted by consultants for the institute are debated by the members and passed as a recommendation on legislative developments for the states. The efforts of the institute are supported by foundations, and the model codes that they have proposed in a number of areas from torts to land use serve as a guide to state efforts to reform the statutory law.

In 1970, further liberalization was undertaken by the states of New York, Hawaii, and Alaska so that the decision on abortion became one between the woman and her physician. Such positions indicated the growing respectability of the claim to legalization, if not the actual pressure of an idea that seemed to be gaining public acceptance.

During the 1960s, the Supreme Court had also indicated a drift that was to culminate in the 1973 decision by their holdings in the cases of *Griswold* v. *Connecticut* (1965) and *United States* v. *Vuitch* (1970). The former established a right of privacy derived from the "penumbras" said to surround the specific guarantees of the Bill of Rights. The latter case demonstrated a concern that the vagueness of abortion statutes might be beyond constitutional limits. The Supreme Court had given signs of hope to those interested in eliminating laws restricting access to abortions. These signs and the political consciousness of the women's movement, which was also being felt at this time, stimulated the hope that eventually led to the challenge of state antiabortion laws.

The Supreme Court's decision in *Roe* v. *Wade* (1973), based as it was on constitutional principles and the authority of the national government, restructured the arena in which the struggle would be carried out. The basis of the Supreme Court decision and the opinion of the Court stimulated a variety of forms of political activity, which are the focus of the following sections. Section A deals with the Supreme Court, the institutional framework within which it operates, and the decisions that constitute the way it enunciates policy. Section B shows the response at the national level to the decision and the ways in which the configuration of state politics was influenced. Section C traces the influence of the decision to the local level through materials from the trial of Dr. Kenneth Edelin in Boston for manslaughter in the death of a fetus he aborted.

SECTION A. THE CONSTITUTIONAL FRAMEWORK

Recent developments in abortion law and policy have as their source the decision in *Roe* v. *Wade*, which was handed down in January of 1973. Consideration of subsequent policy on that issue begins with that decision. The decision itself resulted from the struggles that preceded it in the legal process as well as the political background just enunciated. Its ultimate significance as a policy depends to a great extent on the form that the decision took. The Supreme Court is the head of a diffuse and fragmented court system, with different jurisdictions in each of the states and a separate system for the nation as a whole; it has a unique tradition, a special place in American politics, and its own procedures and personnel; it also decides issues presented to it with particular attention to related issues that it might have previously considered. These three factors provide the background for understanding the decision in *Roe* v. *Wade*, part of which is reproduced in this section.

CHALLENGING THE TEXAS ANTIABORTION LAW

In March of 1970, a single woman, pseudonymously called Jane Roe according to legal decorum, instituted a claim that she had a constitutional right that was being violated by the Texas criminal abortion statute. She sought to have the Texas statute declared unconstitutional and to prevent the District Attorney of Dallas County, Texas, from enforcing it. Roe argued, through her attorney, that she wished to have an abortion that was safe and under clinical conditions but was prevented from doing so by the laws of the state of Texas. She included in her claim a desire to represent, before the law, all others who were in the same situation. She was joined in her claim by a doctor who had been arrested for violating the Texas statute and by a married couple who claimed that they might want to remain childless and felt constrained by the statute.

The Texas statute was first enacted in 1854 and was soon modified into language that remained substantially the same until the challenge to its constitutionality. The statute represented those in effect in most states for over 100 years. It differed from the more recent developments in approximately one fourth of the states, where legislation on the basis of the model provided by the American Law Institute had been enacted.

The Texas Abortion Statute

The Texas statute that was challenged in the Federal District Court comprises Articles 1191–1194 and 1196 of the state's Penal Code. They read as follows:

ARTICLE 1191: ABORTION

If any person shall designedly administer to a pregnant woman or knowingly procure to be administered with her consent any drug or medicine, or shall use towards her any violence or means whatever externally or internally applied, and thereby procure an abortion, he shall be confined in the penitentiary not less than two nor more than five years; if it be done without her consent, the punishment shall be doubled. By "abortion" is meant that the life of the fetus or embryo shall be destroyed in the woman's womb or that a premature birth thereof be caused.

ARTICLE 1192: FURNISHING THE MEANS

Whoever furnishes the means for procuring an abortion knowing the purpose intended is guilty as an accomplice.

ARTICLE 1193: ATTEMPT AT ABORTION

If the means used shall fail to produce an abortion, the offender is nevertheless guilty of an attempt to produce abortion, provided it be shown that such means were calculated to produce that result, and shall be fined not less than one hundred nor more than one thousand dollars.

ARTICLE 1194: MURDER IN PRODUCING ABORTION

If the death of the mother is occasioned by an abortion so produced or by an attempt to effect the same it is murder.

ARTICLE 1196: BY MEDICAL ADVICE

Nothing in this chapter applies to an abortion procured or attempted by medical advice for the purpose of saving the life of the mother.

In an oral presentation before a federal court in Texas, Roe's attorney, cited as Miss Coffee, first made the argument that the Texas statute should be declared unconstitutional in its entirety.

Oral Arguments in Texas

TRANSCRIPT OF ORAL ARGUMENT BEFORE STATUTORY
THREE-JUDGE UNITED STATES DISTRICT COURT FOR THE
NORTHERN DISTRICT OF TEXAS, FILED JULY 30, 1970

IN THE

UNITED STATES DISTRICT COURT

FOR THE NORTHERN DISTRICT OF TEXAS

DALLAS DIVISION

CA NO. 3-3690-B

JANE ROE,

Plaintiff,

—v.—

HENRY WADE,

Defendant.

—v.—

JAMES HUBERT HALLFORD, M.D.,

Intervenor.

CA NO. 3-3691-C

JOHN DOE AND MARY DOE,

Plaintiffs,

—v.—

HENRY WADE,

Defendant.

SOURCE: Brief submitted to the United States Supreme Court in the case of *Roe v. Wade, United States Reports,* Vol. 410, p. 113.

JUDGE GOLDBERG: Do you think the entire statute should be stricken?
MISS COFFEE: Yes.
JUDGE GOLDBERG: Completely?

MISS COFFEE: Yes. I think the Court has no other choice because the scope is so entirely too broad. All the provisions just about are so vague, that I just don't think it's —

JUDGE HUGHES: Suppose we struck out the provision saving the life of the mother in the last section of the law, wouldn't that make the statute constitutional? You would then have that section read, "Nothing in this Chapter applies to an abortion procured or attempted by medical advice."

MISS COFFEE: The thing is — this was not the intent — if the Court should do this, then the Court would be rewriting the statute for the State. There is no indication that the State of Texas intended the statute to read that way.

JUDGE GOLDBERG: Do you know whether this statute was separable? Did it have a separability provision? When was it passed? When was the Abortion statute passed — 1905?

MISS COFFEE: I believe this statute was passed around 1919 — it might be 1905, but the predecessor was passed in 1886, I am told.

JUDGE GOLDBERG: Do you know whether it has a separability provision?

MR. TOLLE: If the Court please, it's 1907, I think.

JUDGE GOLDBERG: Does it have a separability provision?

MISS COFFEE: I don't know, Your Honor.

JUDGE GOLDBERG: Does anyone at the counsel table know?

MR. TOLLE: Not specifically. I believe there is a general provision in the Penal Code providing for separability. I think there is, Judge.

MISS COFFEE: Is the Court worried about —

JUDGE GOLDBERG: We worry about a lot of things. Don't let that worry you.

MISS COFFEE: I was going to suggest if the Court was concerned about there being any criminal sanction against a non-medical personnel performing abortions —

JUDGE GOLDBERG: Perhaps — may I suggest — we may be worried, I don't know — that if we struck it down completely, extricated the whole thing, anybody could perform an abortion any place — in a garage or in an attic or any other place? I know you're going to answer about the medical practice, and we'll get to that a little bit later.

MISS COFFEE: All right, Your Honor. In the case of *University Committee to End the War in Vietnam* versus *Dunn*, a court in Austin, a Three-Judge Federal Court in Austin struck down the Texas Breach of the Peace statute.

JUDGE GOLDBERG: Yes.

MISS COFFEE: They struck down the whole statute, as I understand it, but they stayed the execution of an injunction until the next session of the Legislature out of a Special Order —

JUDGE GOLDBERG: You are suggesting we might do that here?

MISS COFFEE: That's a possibility. I think the statute is so bad the Court is just really going to have to strike it all down. I don't think it's really worth salvaging.

ALL THE WAY TO THE SUPREME COURT

The argument (or brief) presented to the Supreme Court by Attorney Sarah Weddington in behalf of Jane Roe was filed on 18 August 1971. It was technically a request for a "writ of certiorari," which is a legal tool by which most of the cases that the Supreme Court looks at are called up for review from the lower courts. Weddington's 145-page brief claimed that Jane Roe "had only a tenth grade education and no well-paying job which might provide sufficient funds to travel to another jurisdiction for a legal abortion in a safe clinical setting." She further argued in her briefs and in two oral presentations before the Supreme Court that the right to seek and receive medical care is a fundamental personal liberty; the Texas abortion law violated the right to privacy; it advanced no compelling interest of the state; it was unconstitutionally vague; and finally it placed an unconstitutional burden of proof on the physician to justify a decision to perform an abortion. The attorney chose the most reasonable arguments available, but, like most lawyers appealing a case, she did not leave anything out that might move the Court to decide in favor of her client. Appended to the *Roe* brief were 477 pages of supplementary materials including legal, medical, and social scientific evidence in support of her claim. In addition, there were about 20 briefs filed by interested parties seeking to put one idea or another before the Supreme Court. Henry Wade, the District Attorney of Dallas County, represented the state of Texas with members of the state Attorney General's office.

Biographies of the Supreme Court Justices

Nine men sat in judgment of the appeal from the United States District Court for the Northern District of Texas. They had been appointed by Presidents Roosevelt, Eisenhower, Kennedy, and Nixon, with the confirmation of the Senate of the United States. They were of varying ages and backgrounds.

WARREN E. BURGER, the Chief Justice, was born in Minnesota in 1907. He did his undergraduate study at the University of Minnesota and studied law at St. Paul College of Law. He served as Assistant Attorney General of the United States and as a Judge of the Court of Appeals for the District of Columbia before being appointed by Richard Nixon in 1969.

WILLIAM O. DOUGLAS was born in Minnesota in 1898 and received his undergraduate education at Whitman College in Washington state and his law degree from Columbia University. He taught law for 12 years, first at Columbia and then at Yale, and served as chairman of the Securities and Exchange Commission before being appointed to the Court by Franklin Roosevelt in 1939.

WILLIAM BRENNAN, JR., was born in New Jersey in 1906 and educated at the University of Pennsylvania and at Harvard Law School. He served in the Army and on the New Jersey Supreme Court before being named to the Supreme Court by Dwight Eisenhower in 1956.

POTTER STEWART was born in Michigan in 1915 but has always made his home in Ohio. He received both his A.B. and LL.B. from Yale. He served as a Judge on the Court of Appeals for the Sixth Circut before being appointed to the Supreme Court by Dwight Eisenhower in 1958.

BYRON R. WHITE was born in Colorado in 1917. He was educated at the University of Colorado and Yale Law School and served as Deputy Attorney General of the United States before being named to the Supreme Court by John Kennedy in 1962.

THURGOOD MARSHALL was born in Baltimore, Maryland, in 1908. He did his undergraduate study at Lincoln University and received his law degree from Howard University. He served as Chief Legal Officer for the NAACP until his appointment to the U.S. Court of Appeals for the Second Circuit and later as Solicitor General of the United States. Lyndon Johnson nominated him to the Supreme Court in 1967.

HARRY A. BLACKMUN was born in Illinois in 1908 and received both his undergraduate and his legal education at Harvard University. He practiced and taught law in Minnesota until being named to the U.S. Court of Appeals for the Eighth Circuit. He was nominated to the Supreme Court by Richard Nixon in 1970.

LEWIS F. POWELL, JR., was born in 1907 in Virginia. He received his undergraduate and law degrees from Washington and Lee University, practiced law in Virginia, and served as President of the American Bar Association, the American College of Trial Lawyers, and the American Bar Foundation before being nominated to the Supreme Court by Richard Nixon in 1972.

WILLIAM H. REHNQUIST was born in Wisconsin in 1924 and received his undergraduate and law degrees from Stanford University. He practiced law in Arizona before coming to Washington to serve as Assistant Attorney General under Richard Nixon, who appointed him to the Supreme Court in 1972.

The variety of backgrounds, experiences, and attitudes evident among the members of the nation's highest court are some of the factors that may have an effect on the way the justices vote. Justice White, who had experience as a prosecutor, often sides with the government in matters dealing with criminal law. Justice Marshall, who presented the NAACP's case in *Brown* v. *Board of Education*, which held segregated schools unconstitutional, has revealed both in opinions and in oral argument a sensitivity to constitutional protections against racial discrimination. But the Supreme Court deals with complicated legal issues that circumscribe its choices. The justices are not asked their opinion on abortion, but more specifically, their assessment of a particular claim concerning the constitutionality of a state law. In this form, the question raises issues on substantially more than whether a woman ought to be able to have an abortion.

In appointing justices to the Supreme Court, the President can only make a rough assessment of how they are likely to act once they take their place for life on the nation's highest court. President Eisenhower called his appointment of progressive Chief Justice Earl Warren the biggest mistake he made as President. In the abortion case, of the four "law and order" justices appointed by President Nixon, three voted with the majority to strike down the Texas statute and more than a score of similar state laws. Although his appointees were supposed to be "restrained" judges, the decision stands as one of the Court's most expansive in its effect on the legislative prerogatives of the states.

The following selection is from the opinion of this Court on the constitutionality of state laws prohibiting abortion.

The Opinion of the United States Supreme Court in Roe v. Wade

ROE ET AL. (Appellants) v. WADE, DISTRICT ATTORNEY OF DALLAS COUNTY (Appellee)

APPEAL FROM THE UNITED STATES DISTRICT COURT FOR THE
NORTHERN DISTICT OF TEXAS

No. 70–18. Argued December 13, 1971 — Reargued October 11, 1972
— Decided January 22, 1973

Blackmun, J., delivered the opinion of the Court, in which Burger, C. J., and Douglas, Brennan, Stewart, Marshall, and Powell, JJ., joined. Burger, C. J., ... , Douglas, J., ... , and Stewart, J. ... , filed concurring opinions. White, J., filed a dissenting opinion, in which Rehnquist, J., joined . . . . Rehnquist, J., filed a dissenting opinion . . . .

MR. JUSTICE BLACKMUN delivered the opinion of the Court.

This Texas federal appeal and its Georgia companion, *Doe* v. *Bolton* . . . present constitutional challenges to state criminal abortion legislation. The Texas statutes under attack here are typical of those that have been in effect in many States for approximately a century. The Georgia statutes, in contrast, have a modern cast and are a legislative product that, to an extent at least, obviously reflects the influences of recent attitudinal change, of advancing medical knowledge and techniques, and of new thinking about an old issue.

Our task, of course, is to resolve the issue by constitutional measurement, free of emotion and of predilection. We seek earnestly to do this, and, because we do, we have inquired into, and in this opinion place some emphasis upon, medical and medical-legal history and what that history reveals about man's attitudes toward the abortion procedure over the centuries . . . .

The appellee notes ... that the record does not disclose that Roe was pregnant at the time of the District Court hearing on May 22, 1970, ... or on the following June 17 when the court's opinion and judgment were filed. And he suggests that Roe's case must now be moot because she and all other members of her class are no longer subject to any 1970 pregnancy.

. . .

SOURCE: *United States Reports*, Vol. 410, p. 113.

The usual rule in federal cases is that an actual controversy must exist at stages of appellate or certiorari review, and not simply at the date the action is initiated. *United States* v. *Munsingwear, Inc.,* 340 U. S. 36 (1950); *Golden* v. *Zwickler,*... ; *SEC* v. *Medical Committee for Human Rights,* 404 U. S. 403 (1972).

But when, as here, pregnancy is a significant fact in the litigation, the normal 266-day human gestation period is so short that the pregnancy will come to term before the usual appellate process is complete. If that termination makes a case moot, pregnancy litigation seldom will survive much beyond the trial stage, and appellate review will be effectively denied. Our law should not be that rigid. Pregnancy often comes more than once to the same woman, and in the general population, if man is to survive, it will always be with us. Pregnancy provides a classic justification for a conclusion of nonmootness. It truly could be "capable of repetition, yet evading review." *Southern Pacific Terminal Co.* v. *ICC,* 219 U. S. 498, 515 (1911). See *Moore* v. *Ogilvie,* 394 U. S. 814, 816 (1969); *Carroll* v. *Princess Anne,* 393 U. S. 175, 178–179 (1968); *United States* v. *W. T. Grant Co.,* 345 U. S. 629, 632–633 (1953).

. . .

The principal thrust of appellant's attack on the Texas statutes is that they improperly invade a right, said to be possessed by the pregnant woman, to choose to terminate her pregnancy. Appellant would discover this right in the concept of personal "liberty" embodied in the Fourteenth Amendment's Due Process Clause; or in personal, marital, familial, and sexual privacy said to be protected by the Bill of Rights or its penumbras, see *Griswold* v. *Connecticut,* 381 U. S. 479 (1965); *Eisenstadt* v. *Baird,* 405 U. S. 438 (1972); *id.,* at 460 (White, J., concurring in result); or among those rights reserved to the people by the Ninth Amendment, *Griswold* v. *Connecticut,* 381 U. S., at 486 (Goldberg, J., concurring). Before addressing this claim, we feel it desirable briefly to survey, in several aspects, the history of abortion, for such insight as that history may afford us, and then to examine the state purposes and interests behind the criminal abortion laws.

. . .

It perhaps is not generally appreciated that the restrictive criminal abortion laws in effect in a majority of States today are of relatively recent vintage. Those laws, generally proscribing abortion or its attempt at any time during pregnancy except when necessary to preserve the pregnant woman's life, are not of ancient or even of common-law origin. Instead, they derive from statutory changes effected, for the most part, in the latter half of the 19th century.

... Why did not the authority of Hippocrates dissuade abortion practice in his time and that of Rome? The late Dr. Edelstein provides us with a theory: The Oath was not uncontested even in Hippocrates' day; only the Pythagorean school of philosophers frowned upon the related act of suicide. Most Greek thinkers, on the other hand, commended abortion, at least prior to viability. See Plato, *Republic*, V, 461; Aristotle, *Politics*, VII, 1335b 25. For the Pythagoreans, however, it was a matter of dogma. For them the embryo was animate from the moment of conception, and abortion meant destruction of a living being. The abortion clause of the Oath, therefore, "echoes Pythagorean doctrines," and "[i]n no other stratum of Greek opinion were such views held or proposed in the same spirit of uncompromising austerity."

. . . It is undisputed that at common law, abortion performed *before* "quickening" — the first recognizable movement of the fetus *in utero*, appearing usually from the 16th to the 18th week of pregnancy — was not an indictable offense. The absence of a common-law crime for pre-quickening abortion appears to have developed from a confluence of earlier philosophical, theological, and civil and canon law concepts of when life begins. These disciplines variously approached the question in terms of the point at which the embryo or fetus became "formed" or recognizably human, or in terms of when a "person" came into being, that is, infused with a "soul" or "animated."

. . . Due to continued uncertainty about the precise time when animation occurred, to the lack of any empirical basis for the 40–80-day view, and perhaps to Aquinas' definition of movement as one of the two first principles of life, Bracton focused upon quickening as the critical point. The significance of quickening was echoed by later common-law scholars and found its way into the received common law in this country.

Whether abortion of a *quick* fetus was a felony at common law, or even a lesser crime, is still disputed. Bracton, writing early in the 13th century, thought it homicide. But the later and predominant view, following the great common-law scholars, has been that it was, at most, a lesser offense. In a frequently cited passage, Coke took the position that abortion of a woman "quick with childe" is "a great misprision, and no murder." Blackstone followed, saying that while abortion after quickening had once been considered manslaughter (though not murder), "modern law" took a less severe view. A recent review of the common-law precedents argues, however, that those precedents contradict Coke and that even post-quickening abortion was never established as a common-law crime. This is of some importance because while most American courts ruled . . . that abortion of an unquickened fetus was not criminal under their received common law, others followed Coke in stating that abortion of a quick fetus was a "misprision," a term they translated to mean "misdemeanor."

. . . In this country, the law in effect in all but a few States until mid-19th century was the pre-existing English common law. Connecticut, the first State to enact abortion legislation, adopted in 1821 that part of Lord Ellenborough's Act that related to a woman "quick with child." The death penalty was not imposed. Abortion before quickening was made a crime in that State only in 1860. In 1828, New York enacted legislation that, in two respects, was to serve as a model for early anti-abortion statutes. First, while barring destruction of an unquickened fetus as well as a quick fetus, it made the former only a misdemeanor, but the latter second-degree manslaughter. Second, it incorporated a concept of therapeutic abortion by providing that an abortion was excused if it "shall have been necessary to preserve the life of such mother, or shall have been advised by two physicians to be necessary for such purpose." By 1840, when Texas had received the common law, only eight American States had statutes dealing with abortion. It was not until after the War Between the States that legislation began generally to replace the common law. Most of these initial statutes dealt severely with abortion after quickening but were lenient with it before quickening . . . . By the end of the 1950s, a large majority of the jurisdictions banned abortion, however and whenever performed, unless done to save or preserve the life of the mother . . . .

Three reasons have been advanced to explain historically the enactment of criminal abortion laws in the 19th century and to justify their continued existence.

. . .

It has been argued occasionally that these laws were the product of a Victorian social concern to discourage illicit sexual conduct. Texas, however, does not advance this justification in the present case, and it appears that no court or commentator has taken the argument seriously. The appellants and *amici* contend, moreover, that this is not a proper state purpose at all and suggest that, if it were, the Texas statutes are overbroad in protecting it since the law fails to distinguish between married and unwed mothers.

A second reason is concerned with abortion as a medical procedure. When most criminal abortion laws were first enacted, the procedure was a hazardous one for the woman.

. . .

The third reason is the State's interest — some phrase it in terms of duty — in protecting prenatal life. Some of the argument for this justification rests on the theory that a new human life is present from the moment of conception. The State's interest and general obligation to protect life then extends, it is argued, to prenatal life. Only when the life of the pregnant mother herself is at stake, balanced against the life she carries within her, should the interest of the embryo or fetus not prevail. Logically, of course, a legitimate state interest in this area need not stand or fall on acceptance of the belief that life begins at conception or at some other point prior to live birth. In assessing the State's interest, recognition may be given to the less rigid claim that as long as at least *potential* life is involved, the State may assert interests beyond the protection of the pregnant woman alone.

. . .

The Constitution does not explicitly mention any right of privacy. In a line of decisions, however, going back perhaps as far as *Union Pacific R. Co.* v. *Botsford*, 141 U. S. 250, 251 (1891), the Court has recognized that a right of personal privacy, or a guarantee of certain areas or zones of privacy, does exist under the Constitution. In varying contexts, the Court or individual Justices have, indeed, found at least the roots of that right in the First Amendment, *Stanley* v. *Georgia*, 394 U. S. 557, 564 (1969); in the Fourth and Fifth Amendments, *Terry* v. *Ohio*, 392 U. S. 1, 8–9 (1968), *Katz* v. *United States*, 389 U. S. 347, 350 (1967), *Boyd* v. *United States*, 116 U. S. 616 (1886), see *Olmstead* v. *United States*, 277 U. S. 438, 478 (1928) (Brandeis, J., dissenting); in the penumbras of the Bill of Rights, *Griswold* v. *Connecticut*, 381 U. S., at 484–485; in the Ninth Amendment, *id.*, at 486 (Goldberg, J., concurring); or in the concept of liberty guaranteed by the first section of the Fourteenth Amendment, see *Meyer* v. *Nebraska*, 262 U. S. 390, 399 (1923). These decisions make it clear that only personal rights that can be deemed "fundamental" or "implicit in the concept of ordered liberty," *Palko* v. *Connecticut*, 302 U. S. 319, 325 (1937), are included in this guarantee of personal privacy. They also make it clear that the right has some extension to activities relating to marriage, *Loving* v. *Virginia*, 388 U. S. 1, 12 (1967); procreation, *Skinner* v. *Oklahoma*, 316 U. S. 535, 541–542 (1942); contraception, *Eisenstadt* v. *Baird*, 405 U. S., at 453–454; *id.*, at 460, 463–465 (White, J., concurring in result); family relationships, *Prince* v. *Massachusetts*, 321 U. S. 158, 166 (1944); and child rearing and education, *Pierce* v. *Society of Sisters*, 268 U. S. 510, 535 (1925), *Meyer* v. *Nebraska*, *supra*.

This right of privacy . . . is broad enough to encompass a woman's decision whether or not to terminate her pregnancy. . . .

On the basis of elements such as these, appellant and some *amici* argue that the woman's right is absolute and that she is entitled to terminate her pregnancy at whatever time, in whatever way, and for whatever reason she alone chooses. With this we do not agree. Appellant's arguments that Texas either has no valid interest at all in regulating the abortion decision, or no interest strong enough to support any limitation upon the woman's sole determination, are unpersuasive. The Court's decisions recognizing a right of privacy also acknowledge that some state regulation in areas protected by that right is appropriate. As noted above, a State may properly assert important interests in safeguarding health, in maintaining medical standards, and in protecting potential life. At some point in pregnancy, these respective interests become sufficiently compelling to sustain regulation of the factors that govern the abortion decision. The privacy right involved, therefore, cannot be said to be absolute . . . .

Where certain "fundamental rights" are involved, the Court has held that regulation limiting these rights may be justified only by a "compelling state interest," . . . and that legislative enactments must be narrowly drawn to express only the legitimate state interests at stake. *Griswold v. Connecticut*, 381 U. S., at 485; *Aptheker v. Secretary of State*, 378 U. S. 500, 508 (1964); *Cantwell v. Connecticut*, 310 U. S. 296, 307–308 (1940); see *Eisenstadt v. Baird*.

In view of all this, we do not agree that, by adopting one theory of life, Texas may override the rights of the pregnant woman that are at stake. We repeat, however, that the State does have an important and legitimate interest in preserving and protecting the health of the pregnant woman, whether she be a resident of the State or a nonresident who seeks medical consultation and treatment there, and that it has still *another* important and legitimate interest in protecting the potentiality of human life. These interests are separate and distinct. Each grows in substantiality as the woman approaches term and, at a point during pregnancy, each becomes "compelling."

With respect to the State's important and legitimate interest in the health of the mother, the "compelling" point, in the light of present medical knowledge, is at approximately the end of the first trimester. This is so because of the now-established medical fact, referred to above . . . , that until the end of the first trimester mortality in abortion may be less than mortality in normal childbirth. It follows that, from and after this point, a State may regulate the abortion procedure to the extent that the regulation reasonably relates to the preservation and protection of maternal health. Examples of permissible state regulation in this area are requirements as to the qualifications of the person who is to perform the abortion; as to the licensure of that person; as to the facility in which the procedure is to be performed, that is, whether it must be a hospital or may be a clinic or some other place of less-than-hospital status; as to the licensing of the facility; and the like.

This means, on the other hand, that, for the period of pregnancy prior to this "compelling" point, the attending physician, in consultation with his patient, is free to determine, without regulation by the State, that, in his medical judgment, the patient's pregnancy should be terminated. If that decision is reached, the judgment may be effectuated by an abortion free of interference by the State.

With respect to the State's important and legitimate interest in potential life, the "compelling" point is at viability. This is so because the fetus then presumably has the capability of meaningful life outside the mother's womb. State regulation protective of fetal life after viability thus has both logical and biological justifications. If the State is interested in protecting fetal life after viability, it may go so far as to proscribe abortion during that period, except when it is necessary to preserve the life or health of the mother.

Measured against these standards, Art. 1196 of the Texas Penal Code, in restricting legal abortions to those "procured or attempted by medical advice for the purpose of saving the life of the mother," sweeps too broadly. The statute makes no distinction between abortions performed early in pregnancy and those performed later, and it limits to a single reason, "saving" the mother's life, the legal justification for the procedure. The statute, therefore, cannot survive the constitutional attack made upon it here.

. . .

Our conclusion that Art. 1196 is unconstitutional means, of course, that the Texas abortion statutes, as a unit, must fall. The exception of Art. 1196 cannot be struck down separately, for then the State would be left with a statute proscribing all abortion procedures no matter how medically urgent the case.

. . .

To summarize and to repeat:

. . . A state criminal abortion statute of the current Texas type, that excepts from criminality only a *life-saving* procedure on behalf of the mother, without regard to pregnancy stage and without recognition of the other interests involved, is violative of the Due Process Clause of the Fourteenth Amendment.

. . .

Mr. Justice Stewart, concurring.

. . .

The asserted state interests are protection of the health and safety of the pregnant woman, and protection of the potential future human life within her. These are legitimate objectives, amply sufficient to permit a State to regulate abortions as it does other surgical procedures, and perhaps sufficient to permit a State to regulate abortions more stringently or even to prohibit them in the late stages of pregnancy. But such legislation is not before us, and I think the Court today has thoroughly demonstrated that these state interests cannot constitutionally support the broad abridgment of personal liberty worked by the existing Texas law. Accordingly, I join the Court's opinion holding that that law is invalid under the Due Process Clause of the Fourteenth Amendment.

Mr. Justice Rehnquist, dissenting.

· · ·

Nothing in the Court's opinion indicates that Texas might not constitutionally apply its proscription of abortion as written to a woman in that stage of pregnancy. Nonetheless, the Court uses her complaint against the Texas statute as a fulcrum for deciding that States may impose virtually no restrictions on medical abortions performed during the *first* trimester of pregnancy. In deciding such a hypothetical lawsuit, the Court departs from the longstanding admonition that it should never "formulate a rule of constitutional law broader than is required by the precise facts to which it is to be applied." *Liverpool, New York & Philadelphia S. S. Co.* v. *Commissioners of Emigration*, 113 U. S. 33, 39 (1885). See also *Ashwander* v. *TVA*, 297 U. S. 288, 345 (1936) (Brandeis, J., concurring).

SECTION B. THE FEDERAL AND STATE RESPONSES TO THE COURT'S DECISION

A decision of the Supreme Court is the law of the land. But laws are not always followed, much less accepted. Supreme Court decisions apply only to the case at hand. Yet, by indicating how the Court will treat a particular challenge, the decision and the Court's explanation are guides to the legal rights of persons in similar situations and they establish a framework for subsequent political activity on the issue at all levels of government. The more direct and explicit is a challenge to the Court's decision, the more clearly it flaunts the authority of the national government. But there is no requirement for adherence to the spirit of the ruling, and there are numerous ways in which authorities hostile to a ruling may inhibit the realization of its spirit. Constitutional decisions are not always clear, and there are often loopholes left open; they often require executive action and congressional support in order to be effected; and there is always the possibility of a constitutional amendment.

The following selections indicate ways in which policy makers sought to circumvent the legal framework presented by the Supreme Court decision in *Roe* v. *Wade*. At the federal level, the response to the decision by opponents of the legalization of abortion took the form of attempts to amend the United States Constitution and efforts to attach antiabortion provisions to various statutes and appropriation bills in Congress. The following documents and materials reflect these responses. The first is a report of the United States Commission on Civil Rights. It deals with the legal developments relating to abortion up until April 1975. The report is useful both because it reveals a unique influence on the policy making process and because it summarizes the congressional activities to circumvent the decision, against a background of federal court decisions working out some of the issues left unresolved but clearly influenced by the Supreme Court's abortion decision.

THE FEDERAL RESPONSE

CONSTITUTIONAL ASPECTS
OF THE
RIGHT TO LIMIT CHILDBEARING

REPORT OF THE UNITED STATES COMMISSION ON CIVIL RIGHTS
APRIL 1975

The Court left a number of questions unanswered, some deliberately, in holding that the decision to have an abortion in the first trimester rests with the woman and her physician. Such questions as whether the consent of husbands, or the parents of a minor, can be required, whether public hospitals must permit or perform desired abortions, and whether public assistance programs must pay for them are being raised and are gradually winding their way through the courts. Where court decisions have been made, they have usually, but not always, struck down other-person consent requirements, denial of the use of government-owned hospital facilities, and other State legislative measures which would restrict access to abortion.[1]

[1]States may not limit/prohibit Medicaid payments: *Ryan v Klein*, 412 U.S. 924, vacated to be conformed with *Roe* and *Doe*, 412 U.S. 925 (1973). Public hospitals may not refuse to perform/permit abortions or sterilizations: *Doe v. Hale Hosp.*, 500 F.2d 144 (1st Cir. 1974). Private hospitals may refuse to permit abortions or sterilizations: *Allen v. Sisters of St. Joseph*, 361 F.Supp. 1212, 1213 (N.D. Texas 1973). Consent of husband, putative father, or parents not required for abortion or sterilization: *Murray v. Vandevander*, 522 P.2d 302 (Okla. Ct. App. 1974). Restrictions must comport with trimester system established in *Roe* and *Doe*: *Nelson v. Planned Parenthood Center of Tucson Inc.*, 19 Ariz. App. 142,

At the Federal level, a number of proposed constitutional amendments have been introduced in the Congress to override the Supreme Court decision by imposing an absolute ban on abortion, or by permitting States to prohibit abortion in any way they see fit, despite the Court decision . . . .

S.J. Res. 119, 93rd Congress, 1st Session (May 31, 1973) introduced by Senator Buckley (C.R. N.Y.); S.J. Res. 10, 94th Congress, 1st Session (January 23, 1975) introduced by Senator Buckley:

Joint Resolution, Proposing an amendment to the Constitution of the United States for the protection of unborn children and other persons.

Resolved by the Senate and House of Representatives of the United States of America in Congress assembled (two-thirds of each House concurring therein), that the following article is proposed as an amendment to the Constitution of the United States, which shall be valid to all intents and purposes as part of the Constitution when ratified by the legislatures of three-fourths of the several States within seven years from the date of its submission by the Congress:

"ARTICLE —

"Section 1.   With respect to the right to life, the word 'person,' as used in this article and in the fifth and fourteenth articles of amendment to the Constitution of the United States, applies to all human beings, including their unborn offspring at every stage of their biological development, irrespective of age, health, function, or condition of dependency.

"Section 2.   This article shall not apply in an emergency when a reasonable medical certainty exists that continuation of the pregnancy will cause the death of the mother.

"Section 3.   Congress and the several States shall have the power to enforce this article by appropriate legislation within their respective jurisdictions."

In the Congress, some members have attempted to attach restrictive anti-abortion riders to seemingly non-abortion-related bills. The legislation enacted includes: the abortion-related "conscience clause" in the Health

---

505 P.2d 580 (1973). States may not impose restrictions based upon a redefinition of "viability": *Doe v. Israel,* 282 F.2d 157 (1st Cir. 1973). Statutes may not limit/ prohibit dissemination of information or advertising on abortion: *Mitchell Family Planning Inc.* v. *City of Royal Oak,* 335 F.Supp. 738 (E.D. Mich. 1972). AFDC [Aid to Families with Dependent Children] cannot be denied to unborn children where mother chooses not to terminate pregacy: *Alcala v. Burns,* 494 F.2d 743 (8th Cir. 1974).

Programs Extension Act of 1973; an abortion funding ban in the Foreign Assistance Act of 1973; a fetal research ban included in the National Science Foundation Authorization Act of 1974; a limited fetal research ban in the National Research Awards and Protection of Human Subjects Act, and a provision in the Legal Services Corporation Act prohibiting legal services attorneys from handling abortion-related cases.

. . .

The "conscience clause" amendment prohibits the withholding of Federal funds authorized by the act from hospitals, both public and private, which refuse to perform abortions or sterilizations on the basis of religious or moral beliefs. This statute flies in the face of the decisions in *Doe* and *Roe* governing access to abortions as well as the rulings of several Federal and State courts which, following *Roe* and *Doe*, have declared unconstitutional the refusal of public hospitals to permit the performance of abortions. Such refusal, the Supreme Court has decided, is a deprivation of the right to privacy and liberty in matters relating to marriage, sex, procreation, and the family; all in violation of the First, Fourth, Fifth, Ninth, and Fourteenth Amendments to the Constitution.

The Foreign Assistance Act provides that none of the funds made available can be used to pay for abortion as a method of family planning. This section is designed to export forcibly American anti-abortion views to recipients of aid abroad even when they regard abortion as a means of solving overpopulation problems and even when other methods of family planning are funded. The fetal research bans in the National Science Foundation Appropriations Act and the National Research Service Awards and Protection of Human Subjects Act are designed, contrary to the decisions of the Supreme Court, to impose the view that fetuses are human beings, and to restrict the availability of physicians to perform abortions on the assumption that the need to use fetuses in medical research is an abortion incentive.

The Legal Services Corporation Act, in straightforward fashion, prohibits legal services attorneys from handling abortion-related cases in yet another effort to restrict the use of abortion procedures. The proposed amendments to the Community Services Act of 1974 and the Social Security Act Medicaid Provisions, to prohibit any use of funds for abortion, would put poor women in the same position they were in before *Doe* v. *Bolton* was decided — unable to pay for therapeutic abortions, and thus compelled to seek out illicit practitioners or not to abort at all.

The last anti-abortion effort by the Congress in 1974 involved the Department of Labor and the Department of Health, Education and Welfare appropriations bill, H.R. 15580, 93d Cong., 2d Sess. (1974).

The following selection from the *Congressional Record* concerns a subsequent attempt by Senator Bartlett to attach an antiabortion amendment to the Social Security Act. The amendment was to be attached to Senate Bill 66 and the debate took place on the floor of the Senate on 10 April 1975. The *Record* is not always an accurate representation of what went on in debate because the members of Congress have an opportunity to clean up what they have said. They cannot of course change what others said, and, in the case of tightly integrated materials like those on the Bartlett amendment, the record provides a reasonably sound approximation of what occurred.

Senate Debate on Antiabortion Amendment to the Social Security Act

Mr. Bartlett: Mr. President, I call up my amendment No. 336.

The Presiding Officer: The amendment will be stated.

The legislative clerk read as follows:

The Senator from Oklahoma (Mr. Bartlett) proposes an amendment numbered 336:

At the end of the bill add a new section as follows:

Sec. — . No funds authorized under the Social Security Act may be used to pay for or encourage the performance of abortions, except such abortions as are necessary to save the life of a mother.

The Presiding Officer: Is this an amendment for which there is a 2 hour time limitation agreement?

Mr. Bartlett: That is correct. This is the amendment upon which the time agreement was reached.

Mr. President, time and time again, the U.S. Congress has gone on record opposing the use of Federal dollars to finance abortions. We have done this in defense bills, foreign aid bills, and HEW bills.

Presently our law prohibits HEW from administering Federal funds as a means of family planning under the Family Planning Act of 1970.

Unfortunately, the Family Planning Act just scratches the surface of eliminating the Federal Government from the abortion business; and evidently the record of Congress' opposition to abortion financing has gone unheeded.

The last records which were made available to me indicate that in 1973

SOURCE: The *Congressional Record*, 10 April 1975.

our Department of Health, Education, and Welfare spent some $40 to $50 million to pay for approximately 270,000 abortions.

Reports I have recently received indicate about the same record for 1974. They do fail to provide us accurate figures in either case.

Mr. President, after learning this information, I introduced last fall an amendment to the HEW appropriations bill which would prohibit the use of HEW funds, our tax dollars, from being used for abortions. This amendment passed the Senate on a voice vote after a motion to table failed in a 50 to 34 vote.

However, the amendment was deleted in conference primarily because the conferees ruled it was substantive legislation in an appropriation bill. However, a majority of the conferees indicated their support for the measure. In their report they said:

A majority of the Conferees strongly support the apparent intent of the Senate amendment to prohibit the use of public funds to pay for or encourage abortions. Nevertheless, they are persuaded that an annual appropriation bill is an improper vehicle for such a controversial and far-reaching legislative provision whose implications and ramifications are not clear, whose constitutionality has been challenged, and on which on hearings have been held. The rules and traditions of both the House and the Senate militate against the inclusion of legislative language in appropriation bills. The Conferees urge the appropriate legislative committees of the Congress to give early consideration to the enactment into basic law of carefully drawn legislation dealing with the subject of abortion.

Consistent with the wishes of the conference, I am offering this amendment to an appropriate authorization bill.

The Supreme Court dodged the issue of when human life begins by saying:

When those trained in the respective disciplines of medicine, philosophy, and theology are unable to arrive at any consensus, the judiciary at this point in the development of man's knowledge is not in a position to speculate as to the answer. We need not resolve the difficult question of when life begins.

Now, although the Supreme Court may find that question difficult to answer, as a matter of fact there is virtually unanimous consent among sciences, biologists, philosophers, and theologians as to when life does begin. Life begins at the moment of conception when the ovum is fertilized by the sperm, forming that unique genetic organism called the zygote or fetus. From that moment forward, life, the product of God and two human beings, is in existence.

Congress has a real opportunity by passing this amendment to guarantee the right to life of thousands of the unborn of the poor who otherwise will lose their lives.

This Congress would be guaranteeing for many the challenge of the

Declaration of Independence that governments should guarantee the right to human life.

Mr. President, I reserve the remainder of my time.

Mr. Kennedy: Mr. President, at some later time during the course of the debate, a motion will be made to table this amendment, but I do think it is appropriate for those who have views on this issue — and I know there are those who have extremely strong views — to be able to express them during the course of the debate.

I think, quite frankly, as appropriate as it may be as a public policy issue for us to consider the question of the use of taxpayers' funds in support of this particular procedure, this is not the place to resolve the issue. So I am opposed to the amendment on the basis of the procedure that is being followed.

This amendment has not been the subject of any hearings, either in our Health Committee or even in the Committee on Finance. Since this is an amendment to the Social Security Act, the Finance Committee should have hearings on this issue, and I have no knowledge of whether the chairman of the Finance Committee is willing to even consider it.

But it does seem to me appropriate, as we talk about this issue of abortion that we also consider the services that are being provided within the various health programs such as the medicaid programs for maternity care and delivery; because there have been six different court decisions that have said that if the Federal Government is going to make a decision to supply maternity care and pay for deliveries on the one hand, and make that decision as a matter of Federal policy, there are serious constitutional questions whether we can deny the opportunity to someone who wants to use Federal funds for an abortion.

This is a 14th amendment issue. It is an equal rights issue. It is an issue, I think, of very great importance and significance. As I say, there are six different district court decisions at the present time that have held that if we are going to fund maternity care and delivery on the one hand, we cannot deny funds for abortion on the other hand.

. . .

Mr. Kennedy: If a medical judgment were made that the physiological impact of an IUD was post-fertilization, would the Senator prohibit the IUD under the language of his amendment?

Mr. Bartlett: If the IUDs would be determined to be abortions, then this would prohibit it.

Mr. Kennedy: Under whose interpretation that it would be an abortion?

Mr. Bartlett: Under the record I am making on this bill, in my interpretation.

Mr. Kennedy: And, as the Senator knows, at the present time there is a very substantial body of medical opinion that believes that that is exactly the case. Of course it is not a medical certainty, but there is a very substantial body of medical opinion that believes that is the case. Under the Senator's amendment, then, he would prohibit the morning after pill and he would prohibit the use of an IUD.

Mr. Bartlett: Let me say, in complete answer to the distinguished Senator, that I agree that there is a substantial number of people who agree that the morning after pill is committing an abortion. There are those who do not.

Mr. Kennedy: How are we to know? How does the Senator's amendment give us the answer? The Senator just said a minute ago that it would be barred, and now the Senator is kind of qualifying it. What is the HEW person supposed to interpret from this legislative history?

Mr. Bartlett: No. I am saying if it creates an abortion it would be barred.

Mr. Kennedy: But how are we going to know? The Senator does not define abortion in his amendment.

Mr. Bartlett: Well, if there would ever need to be a decision it could, of course, go to court.

Mr. Kennedy: How is the court going to know? They read the legislative history, and we have two different answers.

Mr. Bartlett: The court, of course, is going to know. They created, of course, the moral issue that is —

Mr. Kennedy: How do we know what the Senator's amendment means?

Mr. Bartlett: So I do not think the Supreme Court would find any difficulty at all in coming to a conclusion on this matter.

Mr. Kennedy: Well, they read the legislative history, and it has been back and forth just in the time we have had it here.

. . .

Mr. Buckley: Mr. President, as a cosponsor of the amendment introduced by the Senator from Oklahoma, I would like to say just a few words in support of this amendment.

There are two points that should be raised about such a charge. First, it is simply not true that denying tax dollars for practices held to be rights by Supreme Court decisions is discriminatory. The taxpayer is under no obligation to fund with his money any and all rights. Traditional congressional policy prohibits this Federal financing, a policy which was first explicitly stated in the Family Planning Act of 1970 and reiterated in the first session of the 93rd Congress by the enactment into law of an amendment proscribing the use of foreign aid funds for abortion. Both Houses of Congress are repeatedly on record as opposing Government funds for abortion.

The issue of Federal funding is wholly distinct from the constitutional question decided by the Supreme Court on January 22, 1973. It by no means follows from the fact that a woman is now legally permitted to seek an abortion, that the Federal Government is constitutionally or otherwise obligated to pay for it. It is apparent that abortion is now being promoted as a new-found panacea to certain social and economic problems. Several years ago, the arguments favoring liberalized abortion were couched almost exclusively in terms of the woman's "right to privacy." In the past few years, especially since the Supreme Court's ruling, the arguments for abortion have acquired a new and ominous focus, one that emphasizes the social, economic, and political utility of abortion. Abortions in general and publically funded abortions in particular, are now being advanced as a socially "progressive" and "enlightened" solution to the problems of poverty and welfare. When abortions are openly defended on the explicit grounds that they help to limit the welfare population and reduce public expenditures, I submit we are traveling rapidly down a road that will subject all human life, born or unborn, to the risks of some social planner's cost/benefit calculus. This reduces itself to the simple argument that the way to eliminate people's problems is to eliminate people.

. . .

The Presiding Officer: Who yields time?

Mr. Kennedy: I yield 5 minutes to the Senator from Illinois.

Mr. Percy: Mr. President, last year when an antiabortion amendment was attached to the Labor-HEW appropriations bill, the U.S. Commission on Civil Rights indicated its intention to report on the constitutional aspects of the right to limit childbearing. Because similar amendments to S. 66 have been offered, I wrote to Dr. Arthur S. Flemming, the Chairman of the Commission, asking about the report which will be released next week.

Dr. Flemming's response is vital to the consideration of antiabortion legislation and I wish to share it with my colleagues. I have placed a copy of Dr. Flemming's letter on the desk of each of my colleagues. I urge their careful reading of it. . . . Mr. President, I wish to read just two sentences from that letter. Dr. Flemming said:

One of the report's three major recommendations is that "Congress should reject anti-abortion legislation and amendments, and repeal those which have been enacted, which undermine the constitutional right to limit childbearing." The commission makes this recommendation, and urges the Senate specifically to reject the proposed Bartlett amendments to S. 66.

Mr. President, Senator Bartlett's antiabortion amendment must not be attached to S. 66. I fully support the action to table this amendment.

Mr. Kennedy: Mr. President, I yield 10 minutes to the Senator from New York.

Mr. Javits: Mr. President, I think that the arguments which have been made have been very elucidating, but, as *I* shall make the motion to table, I think it is very important to specify why tabling, which is sometimes not greeted too happily by my colleagues, is uniquely appropriate in this situation.

First, Mr. President, notwithstanding what my beloved friend Senator Pastore has said, the fact is that Federal money is being spent for medical treatment which would be defined by Senator Pastore and his colleagues as abortion right now. It is not something that will happen, it is going on right now. Hence, if we stop it, we are affirmatively acting to perpetrate a discrimination upon the poor women of America. It is as bold as that.

That has been borne out by Senator Buckley's figures. Without arguing the accuracy of the statistics and even if we concede that 28 percent of all money that is spent for abortion is Federal money, the fact remains that 72 percent is not Federal money. So if we abandon it now, that 28 percent of women utilizing Federal money will be discriminated against, because they cannot otherwise afford it.

What does Senator Pastore say to that? He says "Let them eat cake or get charity." That is the argument. You cannot defend it on any moral or humanitarian ground. And, Mr. President, we are at least 50 years beyond that time . . . .

Mr. President, I move to lay the amendment on the table, and I demand the yeas and nays.

The Presiding Officer: Is there a sufficient second? There is a sufficient second.

The yeas and nays were ordered.

The Presiding Officer . . . On this question the yeas and nays have been ordered, and the clerk will call the roll.

The legislative clerk called the roll.

Mr. Randolph (after having voted in the negative): On this vote, I have voted "no." I have a live pair with the Senator from Hawaii (Mr. Inouye). If he were present, he would vote "aye." I therefore withdraw my vote.

Mr. Robert C. Byrd: I announce that the Senator from Nevada (Mr. Cannon), the Senator from Hawaii (Mr. Inouye), the Senator from Washington (Mr. Magnuson), and the Senator from North Carolina (Mr. Morgan) are necessarily absent.

I also announce that the Senator from Montana (Mr. Metcalf) is absent because of death in the family.

I further announce that, if present and voting, the Senator from Washington (Mr. Magnuson) would vote "yea."

Mr. Griffin: I announce that the Senator from Tennessee (Mr. Baker), the Senator from Pennsylvania (Mr. Hugh Scott), and the Senator from Ohio (Mr. Taft) are necessarily absent.

I further announce that, if present and voting, the Senator from Pennsylvania (Mr. Hugh Scott), and the Senator from Ohio (Mr. Taft) would each vote "yea."

The result was announced — yeas 54, nays 36, as follows:

[Rollcall Vote No. 130 Leg.]

YEAS—54

Abóurezk	Hart, Phillip A.	Nunn
Bayh	Haskell	Packwood
Beall	Hathaway	Pearson
Bentsen	Hollings	Pell
Brock	Huddleston	Percy
Brooke	Humphrey	Ribicoff
Bumpers	Jackson	Scott, William L.
Burdick	Javits	Stafford
Byrd, Robert C.	Kennedy	Stevens
Case	Laxalt	Stevenson
Chiles	Leahy	Symington
Clark	Mansfield	Talmadge
Cranston	Mathias	Tower
Culver	McGovern	Tunney
Fong	McIntyre	Weicker
Ford	Mondale	Williams
Glenn	Moss	
Gravel	Muskie	
Hart, Gary W.	Nelson	

NAYS—36

Allen	Fannin	McClure
Bartlett	Garn	McGee
Bellmon	Goldwater	Montoya
Biden	Griffin	Pastore
Buckley	Hansen	Proxmire
Byrd, Harry F., Jr.	Hartke	Roth
Church	Hatfield	Schweiker
Curtis	Helms	Sparkman
Dole	Hruska	Stennis
Domenici	Johnston	Stone
Eagleton	Long	Thurmond
Eastland	McClellan	Young

PRESENT AND GIVING A LIVE PAIR, AS PREVIOUSLY RECORDED — 1

Randolph, against.

NOT VOTING — 8

Baker	Magnuson	Scott, Hugh
Cannon	Metcalf	Taft
Inouye	Morgan	

The first vote on Senator Bartlett's amendment in 1974 was 50 senators in favor and 34 against. The vote came in September of 1974, just before the midterm elections. Since the amendment was deleted in conference, Bartlett attempted to attach his amendment to another appropriations bill. In the second vote, only 36 senators supported it, with 54 voting to have it put aside. All the senators who changed their votes went from support of the amendment (or no comment) to opposition. Yet, of these 19, only 5 were up for reelection. The most significant aspect of this switch may be that 4 of the 5 had abstained from recording any position on the 1974 bill. This situation is representative of the considerable confusion about the political affect of the abortion issue. *Congressional Quarterly* has reported that members of Congress view the issue of abortion as a "no win" conflict. The polls show an even split among the population as a whole on the issue. It has been an issue on which most politicians have avoided taking a visible stand. Planned Parenthood Federation published an extensive study on the impact of having taken a position on abortion for the political future of a number of politicians. Among incumbents, it found that a smaller proportion with consistently "antiabortion" voting records were reelected in 1974 (81 percent) than among incumbents with consistently "proabortion" records (98 percent). The figures, although not establishing very clearly the effect of such a stand, suggest that it is not the overwhelmingly negative factor that some are said to fear. The concern among politicians may result at least partially from strong lobbying by antiabortion groups. Strident statements, such as "We can never let it rest — the issue will never die as long as *Roe* and *Doe* stay on the books," made by a lobbyist for the National Committee for a Human Life Amendment Inc., indicate the commitment of these groups. The confusion is clear in a letter sent by Senator Hugh Scott to his constituents in March of 1975.

Dear — :
Many thanks for sharing with me your concerns about my introducing a Constitutional Amendment to restrict abortion. It was good of you to take the time to write.

As you know, my consideration of introducing a Constitutional Amendment to prohibit abortion, except for certain compelling reasons, has met with great opposition from both sides. The "Right to Life" movement considers my proposal too liberal; the feminists consider it restrictive and discriminatory.

In view of the expressed opposition indicating unacceptability from widely opposing points of view, and because the drafting of legislative language to conform to my views appears impossible, I believe it is both useless and unrealistic to pursue this avenue any further.

Again, thank you so much for contacting me.

Sincerely,
Hugh Scott

On 17 September 1976, in the closing days of the term, Congress banned the use of federal funds to pay for abortions "except where the life of the mother would be endangered if the fetus were carried to term."

THE REACTION IN THE STATES

The Supreme Court's decision was based on the federal Constitution and stimulated a reaction at the national level, but it was directed toward legislation in the states. Justice Blackmun's opinion would serve to indicate the nature of the traditional standards regarding the relationship between a right to privacy and the state's power to legislate on the health and welfare of its citizens. It is the states that are primarily responsible for the criminal law. The decision determined the standards that could be set on the conduct of abortions. The states, as a consequence, became a forum for response to the 1973 decision. Abortions did not automatically become available in all of the states as a result of the Supreme Court's decision. Although those who greeted the decision with enthusiasm anticipated that it would mean greater freedom in obtaining an abortion, the decision simply stated when and in what fashion the legislatures of the 50 states could make abortion a crime. The reaction in the states was well reported in the news media, but a view of a number of individual states is needed to understand the effect of the decision on policy. The law of the states at the time of the decision, the attitudes of the population as perceived by public officials, the interested organizations in existence, the state legislative process, and the activities of the lower courts were the primary factors in the response at this level. Some of the responses are reproduced here. They are followed by a lower court decision on a state's effort to circumvent the decision in *Roe* v. *Wade*. The material on state response concludes with a section of the reformulated Massachusetts abortion law passed subsequent to the Supreme Court decision.

The existing state laws and the forces active in each state prior to the decisions supply the context through which the Supreme Court decision was filtered. As already indicated, 30 states had abortion provisions similar to the Texas statute and a number of others reflected the American Law Institute standard. Only the statutes of New York, Hawaii, California, and Washington treated abortion strictly as a medical issue before the Supreme Court's decision and were not in a position to have to rewrite their statutes. In Maine and in Rhode Island, the state abortion laws were under court challenge and the judges in those cases had been awaiting a decision from the United States Supreme Court before handing down their rulings. In Connecticut, a United States District Court ruled the state's antiabortion law unconstitutional. The Supreme Court of Vermont had recently ruled that state's law unconstitutional and legalized abortions until "quickening," which the Attorney General subsequently ruled to occur in the twelfth week of pregnancy.

In Ohio, the President of the Cleveland Area Student Pro-Life Youth was reported in a *Plain Dealer* interview to have advocated support for a constitutional amendment, which he determined to be the only available avenue of response to the Supreme Court ruling. This position recognized the situation in which the prolife forces seemed to find themselves as a result of the Supreme Court's decision. In New York, the state's liberal abortion law, one of the few not overruled by the Supreme Court, had been feeling considerable "prolife" pressure prior to the decision. The law had been repealed once the previous year, only to be vetoed by the Governor. Assembly Speaker Perry B. Duryea was reported by the *New York Times* to have said that "it would be futile to bring repeal legislation up for debate again." According to the *Des Moines Register*, during the week prior to the Court's decision, proabortion leaders in the legislature had agreed to lower the period for legal abortions from 20 weeks to 12 in the hope that the move would broaden support for their proposals. The bill, drafted prior to the decision, had to be redrafted to conform with the Supreme Court ruling, but when the decision was reported, the supporters of the bill decided to "start the process moving toward the floor." An editorial in the *Register* on 24 January 1973 stated:

The Supreme Court's abortion ruling has spared legislators in Iowa and other states the need to hold emotion charged hearings and debates on a volatile issue .... The abortion ruling is a defense of the individual's freedom of choice at a time when individuals and groups are trying to exploit the state's power so they can impose their moral beliefs on the whole population.

The Supreme Court gave proabortion partisans a victory in Iowa that was far more generous than they might have been able to anticipate had they been forced to rely on state support for their proposal.

In each of the states, the Attorney General's office is the major public source for interpretation of judicial decisions. These leaders were generally rather cautious on this issue. In Iowa, Attorney General Richard Turner said that the decision "apparently" made Iowa's law unconstitutional, but he stopped short of declaring abortion to be legal in Iowa. In the same vein, Attorney General Larry Derryberry told reporters in Oklahoma that it was hard to tell what the decision meant and he would have to study it. Both lawmen did indicate that a prosecution for abortion seemed to be unlikely. In Massachusetts, Attorney General Robert H. Quinn, who was interviewed by the *Springfield Union* on 24 January 1973, also stressed that he needed time to study the decision. He said that he did not plan to work for change in the state's statute and noted that the ruling took precedence over existing state law.

Considerable regrouping followed the Court's decision as pro- and antiabortion forces assessed the new legal terrain, but eventually most states did revise their laws. When the states had approved new statutes on abortion, the courts once again had to determine whether they conformed to constitutional protections. The following summary by Arthur H. Bernstein, a hospital attorney in Oakland, California, appeared in June of 1974. It is the sort of widely disseminated legal opinion through which professionals concerned with legal matters get a sense of the legal developments. This report appeared in *Hospitals, Journal of the American Hospital Association.*[1]

While the Supreme Court principles were comprehensible, they were not comprehensive. Many questions were left unanswered. Inevitably, these queries had to be resolved by the lesser courts. An initial challenge to the Supreme Court's action was presented by the Rhode Island legislature. The previous state antiabortion statute having been rendered unconstitutional, a new one was enacted. Its novel approach was to declare that human life begins at the moment of conception. Therefore, from that instant, a fetus would be a person entitled to constitutional protection under the Fourteenth Amendment. Under this condition of law, to permit the mother to choose abortion would violate the rights of a "person," the fetus, and one who participated in an abortion procedure would face criminal sanctions.

[1]Vol. 48, no. 11, p. 108 (June 1, 1974). Reprinted with permission.

The new criminal statute was quickly challenged by three pregnant women. A federal court made short shrift of the enactment. It pointed out that the Supreme Court, in the abortion opinions, had decided that a fetus is not a person and thus cannot be protected by the Fourteenth Amendment. No state legislature can override the Supreme Court's prerogatives in determining the meaning of the Constitution. Rhode Island's Solons were no more successful at "interposition" than certain southern governors had been a decade ago. *Doe* v. *Israel,* 358 F. Supp. 1193 (D.C. R.I., 1973).

Massachusetts passed its new law subsequent to the decision in Rhode Island, and the effort to conform to the Supreme Court's ruling is evident. The provisions of Sections 12I and 12J provide evidence that the legislature was attempting to draw up its statute according to the dictates of Justice Blackmun's opinion. The 24-week period is simply a more explicit statement of the Justice's second trimester division. However, there is also evidence, in Sections 12K, 12L, and 12N, that the state was not ready to facilitate or in any way encourage abortion. The one- to five-year prison term makes abortion a rather serious crime. These stipulations will necessarily have some influence on the application of the new legislation and on the status of abortion in Massachusetts.

THE REVISED MASSACHUSETTS LAW ON ABORTION
(MASSACHUSETTS CODE: Professions and Occupations)

SEC. 12I. ABORTION; PREGNANCY EXISTING FOR LESS THAN 24 WEEKS

If a pregnancy has existed for less than twenty-four weeks no abortion may be performed except by a physician and only if, in the best medical judgment of a physician, the abortion is necessary under all attendant circumstances.
Added by St.1974, c. 706, Sec. 1.

. . .

SEC. 12J. ABORTION; PREGNANCY EXISTING FOR 24 WEEKS OR MORE

If a pregnancy has existed for twenty-four weeks or more, no abortion may be performed except by a physician and only if it is necessary to save the life of the mother, or if a continuation of her pregnancy will impose on her a substantial risk of grave impairment of her physical or mental health.
Added by St.1974, c. 706, Sec. 1.

. . .

SEC. 12K. VIOLATION OF SECTIONS 12I OR 12J; PUNISHMENT

Any person who violates the provisions of sections twelve I or twelve J shall be punished by imprisonment for not less than one year nor more than five years. Conduct which violates the provisions of this act, which also violates any other criminal laws of the commonwealth, may be punished either under the provisions of this act or under such other applicable criminal laws.
Added by St.1974, c. 706, Sec. 1.

. . .

SEC. 12L. ABORTION PERFORMED PURSUANT TO SECTION 12J; PROTECTION OF UNBORN CHILD

If an abortion is performed pursuant to section twelve J, no abortion procedure which is designed to destroy the life of the unborn child or injure the unborn child in its mother's womb may be used unless, in the physician's best medical judgment, all other available procedures would create a greater risk of death or serious bodily harm to the mother either at the time of the abortion, or subsequently as the result of a future pregnancy, than the one being used.
Added by St.1974, c. 706, Sec. 1.

. . .

SEC. 12N. RESTRICTIONS ON ABORTIONS PERFORMED UNDER SECTION 12I OR 12J; EMERGENCY EXCEPTED

Except in an emergency requiring immediate action, no abortion may be performed under sections twelve I or twelve J unless (1) the written informed consent of the proper person or persons has been delivered to the physician performing the abortion as set forth in section twelve P and (2) if the abortion is during or after the thirteenth week of pregnancy it is performed in a hospital duly authorized to provide facilities for general surgery.

Except in an emergency requiring immediate action, no abortion may be performed under section twelve J unless performed in a hospital duly authorized to provide facilities for obstetrical services.
Added by St.1974, c. 706, Sec. 1.

Although state statutes such as these would ordinarily be the intervening form through which a locality confronts an issue upon which the Supreme Court has ruled, there is a time between the Supreme Court's decision and the passage of state legislation during which localities are technically governed directly by the Supreme Court's decision. The final section of this chapter explores such a case in Boston, Massachusetts.

SECTION C. THE TRIAL OF DR. EDELIN

Some attention has been paid to the way in which national policy on abortion structures the state legislative responses and those of the Attorney Generals in each state. But the actual impact on citizens resulting from a judicial decision occurs at the local level, the same level of government from which the appeal to the Supreme Court was first brought. In this sphere, one consideration relevant to understanding legal policy making is the way in which doctrines related to the federal Constitution by a court in Washington, D.C. affect citizens across the country. For instance, the effect of the decision on the number of legal abortions performed in the United States was dramatic. From 1972 through 1974, they increased 54 percent. This does not, of course, mean that there were more abortions, simply that there were more legal ones. By 1974, 900,000 women were taking advantage of the procedure. Untold numbers of others were affected to the extent that the political and social world in which they lived — the world that determined the options they had in their lives — was a different one as a result of the Court's decision. Since a substantial number of abortions were performed in the years when abortions were legally available in only a few states, the figures suggest that the increase due to the Supreme Court decision has come primarily from lower-income women. These women would not have previously been able to make the costly trip to states where abortions were legal. By 1974, abortion had become the second most frequently performed operation in the country. It trailed only tonsillectomies.

The cities and towns that make up this nation are, in many senses of the word, some distance from Washington, D.C. Most are far from the machinery of power. Yet, in the sphere of judicial politics, the hierarchical structure of the courts somewhat minimizes this distance. Although the interests of a locality may be very different from those in Washington, constitutional law dictates the framework of local response or reaction to issues in the legal area. However, it does not determine the imagination or interests of those who would engage in political activity to circumvent the Court's decision. The present case, although the consequences to my mind are unfortunate, is an example of that imagination and those interests struggling to survive in the closely defined space of constitutional doctrine.

Given the attention to government in this collection, it is appropriate to conclude this chapter with the legal process reaching out to an individual. The procedure is an indictment. Presumably some event has occurred, and the official entrusted by the public with the task of administering its laws has decided to act. The indictment is the product of his actions. In this case, the indictment comes from the office of a District Attorney, who is said to have found it politically expedient to begin this particular prosecution.

The controversy arose when antiabortion activists discovered articles printed in the *New England Medical Journal*, which detailed experiments on fetal tissue that had been acquired following abortions at Boston City Hospital. Antiabortion groups brought the experiments to the attention of the politicians in this predominantly Catholic city. A city council hearing on the matter featured representatives of the church and antiabortion speakers. According to the *New York Times*, District Attorney Garrett Byrne, "facing what appeared to be a difficult Democratic primary against the Chairman of the School Committee who was gaining a lot of publicity from his stand against the court mandated busing of city's school children, opened up an investigation." Newman A. Flanagan, the Assistant District Attorney in charge of the case, was also a possible successor to the District Attorney. Flanagan was the one who actually prepared the indictment and conducted the case in the name of "the people." The indictment is the means by which a person is charged with a crime. It is a formal document, which in most cases must be reviewed by a special panel of citizens known as a grand jury. A copy of the document follows.

THE INDICTMENT OF KENNETH EDELIN

COMMONWEALTH OF MASSACHUSETTS

At the Superior Court, begun and held at the City of Boston, within and for the County of Suffolk, for the transaction of Criminal Business, on the first Monday of April, in the year of our Lord one thousand nine hundred and seventy-four.

The Jurors for the Commonwealth of Massachusetts on their oath present that

KENNETH EDELIN

on the third day of October, in the year of our Lord one thousand nine hundred and seventy-three did assault and beat a certain person, to wit: a male child described to the said Jurors as Baby Boy——————, and by such assault and beating did kill the said person.

A TRUE BILL

Assistant District Attorney   Foreman of the Grand Jury
(his signature)   (his signature)

The charge of manslaughter stipulated in the indictment means the killing of a person without malice. Involuntary manslaughter generally involves reckless or careless conduct that results in the death of a person. Conviction on a manslaughter charge could bring a prison sentence up to 20 years, or a $1000 fine and up to two and one-half years in jail. The person to whom the indictment was addressed, and who became the defendant in this trial, was Kenneth Edelin. He was a 36-year-old obstetrician-gynecologist, originally from Washington, D.C., who practiced in Boston City Hospital. Edelin was represented in the proceedings by William P. Homans, Jr., described by the *Boston Globe* as that city's best-known civil rights lawyer. The Judge hearing the case was James P. McGuire. He had come to Suffolk County Superior Court upon the nomination of Massachusetts Governor Francis Sargent. These four men, along with the jury chosen later, would be the dominant participants in the Boston trial.

PRETRIAL MANEUVERS

Prior to the beginning of a trial, the attorneys for each party involved in the case have the opportunity to discuss before a judge whether the case should go to trial and what the ground rules for a trial should be. The material selected is from the verbatim transcripts taken down by the court reporter during these proceedings. It contains pauses, flubs, and mistakes on the part of the attorneys as well as the sometimes remarkable capacity of a capable lawyer to develop a complex line of argument without speaking from a prepared text. These selections deal with the law under which the case will be brought and the Judge's interpretation of how it should be applied. They reveal, perhaps better than any other material, the way in which the decision of the United States Supreme Court influenced how the prosecution in Boston would be conducted.

"Motions" are appeals to the Presiding Judge for answers to certain questions that the attorneys have. The "motion to dismiss" argued that the trial should not be conducted at all because Edelin had performed an abortion after the Supreme Court had made such an operation legal. The Judge refused the request from Edelin's attorney because of the prosecutor's argument that the doctor was not being charged with an abortion, but with manslaughter. The request from the defense for "particulars" and "further specifications," which is contained below, asks the prosecution to provide more information than is contained in the indictment on how the state's law against manslaughter applies to the case. The prosecution responded to this request with its explanation and asked the Judge to "dismiss" the motion. The Judge upheld the appropriateness of the indictment and accepted the prosecution's interpretation of the distinction between manslaughter and abortion. It was a distinction that seems not to have been considered by the Supreme Court in its decision in *Roe* v. *Wade*. It represents the capacity of a locality to proceed on the basis of the laws of the state and the community where they do not conflict with those of the federal government. Particularly important in this regard is that it is the locality that first makes such decisions, and often several years may pass before agents of the federal government have the opportunity to review actions such as these.

Hearing on Motions

COMMONWEALTH OF MASSACHUSETTS

SUFFOLK, SS:

81,823

SUPERIOR COURT

FIRST CRIMINAL SECTION

MCGUIRE, JUDGE

COMMONWEALTH

VS.

KENNETH EDELIN

PRESENT:

NEWMAN A. FLANAGAN, ESQ., ASSISTANT DISTRICT ATTORNEY

WILLIAM P. HOMANS, JR., ESQ.

HEARING ON MOTION TO DISMISS AND OTHER MOTIONS

BOSTON, MASS.

OCTOBER 10, 1974

EDWARD H. GOLDBERG

OFFICIAL COURT REPORTER

Affidavit in Support of Motion for Grand Jury Testimony

I am informed and believe and therefore aver that (1) the "question of when life begins" is a "difficult question" and has not been resolved by the decision of the United States Supreme Court in *Roe* v. *Wade* (1973), (2) that the question of the duty of a physician toward a fetus which is "potentially able to live outside a mother's womb, albeit with artificial aid" is not settled by the decision in *Roe* v. *Wade*, (3) that the definition of what constitutes an abortion, that is, what intentional conduct is included within the definition of "abortion" as explicated in *Roe* v. *Wade* is unsettled, (4) that there are by no means fixed and precise rules from which the weight or height of a fetus can be used to determine fetal age or its life or viability, and (5) that under the decision of the Supreme Judicial Court [of Massachusetts] *Dietrick* v. *Northampton* 138 MA 14 (1884) and others, the question of criminal liability, if any, for the death of a fetus which may or may not be viable at the time it is no longer in its mother's womb, is unsettled.

William P. Homans, Jr., Esq.

Argument in Support of Motion for a "Bill of Particulars"

MR. HOMANS:

As we suggest in our memorandum, may it please the court, and I am now referring to . . . pages 164–165 of *Roe* against *Wade* at 410, U.S. . . . what the court has held in *Roe* against *Wade* is the periods when and the extent to which the Commonwealth, in this case, or any of the other 49 states can regulate or at some stages proscribe abortion and still conform with the 14th Amendment, and to briefly summarize, your honor, at the first trimester, the — there is no permission given by the court to the regulation of abortion by the state other than obviously that it be performed by a qualified physician.

In the second stage of pregnancy, your honor, the court has stated that legislatures must leave the abortion — excuse me, for the second stage, the state in promoting its interest in the health of the mother, may if it chooses, regulate the abortion procedure in ways that are reasonably related to maternal health. I suggest, your honor, that the words, "The state may regulate," could not be clearer and do not apply to what in the absence of a statute a prosecuting attorney for the Commonwealth or for any of the other 49 states can do.

Finally, may it please the court, and I might state parenthetically here that only for the purposes of this argument do we make any concessions that the fetus in this question was viable. We do not concede that for any other purpose, but at the third stage, your honor, that is the stage subsequent to viability, the state, in promoting its interest in the potentiality of human life, may if it chooses, and if it chooses, is important, regulate and even proscribe abortion except where it is necessary and appropriate medical judgment for the preservation of the life or health of the mother, so

SOURCE: This selection, "Motion for a 'Bill of Particulars,' " begins on page 26 of the official transcript, prepared for appeal from the court stenographer's notes.

nowhere, may it please the court, in the opinion of *Roe* against *Wade,* has the Supreme Court set forth guidelines for the regulation of the abortion procedure, except in so far as the regulation is accomplished by the state legislature, and in fact, may it please the court, . . . even after viability the Supreme Court has not said that the state must proscribe, that is forbid, abortions.

It says it may, if it chooses, regulate and even proscribe, but it gives the states leeway within what is permitted by the 14th Amendment to regulate without proscribing abortion after viability, so that the contention of the Commonwealth, your honor, as exemplified in the paragraph which is paragraph 12 of the Commonwealth particulars, that the defendant did not commit manslaughter during the course of an abortion but that he committed the — that he did a hysterotomy, and that that was what constituted manslaughter, falls, I would suggest in the face of the holdings, *Roe* against *Wade;* that until the state has passed a statute, which it certainly had not done on October 3, 1973, until the state has passed a statute which says, "Doctor and patient, you shall not be involved in an abortion in any circumstances following the time the fetus becomes viable," the defendant's conduct, if it is the conduct alleged in the indictment, and if the fetus was viable, as the Commonwealth suggests, was on the date in question protected by the decision in *Roe* against *Wade,* and this, may it please the court, is regardless of whatever may be the answer of the Commonwealth to the particulars which we discussed earlier today.

What has happened, I am afraid, is that the District Attorney's office has attempted to define abortion for itself, has attempted to say, "This is not an abortion." Has attempted to say, "It not being an abortion but a hysterotomy, that it is therefore a crime upon the part of the defendant," because the defendant according to the Commonwealth, did the hysterotomy after the period of viability.

It almost seems to me, your honor, that to state the proposition is to state its fallacy and what is wrong with what the Commonwealth suggests, in effect, your honor, the District Attorney is putting himself in the position of the state legislature . . . .

The defendant was protected by the decision in *Roe* against *Wade.* Unless in some way the Commonwealth can demonstrate other than by saying hysterotomy is not an abortion or that he can't perform an abortion after viability, the defendant is protected by the decision in *Roe* against *Wade.*

The Massachusetts legislature did pass a statute in April of 1974, on the day after Dr. Edelin performed the operation.

Argument in Support of Motion to Dismiss a Request by the Defense for Further Specification in the Indictment

MR. FLANAGAN:

...I respectfully submit that if you take the issues that have been brought to the defendant's attention both by the indictment and by the particulars that were filed, and the Commonwealth stated that the manslaughter was not during the course of an abortion, not after an abortion, nor any thing to do with the abortion, the Commonwealth states that an act which this defendant did, was — had nothing to do with the abortion itself; the Commonwealth stated that this was done in the process of a hysterotomy.

...Well, we are not saying that the *Roe* v. *Wade* is not a case that may well be involved to some extent in this case, but I respectfully submit that the defendant's conduct is not protected under *Roe* v. *Wade*.

The issue isn't the termination of the pregnancy. The issue is once the pregnancy is terminated, what rights does that individual who is alive and kicking, or who is breathing and has circulation, or is a viable child, what rights does that individual have, and I respectfully submit he has every right you and I have and that it's a human being under the Constitution, and if somebody does something to terminate that life, then it is either murder, or in this case the grand jury saw fit to indict and charge him with manslaughter.

...In the *Roe* v. *Wade* case, your honor, the court held that the right of privacy is broad enough to encompass a woman's decision whether or not to terminate her pregnancy. Nowhere did the court state implicitly or explicitly that this right of personal privacy was broad enough to encompass a physician's decision to terminate the life of the child if the human being results from the termination of the pregnancy, and I respectfully submit that in this case you have an individual living after the termination of the pregnancy, and the defendant has no right to terminate that life.

The following is a request for more information on the part of the attorney for the defense, who in this situation believes that the District Attorney ought to explain himself and the grounds for the particular

SOURCE: This selection begins on page 37 of the official transcript with arguments by Assistant District Attorney Newman Flanagan in support of his own motion to dismiss a request by the defense for further specification in the indictment.

charges filed more completely. It is again up to a judge to determine whether the defendant's request must be satisfied. In this case, the request concerns the rather difficult philosophical problems that the indictment raised.

Query in Motion for a "Bill of Particulars"

If the Commonwealth claims that the defendant committed manslaughter after an abortion had been completed, what act upon the part of the defendant constituted completion of the abortion?

Reply of District Attorney's Office

The Commonwealth does not claim that the defendant committed manslaughter during the course of an abortion.

THE JURY

Following the preliminary maneuvering in which each of the attorneys tried to establish the ground rules for the trial to the best advantage of his side, the jury had to be chosen. Jury selection, always a matter of some skill, has recently become something more. In this case, as with many other recent trials of exceptional political significance, the defense commissioned a poll of the population from which the jury would be drawn in order to get a reading on how these citizens felt about the issues likely to arise at the trial. The poll cost $10,000 and was based on telephone interviews with 1000 persons selected in the same fashion as the jury is selected. The poll was conducted by the Decision Research Corporation of Wellesley and showed that 83 percent of the prospective Suffolk County jurors sampled said that they believed in at least some abortions. The poll also showed a significantly smaller percentage of proabortion respondents among people over 50, among those with incomes under $5000, those who did not complete high school, and among Roman Catholics.

Attorney Homans said that he commissioned the poll because he "felt it would possibly persuade the judge to give more than the usual attention to examination of prospective jurors." Homans was critical of the jury selection process in Massachusetts, which leaves the selection primarily up to the judge. His position is revealed in the following selection from an interview in the *Harvard Political Review:*[1]

HPR: Do you have any thoughts about changing the court system. I'm thinking here in particular about the Edelin trial. It seemed like a good deal of the evidence was in your favor, and that the judge was definitely in your favor, at least in his instructions to the jury. It seemed as if the jury was biased and that was the reason you lost the case.

HOMANS: Well, that part of the Edelin case focused for me the major thing that I object to about the court system in Massachusetts: the extremely restrictive way in which the Massachusetts' courts regulate the manner in which juries are selected. Massachusetts probably has the most backward system of jury selection of any jurisdiction in the country.

There's a case that came down a week ago — it's sitting on the front desk — where the judge finally agreed that the defendant has a right — he's a black defendant — to have the members of the jury asked whether they have any biases or prejudices which would make them treat him any differently than they would a white man. But this is a very grudging decision on the part of the court. It's less a matter of constitutional law, than that people have been pestering them so much about it. Now in the Edelin case we did have a pretty good jury selection procedure. Judge McGuire went out of his way.

I've just been reading about the Attica case in Buffalo. It took four or five weeks to choose the jury because the lawyers participated in the jury selection process.

HPR: Do you think that's a better system?

HOMANS: In given cases, yes. If you've got a case like the New Haven Panthers case or the New York Panthers case or the Edelin case, in which there are issues which people are aware of either through publicity or because they're issues close to them, I don't think it should matter how long it takes to pick a jury. If it takes six weeks in a given case to get a jury, that doesn't mean it will take it in every case. If justice can't be obtained without taking a long time to pick a jury, there's no reason that time should be a deciding factor.

Courts and judges have talked too much about moving things along, getting things going faster, and cleaning up the congestion in the courts.

[1]"William Homans on Law and Politics," an interview conducted by Mark J. Saylor, *Harvard Political Review*, 3, No. 4 (Summer 1975), p. 22.

They've become so obsessed with considerations of time that they tend to forget considerations in deciding factual questions carefully and fairly, which the jury selection process is designed to accomplish.

In addition to these matters, Homans indicated, in an interview in the *Boston Globe* on 19 February 1975, that the poll had been a significant factor in his request for a jury trial and his decision not to ask for a change of venue.

A criticism directed at this particular poll and perhaps its greatest limitation was that, although it tapped general attitudes about abortion, it did not deal with specific questions upon which the trial rested: (1) What are the doctor's duties to keep a fetus alive? (2) How would a photograph of a fetus with most of the physical attributes of a child affect your opinion on abortion . . . or your answer to the first question?

During the jury selection, or voir dire, the challenge for the judge is to discover prejudice of one sort or another where it might influence the capacity of a juror to make an impartial determination of guilt or innocence on the basis of the evidence produced at the trial. The following transcript from the voir dire was taken from the fourth day of the trial, Thursday, 9 January 1975. It vividly reveals the problem of discovering bias in jurors. The juror not only has to be biased, but it seems that he or she has to admit to the bias and not be talked out of it by the judge.

A Selection from the Voir Dire

Voir dire questioning of prospective juror Number 51 appears below. The questioning was conducted by Judge McGuire, who presided at the trial.

JUDGE: Do you have any interest in the case, any personal interest?
No. 51: No.
JUDGE: Have you read or seen anything in the papers about the case?
No. 51: No.
JUDGE: Are you conscious of any bias?
No. 51: No.
JUDGE: Have you formed an opinion about the case?
No. 51: No.

JUDGE: Do you have any opinions concerning abortion?

No. 51: Yes, sir.

JUDGE: What?

No. 51: I am against it.

JUDGE: All right. You are opposed, you are against it. Let me explain to you, sir, that in the Commonwealth under the practice we have in the trial of cases, the jury is the sole determiner of the facts of the case. But you are obliged to take the law that's applicable to that case from the Court, from the Court's interpretation of the law, and to be guided by or to follow the Court's statement as to the applicable laws that must be accepted by you for the purpose of a case. Would you be able to approach the evidence in this case and form a fair and unbiased opinion thereon and accept the instructions as given you by the Court as to the law in the case?

No. 51: I don't think so.

JUDGE: Why not?

No. 51: Because I don't believe in abortion.

JUDGE: But you believe in the fair determination of cases, don't you?

No. 51: Yes.

JUDGE: Well, I repeat to you, despite any personal views of yours, if I instructed you as to the law in this case, and it was different than your personal belief, would you be able to put aside your personal belief and accept the law as I give it to you?

No. 51: Yes.

JUDGE: Now, would you be influenced, or indeed would you tend to be influenced, by any private or personal belief if the instructions I gave you were different than your personal or private belief? Could you reach a fair and impartial judgment in relation to this case.

No. 51: I don't think so.

JUDGE: This Juror is excused for cause.

Two articles on the jury from a Boston newspaper provide a basis for understanding the crucial decision process at the trial. The backgrounds are offered here, as they were for the justices on the Supreme Court, in order to indicate the part of the community that will make the decision as to the guilt or innocence of the accused doctor. There is an expectation that jurors, more than judges, will exercise a "personal" judgment in the decision, yet the legal process limits the choices open to the jury and the evidence upon which they are presumed to make those choices. The second article describes the sorts of things that the jurors understood to have influenced their decision.

PROFILE OF A JURY

GARY GRIFFITH

The 16 jurors now impaneled for the trial of Kenneth Edelin are neither representative of Suffolk County or Kenneth Edelin's peers. All are white. Thirteen are male. At least 12, and possibly more, Roman Catholic.

Only 12 will sit on the final jury. Four alternates were chosen because the trial is expected to last several weeks, and it is not unusual for some to be excused for reasons of illness or family emergency. The final 12 will be made up of the foreman and 11 others drawn by lot. It is not impossible that Kenneth Edelin will be judged by 12 white Catholic males; at least 9 men and 8 Catholics will sit on the final jury.

It is not, of course, suggested here that all Catholics are prejudiced against doctors who perform abortions or that all whites are prejudiced against blacks; but only that Catholics, whose church teaches that life begins at conception and that abortion is morally wrong, are somewhat prone to be prejudiced against abortion, just as whites, who have grown up in a society they have dominated, are somewhat prone to be prejudiced against blacks.

Sixty-nine prospective jurors, including 22 women, were examined by Judge McGuire and asked about their opinion on abortion, the existence of any prejudice in the case, and the extent to which their personal or religious beliefs might influence them. Forty were excused by the judge for various reasons, 13 others were excused by peremptory challenges by the prosecution and defense.

The 16 who were selected have been sequestered at the Lenox Hotel in Boston. The information below comes from their answers to questions asked of them by Judge McGuire, from members of their families, and from various parish officials in the archdiocese of Boston.

The jury members, in order of selection, are:

Michael R. Seifart, 25, an equipment installer for New England Telephone Co., is stockily built, with collar-length reddish-blonde hair and a bushy mustache. He is married and has one daughter, his wife works at Dunkin Donuts. He is Roman Catholic, a member of St. Matthew's Parish in Dorchester, and said he wasn't sure whether or not abortion should be legalized.

Joyce Lovetere, a secretary for the Massachusetts Department of Trans-

SOURCE: *The Real Paper*, January 22, 1975. The article lists only 15 jurors.

portation, celebrated her 22nd birthday on Friday, January 17 while sequestered as a member of the jury. She is single, attractive, lives at home with her parents in Revere and attended Beverly Community College for one year. She enjoys camping, skiing and outdoor sports, is not a strict Catholic but attends church at St. Anthony's. She said she couldn't say whether she was for or against abortion and that it depended on the circumstances.

Liberty Ann Conlin of West Roxbury is a housewife and mother of four. Her husband is a labor foreman in the construction trade. She said she had no opinion on abortion.

William F. Sokolowski, 26, works as a laborer at Maids Meats in Cambridge and lives in Dorchester. He is large framed with hair over his ears and a dark mustache. He is Roman Catholic but does not attend any particular church, is single, plays softball on a tavern team, and expressed no opinion on abortion.

Michael Ciano is short and slightly built, wears a sparse beard and collar-length hair with bangs that make him appear much younger than 32. He works as a materials handler for Electronics Corporation of America in Cambridge, is single, Roman Catholic, and used to attend St. Joseph's Church in Roxbury before moving to East Boston. He said about abortion: "I have my opinion and they have theirs."

Paul Kolesinski, 34, wears slick hair, is a graduate of Boston Trade High, and works as a shipbuilder at the Boston Naval Shipyard. About abortion, he said: "I think it's wrong," but after additional questioning said that he would be able to decide the case on the evidence and the charge from the judge. He and his wife are Roman Catholic, belong to St. Monica's Parish, but attend church at St. Augustine's in South Boston.

Frederick J. Spencer of West Roxbury is married, works as a field service engineer for Teradyne, Inc., wears his hair combed straight back and conservative suits. He said he had no strong feelings about abortion but thought perhaps that too many were done.

Vincent B. Shea, the jury foreman, is 51 and looks younger. The father of four daughters aged 9 to 18, he lives with his wife in Dorchester, works as an MBTA mechanic, and is a sports fan and bowler. He is Roman Catholic, a graduate of Nazareth Grammar School and South Boston High and is a member of St. Gregory's Parish. He said he thought abortions were not wrong if they were properly performed.

Paul A. Holland, a thickly-built man with graying brown hair, is married, has four children, and works as a customer contact clerk for Boston Edison. He is Roman Catholic and a member of St. Margaret's Parish in Dorchester. He said he has no opinion on abortion.

Herbert A. Ladue, a short, balding man of 49, is a graduate of Jamaica Plain High School and a custodian at the JFK Federal Building. Married and the father of two children, he is Roman Catholic and a member of Our Lady of Lourdes Parish in Jamaica Plain. He said about abortion: "In some cases I'm not sure."

Anthony Alessi, 30, a foreman for the New England Telephone Company, is also a graduate of Jamaica Plain High and attends Northeastern University three nights a week studying business administration. Married to a Roman Catholic and the father of three children, he is a Baptist and said he never had strong feelings one way or the other about abortion.

Ralph P. Mischley, 28, a senior draftsman for C.E. Maguire, Inc., in Waltham, is a graduate of Alpina Central Catholic High School in Alpina, Michigan, and like Alessi, attends Northeastern University at night, where he is studying civil engineering. He is married, the father of two children, and the only juror who mentioned his religion in court. He is a member of St. Gregory's Parish in Mattapan and said he had never really thought about the subject of abortion before but added: "I suppose if it would injure the mother's health, I'd rather see the mother survive."

Michael Galante, a stocky, balding man of 61 with a graying mustache, is a press operator for Sintered Metals, Inc. Married and without children, he plays the piano and composes music, is a Roman Catholic and a member of St. Mary Star of the Sea Parish in East Boston. He said he thought abortions should only be performed if absolutely necessary.

Lillian E. Connors, a gray-haired, retired switchboard operator, is married, the mother of one, Roman Catholic, and a member of St. John the Evangelist Parish in Winthrop. She said about abortion: "I believe where it's legal it's all right."

John G. Kelley, a bank teller for the First National Bank of Boston is single, Roman Catholic, and a member of Our Lady of Presentation Parish in Brighton. He said about abortion: "I'm against it, but if a woman wants one, that's her choice."

Postconviction Interviews with the Trial Jurors

The following selection contains a discussion of the trial and postconviction statements from the jury.

THE EDELIN JURY: SIDE-STEPPING
THE REASONABLE DOUBTS

GARY GRIFFITH

At lunchtime on Saturday, February 15, the Brigham's across the street from the Suffolk County Courthouse was packed with reporters and spectators from the Edelin trial, all of us waiting for the jury to reach their decision, and most of us more worried about our lunch than the verdict.

The jury had been out since 12:30 on Friday afternoon, and the question now, as we sat at the red-white-and-blue counters trying to find someone to take our sandwich orders, was not what determination the jurors would reach, but only how long it would take them to reach it. A verdict of not guilty seemed certain; both the evidence and the charge from the judge had been too good for anything else.

On the evidence alone, it appeared clear that Kenneth Edelin had done nothing more than merely perform a legal abortion according to proper medical procedure, and the verdict of not guilty seemed certain. But the charge from Judge James McGuire had clinched it. McGuire had narrowed everything down to one or two issues — exactly the ones that the defense had anticipated.

In his 90-minute charge on Friday morning, he had made it completely clear that at the time of the operation in question, there was no state law regulating abortion, and that the Supreme Court's ruling in January, 1973, "was absolutely controlling on the subject of abortion."

Edelin, he had said, was charged with manslaughter — the unlawful killing of another without malice, but with conduct so reckless, wanton, or grossly negligent, that it would cause death. Mere "carelessness or negligence," he had said, was "not sufficient to prove manslaughter."

Then he had gone on to echo what the defense had been arguing from the start of the trial — that a charge of manslaughter could not apply to the death of a fetus *in utero*, that a fetus was not a person in the eyes of the law, and that for Edelin to be convicted, the prosecution would have to show that the fetus had not only been "born" — which it had not — but that it had also been born alive.

"If there had been no person in this case," Judge McGuire told the jury on Friday morning, "there could not be any conviction in the crime of manslaughter." Unborn persons, he said, could not be the subject of man-

SOURCE: *The Real Paper*, February 26, 1975, p. 4.

slaughter, and he defined birth as "the process which causes the emergence of a new individual outside the mother."

One of the prosecution's key arguments had been that "birth" could occur inside the uterus, when the placenta was detached from the uterine wall, thus putting the fetus on its own systems, but McGuire's definition negated that.

Then McGuire had set up the conditions which would have to apply for Edelin to be convicted.

"In order for the defendant to be found guilty in this case," he said, "you must be satisfied beyond a reasonable doubt that the defendant caused the death of a person who had been alive outside the body of his or her mother.

"If you believe beyond a reasonable doubt," he went on, "that the defendant, by his conduct, caused the death of a person, you may find the defendant guilty of the crime of manslaughter, if that death was caused by wanton or reckless conduct on the part of the defendant.

"If, on the other hand, you do not find beyond a reasonable doubt that the defendant by his conduct caused the death of a person, then you must acquit him of the crime charged.

"And if you find that even though death occurred, it was not due beyond a reasonable doubt to any wanton or reckless conduct on the part of the defendant, then likewise you must acquit."

The charge, it seemed, could not have been much better if Edelin himself had delivered it. Everything was simple now — the complicated question of viability was not an issue, nor was its gestational age or the definition of "birth" — all that mattered now was whether or not the fetus had ever been alive outside the uterus, and McGuire went on to review the key testimony, even though he said he was only giving examples of how testimony could be conflicting.

"You've heard for example," McGuire stated, "conflicting evidence from numerous witnesses as to whether or not the subject showed any signs of life or had any signs of respiration outside the body of its putative mother.

"Dr. Gimenez," he said, "a prosecution witness, testified in substance that after removal from the putative mother, the baby showed no signs of life such as breathing." Dr. Enrique Gimenez-Jimeno, the only eyewitness called by the prosecution, had been damaging to the defense on every issue but this crucial one.

"In the opinion of others," McGuire continued, "such as Dr. Barnes, the baby was stillborn." Dr. Allan Barnes, vice president for medical affairs at the Rockefeller Foundation, had been called by the defense and had reached his opinion from an examination of the medical records.

"Dr. Benirshke," said McGuire, "gave the opinion that the baby had not taken any extrauterine breaths." Dr. Kurt Benirshke, a former assistant in pathology at Harvard Medical School, the former chairman of the pathology department at Dartmouth Medical School, now a professor of reproductive medicine at the University of California at San Diego and the author of some 200 articles on neonatal pathology, fetal pathology, the pathology of the placenta, and embryonic development, had been called by the defense. He had been sent slides of the fetal lung tissue from the autopsy and had used these slides in the courtroom to demonstrate that the precipitates of protein and cellular material in the amniotic fluid in the lungs would have been displaced by air bubbles if the fetus had breathed, but he showed that they were not.

"Dr. Pritchard," Judge McGuire went on, "thought in his opinion, or so testified, that the fetus was dead prior to the hysterotomy, after the third attempt at amniosentesis." Dr. Jack Pritchard, one of the last witnesses to testify for the defense, was the co-author of "Williams' Obstetrics," the most widely-used text in the field. "Amniosentesis" is the medical term for the taps of amniotic fluid taken with a hypodermic needle through the abdomen of the patient prior to an abortion by saline infusion, and numerous taps were attempted on three occasions before Edelin performed the hysterotomy operation. All drew blood instead of amniotic fluid, and in Pritchard's opinion, these had probably caused the death of the fetus before Edelin even made an incision into the uterus.

"On the other hand," he said, "Dr. Ward testified and stated that the subject breathed outside the putative mother's body." Dr. John F. Ward, the prosecution's final witness, a pathologist from Pittsburgh and a member of a Pennsylvania group called People Concerned for the Unborn Child, was the only witness who said that the fetus had breathed air. His opinion was based on an examination of the lung tissue, which showed some expanded alveoli, or air sacs.

Judge McGuire concluded, "Dr. Curtis likewise testified for the prosecution that there was respiratory activity on the part of the subject postnatally." Here, however, McGuire seemed to be wrong. Dr. George Curtis, the medical examiner for Suffolk County, had said the alveoli were partially expanded, and that the expansion showed "there was inhalation and expiration of the lungs taking place." But on cross-examination, Curtis stated that the expansion could just as easily have been caused by *intrauterine* inspiration and expiration of amniotic fluid, a phenomenon known as fetal respiration.

Still, however, it was certainly a charge that Edelin and his attorneys were happy with, and one that was definitely defense-oriented. Finding "beyond a reasonable doubt" that the fetus in question had been alive outside the uterus was going to be difficult at best.

After telling the jurors to "take whatever time you need to reach your verdict," Judge McGuire ended his charge, and Paul Leary, the court clerk, prepared to draw elimination lots to see which of the 16 jurors would become the four alternates — a procedure which now seems to have been crucial, and one that bothered at least a couple of us in the back of the courtroom.

THE FOREMAN'S NOTE

Leary explained to the court and the jury that he was putting the names of 15 of the jurors — everyone but the foreman — into the small wooden barrel on top of the clerk's desk, then closed the lid and gave it a spin.

Two days earlier, in a casual conversation in the corridor, I had asked Charles Dunn, a special assistant district attorney, and one of the four prosecuting the Edelin case, who he would like to see eliminated, if the choice were up to the prosecution.

"The little guy with the whiskers, first of all," he said.

"Ciano?" I asked, and Dunn affirmed the question. Michael Ciano, a materials handler for the Electronics Corporation of America, had worn a beard and bangs through most of the trial, but came down clean shaven on the day of the closing arguments.

"Who else?" I asked Dunn.

"The other guy with the whiskers," he said. "The first one." That was Michael Seifart, a telephone installer for New England Bell, who wore a bushy, reddish-blond mustache and long bushy sideburns.

"Who else?" I asked.

No one he could think of, Dunn said.

When Leary drew the names out, the first one he read was Frederick Spencer, a field service engineer for Teradyne, and perhaps the only college graduate of the 16.

The second was Ralph Mischley, a 28-year-old draftsman who was attending Northeastern University at night.

The third was Michael Ciano.

The fourth was Michael Seifart.

The rest, nine men and three women, all white, and at least ten out of the twelve Roman Catholic, would deliberate on the verdict. The two jurors that the prosecution wanted off the jury were among the four to be eliminated. But Joyce Lovetere, the youngest woman on the jury, and the one the defense had hoped would be the strongest voice — was still on the jury — and besides, even with the other 11 who would be deliberating, it seemed impossible that they could bring back anything but a not-guilty verdict.

Many of us expected it to come back within two or three hours, but it did not. At 5 p.m., we were told that the jurors were going to dinner and then to bed, and the courtroom was closed.

There were two main theories then: one was that the longer it would take, the worse it would be for Edelin; the other was that the jurors didn't understand the charge. Both proved true.

Shortly after 11:30 on Saturday morning, Judge McGuire called the jury back into the courtroom and announced that he had received a note from the foreman requesting a copy of the latter part of his instructions to them, including "the law involved and the specific charge."

McGuire, however, told them that he could not give them the entire latter portion of his charge without putting undue stress on the testimony he had cited, and denied their request. He added, though, that they could send him another note requesting specifics, if they cared to.

At noon, we were told that the jury was having their lunch, and we did the same, converging on Brigham's in a group, and expecting the jury to send down another note after lunch. A verdict, we thought, would not come for several more hours.

However, when those of us who had been served late, or who had dawdled over a cup of coffee, returned to the courthouse and got off the elevators on the ninth floor, we found the television lights on in the corridor and a crowd pressed around them. "I'm never surprised at a verdict one way or another," Newman Flanagan was saying into the microphones. "I think that as a practical matter in this case, the Commonwealth introduced evidence, that, if believed, would warrant finding the defendant guilty, and the jury believed sufficient evidence to find the defendant guilty."

Inside the courtroom Edelin and Homans were sitting up on the defense table, smoking cigarettes and staring at the back of the courtroom. Edelin's sister was crying, so were several other women and several men. After six weeks of hearing testimony, we had missed the final moment. The verdict was guilty. The trial was over. The rest we would get quickly from the others — how the foreman had shouted out the word, how the back of the courtroom had exploded in disbelief, how Michael Ciano had broken into tears, how the jury had been polled and how each of them had said the word . . . guilty . . . guilty . . . .

WRONG PLACE AT THE WRONG TIME

"Three broads on the jury," Paul Holland was saying, sitting in one of the rough-hewn booths and drinking a Michelob beer, "and look who I get for a roommate!" He laughed and pointed across the table at William Sokolowski, another of the 12 final jurors. We were at the Lenox Hotel Bar in Copley Square, where the jurors were gathered together for a farewell party.

Holland, a customer contact clerk for Boston Edison, lives in Dorchester and sends his children to Catholic school. Sokolowski, a 24-year-old meatcutter who grew a goatee during the trial "out of boredom" as he says, lives a few blocks away. Also in the booth with us was alternate juror Michael Seifart, who had little to say except that he would have liked to have "made my views known." Larry King, a reporter from the *Globe*, and Greg Pilkington, a reporter from Channel 2. Several other jurors were either sitting at the bar, declining to be interviewed, or walking around saying their goodbyes. "What a Difference a Day Makes," was coming over the Muzak speakers.

"Did you understand the charge from the judge," I asked after the introductions, "as to what the issue was."

"The charge was clear," Holland nodded.

"The charge was manslaughter," said Sokolowski, swirling the ice in his 7-and-7, Seagram's Seven Crown and Seven Up.

"Then," said Holland, "when he gave his edict, if you will, or whatever you want to call it, as to what manslaughter entailed, we had to decide if this fell within that realm."

"And what did manslaughter entail?" I asked.

"To be honest with you," said Holland, taking a sip of his beer, " — and I'm not ducking you — right now I'm so fatigued I don't know. In a couple of hours from now, I could tell you, but right now I couldn't say."

I asked Sokolowski the same question.

"I feel just like him," he said.

Francis McLaughlin, a bartender at Logan Airport, and another of the final 12 jurors, ducked his head into the booth on his way to the lobby. "I'm on national TV now, kids," he laughed, and three hours later he would be, telling some 30 million viewers that "negligence" was the issue and that "I don't think he done a thorough job examining the baby once it was removed . . . ."

As he walked by toward the cameras, Holland shouted after him, "Ya never thought you'd make good, huh Frank?" From that point on, Holland would do much of the talking.

"What do you think was the most important piece of evidence?" I asked when McLaughlin had gone.

"I don't know if there was any particular piece of evidence that was more outstanding than the other," said Holland. "When you put it all together, there was evidently enough there to make us reach the decision we reached."

"There must have been *something*," said Larry King, "that was a hinge or a key about that thin dividing line between being a person or not."

"I think it would have to be a consensus," said Holland, "to reach a verdict, everybody had to reach a decision in their own mind."

"Well how would *you* define a person?" asked Pilkington.

"How would I define a person?" Holland repeated, then paused to light a cigarette. "I don't know if I'm qualified to define a person in words."

"Well what kinds of things would you say?" Pilkington went on.

"I don't know," said Holland, and he paused again. "I know what I *think* a person should be —"

"What do you think?" asked Pilkington:

"I don't think it's relevant," said Holland after another long pause. Then he added, "As far as talking to you people. It was relevant up there, but I don't think it's relevant here."

Sokolowski felt the same way.

Liberty Ann Conlin, a middle-aged housewife from West Roxbury and another of the 12, came over to kiss the boys goodbye, and the conversation turned back to definitions again when she had gone.

"How would you define manslaughter?" asked Pilkington.

"We're not lawyers," said Sokolowski.

"As it pertains to this case?" asked Holland. The rest of us nodded, but there wasn't any answer coming.

"But it has to deal with a person?" asked King, trying to be helpful.

"Can't be a crime unless it's a person," said Holland, "If you kill a fish, it ain't manslaughter."

That answered a lot of our other questions. Sokolowski felt the same way.

After another round of drinks, and after questions about the photograph of the fetus, which both Holland and Sokolowski said had helped them to determine whether it was a person or not, and questions about the note to the judge, which they said "had worked itself out," we asked if viability became an issue.

"Yes it did," said Holland.

"All through it," said Sokolowski.

"It had to be," Holland added.

"Did the jurors ever come up with an age or weight when a fetus becomes viable?" I asked.

"If all those doctors couldn't come up with a figure," said Sokolowski, "far be it from me —"

"So in other words, you didn't?"

"No," said Sokolowski.

"But you just kind of decided in a general way that it was viable?" asked Pilkington.

"I didn't say that," said Sokolowski.

"Well," said Pilkington, "did you decide it wasn't viable? Or did you you just not decide that one way or another?"

"Let's put it this way," said Sokolowski, "he had a chance."

"Well, gentlemen," said Holland, "can we conclude it and let's talk about girls or something else?"

There was another long pause until Pilkington came up with a sort of compromise question.

"How were the women on the jury?" he asked. "Did they have a different point of view at all?"

"No," said Holland.

"I wouldn't think so," said Sokolowski. We would learn later that the voting in the jury had been 8–4, then 9–3, then 11–1 in less than an hour, and that the one holdout had been John Kelly, a bank teller from Brighton. The issue that Kelly would cite was the same that McLaughlin had referred to on television, that Edelin had been negligent and that he should have given more attention to the fetus after its removal from the uterus. Edelin had testified that he had touched his fingers to the anterior chest wall to check for a heartbeat, then turned his attention back to the patient, and the closing of the incision. The majority of the jurors, according to Kelly, believed that Edelin could have done more. Holland and Sokolowski did not volunteer that information, and when we had asked them if there was "some feeling that Dr. Edelin should have done something that he didn't do?" Holland answered only that "That was discussed."

The rest of the bar-booth conversation dealt with the six weeks of lock-up, during which the jurors were only allowed to correspond with their families by mail, could not see any newspapers at all, and were not allowed to watch television, "except for the hockey games and the Superbowl."

"So what did you do the rest of the time," I asked.

Holland pumped his left arm up and down a couple of times and that drew a laugh from the table.

"We played some practical jokes," said Sokolowski, "that kind of stuff."

"Like what?" I asked.

"Fillin' up one of the girl's beds with lobsters," he said, and that drew another laugh. "The shells."

"Whose bed," I asked, just for the record, and that drew a laugh, too. There was only one young woman on the jury, Joyce Lovetere, who turned 22 during the trial, and she too came through the bar later to kiss the boys goodbye.

"I think it was toughest on her," said Michael Seifart. "She's getting married in August."

Ralph Mischley, another of the alternates, came by the booth with his wife and two children, to shake hands and say goodbye. Before he could leave, Anthony Alessi, one of the twelve, got off his barstool and came over to put his arm around Mischley's wife. "This is the sex maniac we heard about," he joked, and the boys in the booth got a laugh about that, too.

Mischley left, and so did Alessi, but not before one final joke. "Dorchester!" he laughed at Holland and Sokolowski.

"Mission Hill ain't no better!" Sokolowski laughed back, and the party came to an end.

"So now that you've been through it all," I asked, "do you feel that the jury system works pretty well?"

"It's the greatest system in the world," said Paul Holland.

Sokolowski felt the same way.

But the landmark trial of Dr. Kenneth Edelin had not been decided on the legal issues at all; the charge from the judge had not been understood; and the jury that had decided it hadn't seemed to have paid much attention to the testimony.

Dick Gaines of UPI opened his notebook and read us a quote he had gotten from McLaughlin, the newly-made TV star, at the bar: "I got nothing against Dr. Edelin. What he did's been going on for thousands of years and will be going on for thousands of years more. He was just unlucky, he was in the wrong place at the wrong time. Maybe he did the thing wrong. He's a good guy, so he aborted a broad, maybe he didn't do it right."

Gaines shook his head. "That's supposed to comply with beyond a reasonable doubt?"

THE REACTION TO THE VERDICT AND THE APPEAL

Responding to the verdict, the *Washington Post* published the following editorial:[1]

By convicting Dr. Kenneth C. Edelin for manslaughter, the State of Massachusetts has brought disgrace to itself and to the whole judicial system. The charge against the doctor should never have been brought by the prosecutor. The trial judge should never have allowed the case to go to the jury. And the jury's verdict, itself, is suspect. While we believe the conviction will not stand on appeal because it is constitutionally invalid, the wrong which has been committed in Massachusetts against Dr. Edelin, the medical profession and the law itself cannot be fully repaired .... The demonstration of raw power that has been permitted to go on this month in a Boston courtroom, unfortunately, is not unique. It has occurred before when prosecutors and judges used the processes of the law to harass those whose views they would not tolerate. But that does not excuse it.

As mentioned in the editorial, Edelin is entitled to an appeal. The appeal in this case, since the trial was in a state court, will go to the Massachusetts Supreme Judicial Court. Having prepared for the appeal

[1]*The Washington Post*, February 18, 1975. Reprinted with permission.

since very soon after the trial, Edelin's attorneys filed the final briefs on 24 October 1974. The appeal, like that of Jane Roe who first appealed the abortion statute of the state of Texas, claims that there is something wrong that has to be rectified. In this case, the appeal is not over the state statute, but the conduct of the trial and the participants in the trial. According to a story by Pam Lowry in the December edition of *The Docket*, a newspaper published by the Civil Liberties Union of Massachusetts:[2]

The appeal brief first attacks the prosecution as "defective from inception," and then proceeds to challenge specifically the legal theories which the prosecution advanced. The brief pays particular attention to the element which defense counsel believe had the greatest influence on the course of the trial and which resulted in "a mass of evidential errors in the admission of evidence."

This element deals with the response of the District Attorney to the motion for particulars that is reprinted at the beginning of this section. It was that response, the defense is claiming, that allowed the trial to be conducted in a fashion inconsistent with national law on abortion as dictated by the decision in *Roe v. Wade*. The court may choose to consider other matters brought to its attention by the prosecution in response to the appeal, but whether it decides on the basis of the prosecutor's theory that this event was not an abortion or with reference to the conduct of the trial, the outcome will add another consideration to public policy on abortion. The decision by the highest court in Massachusetts is likely to become the basis for an appeal to the Supreme Court of the United States, no matter who wins in the state. In this regard, the whole process of making public policy has come full circle, with the issues demanding resolution at the local level being reordered as a result of events and ways of proceeding in the constitutional system.

The impact of the Edelin decision on the public policy toward abortion has been subtle compared to the national attention and sensational coverage that the trial received in the media. Family planning counselors report that few abortions are done as late as the one performed by Dr. Edelin. The Boston doctor was unusual in his willingness to take the risks of a live birth that come with late term pregnancies. Since the trial, the availability of doctors willing to take the now more

[2]Pam Lowry, *The Docket* (December 1975). Reprinted with permission.

visible risk of a prosecution for manslaughter has probably lessened. The influence of the trial on abortion policy depends on the number of doctors who might have taken chances with late term pregnancies but have been held back by knowledge that prosecution is possible. It further depends on the response of hospitals to the risks involved and on the sorts of guidelines they set for late term abortions. In another sense, it hinges on the extent to which the decision in the case of Kenneth Edelin focused attention on an area not directly dealt with by the Supreme Court: the possibility that an abortion may produce a live birth. That risk has certainly always existed, and as medical technology, both in performing abortions and in sustaining life, develops, this consideration seems likely to remain one of the most important aspects of the national policy on abortion.

On 17 December 1976 the Supreme Judicial Court of Massachusetts reversed Kenneth Edelin's conviction for manslaughter. The ruling cited insufficient evidence for a conviction and advised caution in the use of criminal statutes in this area because they "necessarily trench on professional practice and constitutional freedoms."

FURTHER READINGS FOR CHAPTER 1

Becker, Theodore L., and Malcolm M. Feeley, eds., *The Impact of Supreme Court Decisions*, 2nd ed. (New York: Oxford University Press, 1973). A series of articles explaining what happens after a Supreme Court decision is handed down.

Lader, Lawrence, *Abortion II: Making the Revolution* (Boston: Beacon Press, 1974). A discussion of the political efforts behind the change in abortion policy.

Rohde, David W., and Harold J. Spaeth, *Supreme Court Decision Making* (San Francisco: W. H. Freeman and Company, 1975). The emphasis in this book is on how the Supreme Court operates, with an effort to explain what causes the judges to decide as they do.

Chapter 2 Congress and the Budgetary Process

The Politics of Military Appropriations

DAVID FOURNEY, EDITOR

The Constitution accords to Congress the responsibility for keeping track of expenditures of the national treasury. It has been at a disadvantage because of its large size and fragmented procedure for making decisions. It has generally responded to, rather than initiated, policy and its knowledge of the overall shape of the nation's financial affairs has been dependent on the President. With regard to military spending in particular, it has played a subordinate role to the executive branch. Here the size of the outlays and their technical nature has led to dominance by Pentagon officials and the President's budget experts. Beginning with consideration of the 1976 budget, Congress attempted to institutionalize the power it has acquired relative to the President following its ouster of President Nixon.

By writing a new law to control the budgetary process, in 1974 Congress hoped to set overall limits on expenditures and revenues. Notwithstanding the President's formulation of the budget, which means that the administration's budget will still be the starting point, Congress launched a plan that may stem executive dominance of fiscal matters. For the first time, it would establish a group of experts who would look at the entire issue of federal moneys, assess their effect on employment and inflation, and recommend to Congress strict guidelines within which to make the subsequent more specific budget decisions. Congress would try to watch what the group was doing by passing a resolution on the maximums and minimums twice a year. These mechanisms were planned in order to introduce congressional initiative into the budgetary process and to make it meaningful by encouraging unified action. The relation of these developments to congressional decision making on military spending is the subject of this chapter.

Throughout the many budget reviews of past years, Congress has not generally tampered with the recommendations of the Pentagon. The usual budget cut by Congress amounted to about 5 percent of the initial request. This allowed a small percentage increase for the military each year. It has been suggested that the Pentagon presented a padded budget in anticipation of congressional cuts.

The reform movement in Congress to break up the iron hand of seniority governing the important committee chairmanships was seen by some as a movement away from congressional acquiescence to the requests of the military. A very staunch supporter of military spending was removed from the chairmanship of the House Armed Services Committee. But the replacement, Melvin Price, had himself been a strong supporter of previous military requests. Even though five new members were added to the committee, an adversary position to military spending was not established. This committee, even with all the pressures upon them for massive cuts at a time of inflation, kept the original budget request essentially as it had come down to them. They approved HR 6674 by a vote of 32 to 6.

Three indirect considerations have come to play a significant role in the politics of military spending. The first is a general concern about the effect of government spending on inflation (see Chapter 5). In the past, the military has often been exempt from national belt tightening. But, for fiscal year (FY) 1976, Congress declared a determination to offset the momentum of billions of dollars towards deficit spending. The Congress empowered itself with a check on the budget through the oversight capability of its newly formed Budget Committee. The chairman of the committee, Senator Edmund Muskie, successfully defeated the first military spending bill by invoking budget ceilings set earlier in the year. An indication that the Budget Committee was not isolating military requests for cuts in favor of domestic programs was Muskie's recommendations for defeat of a school lunch program because it too overran the limits of the budget ceilings.

A second matter is the ability of corporations to influence budget decisions. It is a result of the system fostered and supervised by the government itself. There are very few possible companies that benefit directly from defense spending. Because of the highly technical nature of developing weapons systems, the bulk of defense contracts are concentrated in larger firms. The defense market operates in a fashion different from the general contract process. Contracts are not decided by competition but are negotiated with only one or a few companies. The contracting and procurement setup has partly contributed to the mismanagement problems that have been associated with large defense programs. There has been some concern that these companies command an unfair advantage with their access to government and their special relationship to the Pentagon.

Finally, another sensitive area is the relationship between the private corporations and the international weapons trade. The arms manufacturers, whose research and development costs are paid for by the federal government, have been able to maintain almost total control, in conjunction with the Pentagon, over the negotiation of worldwide arms sales. The Congress would like these activities to be channeled through it. It has expressed a concern that the United States will have to respond to a threat resulting from unchecked arms proliferation. With each billion dollar shipment abroad, the United States comes closer to having to face the issue of control over this aspect of foreign policy.

In FY 1976, the federal budget was around 370 billion dollars, while the entire national economy, as measured by the gross national product (GNP), is placed at a trillion dollars. Domestic social programs and the Social Security system have come to account for an increasing portion of the federal budget. The military states that its estimated outlays of 100 billion dollars would comprise merely 26.6 percent of the federal budget, or 5 percent of the capacity output of the GNP. The share of defense spending in comparison to the total amount of federal spending has decreased in recent years. Nevertheless, the military budget has been rising every year. The final approved outlay figure for FY 1976 represents more than a 7 billion dollar, or an 8 percent, increase over what the Pentagon got from Congress the year before.

There are two types of figures cited when dealing with defense spending. The 104.7 billion dollars requested by the Defense Department for 1976 is considered the "total obligational authority." It consists of the annual appropriation granted by Congress and any unused appropriations from previous years. A lower figure often noted is the "total outlay," or funds actually paid out for programs approved in a given year. The outlay expenditure for the military in FY 1976 was around 97.9 billion dollars. The final authorization approved by Congress for FY 1976 was 90.5 billion dollars. These figures change during budget consideration as they are revised by congressional committees.

Because many figures and percentages are employed in the consideration of the military budget, the nature and credibility of the computations is often a matter of discussion. One antidefense lobby, SANE (A Citizens' Organization for a Sane World), objects to the way the Pentagon figures the actual defense demand on the federal budget. This organization has calculated that the government is spending more on the military than on any other domestic program. The defense budget, it argues, consumes up to 54 percent of the total federal budget. SANE includes related expenses of veteran payments and interest on the national debt that is attributed to past wars.

The discrepancy is partially a result of the change in federal accounting practices in 1968. At one time, the federal budget represented the expenditures of federal agencies and programs that had a direct effect upon the tax dollar. Now, defense spending can claim a smaller share of the budget because another category of trust monies has been added in: budget outlays that are fixed and automatically paid out unless fundamental legislative changes are made. They include Social Security and Medicare, railroad retirement, and the highway trust fund. Critics of the military's claims point out that such programs are financed by separate taxes and should therefore be considered separately.

SECTION A. REALIZING CONGRESSIONAL BUDGETARY POWER

In January, the President submits a budget to Congress detailing all expenditures to be made by the federal government for the next fiscal year. Prior to the consideration of the 1976 budget, Congress dealt with individual authorization through its various committees with little systematic attention to what the total national expenditure should have been. In 1974, procedural changes were made in the budgetary process by the Congressional Budget and Impoundment Control Act. According to the act, at the beginning of each period of budget review, the Congress decides what level of expenditure is desirable for the economy. The spending ceilings are proposed by a new budget committee in each house of Congress and a professional Congressional Budget Office. All committees have to keep within the limits set by this committee in evaluating the requests that come before them during consideration of the federal budget. This setup integrates the various committees under a unified economic strategy and gives Congress more time to complete action on a budget bill.

The goal of this act was to gain more leverage in bargaining with the executive departments and the President's Office of Management and Budget through equalization of the expertise, initiative, and unity of the decision making process in Congress. The Budget Committee was only able to send one defense bill back for committee reconsideration in FY 1976; however, the final congressional outlay appropriation for defense was well within the limits set in the budget ceilings. The effort of the Budget Office was to provide the Congress with "some alternatives and analysis." It took care to appear to present objective alternatives and claimed to "take no policy position," according to the Director, Dr. Alice Rivlin. Congress also set a series of deadlines for itself in order to bring divergent committees into a consistent decision making pattern, one that could be monitored. In the first year of operation, the Congress passed its final resolution three months after the date that it had set for itself. The final budget allocation of 374.9 billion dollars was 7 billion dollars over its original ceiling.

Burton Moyer, author of the first article below, is a senior specialist in the Directorate for Banking, International Finance, and Professional Development of the Office of the Secretary of Defense. The selection first appeared in a membership publication of the American Defense Preparedness Association during August 1975. This association is dedicated to a "strong defense oriented society," and is based in Washington, D.C. Moyer outlines the defense budget timetable and the implications of the congressional reforms. The selection following Moyer's is an article about Dr. Alice Rivlin, which is followed by a letter from Senator Muskie to her. The letter was included in a report of the House Committee on the Budget. It requests an investigation into Department of Defense techniques for deriving inflation and real purchasing power calculations. The subsequent investigation found the techniques to be reasonable but set a precedent for a close watch on Pentagon figures.

It is not surprising that the Department of Defense has taken considerable interest in Congress' new budgetary process. If this process works the way that it is supposed to, it will shift some of the initiative for budgetary decisions from the President and the Pentagon over to Congress. Defense is not without friends in the important Congressional committees, but the new procedure will transfer some of the committee power to congressional leadership and to the professionals charged with assessing the entire budget.

THE DEPARTMENT OF DEFENSE
AND THE NEW BUDGET PROCESS

BURTON B. MOYER, JR.

One of the major motivations of people everywhere is the need for a sense of personal worth. It is my belief that this need was one significant factor in the approval by Congress of the Congressional Budget and Impoundment Control Act of 1974. Congress seeks through this legislation to make itself a more effective partner of the executive branch in the governing of the United States.

In describing this effort by Congress to strengthen its performance, five major aspects can be identified that should help in an understanding of the new budget process.

These factors are: (1) the background and (2) the nature of the new budget process; (3) the 1975 "trial run"; (4) authorizations and the new budget process; and (5) the impact of this process on the Department of Defense.

Since 1921, Congress has exercised the power of the purse by piecemeal response to the President's budget. Each spending measure has been considered on its own merits, but rarely has this consideration extended to its relation to total Federal spending.

Even though annual appropriation requests usually have been cut, total

SOURCE: Reprinted from the July-August 1975 issue of *National Defense*, by permission of the editors. Copyright © 1975, American Defense Preparedness Association, Washington, D.C.

spending regularly has exceeded the executive budget. From 1971 through 1974, the President's January budget messages called for congressional budget reform. The 1973 message charged that Congress "must accept responsibility for the budget totals . . . (or) the responsibility for increased taxes, higher interest rates, higher inflation, or all three."

Responding in large part to this criticism, Congress approved the Congressional Budget and Impoundment Control Act in June of 1974. The President signed it into law on July 12, 1974.

The new law creates a congressional budget process that requires Congress to make mathematically consistent annual decisions about total Federal budget authority, outlays, revenues, public debt levels, and budget surplus or deficit. Then its customary decisions about annual appropriations and other spending authority for each Federal program must fall within the levels it establishes for total budget authority and outlays.

To help Congress meet these new responsibilities, the law authorizes House and Senate Budget Committees and a Congressional Budget Office to serve both Houses. It also provides detailed procedures and deadlines for the new budget process, and it shifts from a July–June fiscal year to an October–September fiscal year starting in the fall of 1976.

Some sense of the complexity of the new process may be gained from the accompanying charts on the budget process — old style (Figure 1) and the budget process — new style (Figure 2).

The "budget process — old style" is easy to depict. The President's budget goes to the committees responsible for authorizations and appropriations. After the necessary legislation has been approved, the Office of Management and Budget [OMB] apportions the funds, and the Department spends the money.

In the new-style budget process, the new activities are shown across the top line of the chart. The new activities parallel the initial consideration of authorization and appropriation bills. They include:

• The Congressional Budget Office (CBO) report of its findings in regard to national budget priorities and alternative levels for revenues, new budget authority, outlays, and related surpluses or deficits.

• The first budget resolution, in which Congress approves tentative congressional budget targets. These must include total budget authority and outlays, authority and outlays by major functional categories, recommended revenues, proposed public debt limits, and recommended budget surplus or deficit.

Then, after the authorization and appropriation bills have been approved:

• The fall budget resolution, in which Congress makes its final decisions in regard to budget authority, outlays, revenues, debt limits, and surplus or deficit.

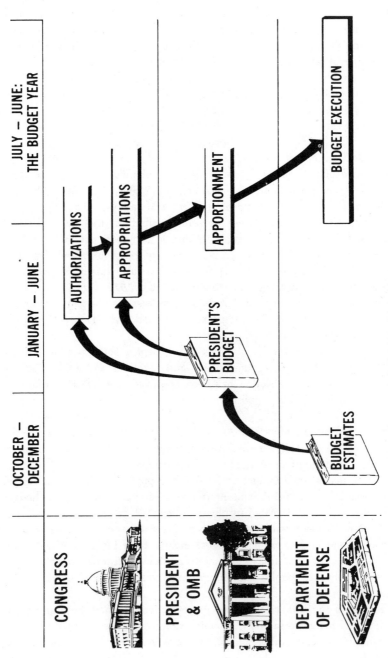

Fig. 1. Chart of national budget process—old style.

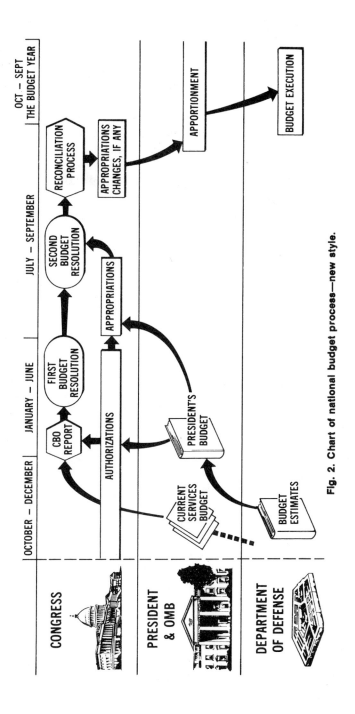

Fig. 2. Chart of national budget process—new style.

• The fall reconciliation bill, which effects the necessary changes, if any, in budget authority, revenues, and debt limits.

The first full test of the new process will start this coming fall, when the President submits his current services estimates for fiscal year 1977. Even now, however, Congress is hard at work on a trial run that has produced tentative congressional budget targets for fiscal 1976.

In this trial run, the House and Senate Budget Committees released their recommendations in mid-April, and both Houses acted upon those recommendations by May 1st. A conference committee adjusted the differences in the House and Senate resolutions in early May, and the recommendations made by the conferees were approved on May 14, 1975.

The approved targets now serve as guidelines — but not ceilings — as Congress responds to the President's budget by approving agency appropriations and spending authority for fiscal 1976.

Comparing these congressional budget targets with the President's January budget estimates, we find that Congress proposed $395.8 billion in new budget authority, an increase of 2.6 per cent over the President's estimate of $385.8 billion. In estimated outlays, Congress anticipates $367 billion, an increase of 5 per cent over the President's estimate of $349.4 billion.

In contrast to these proposed increases in total spending, the conference report on the budget resolution recommends reductions in the amounts for national defense. The conference report target for new budget authority is $100.7 billion, a cut of 6.5 per cent from the President's estimate of $107.7. The conference report estimate for outlays is $90.7 billion, a cut of 3.5 per cent from the President's estimate of $94 billion.

The conference report describes these reductions in the following manner: "All funds requested for military assistance to South Vietnam and Cambodia were deleted from fiscal 1976 estimates, including the outlay effect of the 1975 supplemental request.... The balance of the reductions are the result of revised inflation estimates, reduction in program growth, and financial adjustments."

The Armed Services and Appropriations Committees now must report out authorizing and appropriating legislation that may or may not follow the national-defense spending targets of the conference report. The point to remember is that increases in one category of Federal spending must be accompanied by decreases in another category, or by increases in revenues, if Congress is to achieve its target for the budget deficit as well as [its] target for the public debt.

The final steps in the trial run will be taken in September or later when Congress has completed action on all or most of the spending legislation for fiscal 1976. At that time, the Budget Committees will propose a final budget resolution. It will affirm or amend the earlier targets, and it will provide cuts in spending or increases in revenues or the public debt, if either of these are needed to achieve the final congressional budget levels.

Once the final levels for fiscal 1976 have been approved, it will not be in order for either House to consider legislation that increases spending or decreases revenues without a new budget resolution that establishes new levels for the fiscal year.

The new law provides two important deadlines for annual authorization legislation to enable Congress to complete action on appropriation bills and other spending authority before it considers the September budget resolution. First, authorization bills must be reported out by the appropriate legislative committees on or before May 15th of each year. Secondly, the executive branch of the Government must submit its authorization estimates by May 15th of the previous year.

In anticipation of the year-in-advance requirement, the Department of Defense formulated its authorization estimates for fiscal 1977 last fall, along with budgets for fiscal 1976 and the transition quarter. (The transition quarter is the period from July 1 through September 30, 1976, which falls between the old-style fiscal 1976 and the new-style fiscal 1977.) Consequently, Defense was able to send to Congress on February 5, 1975, a package containing its procurement, research, and personnel authorization estimates for fiscal 1976, for the transition quarter, and for fiscal 1977.

Nevertheless, both the House and Senate Armed Services Committees are reporting out only the fiscal 1976 and transition authorizations at this time. It seems likely that they will not act on the fiscal 1977 estimates until after the President submits his full budget in January of 1976. Such a delay should not endanger the congressional budget schedule, as long as the fiscal 1977 authorizations are reported out not later than May 15, 1976, and approved in early summer. There will still be time to get the fiscal 1977 appropriations approved before the fall budget resolution and reconciliation process.

Obviously, this year's trial run will prepare Defense officials for the full implementation of the congressional budget process in 1976.

In past years we have monitored congressional action on Defense programs by looking to congressional reports and debates on our authorization and appropriation bills. This year we are learning to watch also the congressional reports and debates in regard to the May spending targets and the fall spending ceilings. Their relation to the President's budget will give us advance information in regard to probable congressional decisions on Defense spending.

For the program manager, the year-ahead request for authorizations means that each fall he must be able to produce budget quality estimates for both the budget year and the first out year. If in return, he gets both authorizations and appropriations approved by the beginning of the budget year, his longer-range commitment may be well worth the risks involved.

For Congress, the test of process will come each fall after it has completed action on the individual bills for the fiscal year. Will it affirm its earlier spending targets and direct any cuts in spending that may be needed to achieve those targets? Or will it amend its targets and provide for increases in revenues or in the public debt to take care of appropriations or other spending authority that exceeds the May guidelines?

It appears likely that the success or failure of the new process cannot be assessed until we have experienced at least this year's trial run and the first year of full implementation of the new method.

CONGRESS REPORT/ALICE RIVLIN NAMED CHIEF OF CONGRESSIONAL BUDGET OFFICE

JOEL HAVEMANN

After months of haggling, Congress finally has placed Alice M. Rivlin, an economist with a record of support for social programs and opposition to high defense spending, in charge of the new Congressional Budget Office (CBO).

Rivlin, formerly a senior fellow at the Brookings Institution, was the choice of Senate and House Budget Committees to be director of the office that Congress hopes will become something of a congressional counterpart to the White House Office of Management and Budget (OMB). The CBO is supposed to help the Budget Committees and Congress as a whole to select spending and revenue totals and choose spending priorities.

Since her appointment to the $40,000 a year position on Feb. 24, Rivlin has declined to discuss her views on President Ford's proposed fiscal 1976 budget: she maintains that her job is to provide the Congress with information and policy options, not with her opinions. But as recently as last summer she spoke out against Ford's proposed spending cuts, especially in human resources programs.

SELECTION PROCESS

When the 93rd Congress adjourned last December, Rivlin was the first choice of the Senate Budget Committee for the CBO job. But she was the

SOURCE: *National Journal Reports* (March 1, 1975), p. 332. Copyright © 1975. Reprinted by permission.

third choice of the House Budget Committee, which favored Phillip S. (Sam) Hughes, assistant comptroller general at the General Accounting Office (GAO).

In the new 94th Congress, Rep. Al Ullman, D–Ore., quit as chairman of the House Budget Committee to take over the Ways and Means Committee. He was replaced on Feb. 5 by Rep. Brock Adams, D–Wash., who immediately began negotiating with Sen. Edmund S. Muskie, D–Maine, chairman of the Senate Budget Committee, about the CBO job.

Adams and Muskie ruled out John C. Sawhill, former administrator of the Federal Energy Administration (FEA), who had been the second choice of both Budget Committees in the 93rd Congress. In the eyes of the committees, Sawhill's biggest drawback was that he had worked for the Republican Administration.

The two chairmen discussed the possibility of making either Hughes or Rivlin the deputy to the other at the CBO, but both candidates declined to serve as deputy. Finally, Adams, who had been given full negotiating powers by his committee, broke the stalemate by accepting Rivlin.

"We believe we are starting this organization off with real class," said House Speaker Carl Albert, D–Okla., when he announced Rivlin's appointment on Feb. 24.

PLANS

In an interview, Rivlin said her first job was to hire a staff. She said she will try to start out with "maybe half a dozen very top senior people."

She said she is not sure whether the CBO ever will have a staff of 150, the number that was discussed during formulation of the Congressional Budget and Impoundment Control Act (88 Stat 297), which established the CBO. "I want to get the best people," she said, "and there aren't that many top people available immediately."

She promised to hire a balanced staff representing all parts of the political spectrum except the "lunatic fringe" at both ends. She said the staff must be responsive to the Republican minority as well as the Democratic majority.

Rivlin said the CBO will not be able to help Congress adopt a budget resolution this year laying out total spending and revenue targets for fiscal 1976. For fiscal 1977, she said, the CBO should be prepared to present the Congress with a range of budgetary options, but not in as great detail as the OMB prepares the President's budget.

Rivlin said she hopes for good relations with the Budget Committee staffs. "We'll provide more analysis and a lot of the basic numbers," she said. "They will in a sense be our customers."

Rivlin said the CBO must supply the Congress with budget options, not recommendations, and so she will not state her own budgetary views. "That's one of the costs of taking this job," she said.

But last Aug. 22, when Ford was proposing cuts in the fiscal 1975 budget, Rivlin told the Senate Budget Committee — that she opposed budget cuts. She said the cuts would make unemployment worse while doing little to stop inflation. She recommended more public employment programs and a guaranteed income.

"It would be much in the national interest to shift public resources gradually from defense to domestic programs," she said. "I also believe that the threat of inflation will be with us for many years to come and that it is important to reorient domestic priorities so as to reduce the hardship that both inflation and unemployment bring to low-income people."

BACKGROUND

Rivlin, 43, earned her bachelor's degree from Bryn Mawr College and her Ph.D. in economics from Radcliffe College. She joined Brookings in 1957 and became a senior fellow in 1963. She is an author of three Brookings volumes on the 1972, 1973, and 1974 budgets, *Setting National Priorities.*

During the Johnson Administration she served in the HEW Department as deputy assistant secretary for program analysis from 1966 to 1968 and assistant secretary for planning evaluation from 1968 to 1969.

Her husband, Lewis, is a member of the law firm of Peabody, Rivlin and Lambert. She has a daughter and two sons.

The following letter from Senator Muskie to Alice Rivlin was included in a report of the House Committee on the Budget. Senator Muskie is the head of the Joint Committee on the Budget. The letter is an example of the flow of information from political leaders to the professionals in the budget office, and it indicates something of the new power of the professional analyst in the process. The investigation mentioned was conducted by the Congressional Budget Office (CBO) and it found the Department of Defense calculations to be reasonable, but the CBO, in applying their own authorities to the challenge of overseeing the technicalities of the defense budget, set a precedent for a more active congressional role in the process.

LETTER TO DR. ALICE RIVLIN FROM SENATOR MUSKIE
AND REPRESENTATIVE ADAMS

Dr. Alice Rivlin,
Director, Congressional Budget Office,
Washington, D.C.

Dear Alice:

In considering the fiscal 1976 budget request for National Defense, the Budget Committees encountered serious difficulties interpreting the methods used to compute estimates of price changes. We think it is desirable to formulate a policy which will eliminate these problems. Therefore, we would like you to undertake a study of the budgetary treatment of price changes and provide a report to the House and Senate Budget Committees.

This study should include, but not be limited to, the following elements:

a. Determine the methods now used by the Department of Defense to measure, project, and budget for price changes.

b. Review present OMB policy on formulating and allowing for inflation in the budgeting process, and compare this with the methods used by the Defense Department.

e. Determine the appropriateness of current deflators used for measuring price changes in DoD purchases, and examine the implications of using alternative measures which may be more specific or more general in nature. One matter of interest is the historical relationship between current (or more specific) DoD deflators and common measures of general inflation, including the reasons for fluctuations in this relationship. A second matter of interest is the historical reliability of DoD price change estimates, with an eye toward methodological changes which might improve reliability.

d. Determine whether there is "double counting" of the allowance for inflation in the budget resulting from such an adjustment being more than once during the pricing and budgeting process.

e. Assess the appropriateness of comparing "constant dollar" defense budgets from year to year and over a 10 or 20 year period.

f. Examine alternative methods of including in the budget request a full estimate of pay raises anticipated during the budget year.

g. Review of the pricing guidance provided in formulating the FY 1976 and Transition Quarter defense budgets, and provide updated estimates of anticipated price changes, together with an estimate of the budgetary impact, for that budget period and for fiscal 1977. We would appreciate your providing this part of the study to the Budget Committees by August 15, 1975.

h. As a result of the review, you may want to examine practices and policies with reference to price changes in other areas of the Federal program and budget.

Mr. John F. Cove of the House Committee on the Budget and Mr. Andrew Hamilton of the Senate Committee on the Budget will be your points of contact.

We would appreciate your providing this study by November 30, 1975. With warm regards.

Sincerely,

EDMUND S. MUSKIE,

Chairman, Committee on the Budget, U.S. Senate

BROCK K. ADAMS,

Chairman, Committee on the Budget, U.S. House of Representatives

SECTION B. THE MILITARY IN CONGRESS

The military budget comes to Congress from the executive branch. The proposals are conceived in the military departments and reviewed by the various civilian secretaries. The Secretary of Defense submits the proposal to the President and the allocations are balanced with other national priorities. Thus, the President's sense of the priorities and place of military expenditures in national policy set the framework to which Congress must direct its attention. When performing this function, Gerald Ford demonstrated a strong commitment to the military. He placed the military in opposition to welfare and social services, which had been increasing while the military budget declined. He voiced alarm at the switch from national defense to social programs, yet the development of the military budget as well as its presentation to Congress depended upon the acumen of his Secretary of Defense.

Although the executive branch prepares the budget, neither the Office of Management and Budget nor the Council of Economic Advisers has had significant impact on the details of the military budget. The influence of the President is exerted through his Secretary of Defense, who must master the specifics and justify the budget in Congress. When the Secretary goes before Congress, he represents the desires of the armed services as interpreted in a national budget proposal consistent with executive priorities. As a result of this function, President Ford appointed Donald Rumsfeld as Secretary of Defense, removing the rather more independent James Schlesinger, an appointee of Richard Nixon. Ford explained that he sought a proven member of his "team." In the selection reprinted below, Secretary Schlesinger argues for the budget that was being developed when Ford took office. When asked repeatedly to speculate about where cuts could be made, he argued that the request was already at the lowest possible point, since it had come down from the original armed services recommendation of 112 billion dollars, which, he argued, was needed to keep the system functioning at a satisfactory level.

The Congress begins analyzing the budget shortly after it is received from the President. The total defense budget is drafted into several bills, such as the one for military procurement, research, and development reprinted below. This procurement bill, HR 6674, was first introduced on 5 May 1975. Hearings were held in the House Armed Services Committee and the bill was passed 20 May 1975, superseding two earlier authorization bills. Representing about one third of the entire defense budget, the bill covers the area most vulnerable to cost cutting. Other areas of the budget, such as manpower and personnel-related costs, are not as open to negotiation.

Dozens of standing committees and subcommittees in both houses of Congress evaluate the initial requests for program authorization. Published reports of the hearings cover many thousands of pages and are dominated by Pentagon testimony. The committees cover such areas as Agriculture, Interior, and Armed Services. The subcommittees of a committee such as Armed Services address more specific matters, such as Central Intelligence, Military Construction, and Preparedness Investigating. Since the authorizations approved in each house are rarely the same, a joint "conference" committee is convened for determining a compromise report. This committee reports a final bill, which must then be approved by each house. In 1976, the House of Representatives approved a procurement bill that was 1.5 billion dollars more than the Senate version, and the conference committee came up with a compromise figure in between the contested amounts. The Senate did not accept the compromise results and sent the bill back to the joint committee for revision.

An article from *Congressional Quarterly* examines the possible effect on the appropriations process of personnel changes in the House Armed Services Committee. This article is followed by a report from the Americans for Democratic Action Newsletter, which scores congressional inability to withstand Pentagon pressure during the early stages of the budgetary process. Excerpts taken from the *Congressional Record* report the Senate debate of 1 August 1975 on the defense spending conference report, the compromise version of HR 6674. The outcome of the first vote was for rejection of the 25.8-billion-dollar procurement bill by a margin of 42–48. The subsequent account by columnists Evans and Novak criticizes the actions of the Budget Committee leadership and their use of budgetary ceilings in defeat of the conference report. On the second attempt, the conference bill was approved. Only 250 million dollars had been shaved off, but the Budget Committee could not stop the bill from passing again and the authorization bill was signed by the President into law.

Once the authorization bill has passed, funds must then be appropriated to match the new authority. Unlike the authorization process, in the second stage, that of appropriation, one committee in each house passes on all bills. As a result of this institutional setup, the subcommittees of the Appropriations Committee are often as important in the final budgetary decision as the Standing Committees with responsibility for the same departments or agencies. Upon approval, the conference report on the appropriations bill is sent to the President for final action before the money can be spent.

Remarks by Congresswoman Holtzman give a view of the plans for the Budget Committee as a control on federal expenditure. Her statement was published in the Budget Committee report on the second concurrent resolution of the budget, 31 October 1975. The figures that Holtzman cites for defense represent the amounts endorsed by the House Budget Committee. The Senate counterpart committee increased the House defense outlay figure by almost 1 billion dollars. This action compounded the budget problems as outlined in Holtzman's response. When the differences between the House and Senate figures are resolved, the final concurrent resolution is considered. It is the last word on federal overall spending.

The final article for this section depicts the connection between lobbyists for the defense industry and the congressional decision making process. The relationship of private business to defense procurement is a factor to be considered in evaluating budget policy making. There are obvious pressures exerted upon (and obvious favors extended to) Congress and the Pentagon from private corporations supporting expanding arms developments. Arms growth is often seen as a means of decreasing unemployment and stimulating the economy, both for the nation in general and for a congressional district. Revelations in the spring of 1976 identified 39 military and civilian officials connected to arms procurement and development who were guests at a hunting lodge operated by Rockwell International, Inc., the prime contractor for the B–1 bomber.

THE PRESIDENT AND THE PENTAGON

Remarks by President Ford to a Dinner Meeting of the Conference Board, 22 January 1975

The Conference Board was founded in 1916 to collect and disseminate information to member industries. In the mid-1970s, the group's leadership positions were filled by a former Secretary of Commerce and the Chairmen of the Boards of Koppers Company, Kraftco, Allied Chemical, AT&T, and Textron. Its trustees included 23 board chairmen, two vice-chairmen, four corporation presidents, and one business school dean. The board has a longstanding interest in national and international policy as it affects business and management; it conducts research and holds conferences on such things as economic trends, budgeting, corporate planning, personnel administration, marketing, and the financing of overseas operations.[1]

Now, I fully realize that many in the Congress will find it very difficult to support spending limitations in programs that they have advocated and sincerely believed in over the years. But in the crisis that we face right now, I think it has to be done.

And I might say — to provide some incentive and cooperation — as a starter I intend to invite to the White House, at their earliest convenience, members of the new budget committees of the Senate and House to confer with me on the problems that I have outlined.

To continue the course that we are on is wrong; we definitely need a redirection. And this brings me to the . . . direction of defense policy. There is a fashionable line of thinking in America today, as widespread as it is false, that all we need to do to get Federal spending back in line is to hack

---

[1]These remarks by President Ford are reprinted from *Weekly Compilation of Presidential Documents*, Federal Register Office, National Archives and Record Service, General Services Administration. U.S. Government Printing Office.

away at the defense establishment. There is nothing new about this approach. Unfortunately, it is an error that seems to be endemic to Western democracies in times of peace. Again and again, while totalitarian powers of one kind or another have maintained or expanded their military strength in peacetime, the democracies, primarily in the West, have neglected strong national and allied defense, hoping for the best, but seldom preparing for the worst.

In our own case, defense outlays have remained virtually level in constant dollars from 1969 to 1974. Since 1969, our military manpower has been reduced by over 40 percent. If I recall the figures correctly, about 1,200,000 less in active duty in our military.

In 1968, for example, at the peak of the Vietnam war, personnel costs for the Department of Defense were only 42 percent of total military expenditures. This fiscal year, 1975, personnel costs have risen to 55 percent of the $85 billion defense budget, in other words, from 42 to 55 percent in the short span of approximately 4 to 5 years.

This dramatic shift in how we allocate our defense dollars has prevented us from doing all we should in research and development and the procurement of modern weapons and equipment. In many areas, as a consequence, our military services are faced with a very serious bloc obsolescence in arms as well as material.

You know, the fashion is to deride excessive defense spending. The fact of the matter is that defense outlays have been a dwindling part of our gross national product, falling from an 8 to 9 percent in 1969 to less than 6 percent by 1976.

If the current declining defense trend continues, we will soon see the day, and so will others, when our country no longer has the strength necessary to guarantee our freedom, to guarantee our security in an uneasy world.

We cannot let this happen. The defense budget I am about to propose to the Congress will not let this happen.

STATEMENT OF HON. JAMES R. SCHLESINGER, SECRETARY OF DEFENSE

Secretary Schlesinger: Thank you, Mr. Chairman.

Mr. Chairman, members of the committee.

I present today the President's request to the Congress for total obligational authority in fiscal year 1976 of $104.7 billion, and associated outlays of $92.8 billion.

I should like to emphasize at the outset, Mr. Chairman, that these totals

SOURCE: House Armed Services Committee Hearings, 18 February 1975.

are contingent upon certain legislation that the President has suggested to the Congress, in particular, the 5-percent cap on pay that he has suggested for all uniformed military, civilian, and retired personnel. If we are to follow the CPI [Consumer Price Index] index in raising pay, and this legislation is not forthcoming from the Congress, the total effect would be the need for an additional $1.8 billion in outlays and in TOA.

In addition, the President has submitted to the Congress a request to produce oil from the Naval Petroleum Reserves at Elk Hills, which would bring in approximately $400 million in outlays.

If the Congress gives the President this legislation, we would be in a position to achieve the estimates as submitted. But I should underscore that the full request in detail, without this legislation, would amount to $106.4 billion in TOA, and $95 billion in outlays; these are the figures that have been bruited about in the press.

These sums are substantial, Mr. Chairman, but they are not so substantial in relation to an economy that is expanding, in terms of capacity, at a rate that continues to escape the ability of our citizenry to grasp.

It was 3 or 4 years ago, Mr. Chairman, that this economy passed the trillion-dollar mark. In fiscal year 1976, the capacity output in the economy will amount to $1.84 trillion.

The request that lies before this committee amounts to 5 percent of capacity GNP, and about 5.8 percent of the much lower level of GNP that we expect to see next year, given the lower levels of employment. This is the lowest budget percentage for defense, if we exclude retired pay, since 1940.

In addition to that, the proportion of our population under arms is the lowest since 1940. Also, the proportion of Federal spending is the smallest since 1940, if we leave out the sale of war-surplus commodities in the postwar period. We have the smallest percentage of the labor force since 1940. As you know, 1940 was one year before Pearl Harbor.

We have, Mr. Chairman, been chopping away each year, through inflation, through congressional cuts, and in earlier years, through executive requests, at the size of the Defense budget. And in many respects, we are now very thin in military power.

It is these matters that I would hope the committee will keep in mind.

I do not want to indulge in any soothing or reassuring remarks, or indicate that we can do more and more, that we can maintain the balance with what is a gradual attrition in terms of real resources.

As we know, there has been a major impact, caused by pay and price increases, on the Department of Defense, reflected in the shrinkage of manpower by 1½ million men since 1968, and 600,000 men since prior to Vietnam.

As the members of the committee know, manpower is our highest cost. The requests for fiscal year 1976 just manage to counterbalance the effects of unanticipated inflation in the prior fiscal year.

. . .

Now, Mr. Chairman, we have, of course, no purpose in maintaining a Department of Defense simply to provide opportunities to military men, or a free-floating Defense Establishment. Our Defense Establishment is intimately related to the foreign policy of this Nation. A smaller Defense Establishment, given external problems and external threats, means that we live with a higher level of risk if we attempt to implement certain types of commitments.

The United States has since 1945 been the mainstay of a worldwide military equilibrium designed to protect free nations around the world. The military balance, which we must watch carefully in forms of the fulfillment of our foreign policy objectives, has been shifting adversely.

. . .

The Soviet Union has been growing in terms of constant-dollar expenditures or constant-ruble expenditures by approximately 3 to 5 percent a year . . . . There has been a gradual, steady increase in Soviet military capability. And the Soviet view of détente, I might remind the committee, is that it is a consequence of the expansion of Soviet military power.

. . .

At the present time, according to the estimates of the Central Intelligence Agency, the Soviet Union is outspending the United States by approximately 25 percent, if we leave out retired pay and pensions, and by 20 percent if we include retired pay.

In terms of military manpower, the Soviets have passed the 4-million level in a period during which the United States has reduced its own forces to 2.1 million.

Mr. Chairman, when we talk about maintaining a worldwide military balance, we must keep in mind that we are not talking about the capability of Cuba or Guatemala or Chad. We are talking about the other superpower, if we are concerned with military balance, and the role of the United States as a military power, hopefully second to none.

. . .

We can live with adjustments in any particular year, but when there are continuous trends of expansion of Soviet capabilities and shrinkage of U.S. capabilities, in terms of expenditures, ultimately the effect must be, if those trends are not reversed, to allow military preponderance for the Soviet Union in the Eastern Hemisphere.

. . .

I think that in 1968, if somebody had proposed that real expenditures of the Department of Defense be reduced by 40 percent, that suggestion, as a policy, would have been dismissed as preposterous. Yet, as a result of the annual cutbacks over a period of years, through a process of erosion, we have arrived at that point.

We are approximately 20 percent below the fiscal year 1964 budget. In terms of investment, we are less than half of what we were in fiscal year 1968, and we are down by about 40 percent compared to fiscal year 1964.

. . .

In terms of total public spending, if we include State and local expenditures, national defense is now down to 16 percent of the total. That is the lowest point since before Pearl Harbor.

Social and economic programs have grown substantially, once again reflecting a dramatic change in priorities.

Mr. Chairman, last year we came before this committee and submitted a supplemental which was directed toward the material readiness of our forces. Most of that supplemental was chopped away.

In fiscal year 1975, we absorbed within the O&M [Operation and Maintenance] account, which is not protected against inflation, major reductions in purchasing power. As a result, we have had to curtail substantially certain classes of operations, as well as exercises. Our material readiness in many ways is less satisfactory than it was a year ago.

. . .

We have attempted in this budget request to come back most of the way to the level of operations which was projected in the fiscal year 1975 request prior to the major impact of inflation.

. . . We continue, Mr. Chairman, to have great concern with regard to the problem of efficiency. We have, as you know, with the support of the Congress, been engaged in the reduction of headquarters. This is an attempt to readjust the direction of expenditures within the Department of Defense to obtain more combat power per dollar.

We have been reducing Service headquarters. We have been reducing support forces. And in the course of this, we have, I think, achieved programs that provide a greater degree of combat power than we previously had.

. . .

Mr. Chairman, to summarize: There is sometimes some confusion on these matters between Federal funds expenditures, administrative budget expenditures, and the like.

While I think it is necessary in this country to have differences of opinion about what is appropriate policy, we ought to have no differences of opinion about the facts. The facts show a very substantial trend against the Department of Defense in terms of overall public spending, in terms of

Federal funds expenditures, and in terms of unified budget expenditures.

As I have indicated, Mr. Chairman, we are, relatively speaking, in the weakest position since the post-World War II demobilization, a period of time when the United States possessed a nuclear monopoly and when the Soviet Union was recovering from major wartime losses.

If this committee continues to be meticulously concerned about the requirements of national security, and the worldwide military balance, I am sure you will recognize that these requests, which reflect a substantial change in the priorities of the nation, are reasonable and necessary to maintain the foreign policy role for which the United States has acquired responsibility. Without the United States, much of the free world, however you way wish to define it, outside of the Western Hemisphere, will succomb to external hegemony.

There is no power, Mr. Chairman, other than the United States that can maintain this worldwide military balance. If the United States proceeds to "drop the torch," there is none other to pick it up.

These are the responsibilities which I keenly feel, and I am sure that the members of this committee also feel, in equal degree.

Mr. Chairman, this concludes my formal remarks. I am prepared for any questions you may have, or General Brown is prepared to respond in any way the committee directs.

The Military Procurement Bill

94TH CONGRESS, 1ST SESSION: H. R. 6674 [REPORT NO. 94–199]
IN THE HOUSE OF REPRESENTATIVES: MAY 5, 1975; MAY 10, 1975

MAY 5, 1975: Mr. Price introduced the following bill; which was referred to the Committee on Armed Services.

MAY 10, 1975: Reported without amendment, committed to the Committee of the Whole House on the State of the Union, and ordered to be printed

A BILL

To authorize appropriations during the fiscal year 1976, and the period beginning July 1, 1976, and ending September 30, 1976, for procurement of aircraft, missiles, naval vessels, tracked combat vehicles, torpedoes, and other weapons, and research, development, test and evaluation for the Armed Forces, and to prescribe the authorized personnel strength for each

94TH CONGRESS
1ST SESSION

H. R. 6674

[Report No. 94–199]

IN THE HOUSE OF REPRESENTATIVES

MAY 5, 1975

Mr. PRICE introduced the following bill; which was referred to the Committee on Armed Services

MAY 10, 1975

Reported without amendment, committed to the Committee of the Whole House on the State of the Union, and ordered to be printed

A BILL

To authorize appropriations during the fiscal year 1976, and the period beginning July 1, 1976, and ending September 30, 1976, for procurement of aircraft, missiles, naval vessels, tracked combat vehicles, torpedoes, and other weapons, and research, development, test and evaluation for the Armed Forces, and to prescribe the authorized personnel strength for each active duty component and of the Selected Reserve of each Reserve component of the Armed Forces and of civilian personnel of the Department of Defense, and to authorize the military training student loads and for other purposes.

1   *Be it enacted by the Senate and House of Representa-*

2 *tives of the United States of America in Congress assembled,*

3   TITLE I—PROCUREMENT

4   SEC. 101. Funds are hereby authorized to be appro-

5 priated for the use of the Armed Forces of the United States

active duty component and of the Selected Reserve of each Reserve component of the Armed Forces and of civilian personnel of the Department of Defense, and to authorize the military training student loads and for other purposes.

Be it enacted by the Senate and House of Representatives of the United States of America in Congress assembled,

TITLE I — PROCUREMENT

Sec. 101. Funds are hereby authorized to be appropriated for the use of the Armed Forces of the United States for procurement of aircraft, missiles, naval vessels, tracked combat vehicles, torpedoes, and other weapons as authorized by law, in amounts as follows:

(a) (1) During the fiscal year 1976:

AIRCRAFT

For aircraft: For the Army, $362,300,000, however, no funds authorized for procurement of Army aircraft shall be obligated for AH-1S aircraft; for the Navy and Marine Corps, $3,056,600,000; for the Air Force, $4,445,-250,000, of which $115,000,000 shall be used only for the procurement of A-7D aircraft for the National Guard.

(2) During the period July 1, 1976, to September 30, 1976:

AIRCRAFT

For aircraft: For the Army, $59,400,000; for the Navy and the Marine Corps, $585,500,000; for the Air Force, $886,300,000.

(b) (1) During the fiscal year 1976:

MISSILES

For missiles: For the Army, $455,600,000, except, that no funds authorized for appropriation by this or any other Act shall be obligated or expended for development or production of a nonnuclear Lance warhead for any other nation, until a nonnuclear warhead for the Lance missile system for the United States Army has been certified for production by the Department of Defense; for the Navy, $1,000,500,000; for the Marine Corps, $52,900,000; for the Air Force, $1,768,500,000.

(2) During the period July 1, 1976, to September 30, 1976:

MISSILES

For missiles: For the Army, $56,500,000; for the Navy, $309,100,000; for the Marine Corps, $10,700,000; for the Air Force, $277,400,000.

(c) (1) During the fiscal year 1976:

NAVAL VESSELS

For naval vessels: For the Navy, $4,422,400,000.

(2) During the period July 1, 1976, to September 30, 1976:

NAVAL VESSELS

For naval vessels: For the Navy, $474,200,000.

(d) (1) During the fiscal year 1976:

TRACKED COMBAT VEHICLES

For tracked combat vehicles: For the Army, $915,000,000; for the Marine Corps, $101,500,000.

(2) During the period July 1, 1976, to September 30, 1976:

TRACKED COMBAT VEHICLES

For tracked combat vehicles: For the Army, $272,600,000; for the Marine Corps, $400,000.

(e) (1) During the fiscal year 1976:

TORPEDOES

For torpedoes and related support equipment: For the Navy $197,400,000.

(2) During the period July 1, 1976 to September 30, 1976:

TORPEDOES

For torpedoes and related support equipment: For the Navy, $19,200,000.

(f) (1) During the fiscal year 1976:

OTHER WEAPONS

For other weapons: For the Army, $74,300,000; for the Navy, $26,-300,000; for the Marine Corps, $100,000.

(2) During the period July 1, 1976 to September 30, 1976:

OTHER WEAPONS

For other weapons: For the Army, $9,700,000; for the Navy, $4,400,000.

TITLE II — RESEARCH, DEVELOPMENT, TEST AND EVALUATION

Sec. 201. Funds are hereby authorized to be appropriated for the use of the Armed Forces of the United States for research, development, test and evaluation, as authorized by law, in amounts as follows:

(a) (1) During the fiscal year 1976: for the Army, $2,049,228,000; for the Navy (including the Marine Corps), $3,268,661,000, of which no funds will be expended for AEGIS or the Combat System Engineering Development Site for AEGIS until the Secretary of Defense provides to the Committee on Armed Services of the House and Senate a plan that identifies the nuclear platform and funding for AEGIS fleet implementation during or prior to 1981; for the Air Force, $3,760,691,000; and for the Defense Agencies, $581,793,000; of which $25,000,000 is authorized for the activities of the Director of Test and Evaluation, Defense.

(2) During the period July 1, 1976, to September 30, 1976:

for the Army: $535,017,000;

for the Navy (including the Marine Corps), $849,730,000;

for the Air Force, $982,677,000; and

for the Defense Agencies, $141,193,000; of which $3,400,000 is authorized for the activities of the Director of Test and Evaluation, Defense.

TITLE III — ACTIVE FORCES

Sec. 301. Each component of the Armed Forces is authorized an end strength for active duty personnel as follows:

(a) (1) For the fiscal year beginning July 1, 1975, and ending June 30, 1976:

(A) Army, 785,000.

(B) The Navy, 528,651.

(C) The Marine Corps, 196,303.

(D) The Air Force, 590,000.

(2) For the period beginning July 1, 1976, and ending September 30, 1976;

(A) The Army, 793,000.
(B) The Navy, 535,860.
(C) The Marine Corps, 196,498.
(D) The Air Force, 590,000.

TITLE IV — RESERVE FORCES

Sec. 401. The Selected Reserve of each Reserve component of the Armed Forces will be programmed to attain average strength of not less than the following:

(a) (1) For the fiscal year beginning July 1, 1975, and ending June 30, 1976:
(A) The Army National Guard of the United States, 400,000.
(B) The Army Reserve, 226,000.
(C) The Naval Reserve, 112,000.
(D) The Marine Corps Reserve, 32,481.
(E) The Air National Guard of the United States, 94,879.
(F) The Air Force Reserve, 51,789.
(G) The Coast Guard Reserve, 11,700.

(2) For the period beginning July 1, 1976, and ending September 30, 1976:
(A) The Army National Guard of the United States, 400,000.
(B) The Army Reserve, 226,000.
(C) The Naval Reserve, 112,000.
(D) The Marine Corps Reserve, 33,013.
(E) The Air National Guard of the United States, 94,543.
(F) The Air Force Reserve, 53,642.
(G) The Coast Guard Reserve, 11,700.

Sec. 402. The average strengths prescribed by section 401 of this title for the Selected Reserve of any Reserve component shall be proportionately reduced by (1) the total authorized strength of units organized to serve as units of the Selected Reserve of such component which are on active duty (other than for training) at any time during the fiscal year or other period, and (2) the total number of individual members not in units organized to serve as units of the Selected Reserve of such component who are on active duty (other than for training or for unsatisfactory participation in training) without their consent at any time during the fiscal year or other period. Whenever such units or such individual members are released from active duty during any fiscal year or other period, the average strength for such fiscal year or other period for the Selected Reserve of such Reserve component shall be proportionately increased by the total authorized strength of such units and by the total number of such individual members.

THE POLITICS OF THE BUDGET PROCESS

An inquiry into changes in congressional power bearing on the military authorization bills introduces the political considerations that will determine the actual operation of the new budgetary process. The sources themselves are important barometers of activities in Congress. *Congressional Quarterly* is widely consulted by legislators and their staffs as a guide to what is happening in the maze of Washington politics. The *ADA Newsletter* is one of many reports from particular groups that articulate policy stands and evaluate congressional action. Like other groups, the ADA maintains a record of the ways legislators vote on important issues. Rowland Evans and Robert Novak's column from the *Washington Post* expresses opinion that circulates outside of Washington as well as being a force in the capital.

A CHANGE OF STYLE ON HOUSE ARMED SERVICES

Many members of the House this year are anxious to do battle with the Pentagon over its fiscal 1976 $106.3–billion budget request, a third of which must be approved by the Armed Services Committee.

Recognizing the concerns of military spending critics, liberals, and many House freshmen over higher expenditures for military programs, Melvin Price (D–Ill.), the new chairman of Armed Services, has promised that under his leadership the committee will "give attention to any position taken by the Democratic caucus" on defense issues. Moreover, Price has indicated that his committee will probably take its lead on military spending authorizations from the new House Budget Committee that was established in 1974 to allow more responsible congressional consideration of the federal budget and economic policy.

Nevertheless, Price declared after his selection as chairman Jan. 22 that his committee "will attempt to give to the Defense Department whatever is necessary to maintain an adequate defense establishment," a position that has reflected his attitude toward defense spending ever since he was elected to Congress in 1944 and one that is endorsed by a majority of the panel's members.

That statement also echoes the views of F. Edward Hebert (D–La.), Price's predecessor, who was deposed as chairman by the Democratic caucus Jan. 16. Both have emphasized the need for a strong national defense and have

Source: Reprinted from *Congressional Quarterly Weekly Report*, 15 February 1975, pp. 336–341.

consistently voted for most of the Pentagon's more controversial programs and against large reductions in military spending. But Price on occasion has chastised the Defense Department for cost overruns and lack of candor about some of its requests.

The difference between the two Democrats, according to members of the committee interviewed by Congressional Quarterly, is in their style and personality. "I can't tell any difference [between them] on their views," said Floyd V. Hicks (D–Wash.), a member of Price's Research and Development Subcommittee. "Style is the difference. Price is soft-spoken, but you'll still get a 'no' from him."

While Hebert ran into trouble with the House freshmen during a meeting in January by referring to them as "boys" and "girls." Price has never been autocratic in his relations with the subcommittee, Hicks said. And other members of the Armed Services Committee as well as the Joint Atomic Energy Committee, which he chaired in the 93rd Congress, cite Price's fairness to all members.

Committee's New Look

Under Price's leadership, members of the committee anticipate greater freedom to scrutinize military projects they feel are too expensive or not essential to defense needs. In addition, they expect an increase in professional staff who are capable of ferreting out technical data and information from Defense Department officials.

But the workload of the committee, some members say, prevents a thorough examination of the Pentagon's requests, and committee rules still bar access by members' staff to classified data that they say is necessary in determining whether a defense project is essential.

The committee membership remains basically pro-military, which may put the panel on a collision course not only with some of its own members but also with an increasing number in the House who are critical of defense budget projections for fiscal 1976 and beyond.

Three members of the Armed Services Committee, all critics of recent Pentagon spending levels, welcomed Price's leadership of the panel. "I'm positive that the subcommittee chairmen will be stronger under Price," Robert L. Leggett (D–Calif.) told CQ. "I would hope that we can take military projects that the House and Senate have singled out and then conduct an in depth review. Before, we went through page after page of the bill without focus."

"Hebert's defeat means procedural fairness in the committee," said Les Aspin (D–Wis.), one of the panel's most severe critics. "It will mean that the committee will follow more closely the caucus' wishes."

Patricia Schroeder (D–Colo.) also anticipates fairness by Price, particularly during the selection of House conferees to resolve Senate and House differences on defense legislation. While Hebert was criticized for selecting the most senior, pro-military members of the committee for conference sessions — although amendments by junior members of his committee to cut military spending occasionally were on the conference agenda — Schroeder said she did not think conferee selection would be an issue with Price.

ARMED SERVICES LEGISLATIVE ROLE

Whatever course Price follows in chairing the Armed Services Committee, he will preside over a panel whose operations and influence have expanded greatly since it was created by the Legislative Reorganization Act of 1946. At that time the committee had jurisdiction only over military organization, policy and manpower through the draft. The committee did review plans for developing new weapons systems, but it was the Appropriations Committee which both authorized and appropriated funds for specific Pentagon arms programs.

In 1959, the committee assumed responsibility from the Appropriations Committee for setting ceilings on funds appropriated for the purchase of aircraft, missiles, and ships. This was a major breakthrough, giving the committee power to authorize appropriations for about 15 per cent of the Defense Department's annual expenditures.

By the late 1960s, the Armed Services Committee was acting on legislation authorizing funds for the following research, development, testing and evaluation of weapons and communications projects; procurement of all weapons and weapons systems — aircraft, missiles, naval vessels, tracked combat vehicles, and torpedoes; active duty personnel salaries; military construction programs, including family housing; and military assistance to South Vietnam.

Of the $85.2 billion appropriated by Congress in fiscal 1975 for the Defense Department, 30 per cent ($24.8 billion) received prior authorization by the committee. The panel does not authorize funds annually for operation and maintenance of the armed forces ($25.3 billion in fiscal 1975), for retired military personnel benefits and pensions ($6 billion) or for active duty military personnel benefits and salaries ($24.2 billion), all of which are approved directly by the Appropriations Committee . . . .

Besides approving authorizations for weapons procurement, research, and construction each year, legislation which occupies the bulk of its time, the committee acts on a wide range of other matters. In 1974 the committee considered legislation revising the pay structure of medical officers, held hearings on the extent of bombing of North Vietnam in late 1972 and early 1973, revised special-pay bonuses for members of the armed services and authorized the military bands to sell tapes and records in connection with the 1976 Bicentennial celebrations.

In addition, special subcommittees of the Armed Services panel held hearings on the admission of women to the service academies, requests for transfers of naval vessels to other nations, and Central Intelligence Agency activities.

Committee Workload

With the dramatic increase in the committee's responsibilities and workload has come criticism that the panel's resources and manpower are spread too thin to review adequately the Pentagon's budget requests and probe the technical data submitted by the department in support of its projects. "You can sit there year after year and just begin to learn the acronyms for all the Pentagon programs," said Hicks. "You just don't have a grasp on everything. The little things, which amount to millions, just go by."

Yet the committee attributes part of its difficulties to the "non-responsiveness" of Pentagon officials in submitting required reports and the department's "too often inaccurate" cost estimates. In its 1974 report on the fiscal 1975 procurement bill (HR 14592 — H Rept 93–1035), the committee said it had to ask the same questions repeatedly in order to "ascertain actual system costs."

During 1974 hearings on the research and development section of HR 14592, William L. Dickinson (R–Ala.) complained to Lt. Gen. Alfred Starbird (Ret.), a deputy director in the Defense Department's Office of Research and Engineering, that the committee members lacked the expertise to probe Pentagon requests. "You have to be pretty smart to know what the question is that will get the answer you are seeking. And I don't think for a minute that the services knock themselves out trying to help you ask the right questions, unless they are anxious to have you ask that question."

Budget Cuts

While the committee members bicker with the Defense Department each year, the authorization bills reported to the House by the panel are always just slightly below the Pentagon requests. Between 1972 and 1975, according to a study by a committee member who did not wish to be identified, the amounts authorized for weapons procurement in the legislation reported by the committee averaged 98.5 per cent of the totals requested. In comparison, the Senate Armed Services Committee granted 93.9 per cent of the Pentagon budget requests and Congress approved 90.8 per cent.

WHITE HOUSE, PENTAGON VIEWS

Although "There is hardly a particle of difference philosophically between Representatives Hebert and Price in regard to national defense," a White House staff member noted, "there are bound to be changes" in the committee's approach to defense issues because of the new line-up in Congress. "All committee chairmen are on notice that they had better be responsive to the freshmen and king caucus."

On the other hand, this source said, the Armed Services Committee "would appear to be less affected by the new liberal taint in the House." The two new Republicans on the committee are considered "solid conservatives," and the majority of the panel has consistently supported Pentagon requests.

The Defense Department, meanwhile, has been described as "rattled" and "shaken" with the change in the committee's leadership — but not because of any difference in the views of Price and Hebert. The Pentagon now realizes that "chairmen with whom they get along can be knocked off now and then," according to one Pentagon public information employee, and it is "no longer automatic for members who were waiting in the wings to become chairmen" to achieve leadership posts.

PENTAGON WINS AGAIN

JOHN ISAACS

The Senate and House concluded their first series of major military spending votes in the 94th Congress by the first week in June, and the Pentagon emerged with a clear victory. Amendment after amendment designed to limit the huge increase in the military budget went down to defeat. Votes on amendments to the military authorization bill were a disaster for those seeking reductions in the Pentagon's fiscal 1976 budget.

All budget cutting amendments in the House went down to defeat, including Rep. Les Aspin's (D–Wis.) ceiling amendment setting a dollar limit on overall spending for weapons programs. The Aspin amendment lost on a relatively close vote; amendments to cut back or kill weapons programs, however, were defeated by large margins.

In the Senate, Pentagon critics won a few small victories, including one

SOURCE: This article by John Isaacs, then legislative representative of the Americans for Democratic Action, appeared in ADA's *Legislative Newsletter*, June 15, 1975.

amendment to limit testing of a new nuclear warhead and another to cut the size of the Department of Defense (DOD) civilian bureaucracy. Yet a major attempt to cut out money for all counterforce programs failed, as did an effort to set a ceiling on the Pentagon's budget. Attempts to trim money for the B–1 bomber, AWACS, Minutemen III missiles, site defense, and other major systems all crashed down in defeat.

THE SETTING FOR THE VOTES

The Pentagon tried a new tack this year: requesting a budgetary increase that was so large that even if the House and Senate Armed Services Committees did not grant the entire request, the military budget still would rise considerably. The Pentagon requested a 17.5 percent increase in total obligational authority — to $104.7 billion in fiscal 1976 — and a 35 percent hike in money for weapons procurement and research and development. The size of its request was startling.

Making larger cuts than usual, the House and Senate Armed Services Committees boasted of their accomplishments. The press generally picked up on the theme of the committees' success in trimming the Pentagon's budget requests, failing to point out that the House committee allowed the Pentagon an enormous 27 percent increase over its budget of last year and that the Senate committee allowed it an increase of 20 percent.

The influx of liberal freshmen in the House, the more moderate Senate Armed Services Committee, and the fact that Pentagon critics in both Houses were better organized should have helped build support for this year's budget cutting amendments to the military authorization bill. Ultimately, however, these factors did not prove decisive.

The conclusion of the Indochina debacle, followed by the Ford Administration's gunboat diplomacy in the Mayaguez incident, completely changed the atmosphere and mood of Congress. In the face of a challenge to America's credibility — President Ford and Secretary of State Kissinger did all they could to make Members believe that such a challenge existed — many Members became reluctant to vote for military reductions. There was tremendous sensitivity to the "isolationist" charge bandied about by various cabinet officers. The spirit of a strong, new Congress willing to challenge misguided Administration policies, at least on foreign policy and military issues, faded fast.

Another negative factor was the economy. Massive unemployment throughout the nation made many Members fearful of voting to cut programs which might exacerbate unemployment in their districts. Finally, there was the rush of some major newspapers, particularly the *Washington Post* and the *New York Times*, to get back on the "establishment team" by supporting the Administration on the military budget and on the Mayaguez affair after years of strong opposition to several Administration's Indochina policies.

THE HOUSE VOTES

The House considered the military authorization bill on May 19–20, only days after the Mayaguez incident. The hallowed halls of the House were still echoing Members' jingoistic speeches about the need to demonstrate America's strength to the rest of the world.

The major weapons system fight in the House came on the B–1 bomber. The strategy of Pentagon opponents had been for Rep. Thomas Downey (D–N.Y.) to offer an amendment to cut out all $749 million in money for procurement and research and development of the B–1 in FY 1976, and then for Rep. Aspin to offer a more modest amendment to trim the $77 million in procurement money. This two-pronged approach was aimed at picking up support for the Aspin amendment. Unfortunately, however, a parliamentary tangle prevented Downey from offering his amendment.

As a result, the House easily defeated the Aspin B–1 amendment, 164–227. Still, this year's vote showed a significant 70 vote pickup from only 94 votes in favor of an amendment to kill the B–1 bomber in 1974. In fact, it was the highest vote ever against a major weapons system on a military authorization bill. Democratic freshmen voted 57–15 for the amendment, providing significant new support. Yet there still is substantial reluctance among many Members in the House to challenge the Pentagon on any weapons program.

The final significant House vote came on the Aspin ceiling amendment which would have set a dollar limit on weapons program spending $1.9 billion below the level approved by the Armed Services Committee. Aspin had won handily with a similar amendment in 1973, but lost by 24 votes in 1974.

This year, the amendment failed 183–216, despite a 55–16 freshman margin in its favor. A number of moderate Democrats and Republicans like Reps. Richard Bolling (D–Mo.), Thomas Foley (D–Wash.) and Joel Pritchard (R–Wash.) abandoned their previous support. Bolling, in fact, in an action reminiscent of his earlier efforts against amendments to stop the Vietnam war, helped lead the fight against this amendment.

None of the House votes on other military budget cutting amendments was close. An amendment by Rep. Ronald Dellums (D–Calif.) to reduce America's overseas troop levels by a modest 70,000 troops was crushed 95–311, with liberals, moderates, and conservatives climbing all over each other to demonstrate that they would not turn "isolationist." Even Rep. Thomas O'Neill (D–Mass.), who for the past two years has sponsored troop cutting amendments of his own, this year voted against such cuts.

Other amendments — to bar testing of the maneuverable re-entry vehicle (MaRV), to delete money for procurement of three airborne warning and control system aircraft (AWACS), to cut money for the A–10 and Trident program — failed by large votes. The one small victory came with passage of an amendment to allow women to enter U.S. military academies. In all it was a bad few days for proponents of military cutbacks.

SENATE TAKES CENTER STAGE

The Senate spent the full week of June 2 debating and voting on the military authorization bill, but its final bill differed only marginally from that produced by the House.

A significant innovation this year was a two day debate on the policies and assumptions underlying the Pentagon's budget requests. Much of the credit for organizing the debate goes to Sen. Alan Cranston (D–Calif.), who was joined by Sen. Edward Kennedy (D–Mass.) and by the three freshman Democrats on Armed Services, John Culver (Iowa), Gary Hart (Colo.), and Patrick Leahy (Vt.).

The basic idea of the debate was to approach the bill in an integrated and analytical way, to discuss weapons systems not just in terms of their destructive capabilities, but also in terms of their relationship to U.S. foreign policy interests. A bipartisan letter signed by both conservatives and liberals invited all Senators to participate.

The final debate hardly could be labeled "great," and some Members could not resist the temptation to ready lengthy prepared statements. Still, this year marked the first time in recent memory that the Senate has approached the Pentagon's budget requests with a serious intent to ask the important questions. There also were some very interesting face-to-face confrontations like Kennedy vs. Sam Nunn (D–Ga.) and McGovern (D–S. Dak.) vs. Goldwater (R–Ariz.).

Even if not many answers were supplied during the debate, a number of highly significant questions were raised and discussed. If a Senate-passed Culver amendment mandating an annual joint State Department–Defense Department report survives the conference committee, this date may be institutionalized.

Counterforce

The most important debate over a weapons system came on an amendment by Sens. Thomas McIntyre (D–N.H.) and Edward Brooke (R–Mass.) to delete $143 million for a series of counterforce programs. These programs, while not costly at present, could lead the U.S. and the Soviet Union to develop first-strike threats against each other's ground-based missile force. By undermining the present confidence that each side has in the survivability of its retaliatory force following an all out attack, counterforce programs could seriously jeopardize nuclear stability. These programs are all in line with Defense Secretary Schlesinger's "Dr. Strangelove" notion that it is possible to fight a little nuclear war without inviting a total nuclear catastrophe.

McIntyre, the moderate Armed Services research and development subcommittee chairman, who last year led a similar counterforce fight and two years ago missed slowing down the Trident submarine program by only two votes, once again developed a beautiful legislative fight on this highly complex strategic issue. Helped by Brooke, Cranston, and Sen. John Pastore (D–R. I.), McIntyre made a careful vote count and undertook an intensive, personalized lobbying campaign aimed especially at winning the support of Senate moderates. Also, specifically at McIntyre's request, the Senate went into a rare secret session to discuss classified arguments on counterforce.

At one point, there did appear to be close to a majority for McIntyre's counterforce amendment. But this support melted away in the last hours before the vote and even during the roll call. Freshman Senator Dale Bumpers (D–Ark.) and Sen. Joseph Montoya (D–N.M.) voted for the amendment the first time around on the roll call, only to switch to the opposition the second time. It is understood that Sen. Strom Thurmond (R–S.C.) got to Montoya in the middle of the roll call with the argument that some of the counterforce money was being spent in Montoya's state. (Two years ago, Montoya similarly made a last-minute switch on the crucial Trident vote, despite a pledge of support for the amendment.) Sens. Frank Moss (D–Utah), Quentin Burdick (D–N. Dak.), and Abraham Ribicoff (D–Conn.), all of whom had appeared to be leaning toward supporting the McIntyre amendment, wound up voting against it. Sen. William Proxmire (D–Wis.) repeated his "nay" vote of last year. A couple of likely "yea" votes were absent.

However, the Senate did conduct a relatively clear debate on a highly complex issue. The base of those opposing these dangerous nuclear programs increased. Also, the way was paved for the more modest amendment to halt MaRV testing sponsored two days later by Sen. Hubert Humphrey (D–Minn.) and Brooke.

The Humphrey amendment, a small consolation prize for opponents of counterforce, was won by a narrow 43 to 41 vote. Sens. Bumpers, Burdick, Moss, Proxmire, and surprisingly, Sens. Henry Bellmon (R–Okla.) and Warren Magnuson (D–Wash.) switched in favor of the amendment, a number of Senators were absent, and two arranged "live pairs" cancelled two no votes. Humphrey again proved his ability to appeal to moderates of the

Senate and enhanced his reputation as one of the few Senators able to get a significant amendment passed on military budget bills. He effectively used the argument that once the MaRV was tested, the Soviet Union would have to operate on the assumption — correct or not — that we actually were deploying the system. As a significant side note, Sen. Lloyd Bentsen (D–Texas), joined with the hawkish Sen. Henry Jackson (D–Wash.) to cast votes in favor of going forward with MaRV testing.

Ceiling Amendment

The other major Senate fight came on a military authorization bill ceiling amendment sponsored by Sens. Stuart Symington (D–Mo.), Kennedy, and Cranston. This amendment was offered before any other in hopes that a success on this vote would enhance prospects for trimming weapons programs on subsequent votes.

Ceiling amendments, which set a dollar limit on overall military spending without specifying which weapons programs are to be cut do have a certain amount of appeal. Many Members of Congress are reluctant to engage in debates on the complex technical aspects of specific weapons systems, preferring instead to set an overall limit on military spending. Also, the ceiling concept has been embodied in the new budget act: Congress now is establishing ceilings on the entire federal budget and on major functional areas like health, agriculture, or national defense. The White House was concerned enough about the appeal of a Pentagon budget ceiling amendment that it launched an intensive lobbying campaign to insure the defeat of such an amendment.

Debate on the ceiling amendment got burdened down with the usual problems. Some Senators like Charles Percy (R–Ill.) refuse to vote for ceiling amendments on principle, saying that the Senate should specify the weapons programs to be cut. Sen. Edmund Muskie (D–Me.) withdrew his support of the amendment on the grounds that it might threaten Maine's ship-building program. Appropriations Committee chairman John McClellan (D–Ark.) thundered against the amendment as impinging upon his committee's power to set military appropriations, using this argument despite the fact that the Appropriations Committee always has been required to set military appropriations in line with limits established by the military authorization bill — ceiling amendment or not. Even Nunn, supposedly the late Sen. Richard Russell's (D–Ga.) successor as reigning Georgia military expert, added to the general confusion over the military spending figures by getting outlays, authorizations, and appropriations confused.

So the ceiling amendment went down to a 36–59 trouncing, again raising questions among liberals over the best strategy for amendments to reduce the Pentagon's budget. An analysis of the ceiling amendment, the counter-force amendments and the votes on AWACS, site defense, B–1, and Minutemen III shows a total of 55 Senators willing to support one amendment or another, but never more than 43 who voted in favor of any one amendment.

A Summing Up

Most major weapons program amendments in the Senate went down to defeat. Thomas Eagleton's (D–Mo.) amendment to hold back production of AWACS failed 38–58. Mike Gravel's (D–Alaska) amendment to bar use of funds for development of a site defense ABM program lost 39–54. McGovern's B–1 amendment was defeated 32–57. A Kennedy–Cranston amendment to delete funds for the procurement of 50 Minutemen III missiles lost 27–56.

A few amendments brightened the otherwise bleak Senate picture: One, of course, was Humphrey's MaRV testing amendment. Proxmire produced an amazing liberal–conservative coalition including Barry Goldwater to win by a close 42–40 margin an amendment mandating a cut of 17,000 DOD civilian personnel. Sen. William Hathaway (D–Me.) won an amendment paralleling the House amendment to permit women in the military academies. Sen. James Abourezk (D–S. Dak.) managed to modify a much abused "feed and forage" act dating back originally to 1820, which the Pentagon had stretched to authorize air operations in Indochina.

There were other positive aspects to the week spent in the bill. Culver got an amendment adopted in committee requiring the Pentagon to provide the life cycle cost (the cost of acquiring, operating, and maintaining a weapon over its useful life) of major weapons systems in order to get more detailed information on true weapons costs.

Culver and the two other freshman Democrats, Gary Hart and Leahy, made a highly positive contribution to the Senate Armed Services Committee, easily justifying the move earlier this year to moderate the committee's conservative majority. These freshmen helped to make the difference on a number of key votes in committee — including votes to delete money for the dangerous binary chemical warfare program and for the F–111 bomber — which kept the amount of money authorized below what it otherwise would have been. They asked a lot of tough questions seldom put to Pentagon witnesses before.

Still the Pentagon got its way in almost all cases. On major weapons systems, where DOD, the White House, defense contractors, the reserves, and the other components of the still very potent military–industrial complex put on the pressure, it is almost impossible to win a vote in Congress. The complexities of the technological systems give the Pentagon an overwhelming advantage over Senators having very little competence in the area; as a result, there is a strong tendency to stick with the recommendations of the Armed Services Committee. In addition, the Pentagon frequently seems to be able to turn the international atmosphere — there almost always is one crisis or another — or the economic situation to its favor. Every program involves jobs in several different districts and states forcing many Members to vote "for jobs." It is not totally impossible to win an amendment on the military bills, if the "atmospherics" are right, the sponsors are effective in appealing to swing votes, and there is the right kind of coalition building; but never let it be said that it's easy.

DEBATE ON THE CONFERENCE REPORT, DEFENSE AUTHORIZATION ACT OF 1976

Mr. STENNIS [Senator John Stennis of Mississippi]: Mr. President, we have worked out a time agreement. This is really a highly important bill with a lot of items in it. I hope we can have the attention of the Senators. This is the military authorization bill, Mr. President, primarily for research and development and military procurement — planes, missiles, submarines, guns, and so forth. We also pass on the ceiling for manpower.

Mr. President, this was an unusual conference in many ways. We met over a period of 2 months and, in round numbers, we had 17 actual meetings of the conferees. As I remember, we also had four separate meetings of the Senate conferees. In the end, we had examined 306 differences in money items, and reached agreement on them and on 43 separate items on language.

. . .

The difference in the amount of money in the House bill and the Senate bill, in round numbers, was that the House was 1.5 billion dollars above our bill. And again in round numbers, it comes out that in the give and take, the adjustments just about offset each other.

Our bill, in round numbers, Mr. President, was 25 billion dollars.

They elected me chairman of the conference. We had studiously tried to stay within the targets of the Senate Budget Committee when we first approved the bill and when we had it on the floor. When we started this conference I announced that we felt a strong obligation in that regard and that our purpose was to stay within those guidelines, even though we did not have a definite figure guideline, and there is none yet. All during this

SOURCE: Reprinted from the *Congressional Record*, 1 August 1975.

conference, I conferred with the chief of staff and other members as to whether or not we were staying within those guidelines and I was advised that we were.

I am able to say now, Mr. President, that our bill, as it was presented to the Senate and as it left the Senate, was within the guidelines, and this bill we present today is within the Senate budget guidelines.

I do not have any doubt about it, according to my understanding and my appraisal of the situation.

I wish the membership was here to hear the arguments on both sides because we have been challenged by the very fine and able chairman of the Budget Committee on that particular point. The Senator from Maine, with whom I have maintained contact, has worked with us on this matter all the way through. I know he is very conscientious in the discharge of his duties in this connection.

Mr. MUSKIE [Senator Edmund Muskie of Maine]: Mr. President, the Senate had pending . . . important conference reports which have major implications for the new congressional budget.

. . .

I will vote against the military procurement conference report because it authorizes military expenditures which translate into appropriations which exceed our congressional budget targets.

. . .

It is no discredit to our Senate conferees on these bills that we vote to reject these reports. Each bill, as it passed the House, exceeded the budget totals to an even greater degree than do these conference reports. The Senate conferees were able to reduce that excess spending but, regrettably, not to eliminate it.

But a vote to approve these conference reports is a vote to exceed the budget targets we set for ourselves in May. It is a vote for a larger deficit.

Mr. BELLMON [Senator Henry Bellmon of Oklahoma]: Mr. President, I find myself in a quandary today. I am completely dedicated to making the newly-adopted budget process work. It is the only available means Congress has to stop the irresponsible accumulation of one huge deficit after another, as has happened every year since I have been in the Senate. This plunge into economic chaos has to be stopped. I consider it to be the greatest threat our country faces today, and therefore, while I have always supported and still support a strong national defense, I intend to oppose, and ask my colleagues to oppose, the Conference Report on H.R. 6674, the Military Procurement Authorization bill. I am mindful of the arguments concerning the military need for various items in this bill and I respect the opinions of my friend, the Senator from Mississippi . . . for I have often voted with [him] on military matters. Yet I am absolutely convinced that this country must be just as strong economically as it must be prepared militarily. Therefore, I must oppose this conference report in the name of fiscal responsibility. Military need must be weighed carefully with other needs and the ability of this Nation to meet the costs of Government.

On May 14, 1975, the Senate approved the first concurrent resolution on the budget. After several months of hearings, economic analysis, and staff study, what was deemed to be the appropriate level of spending for fiscal year 1976 was determined and the Senate overwhelmingly approved those numbers only 78 days ago. We collectively said that budget authority should be $395.8 billion, outlays should be $367.0 billion. Given what we expect in the way of revenues, the level of deficit was determined to be $68.8 billion.

Many of us were not happy with that deficit number, but it mathematically followed once the appropriate spending level was determined. Now we have serious concern that we can hold the deficit down to $68.8 billion.

Mr. President, I do not intend to support or oppose any specific military program. Members of the armed services are far better equipped to decide where military spending is most needed. The responsibility of the budget committee is to set realistic spending levels, and gain congressional approval of those levels. This has been done — we now have the responsibility to see that their spending levels are not exceeded.

As part of the Senate approved budget resolution, it was determined that the national defense function would total $100.7 billion in budget authority and $90.7 billion in outlays. If H.R. 6674 is adopted and if the programs and personnel levels in this bill are fully funded, then I am very much afraid that the defense budget targets will be overshot and our Federal deficit numbers will exceed even the huge $68.8 billion in the congressional budget.

As mentioned by Senator Muskie, it appears that all of the pending requests in the national defense function total $9.6 billion in authority and $5.4 billion in outlays over the budget.

This bill accomplishes about $4.2 billion of the needed cut in budget authority and only $1.3 billion of the necessary reduction in outlays. Since it is not very likely that substantial savings can be found in the military construction operation and maintenance and other defense accounts, nor that the originally anticipated income from the stockpile sales will materialize in total, it is imperative that the military procurement and research and development authorization and appropriation be reduced as much as possible.

It would be simple to allow this authorization to pass by rationalizing that we can cut it later in the appropriations process. But I believe that if we really intend to adhere to the budget act, it is important to apply the budget to authorizations as well as appropriations. This will provide the quickest guidance to the agencies and departments so they can plan and operate accordingly for better efficiency. It eliminates uncertainties for those elements of the budget which have been authorized but may not be appropriated.

In summary, by sending this bill back to conference, we are demonstrating that we are willing to live with the discipline of a budget — that we are willing to take difficult, and sometimes unpopular, positions in order to prevent excessive Government spending to restore confidence in Government which is so needed for our Nation's economic stability.

Mr. Humphrey [Senator Hubert Humphrey of Minnesota]: Mr. President, last year, the Congress passed a bill that drastically changed the Federal budgetary process. The ultimate goal of that legislation was to give Congress a more important role in deciding how large department and agency budgets should be. With the addition of new staff expertise in the Budget Committees and the Congressional Budget Office, the Congress developed an analytical capability on budget matters like it has never had before. The Members of Congress had struck a blow for greater congressional control of the Federal budget and for greater fiscal responsibility.

These goals are surely noble ones. But in the case of this year's national defense function budget, they have been totally lost on the Congress. If the Senate and House continue on their present course, and it appears that they will, expenditures will be authorized in the defense area that are substantially in excess of $100.7 billion goal established by the concurrent budget resolution.

How could Congress fail to hit its own cut mark by a large margin? To see how, I will start with a look at the defense authorization bill for military procurement that is now before us.

The Senate bill authorized $25 billion. The House authorized $26.5 billion. The conference bill comprised at $25.8 billion — more than the Senate version.

Also, the Senate cut defense manpower by 58,300 men. The House made no cut at all. The conference compromise pegged a cut of 32,000 men. An additional budget cut of about $0.2 billion was lost, therefore, by not cutting the 26,300 extra men removed in the Senate version.

All told, then, the Senate cut $1 billion more than the conference version of the procurement and personnel measures. And now this $1 billion additional savings is lost.

Mr. Clark [Senator Joseph Clark of Pennsylvania]: Mr. President, I rise in opposition to the conference report on H.H. 6674, the arms procurement authorization bill which has come back to us with the Senate's contributions almost totally missing.

Granted that the Senate chose to reject nearly all proposed cuts in the Pentagon's proposals for new military spending in fiscal year 1976. I find it nonetheless disturbing that those specific elements in the legislation added by the Senate fared so poorly in the conference. It seems that in almost every instance where the House version was more favorable to the Pentagon than that of the Senate, the House version prevailed.

. . .

Mr. President, I think what disturbs me most about this whole exercise in Government waste and congressional futility is the irony of it. What we are buying is an arsenal of weapons which our leaders, and the leaders of the Soviet Union as well, tell us could never be used without risking the total destruction of both societies, and the rest of the world along with them. They are of no real use to us except to wipe ourselves off the face of the Earth. Yet we willingly drain ever-larger proportions of our precious national resources and manpower into their production year after year. Where will it end?

. . .

And there is another irony. When we take up in the Congress proposals for foreign aid or for a long list of domestic needs, the burden of proof always rests with those proposing such spending. Not so with defense spending. As we learned to our sorrow last month, when it comes to Pentagon programs, the burden of proof rests with those who question their need.

. . .

Mr. President, I think we need to remind ourselves that the Vietnam war has ended. For the first time in more than a decade we are at peace. The $30 billion annnual outlays for Indochina are no more. We face no imminent threat of war, and if we did, I doubt that these expenditures would save us in a nuclear exchange. Our relations with nations such as the Soviet Union and the Peoples Republic of China have never been so relaxed. There are troubles in the world, to be sure, but the worst ones at the moment are economic, not military. Spending money on munitions will not help much in shoring up the dollar or the pound, or in reducing our excessive demand for foreign oil.

Look at the size of the defense budget we are being asked to approve. New spending authority is 18 percent higher than last year's, and overall the Defense Department budget represents 27 percent of the total Federal budget. This is nothing if not shocking.

Just for comparison, we should note that last year's spending authority had a 2-percent growth figure, contrasted with 18 percent this year.

. . .

Now with regard to this conference report, let us look at the items for procurement and for research, development, test, and evaluation. The total is $25.8 billion, the largest increase in such spending we have ever experienced in peacetime. A 24-percent increase, compared to a 3-percent increase last year. And looking at the many new programs in this list, we know that this year's increase is only the beginning. Where seed money is strewn one can be sure bigger demands will grow.

. . .

Now I am not saying that we must stop all research or even all new weapons building. What I am saying is that the defense budget of the United States has gone wild, and we in the Senate are sitting here allowing it [to] go unchecked. The logic of it is wholly absent. Somehow we have gone mad in our preoccupation with expensive gadgetry. And meanwhile we are running up a Federal deficit this year that is nearly as large as the defense budget itself.

One final point and I will conclude my remarks. Last fall there were many political victories around the country, just as there have been for 6 years or so, that rewarded those who campaigned to hold down military spending. What has happened? Where is that mandate reflected, either in the House or the Senate, or in this conference report? I am puzzled. I wonder whether my memory fails me, or whether some people have changed their minds since election day. It is puzzling.

Mr. President, I believe the Senate should reject this conference report and instruct its conferees to restore the items I have mentioned — items not calling for new expenditures, but new restraints. The Defense Department needs to find out that it is a servant of the Congress and the American people, and not the other way around.

THE SENATE SHELL GAME

ROWLAND EVANS AND ROBERT NOVAK

The most recent "scorekeeping" report by the Senate Budget Committee, showing excessive defense spending and reduced non-defense spending, suggests that the much acclaimed congressional budgetary reform is really a Senate shell game to fleece the Pentagon.

In fact, Congress clearly is *reducing* defense spending and increasing non-defense spending. The reason this does not show up in the monthly scorecard is an accounting change by the Senate staff which, at least temporarily, appears to reduce non-defense for future spending by a huge $27 billion.

Source: *Washington Post*, September 18, 1975. "The Senate Shell Game" by Rowland Evans and Robert Novak. Courtesy of Field Newspaper Syndicate.

That accounting change will probably be corrected in time, but the figure juggling reflects a clever anti-Pentagon operation only now becoming clear.

The budgetry reform, while actually cutting Pentagon spending more deeply than domestic programs, gives the opposite impression. If we cut school milk funds, demand liberal budget reformers headed by Sen. Edmund Muskie of Maine, you must reduce missiles and aircraft carriers. The result: enough conservative Republicans joining Muskie to create a new Senate anti-defense coalition endangering long-range defense programs.

Architect of this coalition is Muskie, who preaches "fiscal discipline" but is firmly committed to cutting back the Pentagon and boosting social welfare spending. Such "reordering of priorities" is the goal of Muskie's Senate Budget Committee staff (including its defense specialist, Andrew Hamilton, a former soft-line staffer on the National Security Council).

The game began stacked against defense in the Muskie committee's original targets. The defensive target was set below President Ford's request ($3 billion less for current spending, $7 billion less for new budget authority). The non-defense target was set above President Ford's request ($21 billion more for current spending, $17 billion more for new budget authority).

From that uneven beginning, the Muskie committee moved into a budget accounting quagmire navigable by few technicians and no U.S. senators. The committee's Sept. 2 scorecard shows Congress $4 billion over the committee target in defense budget authority and $9 billion under its target in non-defense budget authority.

How can this be when Congress cuts defense and increases just about everything else? The scorecard answers in a footnote: An accounting change removed $27 billion in long-term authority for public housing. Without that change, non-defense budget authority would be $9 billion above even the Senate's high target. This target may be lowered later to correspond to the accounting change, but the Muskie committee for now has given a false impression of defense profligacy and non-defense parsimony.

This fits Muskie's Senate tactics. On July 10, he rose to oppose a $180 million addition to the school lunch program on grounds it exceeded his committee's targets. He was overwhelmingly supported by the Senate, amid speculation Muskie had turned from spender to tight-fisted fiscal conservative.

That speculation ended when Muskie dropped the other shoe Aug. 1, the last day before the August recess. Muskie again rose in the Senate to reject the defense procurement bill's final version on grounds it exceeded the target by $5.4 billion (a misleading figure partially caused by the Muskie staff's accountancy). Muskie's message: If you cut school lunches, cut defense as well.

Defense advocates scarcely consider swapping free lunches for missiles a fair trade considering the overall rise in social welfare spending. But Muskie's argument enlisted five conservative Republicans — Henry Bellmon of Oklahoma, J. Glenn Beall of Maryland, Robert Dole of Kansas, Pete Domenici of New Mexico, and William Roth of Delaware. They provided the difference as the Senate rejected the bill 48 to 42.

It is no coincidence that all these conservatives except Roth belong to Muskie's budget committee. Relatively junior in seniority, they view the new budgetary process as their avenue to power.

Thus, a new anti-defense coalition has been built on internal Senate politics, on balancing minor social welfare cuts with major defense cuts and on impenetrable budgetary accounting. The Aug. 1 roll call reflects a possible landmark change in Capitol Hill defense politics that deeply worries the Pentagon. On Sept. 5, Muskie helped cement his coalition by successfully opposing the final version of the school lunch bill, thereby perpetuating the notion of tradeoff.

Defense officials hope to break the coalition by convincing its conservative Republicans that they are victimized by figures which magnify defense spending and shrink non-defense spending. But the impulse for stronger national defense immediately following the Indochina debacle seems to be fading. The desire to equate elimination of free school lunches for children of $200-a-week workers with cuts in military preparedness may be irresistible.

THE VIEWS OF THE MEMBERS

Elizabeth Holtzman is a Democratic member of the House of Representatives from New York City. In comparing defense spending to other areas of the economy she concludes that the House Budget Committee is performing poorly in terms of the standards of budgetary supervision called for under the Budget Act. The defense figures that the Congresswoman cites represent only those endorsed by the House Budget Committee. The Senate counterpart committee increased the House outlay by almost 1 billion dollars, compounding the budget problems to which Holtzman addresses herself.

DISSENTING VIEWS OF HON. ELIZABETH HOLTZMAN

This is a timid budget which does not address the serious economic and social problems facing our country.

This budget essentially accepts the spending patterns of the past. It does little except tinker at the margin with problems, instead of asserting new priorities for the Nation. For example, it authorizes spending 45 percent of general revenue funds for defense despite the fact that we are no longer at war.

The budget fails to deal adequately with unemployment. There are more than ten million people who are unemployed or have dropped out of the labor force. The budget endorses a 7.5 percent unemployment rate for 1976. This is a tragic waste of human resources. It translates into an economic loss of over $100 billion in real output during 1976. With our labor force growing at unprecedented rate,[1] our economy must expand considerably more rapidly to provide jobs, housing, education, and health services for more people.

This budget recommends the Congress forego the opportunity to face these issues. It chooses to accept paying for joblessness — $19.1 billion for unemployment compensation, $6.6 billion for food stamps, and $5.8 billion for AFDC — instead of paying for job creation. I believe it is a serious mistake for the Federal budget to choose welfare over work.

While our major cities are continuing to decay and face an increasingly bleak future, this resolution endorses $91.2 billion in outlays for defense. This is $500 million higher than the Committee recommended, and the Congress accepted, in the First Budget Resolution. The present resolution recommends spending $8.3 billion more on defense than we did last year. We are not at war, nor is the threat of war imminent. We should not spend billions in peace-time to support such demonstrably wasteful weapons systems as the B–1 bomber, AWACS, the Trident submarine, and MARVS. Most spending on defense is by definition inflationary; weapons do not enhance our country's economic strength or potential.

The resolution calls for the Department of Defense to absorb 50 percent of the cost of its pay raises ($800 million); that is commendable. But the Committee, by rejecting my amendment for 100 percent absorption (which would have saved another $800 million), failed to take more positive steps to control the Pentagon budget.

SOURCE: Reprinted from Report on Second Concurrent Resolution of the Budget, Fiscal Year 1976. 31 October 1975. House Budget Committee.
[1]During the 1950s the labor force grew at less than 1.5 percent a year; it is now increasing at 2.5 percent annually.

While I know the limitations faced by the Budget Committee because of its short existence and the magnitude and complexity of its task, I believe it has nonetheless failed to use opportunities that were available to effect a significant change in national priorities. Thus, while this budget contains $1.3 billion to support the prices of tobacco, wheat, peanuts, and other commodities, the Committee would not accept my amendment to increase spending for elementary education by $200 million. There have only minimal funding increases for this program, despite the fact that the nation has a 23 percent rate of functional adult illiteracy in recent years.

This resolution fails to address the desperate plight of the most helpless Americans — the poverty stricken, aged, blind, and disabled. The SSI program does not yet provide enough income for these poorest of our citizens, and the Committee rejected my amendment to add $644 million to provide housing allowances and other benefits for SSI beneficiaries. This is not the way a responsible Congress, concerned with this nation's human needs, should behave.

The Committee continues to recommend funds for programs which are unnecessary and unproductive, and which add nothing to our national defense or our national economy. The budget fails to support programs which would strengthen our economy and improve the daily lives of millions of Americans.

The Budget Committee has yet to seize the opporunity given to us under the Budget Act, to make substantial changes in the ways that Federal monies are gathered and spent. This budget is regrettably a weak document.

ARMS LOBBYISTS RELY ON VARIED SOURCES INCLUDING LIBERALS SEEKING TO PROTECT WORKERS' JOBS

RICHARD D. LYONS

WASHINGTON, Oct. 15 — When freshman Representative Philip H. Hayes entered Congress last January he sought to concentrate his legislative efforts on problems of the economy and the control of water pollution, yet found himself embroiled in a totally unexpected area — the politics of munitions.

The idealistic Democrat, who had opposed the Vietnam war and who describes himself as "anything but pro-Pentagon," suddenly was devoting

SOURCE: *The New York Times*, October 20, 1975. © 1975 by The New York Times Company. Reprinted by permission.

much of his time to a successful drive to retain the job of 600 constituents at a naval munitions depot in Crane, Ind.

"I'm all for taking care of my own people," Mr. Hayes said candidly the other day in conceding that he had been forced by practical politics to join 500 or so other members of Congress who find it expedient either to join or at least not buck the national arms lobby.

Mr. Hayes senses that he is in an ideological dilemma because it upsets him to think that "the United States has become the Krupp of the world" — a position that other persons more prominent in national affairs believe exists.

Mr. Hayes is not alone in the dilemma. Political and academic interests seemingly unconnected with the production of weapons find themselves drawn into league with the corporate groups that will over the next 12 months produce $35-billion worth of weapons, spare parts and military services for the United States and 136 other countries.

Leonard Woodcock, the auto workers president who is a pillar of liberal politics and anything but a militarist, actively supported funds for the B-1 bomber. Other labor leaders, such as the late Joseph A. Beirne, once president of the Communications Workers of America, backed the Vietnam war because it meant jobs for the members of their unions. Universities want Pentagon research and development projects continued because they translate to Federal funds to keep their laboratories open.

It would be expected that the nation's corporate giants, as well as possibly 10,000 small businesses serving as subcontractors, would want to promote a munitions business that outsells the munitions business of the rest of the world combined.

The arms lobby is huge, amorphous and powerful. Surrounding the White House and the Pentagon are offices of 221 companies producing weapons that have easy access to the White House and high members of the executive branch of Government. In his first year as President, Gerald R. Ford entertained at the White House the leading executives of 23 large corporations involved in arms production.

The President numbers among his personal friends such prominent lobbyists for arms builders as Rodney W. Markley, Jr. of the Ford Motor Company, William G. Whyte of United States Steel Corporation and Kimberly C. Hallamore of Lear Siegler Inc., whose collective products range from rifles to guided missiles.

During a state dinner for the Shah of Iran in May the guests included Henry Ford 2d, chairman of the Ford Motor Comapny; Robert H. Mulott, chairman of FMC Corporation, and David S. Lewis, chairman of the General Dynamics Corporation. The three companies are major munitions makers and Iran has become the primary purchaser of American-made arms, placing almost $10-billion worth of orders in the United States since 1970.

BIG NAME LEGAL TALENT

For legal talent the major arms makers rely on such former advisers to Presidents as Clark MacGregor, President Nixon's campaign manager who now represents United Aircraft; Clark Clifford, former Secretary of Defense under President Johnson, who has served General Electric, and Nicholas deB. Katzenbach, former Attorney General under President Johnson, now general counsel for International Business Machines. The three companies make a wide variety of military material such as jet engines, helicopters and sophisticated electronics.

Their ability to smooth over difficulties between their employer–clients and the Federal bureaucracy is legendary. According to one tale, Thomas G. Corcoran, a "brain truster" in the Franklin D. Roosevelt Administration, was retained by a defense contractor involved in a multimillion dollar damage suit brought by the Defense Department and settled it with one short telephone call. Mr. Corcoran, however, said that resolution of the dispute actually took him a month.

The arms lobby is also aided by such industrial groups as the Aerospace Industries Association, the Defense Supply Association and the American Defense Preparedness Association, which look after the interests of their members.

More than 1,000 former Pentagon officials work in their area either directly for arms makers or as "consultants" to them. Scores of former Congressmen work here either as lobbyists for major arms makers or for the law firms that handle their legal affairs. They include J. W. Fulbright, former Senator from Arkansas, and John Sherman Cooper, former Senator from Kentucky, both of whom are with law firms in Washington.

Representative Hayes of Indiana conceded that "I'm under pressure to maintain what is euphemistically called a 'strong national defense position' as are other members who have military bases and defense contractors in their areas."

Two of the most persistent critics of runaway arms production are Senator William Proxmire and Representative Les Aspin, Democrats from Wisconsin, a state more noted for dairy farming than munitions making. Their crusade against funds for the Air Force's prize project, the B–1 bomber, led one Pentagon official to jest that it was "a shame that we can't run the B–1 on milk."

"The arms lobby is powerful, but not cohesive," Mr. Aspin said in an interview. "Nobody orchestrates the lobby because all its members are out there fighting for their own piece of turf."

Mr. Aspin, a doctor of philosophy in economics, served as a Pentagon planner before entering Congress four years ago to become the loudest gadfly of the military on Capitol Hill. The lobby, he said, is even more powerful "if the unemployment rate is 8 per cent, rather than 3 per cent."

"When discussing defense appropriations the talk isn't of the relationship between weapons and world defense, it's of jobs and what a specific project will mean to a Congressman's district," he said.

When the lobbyists for North American Rockwell, now named Rockwell International, were promoting the B–1 bomber, Mr. Aspin said, "their biggest selling point was the 192,000 jobs that the program would create."

Representative John F. Seiberling, Democrat of Ohio, was given a list by the B–1 lobbyists showing that companies in his Akron area district stood to gain more than $10-million in business if funds for the plane were approved. However, Mr. Seiberling voted against spending the money.

Funds for the B–1 have been pushed by Congressmen from California, where the plane is being built, and the United Auto Workers, which represents thousands of workers in the depressed aerospace industry there.

"At the urging of the Texas delegation, Congress voted more than $300-million for F–111 and A–7 airplanes that the Pentagon never even asked for," Mr. Aspin said. The production centers for the planes are in Dallas–Fort Worth.

Mr. Aspin said that the most intense lobbying was of members of those Congressional committees that authorize and appropriate funds for the military, such as the House Armed Services Committee, of which he is a member.

MORE OUT THAN IN

As a prime example of Congressional pressure to buy weapons, Pentagon officials testified four years ago that they had been forced by political pressures on Capitol Hill to develop the F–5 jet fighter to equip foreign air forces even though the United States Air Force had no intention of using the plane.

Senator Hubert H. Humphrey, Democrat of Minnesota, complained that $113-million of Federal research and development funds had been invested in the F–5 but that only $3-million of this amount had been recovered through foreign sales.

The F–5 had been sold throughout the Middle East, the Persian Gulf and Latin America by its developer, Northrop Aircraft, which with rival Lockheed has reported the payment of millions of dollars abroad in bribes and commissions on its sales.

One Northrop consultant here is Leonard A. Alne, who last year was director of overseas arms sales for the Pentagon.

Asked if there was indeed an arms lobby in Washington, Mr. Alne answered, "Yes — the 20 major companies have large offices with huge staffs." But he emphatically denied there was anything sinister about their work.

"There is a tendency on the part of the press to look for something shady here, yet these are high-integrity firms that want to educate Washington in the real world," he said.

Discussing the decision by the Governments of Begium, Norway, Denmark and the Netherlands to choose the F–16, an American-built jet fighter, as the standard replacement for its older planes, Mr. Alne said:

"If this General Dynamics aircraft ultimately replaces 2,000 of the 5,000 obsolescent aircraft in the free world that need replacing, the United States would gain about $470-million in recovery of its research and development effort, about 900,000 jobs, over $6-billion in tax receipts, and over $9-billion in balance-of-payments receipts."

He listed such other considerations for approving overseas sales as world peace, foreign policy, diplomatic relations and national security in addition to that of pure economic benefit. While necessary and powerful, he said, the arms lobby is not conspiratorial.

"The cultural response to arms is that the lobby has removed itself so that nothing remains but the grin of the Cheshire cat, but large defense contractors lean over backwards so that they don't get themselves involved in a collusive lobbying effort," he added.

"It's impossible to set up a cabal," he went on. "Why you can't get Lockheed, Grumman and General Dynamics to agree on the time of day."

One Senate aide who has specialized in the economics of armaments said the munitions lobby "is enormously powerful on Capitol Hill."

"Sure they offer contracts for a Congressman's constituents and jobs for the voters back in his district, but they also offer drinks, luncheons, dinners and free plane rides back to the district or to vacation spots at famous watering holes," he continued.

The aide said that some Congressmen who would like to oppose new arms expenditures cannot do so "because it's politically taboo to oppose large defense contractors in one's own state."

"These lobbyists are damned effective," he went on. "They know exactly how to apply the pressure and exactly where to stop so that they don't antagonize the Congressmen they're working on."

Yet there is increasing pressure in both houses of Congress to scrutinize more closely the domestic military budget, as well as the shipment of arms overseas.

In the view of Gene R. Larocque, the retired rear admiral who is director of the Center for Defense Information here, "The uncontrolled, unplanned, hectic efforts of the U.S. Government to sell weapons all over the world, to any country which can afford them, will in the long run reduce our national security."

"In recent years the U.S. has given or sold to foreign governments over 18,000 nuclear-capable missiles, ships and aircraft," he said. "It is now within the capacity of almost every nation to develop or obtain the nuclear weapons to go with the nuclear-capable missiles, ships and aircraft."

As the argument was put by Representative Stephen J. Solarz, Democrat of Brooklyn: "Does it make sense for us to be sending billions and billions of dollars of military hardware to countries against whom we might be engaged in hostilities?"

SECTION C. THE B–1 BOMBER CONTROVERSY

Since 1974, there have been almost 50 new weapon systems up for funding consideration from the three armed services. A number of long-range military programs were contested during consideration of the fiscal year 1976 defense budget. Those generating the most controversy were the Trident submarine, the Airborne Warning Control System, and the B–1 bomber. The arguments concerning the B–1 have been selected for this chapter to confront the reader with the complexity of the issues and with the types of questions raised and the pressures exerted in the process of deciding on any of these programs.

The B–1 is being implemented as a replacement for the B–52, which has been in use for almost 20 years. Continued attention to manned bomber programs has been criticized because of the strategic shift to intercontinental missiles. Critics of the weapon have termed it a "cold war relic." Former Secretary of Defense Robert McNamara impounded the money already funded by Congress for the B–1 bomber because he felt manned strategic bombers were obsolete. The Congress itself challenged the authorization for production of the B–1 in 1973 and in 1974.

Several technical advantages including system flexibility and capability have convinced the Air Force of the need for this particular program. The first article of this section reprints a 1975 speech by the Special Assistant to the Chief of Staff, U.S. Air Force, on the need for a B–1 bomber. A transcript of hearings before the House Subcommittee on the Department of Defense shows how Congress handles the review of technical defense information. The hearings concerned the appropriation request for the B–1. They were presided over by Congressman George H. Mahon, a member of the House since 1934, chairman of the full Appropriations Committee, and one of the most powerful men in Congress. Chairman Mahon was one of the few senior congressmen to survive the challenge to their dominance of the important committees of the House of Representatives. John L. McLucas preceded the questioning with a prepared statement on the B–1 development program. The testimony covered cost requests, advantages, status, and alternatives to the system. The hearings took place 9 June 1975.

As has been indicated, the authorization process is controlled by specialized committees with attention to specific areas in the budget. The committees that oversee appropriations, however, represent a broader spectrum and consequently are not quite so susceptible to influence by any one specific interest group. It is in these committees that the actual figures for specific purchases are finally resolved. The most informed efforts to stop such appropriations also seem to arise during this stage. This is especially true when the President is a supporter of the spending program. His signature is the final step in the budget process.

The Need for the B–1 Bomber: Remarks of Major General H. M. Darmstandler to the Commonwealth Club of California

In my job, I have become very sensitive to public attitudes and to the perceptions one finds on the B–1 bomber. I track pretty closely what the media is disseminating on the B–1. From a factual point of view, I think the B–1 has received adequate and accurate coverage of such public interest

SOURCE: Major General H. M. Darmstandler, Special Assistant to the Chief of Staff, U.S. Air Force, for B–1 Matters, addressed the Commonwealth Club on 24 July 1975.

milestones as contract award, rollout, first flight, and the like. But for a host of other important considerations — such as the need for a manned bomber, the cost of a new bomber, and even its effects on the environment — I think the coverage is poor and, even worse, frequently abounds in misinformation. The editorial treatment is almost uniformly negative.

Then, there are the adversary groups who openly and aggressively campaign against the B–1 bomber. Whatever their motivation, they mix a modicum of fact with a vast array of unsupported assertions and a seemingly endless supply of lurid adjectives. From these, they then draw conclusions to fit their motivations.

As a result, there has grown to be a rich and widespread literature of B–1 mythology. I suppose that wouldn't be so bad if it were recognized for what it is — mythology. But the unfortunate truth is that there is no easy way for the public to discern what is fact and what is myth. Moreover, there seems to be a great American proclivity to believe anything that is in print. . . .

Now, in an effort "to set the record straight," I would like to identify some of the more prevalent myths about the B–1 bomber and explain why they are just that — myths . . . .

First, there are the myths which have to do with the role of the manned bombers in assuring this nation's security. They go something like this: Bombers are obsolete in the missile age.

But are they really obsolete? Hardly. Why not? Because it is the combination of strategic forces together with perceived national resolve which deters a nuclear attack on this country. What does an enemy see when he looks at us? He sees a combination of ready missiles and aircraft. Even more important, he finds it is virtually impossible to plan a surprise first strike that would so incapacitate us that we could not effectively retaliate. Hence, if he is sane, he cannot find a net advantage in attacking us. Deterrence prevails and, indeed, detente is possible.

Now, let me say a little more about how that combination of missiles and aircraft work. Simply stated, an enemy cannot attack both our missiles and our aircraft without giving us sufficient warning to launch one, or the other, or both. If, for example, he were to time all of his warheads to arrive on their targets simultaneously, we would have about a half-hour to get all of our alert bombers and tankers into the air and safely away — a lot more time than is actually needed. Even if the detection of an attack should be in error, those bombers are under positive control and would return to their bases.

But what if an enemy should elect to attack our bomber bases with "short time of flight" submarine launched missiles? Then, he would have to contemplate receiving the full force of our ballistic missiles. In this case you don't have to worry about being in error — that first missile impact at a bomber base would remove any doubt that the attack was real . . . .

There's another popular myth which postulates that bombers are worthless because they would not get to their targets for several hours — enough time for several exchanges of missiles. From a simplistic point of view — considering only speed, time and distance — one might draw such a conclusion. But it would fail to recognize the most important point — that deterrence is the objective. We deter with a combination of forces where each has unique capabilities to survive and to penetrate.

Now, recognizing that deterrence is the primary objective, the unique capability of the bombers to be en route to their targets but recallable could make the difference between success and failure in deterring an all-out missile exchange. Those several hours of en route time could very well be the time needed to negotiate a nonviolent solution.

Think back to the Cuban missile crisis of 1962. We had a combination of strategic missiles and aircraft at that time. But whereas the President was understandably reluctant to launch any of those missiles to demonstrate national resolve, he had no such qualms about increasing the readily visible alert status of the bombers. Rather than being worthless because of time of flight considerations, this characteristic in itself could contribute to their being the most valuable deterrent force in our inventory, and our most important negotiating tool.

Interestingly, those who criticize the bomber for not being able to arrive in time, also criticize it for being able to visit "too much" destruction on an enemy. They say the increased weapon delivery capability of the B–1 adds to already excessive overkill.

Before I get into this one, let me make one point just as firmly as I know how. The primary mission of our strategic forces is not to kill anyone! Their mission is to deter killing. Hence, the more effective our strategic forces are — particularly as perceived by an enemy — the less likely is any nuclear war. Ergo, "overkill" is a myth and "over deterrence" should hardly be viewed as objectionable.

. . .

Then, there are a variety of myths about the B–1 and the environment. Make no mistake, I am just as much concerned about the environment as the Sierra Club — and perhaps there are some Sierra Club members here today. But the B–1 represents a significant improvement in environmental impact.

Take the myth of the B–1 imperiling the ozone layer. The fact is that the B–1 will not operate in the ozone layer except on very rare occasions. Why is that so? Well, first, the primary mission of the B–1 bomber is deterrence and that is achieved by keeping the aircraft on the ground, ready to go. We expect to have a much higher alert rate with the B–1 than with the B–52 — it is designed that way. Second, when we do fly the B–1, we'll be confirming in flight the key mission performance tasks learned and practiced in simulators on the ground. Those tasks include takeoffs, landings, refuelings and low-altitude penetration profiles — none of which come close to the ozone layer. Only on such rare occasions as ferrying the aircraft from one base to another, or a short supersonic dash, would we contact the ozone layer. And only in the latter case would the B–1 make a sonic boom — and that would always be in a controlled area.

Of course, all of us are fuel conscious these days and there are some environmentalists who allege that the supersonic B–1 bomber will be a fuel guzzler. Although the B–1 is fully capable of supersonic flight at medium to high altitudes, that is not its primary mission! The demanding design requirement is high subsonic speed at low altitude where the dense air exerts heavy loads on the aircraft. In normal cruise conditions it is very efficient. One reason is that the B–1 has the most advanced technology engines in the free world. In terms of fuel economy, that translates into a B–1 consuming one-quarter less fuel than a B–52. But by spending more time on alert and less time in the air, the B–1 force of 210 operational aircraft will consume less than one quarter of the fuel used by today's force of 330 B–52s. And, that is a significant saving — close to a half-billion gallons a year!

I might add, the B–1 engines are smokeless and have virtually complete combustion.

There are a variety of other B–1 myths that I won't be able to get to; but, there is one other set of myths that I would like to address briefly before we get to your questions. They involve alternatives to the B–1. For those of you who have heard or read about a modernized B–52, or a stretched FB–111, or a standoff air launched cruise missile that could do the bomber job cheaper, I would like to point out that study after study — by the Air Force and the Department of Defense and by informed independent organizations — have conclusively demonstrated that the B–1 bomber is the most cost-effective way to do the bomber job in the 1980s and beyond.

And, why not? After all, the B–1 was designed with that as its objective. It has a swing wing so it can get off the ground in a hurry but still fly at high speed on the deck. It's hardened against nuclear effects. It's small as seen by radar, and relatively easy to hide with electronic countermeasures. And, it can carry a big weapon load in its three weapon bays and deliver those weapons accurately.

Conversely, even a modernized B–52 will be too big as seen on radar and too slow for the advanced Soviet air defenses that we foresee in the next decade. The FB–111, even if stretched, is just too small. It's too small to have enough range and it's too small to carry a big enough payload. The standoff air launched cruise missile isn't likely to survive in a big, slow carrier aircraft. It also doesn't look like it will offer the flexibility needed to penetrate heavy terminal defenses with high confidence.

So, when you add it all up — the facts, the capabilities, the anticipated defenses — it comes out that the B–1 bomber is the best way to go.

Proceedings in the House
Appropriations Committee

HEARINGS BEFORE A SUBCOMMITTEE OF THE COMMITTEE ON APPROPRIATIONS, HOUSE OF REPRESENTATIVES NINETY-FOURTH CONGRESS, FIRST SESSION

SUBCOMMITTEE ON THE DEPARTMENT OF DEFENSE

GEORGE H. MAHON, TEXAS, *CHAIRMAN*

Robert L. F. Sikes, Florida
Daniel J. Flood, Pennsylvania
Joseph P. Addabbo, New York
John J. McFall, California
John J. Flynt, Jr., Georgia
Robert N. Giaimo, Connecticut

Bill Chappell, Jr., Florida
Bill D. Burlison, Missouri
Jack Edwards, Alabama
J. Kenneth Robinson, Virginia
Jack F. Kemp, New York

UNITED STATES AIR FORCE: B-1 AIRCRAFT PROGRAM

Mr. Mahon: The committee will come to order.

Today, we will consider the fiscal year 1976 and transitional period budget requests for the B–1 bomber. In addition, a fiscal year 1975 repro- gramming request for authority to begin development of the fourth B–1 bomber prototype aircraft will be discussed.

We are pleased to have with us Secretary McLucas, Secretary of the Air Force; General Jones, Chief of Staff of the Air Force; Mr. Walsh and Mr. Aldrige, of Defense Research and Engineering; and other witnesses.

The B–1 bomber has become one of the most controversial programs in the Department of Defense. The issues range from the need for the TRIAD to questions on cost effectiveness, alternatives to the B–1, and the environ- mental impact of a new bomber. Relative to cost, the current estimate to complete development of 4 prototypes and purchase 240 bombers is $20.6

billion in then-year dollars, of which $2 billion has been spent to date.

Mr. Secretary and General Jones, you both have appeared before this committee previously in support of the fiscal year 1976 budget request. At this time, however, we would like to discuss the issues surrounding the B–1 in more detail. . . . As you know, last night the House voted on the B–1 issue. The vote was favorable to the continuation of the B–1 bomber program.

The favorable vote on the bomber was 227 to 164. This doesn't mean everyone is completely satisfied about the B–1 bomber. There are a lot of people who would like to be against it. A lot of people voted for it rather than join in the opposition, feeling they did not want to be associated with anything that smacked of a slowdown in our defense at a time when the Soviet Union is moving forward rather aggressively and ambitiously to acquire greater power and exceed the United States in military strength.

I think everybody has some misgivings, including George Mahon and, I suspect, many of the members of this committee. We are not sure what to do other than to proceed, at least for the time. . . . Present policy provides for limited strategic options in addition to retaining the assured destruction capability. These options provide for attacks against military targets only, as compared with attacks on urban industrial areas. What impact, if any, has this change in policy had upon the system design characteristics of the B–1?

Secretary McLucas: Mr. Chairman, I don't believe it has had any impact on the B–1. The B–1 was laid down before this change that you talk about, or before this elaboration of the change.

General Jones: We have not in the past had a mutually assured destruction philosophy. It has been a matter of emphasis. All along we have had a capability and the plan to target military installations and urban-industrial targets. The B–1, with its great accuracy, ability to penetrate and carry a mix of nuclear weapons, is particularly suited to attacks on military targets.

It certainly fits either concept, whether you put your emphasis on assured destruction or on destruction of military targets, but its greatest utility is in attacking military target systems.

. . .

Mr. Mahon: Is the B–1 almost solely a program made necessary, in your judgment, because of the surging power of the Soviet Union? Is that the only nation really that would cause us to build the B–1?

Secretary McLucas: That is true, Mr. Chairman. We don't think we can justify a program of this cost for any threat other than one of the magnitude you cite.

Mr. Mahon: Later we want to talk about what the Soviet Union is doing in this field.

Would our bomber force be used to strike limited military targets? How would the Soviet Union know if a bomber were going to attack military targets and not urban industrial targets?

General Jones: We have an option as to how to employ the bomber, and particularly the B–1, but our concept now would be to employ them almost solely against military targets, while retaining the option of employing them against urban industrial targets.

Mr. Edwards: Tell me a little about the B–1. How large a crew does it have?

Secretary McLucas: The B–1 has four people in the crew. It will have two extra seats for evaluation and training purposes so in peacetime missions two more people could be trained in addition to the four crew members.

Mr. Edwards: We heard a lot last night on the floor about long lead-time items. This was what the big vote last night was on just before we went home. I never did hear anybody on the floor adequately describe what those items are.

One was arguing that you ought not to buy them now because there are so many modifications coming along that you may not need them by the time you get to that point. Others were arguing that in any case you are going to need this kind of stuff.

What are we talking about?

Secretary McLucas: We are talking about two kinds of costs. By the way, we have the program director here in case we need to elaborate, but basically there are two kinds of costs.

One is this: It takes 42 months between the time you initiate an order until the time you get an airplane. Some of the materials take a long time to be delivered. If you don't want a break in the continuity of your program, it pays to buy those materials in advance so they are available when needed. The other basic items are design and materials for tooling, production tooling to build these airplanes.

Mr. Edwards: Are you making any kind of major modification in your plans that would leave the tooling you order and buy now out of date by the time you get ready to start the full production?

Secretary McLucas: No, sir. I don't believe that criticism is justified. We have learned a lot in the 5 years we have been working on the airplane and we now feel we are in a position to lay down the design of an airplane that will be essentially identical in that preproduction phase to the ones that would come off the production line later.

Mr. Edwards: Now, also there was talk last night about the B–52 G and H, as I recall, that would be used into the 1980s and even into the 1990s, as I recall.

There was also talk last night about the cost of some $20 million per copy to upgrade the B–52 if we were to continue to go with that kind of a plane. I wonder if you would discuss that subject briefly?

Secretary McLucas: We have looked at a number of potential improvements to the B–52, the most basic one being a change to a new engine and other structural modifications. The changes would clean up the drag on the airplane so it could fly a little faster. We would have to replace a lot of the avionics inside of the airplane. All of these modifications that we have envisioned would cost considerably more than the $20 million that was cited. It depends on what year funding you put in it, of course.

As we look at it in the way we compare the B–1 funding, it is more like a $40 million total. Some would be in the first year, some in the next year, and so on, and you have to take inflation into account as people do when they criticize the total cost of the B–1. In any case, you are talking about a significantly changed B–52, an airplane where you spend roughly $40 million each to achieve these improvements. And you do in fact have to make a lot of improvements.

Mr. Edwards: The $40 million figure would compare with the $84 million we are talking about now for the B–1?

Secretary McLucas: That is right, yes.

General Jones: We have already spent $2 billion. If you went that direction, you wouldn't recoup the $2 billion.

Mr. Addabbo: $84 million vis-a-vis $40 million. Per copy?

Secretary McLucas: Yes.

Mr. Burlison: What impact would the Senate Armed Services Committee reduction in the B–1 program have on schedule and total program cost?

General Evans: The impact of their action would be an interruption in program continuity. This interruption will result in the loss of several thousand skilled workers and a delay in the production schedule of about 1 year. The cost to the program is very difficult to estimate since neither we nor commercial aerospace firms have previous experience in managing a major program through such an interruption. Our best estimate is that the loss of learning will add about $235 million to program costs, and that an additional year's exposure to the effects of inflation will cause an additional $640 million increase to total program cost.

In summary, the impact is difficult to quantify but our best estimate shows an increase of about $1 billion in cost, which equates to just over $4 million for each aircraft: and a delay of approximately 1 year in delivery of production aircraft. In addition, a considerable increase in risk to the cost and schedule estimates would occur since the talents and experience of those people lost may no longer be available to the program.

. . .

Mr. Burlison: Does the fiscal year 1976 budget request include any funds to reimburse the B–1 contractors for effort actually performed in fiscal year 1975 and allowable under the limit of Government obligations clause in the contracts?

General Martin: The fiscal year 1976 request contains sufficient funds to cover the contractor's cumulative forecast expenditure and commitments through fiscal year 1976. Rockwell International has informed the Air Force that while the funds available under the fiscal year 1975 limit of Government obligations will be adequate to cover their forecast expenditures through fiscal year 1975, it will not be adequate to cover all of their commitments and they expect an exposure of about $16 million at the end of fiscal year 1975. Therefore, we would expect that some portion of Rockwell's fiscal year 1976 funds, up to $16 million, will be used to fund commitments actually incurred in fiscal year 1975 but paid in fiscal year 1976.

Mr. Burlison: When would the development of a fourth prototype begin, and when would it be completed?

General Evans: Based on our best estimate of current leadtimes, the aircraft will take approximately 42 months to build. If the Congress approves our request to use about $5 million of fiscal year 1975 B–1 funds to start AV No. 4 in June, we expect the aircraft would be completed in November or December 1978.

Mr. Flynt: Thank you, General Martin.

Anti-B–1 Bomber Literature

The Clergy and Laity Concerned is an organization that originated in the struggle to end the Vietnam War. It has come to focus its attention on the B–1 bomber since that conflict ended. The following appeal for support came out after the conclusion of consideration of the FY 1976 budget and it anticipates the struggle over the 1977 budget when the first funds will be requested to produce the bomber.

CLERGY AND LAITY CONCERNED
235 East 49th Street, New York, N. Y. 10017
December 1975

Dear Friend:

CALC exists to assure that your values and your priorities — not just those of big business, the military and government officials — will play a more decisive role in the life of this nation.

As the election year approaches we begin to hear many promises, that *this time* our interests will truly be served. But we will not accept promises. We know that the crucial decisions about our nation's priorities and policies — matters that directly affect the quality of our lives — are too important to be left in the hands of politicians aspiring for office.

That is why CALC continues to plan and implement action programs that will place our priorities before the public and the decision-makers and directly influence the course of public policy.

1976 is our last chance to influence the fate of the B–1 Bomber.

In June, Congress will decide whether or not to approve the production of the Bombers. How they decide is up to us.

For the past two years CALC has concentrated on making the B–1 an issue of public concern — and we've succeeded in making it very visible and highly controversial. But that is not enough to assure that the B–1 won't be built.

The next step requires action. So CALC is launching a major drive to make the opposition of the American people to the B–1 Bomber a matter of public record.

From now until June, the staffs and members of CALC's local, regional and national offices will be on street corners, in community meeting places, in schools and libraries, churches and synagogues, and in the mails to gather as many signed statements as humanly possible. At the right time they'll be turned over to the decision-makers.

CALC now asks you to help launch this massive drive. With your active participation we will succeed. Please add the power of your voice to this effort and sign the enclosed protest. Try to get signatures for the additional forms enclosed, and return them to CALC with the biggest year end contribution you can afford. It *will* make a difference.

SOURCE: The Stop the B–1 Bomber: National Peace Conversion Campaign of Clergy and Laity Concerned in Association with the Washington Square United Methodist Church.

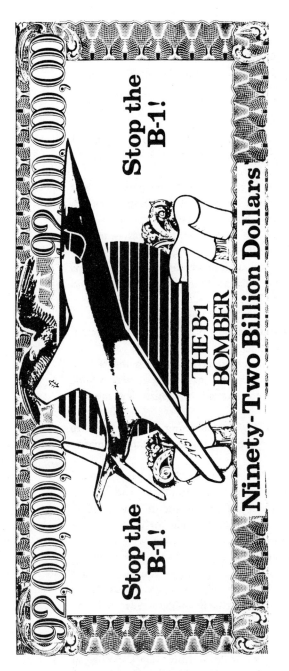

Stop the B-1!

THE B-1 BOMBER

USAF

Stop the B-1!

Ninety-Two Billion Dollars

The Air Force and three of the nation's largest corporations want $92 billion* of our tax money for a supersonic swing-wing swindle.

The corporations are Rockwell International, General Electric and Boeing. The swindle is the B-1 Bomber. The decision is this year.

The B-1 is a manned nuclear bomber proposed as the replacement for the B-52. It is expensive and "a public works project for the aerospace industry rather than a needed weapon for the defense of the United States," according to Senator William Proxmire.

The fleet of 244 B-1 Bombers will cost the average wage earner $1108.43.

I don't want my tax money spent on the B-1.

The money for one B-1, currently $84 million, could fund 25 health care centers, each treating 40,000 people annually. The U.S. is 1st in military power but 18th in doctor-patient ratio.

I'd rather have my tax money spent for things I need than for a fleet of bombers I don't need.

I understand from the Bureau of Labor Statistics that $1 billion spent on human needs would create at least 30,000 more jobs than if the money were spent on the B-1.

I want my tax money spent for jobs and people, not for a flying pork barrel for the weapons industry. Put me on record against the B-1 Bomber.

_____
name

_____
address

_____
city & state

* $92 billion over 30 years includes the cost of 244 bombers armaments, fuel, and operation & maintenance of bombers and tankers.

RETURN TO:

Clergy and Laity Concerned
235 East 49th St.
New York, NY 10017

Wishing you joy in the New Year's struggle for peace and justice, we are,

Yours in peace,
Rabbi Balfour Brickner
Steering Committee
Rev. George Webber
Chairperson

THE B–1 BOMBER: IS IT WORTH $95 BILLION?

The proposed B–1 "penetrating bomber" — designed to get past enemy air defenses — may well be an anachronism in the missile age. Not only is the B–1 a questionable addition to our nuclear forces in this day and time, but it is unusually expensive as well.

It will cost the U.S. more than $90 billion to build and operate the B–1 bomber over its 30 year life. The B–1 is an extravagance that the U.S. cannot afford at a time when hard choices must be made throughout the defense budget.

By 1980, without the proposed B–1, the U.S. will have over 12,000 nuclear weapons on nuclear-powered submarines, land-based missiles, and long-range bombers. The B–1 is not needed for our strategic deterrent.

This year the U.S. Air Force has requested $749.2 million for the B–1. $77.0 million is to begin procurement. The remaining $672.2 million is for research, development, testing and engineering. By the time the bomber is completed, the cost to build 244 B–1s could rise to $25 billion, with each bomber costing about $100 million.

AIR FORCE ARGUMENTS

The Air Force states that the B–1 is needed to replace the "aging" B–52. However, a replacement for the B–52 will not be needed until 1990. The last B–52 was built in 1962. About 260 B–52s will last at least until 1990. B–52s have not been growing obsolete. They have been constantly modernized with improved navigation aids, electronic counter-measures, terrain avoidance equipment, structural rework and numerous other improvements. Only the 80 D model B–52s are approaching the end of their useful life and the Air Force plans to spend $272 million to modify these planes to keep

SOURCE: "The B–1 Bomber," *Defense Monitor*, 4, No. 4 (June 1975): reprinted with permission from the Center for Defense Information, Washington, D.C.

them operating. The late model B–52 Gs and Hs are fully modern and in excellent flying shape. From the Air Force's own data it is clear that the B–1 is an addition to the late model B–52 and FB–111 force of over 300 aircraft that will exist until the 1990s. Replacements, if indeed they are required, will not be needed for fifteen years.

The Air Force states it must have a bomber that could penetrate any possible Soviet air defense system and strike targets anywhere in the Soviet Union. Between one third and one half of the cost of the proposed B–1 will pay for the capability of flying low and fast and evading detection. Late model B–52s will also be able to penetrate Soviet air defenses. More than $3 billion was spent on electronic jamming devices and other equipment to give them that capability.

The fundamental question is: Does the B–1 with its penetrating capability add significantly to the U.S. deterrent? Missiles that can reach their targets quickly and with no opposition provide a more than adequate nuclear strike force.

The Air Force states that the B–1 is needed because it can carry more bombs and missiles than the B–52. However, with a projected U.S. inventory of nuclear weapons of over 12,000 by 1980, the difference between mission loads of a B–1 and a B–52 is insignificant. Existing bombers can deliver over 220,000 Hiroshima equivalents. U.S. strategic forces, counting bombers, ICBMs and SLBMs can deliver a total of over 369,000 Hiroshima equivalents. The deliverable destructive capability will increase dramatically during the next ten years, even without the B–1.

Finally, the Air Force states it needs the B–1 because the Russians are building a similar bomber — something the Air Force calls the Backfire.

The Soviet bomber force of about 160 is quite small. It consists of 100 heavy Bear bombers, all of which are propeller driven, 35 Bison jet bombers, and the Backfire. The Backfire, of which there are up to 20, is an intermediate range aircraft and far less capable than both the B–52 and the B–1. According to Defense Secretary James Schlesinger, the Backfire is intended primarily for use against China and Europe. The relatively ineffective Soviet bomber force can in no way provide justification for the B–1.

MISSILES FOR DETERRENCE

The manned bomber was once the mainstay of our nuclear deterrent force. This is no longer the case. Deterrence is now provided by more reliable, less vulnerable, and less costly Minuteman ICBMs and Poseidon/

Polaris submarine-based missiles. In an era when missiles can reach their targets in 30 minutes, bombers that take eight hours can only play a relatively minor role.

Indeed, a major military drawback of the manned bomber is that existing U.S. strategic employment procedures call for the land-based missiles to cut corridors for bombers through Soviet defenses. The bomber is the only strategic weapon system that is dependent on the other parts of the triad for its own survival and effectiveness. It is far simpler and cheaper for missiles to be used directly on primary targets than in suppressing defenses in aid of the B-1 bomber.

Missiles on submarines and in silos are more controllable than manned bombers. It would be easier to keep a nuclear war from escalating by relying on missiles rather than bombers. Once a bomber has passed its "fail safe" point and is committed to attacking a target in the Soviet Union, it is out of civilian control for at least two hours. Missiles fired from land are only out of civilian control for thirty minutes before they strike their targets. Also missiles in their containers are not as vulnerable to nuclear accidents as manned aircraft, several of which have crashed in the past.

CURRENT BOMBER FORCE

At present the U.S. has almost 500 bombers. 425 of them are B–52s. The others are FB–111s. The FB–111s along with 250–270 late model B–52s will comprise a manned bomber force of over 300 aircraft that will last until the 1990s.

In the 1980s these bombers alone will be able to deliver over 5500 nuclear weapons to the Soviet Union — almost as many weapons as the United States had on all its forces at the signing of the SALT accords in 1972.

(It should be noted that U.S. ICBMs can deliver more than 2000 nuclear weapons and SLBMs more than 5000 nuclear weapons.)

The Soviets, in contrast to the United States, have not allocated substantial resources to long-range bombers. Their bomber force reached a level of 150–200 planes through the 1950s and 1960s. They currently have about 100 propeller-driven heavy bombers and about 60 jet bombers, including the modern Backfire bomber. The small Soviet bomber threat is reflected in the fact that the U.S. has just about dismantled its antibomber defenses. The lack of Soviet interest in heavy bombers provides an opportunity for similar restraint on the part of the U.S. and a potential area for significant arms reduction.

SOVIET AIR DEFENSE

The Soviets have invested heavily in trying to protect themselves against bomber attack. However, the threat to U.S. bombers flying into the Soviet Union is minimal. The Soviet air defense missile network is extensive but has negligible capabilities against low-flying aircraft. Soviet AWACS (Airborne Warning and Control) aircraft for the purpose of detecting bombers and directing interceptors cannot detect low-flying aircraft over land. Soviet Foxbat (Mig 25) interceptor aircraft are ineffective against low-flying bombers. Their radar is intended for a reconnaissance role, not for shooting down bombers. Any breakthrough in Soviet air defense technology that would threaten B–52s would in all likelihood also threaten B–1s.

The Air Force argues that the proposed B–1 will make the Russians allocate greater resources to air defense. That is not a reasonable basis for the U.S. to spend billions needlessly on marginal military capabilities.

TOTAL COST IS $92 BILLION

Congress has a hard time making sound decisions on military programs because it is not provided with complete information by the Defense Department. The full costs of weapons systems are seldom evaluated because these costs are often hidden and spread over many years. Costly programs almost always start small. Today's small research and development program, the tip of the iceberg, is tomorrow's multi-billion dollar weapons system.

The Defense Department has yet to make available to the Congress and the public realistic estimates of the life cycle costs of major weapons. Life cycle cost is the cost of operating and maintaining weapons throughout their lifetime and the cost of associated weapons and equipment in addition to the actual cost of developing and procuring a particular major weapon.

In the absence of Defense Department data, estimates of life cycle costs can only be approximations. But it is clear that the real cost of the B–1 is far more than the current DOD estimate of $21 billion for procurement of the B–1s. Simply the cost of developing and producing the bomber itself has reached $84 million per plane. However, bombers require armament to perform their missions and the Air Force will also need support from tanker aircraft to refuel the B–1s. The cost of operating and maintaining the bombers and the tankers also adds a sizable chunk of money. Combined, these components of life cycle cost add up to $91.5 billion, or $375 million for each B–1 bomber. A new tanker, which may be required, would raise the cost even higher.

LIFE CYLE COST OF B-1 BOMBER FORCE IS $92 BILLION

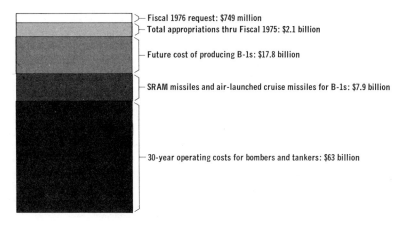

— Fiscal 1976 request: $749 million

— Total appropriations thru Fiscal 1975: $2.1 billion

— Future cost of producing B-1s: $17.8 billion

— SRAM missiles and air-launched cruise missiles for B-1s: $7.9 billion

— 30-year operating costs for bombers and tankers: $63 billion

FAULTY DOD BOMBER STUDY

To counter criticisms that the B–1 may be an extravagant waste of money and that other ways to bomb the USSR might be cheaper, the Defense Department conducted a year-long investigation called the Joint Strategic Bomber Study which, not surprisingly, concluded, that the B–1 is best. The official conclusion appears to be more commercial than analytical: "Of the equal cost forces examined, those containing B–1s performed substantially better. The low-flying, nuclear-hard B–1, with its high quality ECM [electronic counter-measures], out-performed all other vehicles by a wide margin." Critical to the DOD's study was the assumption that the United States needs to spend as much money on bombers as the B–1 costs and in its methodology the study compared only "equal-cost" alternatives. The DOD analysts neglected to examine the question of whether the country needs a bomber fleet in the first place and also made no determination as to whether that capability could be obtained at much less cost. As Senator Thomas McIntyre, Chairman of the Senate Armed Services Research and Development Subcommittee, has commented on the Joint Strategic Bomber Study: "This study, like other incidents in the history of the B–1 program, has led me to fear that there is little or no real consideration within the DOD and Air Force that we may not need the B–1 and that, therefore, we should prudently examine other alternatives for our future bomber force."

Appropriations for the Bomber

PUBLIC LAW 94–106 [H.R. 6674]; OCT. 7, 1975

DEPARTMENT OF DEFENSE APPROPRIATION AUTHORIZATION ACT, 1976

An Act to authorize appropriations during the fiscal year 1976, and the period beginning July 1, 1976, and ending September 30, 1976, for procurement of aircraft, missiles, naval vessels, tracked combat vehicles, torpedoes, and other weapons, and research, development, test and evaluation for the Armed Forces, and to prescribe the authorized personnel strength for each active duty component and of the Selected Reserve of each Reserve Component of the Armed Forces and of civilian personnel of the Department of Defense, and to authorize the military training student loads and for other purposes.

Be it enacted by the Senate and House of Representatives of the United States of America in Congress assembled,

Title I — Procurement.

SEC. 101. Funds are hereby authorized to be appropriated during the fiscal year 1976 for the use of the Armed Forces of the United States for procurement of aircraft, missiles, naval vessels, tracked combat vehicles, torpedoes, and other weapons, as authorized by law, in amounts as follows:

AIRCRAFT

For aircraft: for the Army, $337,500,000; for the Navy and the Marine Corps, $2,997,800,000; for the Air Force, $4,119,000,000, of which amount not to exceed $64,000,000 is authorized for the procurement of only long lead items for the B–1 bomber aircraft. None of the funds authorized by this Act may be obligated or expended for the purpose of entering into any production contract or any other contractual arrangement for production of the B-1 bomber aircraft unless the production of such aircraft is hereafter authorized by law. The funds authorized in this Act for long lead items for the B–1 bomber aircraft do not constitute a production decision or a commitment on the part of Congress for the future production of such aircraft.

In the matter of the B–1, like military purchases generally, there is a psychological barrier between research and development appropriations and money allocated for purchase or procurement. Although $64,000,000 was ultimately appropriated for "parts" for the B–1 in FY 1976, $597,200,000 was appropriated for additional research and development. For FY 1977, the Department of Defense requested $1.5 billion for production of three planes and another 400 million dollars for research and development. The 1977 Congressional Budget Office ceiling for defense looks as if it will include the B–1, and an effort by Democratic members of the House to put production in escrow until the presidential election was over was defeated 210–177 on 9 April 1976. As this book goes to press, the B–1s are ready for production, and unless the public raises a substantial outcry, Rockwell International, Inc., is likely to begin filling orders.

FURTHER READINGS FOR CHAPTER 2

Melman, Seymour, *The Permanent War Economy: American Capitalism in Decline* (New York: Simon & Schuster, 1974). A critique of the impact of large-scale defense spending on the nation's economy and the price paid for it. The discussion, because of its attention to productivity and full employment, ties in well with Chapter 4.

Murphy, Thomas P., *The New Politics Congress* (Lexington, Mass.: Lexington Books, 1974). Relates the political climate, institutional dimensions, and external pressures on Congress, to explain the activities of a new congressional majority.

Polsby, Nelson, and Aaron Wildavsky, *The Politics of the Budgetary Process* (Boston: Little, Brown and Company, 1964). An overview of what is political about the way budgets are made.

Chapter 3 The Presidency

The Policy Agenda, Keeping House, Making Policy

JOHN BRIGHAM, EDITOR

This chapter provides materials bearing on how the President of the United States affects public policy. It is organized around three considerations. The first is the policy agenda, the issues which have become a public concern to such an extent that the President will be expected to address them in some fashion. The second is the occupant of the office and the way in which his personality and his relations with subordinates affect the handling of these issues. The third is the national political environment within which the President operates, particularly electoral politics and the legislative process.

The Presidency is of extraordinary significance. Whether through the negative power most vividly characterized by the veto or in the positive influence on the approach that the government takes to issues, the President has more effect than any single individual on national policy. He can step up the pace of government as President Kennedy did with his injection of "vigor" or slow it down as President Nixon did during Watergate with his "stonewalling." Yet, in his dependence on the three dimensions of political life considered in the following pages, the President is not unlike other public figures. He can redirect but not create national issues; his capacity to deal with issues is dependent on personal and administrative abilities, and the policy he is able to achieve will be the result of his handling of the institutional and the larger political environment. The President's particular relationship to these considerations is the result of his presumed position of leadership.

The following materials deal with energy in general and oil policy in particular, an issue raising domestic as well as foreign policy questions. Section A presents the issue; Section B portrays the President at work; and Section C covers the institutional and political environment in which authoritative policies are developed.

SECTION A. THE "ENERGY CRISIS"

In the winter of 1973–1974, Americans faced what came to be known as the "energy crisis." They had trouble getting gasoline, for which there had been a 30 to 50 percent increase in price in a matter of months. There was talk of rationing, and the national speed limit was reduced in order to save fuel. Americans were also faced with shortages of heating oil, which had taken an even greater jump in price. They were asked by President Nixon to turn down their thermostats, and the media was full of schemes to save energy. Not the existence of a crisis, but the cause, cure, and prevention of its recurrence became the subject of considerable debate throughout the year 1975.

In public discussion at the height of the crisis, responsibility was placed on the foreign oil-producing nations, whose oil embargo against the United States for support of Israel and the price increases that followed had been linked to the crisis in the United States. That such a linkage could be made, indeed that it became the primary focus of attention in the important period during the crisis and immediately after, while people were still fuming about long lines and high prices, is an important factor in understanding the presidential response to the "energy crisis," first by Richard Nixon with his Project Independence and subsequently by Gerald Ford, who continued the rhetoric and the policy of energy self-sufficiency for the United States. Shortly after World War II, when the United States first began importing oil in significant quantities, pressure from the American oil industry and a concern for ready sources of refined domestic petroleum led to the imposition of quotas on imported oil, a policy that was continued for almost three decades. By the late 1960s, however, the American producers had begun to speak of a coming crisis. These corporations had been increasing the production of and dependence on foreign oil at twice the speed of domestic production. The quota system was abandoned by President Nixon in the spring of 1973, and, although the strict notion that domestic production was necessary for national security reasons began to wane, a new concern that undue dependence on foreign production limited the sway of the United States as a world power began to be felt.

The immediate shortages seem in retrospect to have depended as much on national pricing policies and their relation to oil company profits as on external forces. The price controls that the Nixon Administration had imposed as a curb on inflation had a direct effect on oil industry production policies. Immediate profits are not the only industry motivation, and the initial shortages afforded the companies an opportunity to increase their control over the agents of distribution by driving discount and non-company-owned service stations out of business. After the Arab embargo, however, the lid on prices was raised under the convenient cover provided by the Middle Eastern exporters. The "crisis" for the American public raised profits for the ten biggest oil companies by 51 percent and created an environment that enabled the conservationist-imposed ban on the Aslaska pipeline and offshore drilling to be lifted.

Energy Becomes an Issue

Energy surfaced as a political issue as rapidly and dramatically as any that has faced a President. The issue produced a greater impact on public life than most matters of domestic politics. The way in which the lives of millions of Americans were altered by the high prices and shortages of petroleum products, beginning in the winter of 1973–1974, made energy a matter of national concern. When an issue gains prominence of this sort it may be said to have gained a place on the policy agenda, the totality of issues to which policy makers address themselves. As such an issue, energy dictated a response from the President, but throughout much of the crisis President Nixon was preoccupied with the unraveling Watergate scandals. As official responses became clearer, it continued to be evident that Presidential policy making in this area was addressed to the public issue which is revealed in the following news articles.

A President's perception of an issue is many steps removed from a problem existing for the populace or even its manifestations in news reports, and although that perception is even farther from a policy outcome, it constitutes the basis of the official policy which is handed down by the government. The energy policy that resulted at least in part from these perceptions is traced throughout this chapter, as various institutional and perceptual factors shape the ultimate outcome, but the process begins with public reports of a series of events disrupting American life.

MOTORISTS LINE UP FOR GASOLINE HERE

Closing of Service Stations is Anticipated by Drivers Across the Country

DAVID A. ANDELMAN

Anticipating widespread voluntary closings of service stations today, motorists lined up at gasoline pumps throughout the New York area and across the United States yesterday to stock up on fuel.

Cars were three and four deep at the pumps as early as 7 A.M. yesterday, and by mid-afternoon, many of the nation's 220,000 service stations reported such a heavy run on their fuel stocks that they were already running low. Some began closing down well before the cutoff of 9 P.M. yesterday in an effort to assure themselves of some supplies Monday morning.

Many of the motorists were also confronted with higher prices — as much as 2 or 3 cents or more a gallon — at the pumps when they drove in yesterday morning. On Friday, three of the major national oil companies — Shell, Atlantic–Richfield and Sun Oil Company — announced major price increases and others indicated they would follow suit this week.

Surveys in the New York metropolitan area and other scattered regions of the country indicated that in most cases 90 percent or more of the service-station operators intended to observe the voluntary closings from 9 P.M. yesterday to midnight tonight suggested by President Nixon as a means of conserving gasoline.

By 4 P.M., most stations in Manhattan had closed for the weekend and by early evening they were closing in other boroughs. The New York and New Jersey state police reported traffic generally lighter than usual for a Saturday in December, and, on Long Island, the state parkway police reported normal flows.

The New York Automobile Club reported that a telephone survey of

SOURCE: *The New York Times*, December 2, 1973, p. 1. © 1973 by The New York Times Company. Reprinted by permission.

294 stations in the 14 southernmost counties of New York State, including all of New York City, Long Island and Westchester County, showed that the owners of only 31 stations said they would be pumping gas. A similar survey in 11 Southern California counties showed 82 percent planning to close.

"And even that's optimistic because we expect those 31 in New York will run out of gas pretty quickly," said Peter Hahn, a spokesman for the Automobile Club. As for emergencies, he said, the club will provide full road service with the possible exception of gasoline for the stranded. "We'll do everything possible," he said, "but if the pumps are closed, even we can't get it."

In Queens, of 19 service stations surveyed, not one said they would be open today, echoing the similar unanimity found by random surveys throughout the five boroughs and in New Jersey, Westchester County and on Long Island.

The handful of stations in the metropolitan area still open past 9 P.M. were all jammed with cars. The 24th Precinct on Manhattan's Upper West Side dispatched four police officers to West 96th Street where patrons of a Mobil station just east of Riverside Drive, planning to stay open all weekend, were jamming traffic for more than two blocks both east and west. "It was chaos," said Sgt. John Moreno.

At the Knapp Street entrance to Shore Parkway in Brooklyn, where four stations were closed, workers at an open Sunoco station struggled into the night to keep pace with a line of cars around the block.

"They're getting scared," said an attendant preparing to close his station in Smithtown, L.I., last night. "I must have pumped every car on the island tonight."

It was generally with a feeling of resignation that service station owners prepared for the shutdown, marking in some instances the first time their stations would be closed in years.

On Staten Island, Ray Shirley said his Ray-Jay Texaco station would shut down at 9 P.M. after nine years of 24 hour-a-day, 365-days-a-year operation. "We were never closed," he said proudly. "In fact we don't even have a key to the front door."

The closings were first suggested last Sunday by President Nixon who predicted that the one-day moratorium on gasoline sales could save 2.1 million gallons a week.

For the present, the closings are voluntary. But the National Energy Emergency Act that passed the Senate mandates Sunday closings and provides for enforcement. Passage is not, however, expected to be completed for at least two weeks.

The closing concept, however, has not met with uniform acceptance throughout the country.

"You know how I feel about the environmental situation?" asked Kenneth Johnson of Hempstead, L.I., as he waited to fill his tank at the Hess Station on Peninsula Boulevard there. "If we're all going to hell, we might as well drive there."

Elsewhere, throngs besieged service station owners. "I'm being mobbed," shouted Ben Kwinter, proprietor of K & K Service Center on Coney Island Avenue in Brooklyn.

In Albany, when he refused to sell her gasoline, the proprietor of Boopsie's Shell Station said that a small, elderly woman tried to assault him. "She wanted to hit me with an oil can," said the proprietor, George Rickert, "and she started to reach for it. I wanted to sell to my regular customers."

This form of informal rationing and more official types along the major interstate roads were also causing problems for motorists trying to fill up to beat the deadline.

TURNPIKE RATIONING SET

All gasoline stations on the Ohio Turnpike will be observing the Sunday closing hours and Connecticut state police reported traffic already thinning out on the Merritt Parkway and Connecticut Turnpike. On the turnpike, however, gasoline will be sold only for emergencies and, at that, only with permission of the state police.

Stations on the New Jersey Turnpike plan to stay open but will ration cars to five gallons, enforcing the rationing by stamping the toll tickets of motorists after the purchase.

Even private airplane traffic promised to encounter some difficulties, although the sale of aviation fuel was not specifically included in the President's order. Operators of New Jersey's Teterboro Airport said they would sell no aviation fuel to the 450 private planes that use that facility during the Sunday closing hours.

In most areas, emergency service promised to be spotty or even nonexistent. The Connecticut Motor Club appealed to service-station owners who planned to remain open to report to them so that they could supply some gasoline to those in real emergencies.

Elsewhere, around the country, The Associated Press reported stations pumping record quantities of gasoline in preparation for today's close.

In the Boston suburb of Arlington, Mass., Jerry Swinford, the attendant at a Sunoco station, observed that his customers were "not as worried about the supply of gas as they are about the price." On the other hand, Bill Fox, co-owner of four Shell stations in Detroit suburbs was more worried about the $3,600 he figured to lose each month by closing Sundays.

But in Georgia, Doc Bruner is relishing today's ban. He plans to keep his Texaco station open. "Come out here Sunday," he said, "and I'll show you something to behold. Just don't get run over."

Energy Policy Options

In responding publicly to an issue of national concern, the President, as is the case with governmental authorities generally, must present a plan that is linked to an interpretation of the nature of the issue. The government has a limited number of tools of public policy available, and in making a choice the effect on the issue as well as the interests served by a particular policy must be considered. It would be false to give the impression that all responses receive equal treatment. Any of the tools will strike the President as acceptable or unacceptable depending on his experience and the policy orientation of his administration. The selection that follows is from the 1974 Ford Foundation Energy Policy Project's preliminary report entitled *Exploring Energy Choices*. The very manner of presenting the choices indicates this group's assessment of the viability of certain options. Tax policy, for instance, is a familiar tool that has been widely used. The problem for the President is to assess the ways in which it might be applied to the case at hand and the effects that it might have on the groups from whom he gets his support. Public ownership and development, on the other hand, is less familiar to the American experience. As discussed by the research group, it is tied to the existence of resources under government control. This discussion, although limited itself, suggests the range of options at the President's disposal for carrying out a particular policy. It should be a basis for consideration of the relation between perception of the alternatives and the nature of the issue to be faced.

THE RANGE OF OPTIONS IN ENERGY POLICY
(PRELIMINARY REPORT OF THE FORD FOUNDATION)

GOVERNMENT INTERVENTION:
THE USE OF POLICY TOOLS

The economically justified purpose for governmental intervention is to correct inadequate competitive forces and to satisfy public concerns not reflected in market prices. But often in the past government intervention has simply been a response to the power of special interest groups.

Whether the basis for governmental intervention is economic or political, the tools of intervention are pretty much the same: taxes and subsidies, research and development, regulation, and governmental ownership.

Before examining the corrective tools which the government has at its disposal for making changes in energy matters, it must be emphasized that just about everything the government does has some impact on the energy sector. In the past, for example, growth in energy consumption has been very closely associated with growth in the economy. As we have seen, fiscal and monetary policies designed to stimulate or restrain the economy or consumer expenditures can have major effects on the amount of energy produced and consumed. Environmental laws and foreign policies also greatly affect energy supply and demand.

At present, of course, the energy scene is dominated by a package of measures designed to deal with emergency dislocations in supplies. These include moral suasion, price controls and various forms of rationing. While they may take the nation out of the present energy crunch they are a completely inadequate set of tools for developing policies for the future in a way that will satisfy our multiple policy objectives. The government has more effective policy tools it can call upon to correct the inadequacies of the market place with respect to the energy field.

Taxes and Subsidies

The basic function of taxes is to raise revenues. However, in the energy field, tax policies have also been used for decades as a means of encouraging exploration and development — primarily for oil and gas. These policies

SOURCE: *Exploring Energy Choices: A Preliminary Report.* Washington, D.C.: The Ford Foundation, 1974. Pages 23–26. Reprinted from *Exploring Energy Choices* with permission of the Energy Policy Project of The Ford Foundation.

include: (1) the depletion allowance, which allows producers to deduct from taxable income a percentage share of the income from production each year — 22 percent in the case of gas and oil. It permits total deductions many times greater than the actual investment costs over the lifetime of the property; (2) the expensing of intangible costs, under which all development or drilling costs (except for those items which have salvage value) can be written off as current expenses, thus decreasing the current income subject to taxes; (3) the tax credits for payments to foreign governments which offset all payments to foreign governments against American corporate income tax liabilities. One effect of all these tax benefits, which are in effect subsidies to producers, has been to make prices lower than they otherwise would have been for oil.

By increasing retail prices of energy, taxes can be used to curtail demand. Taxes can be used to help clean up the environment by charging polluters for discharging wastes into the air and water. Such taxes would also help balance our energy budget by folding into prices more of the real costs of energy production, thus discouraging wasteful consumption while encouraging suppliers to reduce their pollutants. Excess profits taxes can be used to tax away windfall profits which are determined to be in excess of the level of profits needed to induce additional supplies. The problem is that excess profits taxes are extremely cumbersome to administer and can lead to extravagant and wasteful practices by corporations in order to avoid payment of the taxes. Taxes on imports or exports can also be used to regulate trade in energy.

Governmental investments and subsidies are a most powerful instrument of energy policy. Governmental dollars and guarantees can be used to encourage mass transit, bicycle paths, loans to insulate homes, and all sorts of activities that might save energy or enlarge supply in the future. Subsidies can be indirect, as in the case of the tax treatment of oil and gas production noted above. Or they can be direct, as in the case of R&D, discussed below.

Research and Development

Funds for research leading to development of new energy sources and technologies to conserve energy provide another powerful tool for government policy makers. Energy R&D spending is being increased in a substantial way. We look to new technology for a large part of the solution to future energy problems, but there is little immediate effect from current efforts, because lead times for energy R&D are very long. Results will be felt, not next month or next year, but in 1985 or 2001 AD and beyond. Yet it is essential to invest now in the energy future of the twenty-first century.

Governmental Regulation

This category includes all of the government-imposed standards ranging from licensing, emission standards, state and local utility regulation, regulation of natural gas prices, anti-trust legislation, import and export quotas, etc. The rationale behind regulation as a policy is usually the inadequacy of a market approach.

When regulation is used by government to implement policy, it is usually characterized by the establishment of an administrative agency with a specific mandate guided by legislative standards. Examples are the Environmental Protection Agency, which enforces the standards of the Clean Air and Clean Water Acts, and the Atomic Energy Commission which regulates safety in nuclear plants.

Regulation is a plausible solution where there is a public demand for standards to achieve a clear purpose like environmental protection or price controls. The major shortcoming of regulation is that it rarely performs as well as its proponents expect. Mandates may be ignored for lack of funding. Agencies may be captured by the very groups they are meant to regulate — not necessarily through villainy, but more likely through the gradual development of common interests, a harmonious view of problems, and an interchange of manpower between the regulator and the regulated. Regulatory agencies may also be extremely susceptible to rigidity in substantive and procedural issues, making their responses painfully slow.

Despite these limitations, regulation is sometimes the best way to achieve a desired result, particularly if the market appears incapable of meeting social objectives. Public and legislative vigilance would undoubtedly enable the agencies to better their performance in the carrying out of their mandates.

Public Ownership and Resource Development

Public ownership is a policy tool that has been used sparingly in the United States. Government-owned companies have been established in the electric power industry, and the government is at present the sole proprietor of uranium enrichment plants. In both instances the federal energy role was a by-product of long-accepted federal functions: flood control and regional development for TVA and national defense for atomic energy. Even so, more direct federal action is an option often suggested for development of oil and gas resources on the federal domain, and for other purposes. The extent of public ownership is an important consideration whenever this tool is discussed. Limiting public ownership to a "yardstick" or example-setting function to spur more effective performance in the private sector stops short of subjecting the entire industry to nationalization.

The energy field is characterized by another aspect of public ownership. With the Department of the Interior acting as custodian, the American people own the bulk of the remaining fossil fuel resources in the United States. . . . It is relevant here in the sense that government ownership of the fuels might be a justification for the government to engage directly in their development.

Making Policy Choices

The shortages were the result of a number of circumstances most closely related to Presidential decisions. However, the "crisis" faced by President Nixon and passed on to Gerald Ford became an issue high on the policy agenda. It was an issue over which the national government's control was limited because of the dominance of private power in this area. The following article came out early in a year of energy policy making and indicates something of the public concern directed at corporate policies, a concern that neither Nixon nor Ford faced directly but one that set the stage for the confrontation between the President and Congress.

ATTACKS ON OIL INDUSTRY GROW FIERCER

Energy Crisis Is Cause of Criticism

MICHAEL C. JENSEN

The oil industry, one of the largest and most conspicuous in the country, has always had its share of critics, but the energy crisis, which spawned sharply higher oil and gas prices, as well as shortages and huge profits for the oil companies, has triggered a new series of public attacks.

This has taken the form of antitrust suits by corporations and Government bodies, angry testimony in Congressional hearings, and critical reports by both public and private panels.

In addition, private citizens across the nation, many of them having turned down their thermostats and reduced their speed on the highways to save costly fuel, have focused their outrage on the nation's large producers and refiners.

Even before the energy crisis of 1973–74, the oil industry was a frequent target of critics. It was accused of exerting an inordinate amount of influence through its well-financed lobby in Washington, its powerful political friends in Congress and the White House, and its executives who served as directors for corporations in other industries, banks and financial institutions.

Also widely criticized as preferential was the industry's tax treatment by the Government, characterized by generous depletion allowances. Other critics attacked the industry for despoiling the environment, partly by massive spills.

Many Americans, however, paid little attention to such criticism until their own pocketbooks began to suffer. But when prices for petroleum products began to soar, and oil industry profits skyrocketed even as motorists and homeowners were forced to pay sharply higher prices for gasoline and fuel oil, resentment began to come to the surface.

Today, many private citizens apparently believe that they have done their part to help ease the energy crisis — and may be called upon to do more — but that the big oil companies have not made comparable sacrifices.

"I blame the major oil companies," said George A. Baratta, owner of a small grocery in Miami, and one of a number of energy consumers interviewed in spot checks across the country. "I think they used the Arabs as an excuse to raise prices."

Although the worldwide increase in prices was triggered by members of the Organization of Petroleum Exporting Countries, many of the attacks in this country have been directed at the big American companies. Some of the companies have attempted to redirect the blame, pointing out that they are paying more for the oil they import and that world price levels have risen generally.

Nevertheless, the criticism continues, fueled by the following developments:

Prices for gasoline have risen by about 30 per cent since October, 1973, when the Arab boycott began and home heating oil prices are up by more than 40 per cent.

Profits of many oil companies soared to record levels in the last year, in some cases more than doubling.

Gas station profits also have skyrocketed. While specific results are closely guarded within the industry, some dealers admit privately that their profits have doubled in the last year.

Prices set in world petroleum markets by the major exporting countries have been allowed to dictate price levels in the United States even though this country is nearly two-thirds self-sufficient in its petroleum needs.

Costs for industries that use large amounts of fuel have risen sharply with the result that consumers are paying higher prices for electricity, air fares, and a variety of products. Higher energy costs in general have helped drag the nation into a recession.

ASSOCIATE OF NADER

Like Mr. Baratta, whose soaring utility bills have eaten into his business profits and stretched his household budget, millions of other Americans are apparently dismayed at the current state of energy affairs and are eager to find a villain.

In a recent nationwide survey by the Roper Organization, 63 per cent of the Americans polled cited increased fuel and energy costs as a primary cause of inflation. Sixty per cent said business and industry were making too much profit. The combination, Roper said, was a clear indication that the public believed some of the price increases could have been avoided.

Garry DeLoss, an associate of Ralph Nader, the consumer advocate, charges that the American public has been overcharged by more than $18 billion because the Government allowed domestic energy producers to raise their prices to levels dictated by foreign nations.

Mr. DeLoss asserts that a mandatory Government program limiting energy consumption is necessary, but that it should be characterized by price rollbacks rather than higher prices. The Ford Administration has adopted the opposite view, and expects higher prices to serve as a deterrent to consumption.

At the heart of much of the current criticism is a widespread feeling that the oil companies still are not doing all they can do to make sure that last winter's energy crisis is not repeated.

Critics point out that domestic companies have been allowed by the Government to charge prevailing world prices for much of the crude oil that is pumped out of the ground in this country (the so-called "new, released and stripper" oil), while prices have been fixed at $5.25 a barrel for "old" oil. The higher average price does not seem to have provided sufficient incentive to ease the tight supply situation, they say.

DRILLING ACTIVITY UP

The industry responds that discovering and bringing in new wells take years and that drilling activity already has picked up sharply.

Still, domestic crude oil production is running 5 per cent below levels a year earlier, and expansion of refineries has been modest.

The industry says old fields are running down and new supplies of crude oil are not yet assured. However, some of the industry's money has been used for totally different purposes, such as the Mobil Oil Company's $800-million acquisition of the Marcor Company, which comprises a mass retailer (Montgomery Ward) and a container manufacturer.

What's more, the nation's reliance on Arab oil, far from being reduced since last year, has actually risen — to 8.2 per cent from the 7.7 per cent level that prevailed in October, 1973. According to the Petroleum Industry Research Foundation, if another embargo were imposed, the United States would be in worse shape than ever.

Meanwhile, energy users have been hit with skyrocketing costs, especially those who live in all-electric homes. As a result, many are furious.

"I think it's darned unfair," said James Harrison, a professor of music from Sneden's Landing, New York.

COMPARISONS GIVEN

Mr. Harrison's first utility bill after moving into his all-electric home last winter was $900 for four months of electricity. "It was a rude, rude shock," he said. "We now keep our thermostat down to 60 or 62 degrees all the time. We often wear sweaters around the house and keep small electric heaters next to our working places. It's the cost."

The industry also has been attacked by its own workers.

The Oil, Chemical and Atomic Workers International Union, which says it has about 60,000 members working in the industry, recently charged that workers and consumers were being "robbed blind."

"Oil industry profits are up 146 per cent since 1972," the union said, "360 per cent since 1961. We may be paying more for foreign crude, but we're also paying a lot more for industry profits."

Among the major oil companies reporting profit increases for 1974 were Exxon, up 29 per cent to $3.14-billion; the Standard Oil Company (Indiana), up 90 per cent, and Texaco, Inc., up 23 per cent.

Some, but not all, of the major oil producers noted that their profits had begun to decline as the year ended. Mobil, for example, said fourth quarter earnings were off 51 per cent from year-earlier levels and Texaco was off 29 per cent. Indiana Standard, however, was up 44 per cent in the fourth quarter, and Exxon was up 9 per cent from year-earlier levels.

Contending that oil executives had received salary increases of more than 21 per cent in 1973, the union also said the industry had spent millions of dollars on extraneous matters.

"If the oil companies have all that money to spend on executive raises, outside investments and political contributions, they must be making too much money," the union said. "The money we pay for oil shouldn't go for anything except finding, refining, and delivering oil. The industry can and should lower prices."

In addition to criticism from individuals and workers, the oil industry has been sharply attacked by Congress and its investigators.

The General Accounting Office late last year reported that Government audit officials had estimated that the nation's oil companies may have over-charged their customers by $1 billion to $2 billion by skirting Federal regulations.

IMPACT OF PRICES

The impact of higher prices has been most keenly felt in areas like New England, which relies heavily on imported oil and where severe winters require many homeowners to buy thousands of gallons of fuel oil each year.

Four years ago, Mrs. Rubin G. Baker Jr., who lives with her family in a huge, old 16-room house in Wellfleet, Mass., spent $147 to heat her home in January. Fuel oil had risen to 32.4 cents a gallon, and Mrs. Baker had to reduce her consumption from 746 gallons to 448 gallons to keep the total price for the month roughly even.

How has the reduction been accomplished? During the winter, the Bakers close off all but four rooms on the first floor, where the family lives and sleeps. They keep the thermostat at 66 degrees during the day and at 64 degrees at night. Plastic sheets are tacked over the house's old wooden storm windows, and tinfoil is placed behind radiators as heat reflectors.

Legal moves against the oil companies also have proliferated in the wake of the energy crisis. For example, The New York City Housing Authority earlier this month filed a $100 million Federal suit against 11 major oil companies charging them with restraint of trade and rigging of oil prices. A similar suit was filed last summer by the Lefrak Organization, New York City's largest private landlord, against six major oil companies.

GLOOMY FUTURE SEEN

In addition to price increases already imposed, the future seems gloomy for oil and gas users. The Library of Congress has estimated the various potential legislative, regulatory, administrative and economic developments could add billions more to energy costs. They include:

Decontrol of the price of all crude oil. Cost: $10.2 billion annually.

Increases in the "intra-state" price of natural gas. Cost: $6.8 billion within a year.

Deregulation of "new" natural gas. Cost: $59.9 billion by the end of 1980.

What distresses many Americans is the fact that heavy emphasis is being laid on the need for greater public conservation. Some point out that only a major conservation effort has prevented the recurrence of last year's energy crisis.

Recent figures from the Bureau of Mines indicate that during September, the most recent month available, petroleum products including motor gasoline, jet fuel, heating fuel and oil burned by utilities, declined by 3.8 per cent from year-earlier levels. The FEA adds that demand for all petroleum products through the first 9 months of 1974 was down 4.9 per cent.

According to the Lundberg Survey, an authoritative trade sampling organization headquartered in North Hollywood, Calif., national consumption of gasoline was down by 4.7 per cent in the first eight months of 1974, and down by 5 per cent during the month of August.

VIEW OF EXPERTS

Experts point out that normal growth in energy consumption ranges from 4 per cent to 6 per cent. Thus, the decline in actual consumption, combined with the lack of growth, means the nation is saving about 1 million barrels of oil a day from anticipated consumption, the experts say.

With consumption lagging, stockpiles and inventories of crude oil and many petroleum products have been rebuilt in recent months. Furthermore, refiners are running at only about 85 per cent of their capacity, although that capacity is higher than it was a year ago.

Stocks of crude oil are up about 15 per cent from year-earlier levels, inventories of gasoline are 10 per cent higher, jet fuel stocks are up 6 per cent, and heavy fuel oil used by utilities is up 20 per cent. Home heating stocks are about 4 per cent higher than last year's levels. For the most part, growing inventories have not meant lower prices, however. Although gasoline prices have drifted slightly lower in recent months, they still are about 30 per cent higher than they were when the "crisis" was in its early stages in October, 1973, according to the Federal Energy Administration. Jet fuel prices are up by 75 per cent, home heating fuel has risen more than 40 per cent, and residual fuel has more than doubled on price. Residual oil, of course, is heavily used by utilities, and is reflected in higher electrical bills.

CRITICISM CITED

Skepticism about the energy crisis has been heightened by the criticism of officials in the Government and at foundations and universities.

S. David Freeman, who conducted a detailed study for the Ford Foundation, says the crisis resulted from "a failure of private, corporate energy policies originating in Houston and Dallas and New York, and rubber-stamped over the years by the Congress and a succession of Presidents."

Fred C. Allvine of the University of Georgia, in a book called *Highway Robbery, An Analysis of the Gasoline Crisis,* concludes that "certain large companies played a significant role in creating the shortage."

"They were aided and abetted in so doing by inept management of the oil import program by the executive branch of the Federal Government," he says. "The petroleum product shortages have resulted in the most rapid rise in the price of petroleum products and improvement in earnings occuring over the past 25 years."

While the large oil companies and the Government have come in for most of the criticism, gasoline stations also have been singled out for profitting from the public's discomfort.

PETITION BY CONSUMERS

The Consumers Union of the United States, Inc., has petitioned the Federal Energy Administration for repeal of a Government rule allowing gasoline retailers an additional 3 cents per gallon profit.

The Consumers Union points out that the extra three cents was granted last winter, at a time when the retailers were operating on reduced volume.

However, volume at most gas stations has recovered, the organization points out, and net profits of the stations during the summer of 1974 "were more than double those of the previous summer."

In addition to eliminating the extra 3 cent profit margin, the Consumers Union has asked the FEA to determine the amount of "excessive profits" received by the retailers, and to require that such profits be returned to consumers.

MIXED VIEWS EXPRESSED

As for the major oil companies, analysts are mixed about their prospects for continuing profit gains. Some say the industry's profits will decline slightly from the record levels set last year. Others say domestic earnings of the major companies will continue to show increases, at least during the first six months of 1975.

For one thing, some of the companies have the ability to pass along in the form of higher product prices, allowable increases which they have "banked" rather than imposed.

For another, they can continue to pass through high-priced crude oil, which they produce themselves.

"At this point, we think first-half earnings of the domestic companies will continue to show year-to-year gains," said R. S. Ilacqua of L. F. Rothschild & Company. He said the gains would come from the companies' own crude oil, which could be passed along to customers, and from the companies' ability to pass along to customers much of the higher cost of purchased crude oil.

Mr. Ilacqua warned, however, that inflated operating costs, which could not be passed on to customers under current Government regulations, would limit profit increases.

Meanwhile, growing profits or not, homeowners and motorists face the unhappy prospect of ever-higher prices.

"I vacillate between extreme pessimism and extreme optimism," said Mrs. Paula Newcomb of Sacramento, Calif. "We have to quit producing so many people and use less of our fossil fuels.

"We need legislation," she added, "the kind rich people can't get around."

SECTION B. A PRESIDENT'S DAY

The extraordinarily candid portrait offered in this section focuses on the daily events and personal contacts through which the President's influence is translated into governmental action. With over 2 million employees, the executive branch is a massive bureaucracy responsible for carrying out national policy. The Office of the President alone has thousands of members who provide the information on which policy is made and means of carrying it out. The creation and execution of policy is dependent on the various activities that take place in the White House bringing together those in charge of the executive agencies and those with whom the administration must work. The nature of these activities is a function of the sort of person the President is and the kinds of people he surrounds himself with. In this regard, the institutions matter far less than the sorts of persons involved and the informal relations that emerge in each administration.

The personality of the President is an essential force in the operation of the executive branch and can become the dominant factor in the politics of the entire government. Personality can contribute much to a sense of the spirit of government, exerting a political influence that reaches beyond the formal structure and institutions. The quality was accented by Gerald Ford, whose image as an open and honest man

An official photograph from the White House.

was projected against the background of corruption that preceded him. Perhaps the greatest fear relating to the President's personality concerns the agents of destruction at the disposal of this one person. The concern that the President be cool and detached is associated most often with crisis periods like those surrounding the 1962 confrontation over missiles in Cuba, or the seizure of the American cargo ship Mayaguez by Cambodia in 1974. Such incidents threaten to catapult the country into war within hours. The Presidential personality has also been a factor influencing the degree of openness in an administration and the responsiveness of the executive to shifts in national politics. The personal characteristics of Presidents Wilson, Johnson, and Nixon resulted in administrative postures determining how they responded to the challenges faced by their administrations. Each of these administrations is remembered for the failures that ensued. As a barrier that subordinates must face when making recommendations, personality is a prime determinant of what the President will be told and what he will hear. Finally, personality is a dimension of the power to persuade, which many observers consider a crucial quality for an effective President. It is the medium through which the Chief Executive transmits substantive policy. This aspect of the President, especially as it explains the conduct of the office, illuminates the mysterious process that translates the perception of problems into official policy.

The President has always had a staff. But as the nation has grown, the older advisory positions have become institutionalized and new positions have developed simply to control the various agencies of the executive branch. Not only has George Washington's small Cabinet increased to 12, but it is now complemented by such members of the Executive Office as the Budget Director and the Energy Administrator and such import agency positions as the heads of the Federal Bureau of Investigation and the Environmental Protection Agency. The emphasis here is on the way in which those who surround the President influence how policy issues are perceived and how alternatives are formulated and assessed from day to day. Many of the institutions mentioned in this section play an important role in specific policy areas covered in other chapters of this collection, such as military spending and economic planning. An entire day is included here to show how the ongoing process revolves around the President.

One of the most significant developments — one that has a great impact on the immediate environment of the President — concerns the specialized personal advisers to the President. The staff around the President became the focus of attention as the depths of the Watergate coverup were revealed. Referred to as the "Palace Guard," those men worked for President Nixon and bore much of the responsibility for the misdeeds of his administration. The organization of the subordinates and their relationship to the President determine the President's success in performing his duties. In the section of John Hersey's report which follows, the main staff members are Donald Rumsfeld, at the time the Assistant to the President; Ron Nessen, the President's Press Secretary; Harold Seidman, the Assistant for Economic Affairs; Robert Hartmann, a Counselor to the President who is in charge of speech writers; and John O. Marsh, Jr., the Counselor in overall charge of the President's relations with Congress and various sectors of the public.

When the White House is trying to obtain compliance from the different departments, the staff relies on the prestige of the office and its capacity to bestow favors more readily than on the use of force that stands behind the authority of the President. Thomas Cronin, in a study of the Presidency, has characterized the staff as "middlemen" charged with winning departmental compliance with the President's decisions. The important and complex art of influence is evident in the variety of activities performed by the staff. They are the messengers, the information gatherers, the public relations people, and the appointment secretaries. Cronin has pointed out that the White House Staff differ from department heads not only because of institutional differences but also because of the way they are chosen. Presidents have increasingly assigned campaign aides and personal associates to the White House Staff, while filling Cabinet posts with members of business and professional elites, usually having some public standing. The immediate staff is often made up of less public figures. They are men and women whose allegiance and responsibility has been to the President. Most of the executive branch has other more formal institutional connections and, even though appointed by the President, Cabinet and agency heads must be confirmed by Congress.

The Office of the President in operation reveals a number of things that bear on the President's capacity to deal with policy issues that may arise. The way it is set up determines what he will know about an issue, the extent of consideration he will give it, and the options available to him. These matters will affect, as well as be affected by, issues of public concern as revealed through the media. The President is never forced to respond in a particular way, but his actions may be explained as the individual personality and a "support" mechanism that makes the individual larger than life.

The following selection describes the framework of everyday decisions by showing the Office of the President at work. Here, crucial decisions about energy policy are sandwiched between other policy issues and ceremonial duties. There is little time for deliberation, and most decisions must be understood as judgments on the basis of briefings, the interpretation of advisers, and the intuitive responses of the pivot man, the President. The first matter concerning energy problems deals with the government's Elk Hills oil reserves. The President is presented with a problem. He wants something done. If the staff can accomplish it, the President might not hear of the matter again. If they cannot, he may have to make more specific choices or address his persuasive power more pointedly. In minutes, the issues confronted range over upheaval in Portugal, diplomatic negotiations in Turkey, domestic boat sales, strategy with reference to Congress, policy on assassinations, and a visit from the Maid of Cotton. Decisions are made quickly, generally with little discussion or dissent from the President's advisers.

Energy and the economy get special attention in a meeting of the Economic Policy Board set up by Ford. The spectrum of views is wider here and the deference to the President is not quite so obvious, but all these men (except Federal Reserve Chairman Burns) serve more or less at the President's pleasure. It seems to be more than a coincidence that the Vice-President, who has the greatest national standing independent of the President, is the odd man on the issues Hersey reports. It is Rockefeller who asks questions and to whom many of the other advisers address themselves. This is again a decision making meeting, although it is also evident that the President is taught a number of important lessons on rebates and tax policy.

Later in the day, the matter of the Elk Hills oil reserves comes up again. Here the President is applying the pressure to have a decision carried out. He gives the Secretary of Defense the same instructions that were given earlier to staff member Richard Cheney. In this instance, the President is making a connection with a departmental head instead of the ever present "guard." But there are signs of his frustration with Schlesinger that led to a move later in the year to replace him with Presidential Assistant Rumsfeld and to move Richard Cheney into Rumsfeld's position as Chief of the Palace Guard.

TUESDAY

A HARD-EDGED

CONSERVATIVE VOICE

JOHN HERSEY

7:40 A.M. The President, accompanied by two Secret Service men and a valet carrying the brown suitcase, arrives from the residence. He is dressed today in a flashy suit of bold vertical stripes of shades of gray; he looks a bit drawn this morning. It is raining again.

SOURCE: From *The President*, by John Hersey, pp. 31–54. Copyright © 1975 by John Hersey. Reprinted by permission of Alfred A. Knopf, Inc. Originally appeared in *The New York Times Magazine*.
The day referred to in this selection is Tuesday, 11 March 1975.

7:42 A.M. Brent Scowcroft goes in to show the President dispatches from Henry Kissinger and intelligence messages that have accumulated overnight. I am not invited to join them; the President, in setting the ground rules for my access to him, has specifically excluded these daily foreign-policy and security sessions.

Lieutenant General Scowcroft, who is fifty, is Deputy Assistant to the President for National Security Affairs. This means — though you would never know it to look at him — that he is Henry Kissinger's administrative *alter ego*; when the Secretary of State is away, and he is often away, the general alone speaks for him to the President on foreign and national-security matters. Short, wiry, rooster-quick, with sparkling eyes, he seems a living model of a sprite that must surely dwell in Dr. Henry Kissinger, who cannot possibly be as heavy and lugubrious all the way through as he looks and sounds on the outside. As to point of view, Scowcroft does in some eerie way actually seem to inhabit Kissinger. The general is a rarity — an intellectual soldier. He has a Ph.D. from Columbia in international relations; he has studied at West Point, Lafayette, Georgetown, the Strategic Intelligence School, the Armed Forces Staff College and the National War College; and he has been an assistant professor of Russian history at West Point and professor of political science at the Air Force Academy.

8:30 A.M. Robert Trowbridge Hartmann, with whom I now enter the Oval Office, is one of the President's two Counselors; he is fifty-eight. His explicit areas of responsibility are speechwriting and, vaguely, politics, but he is a long-standing friend of Mr. Ford's and was his Chief of Staff during the Vice Presidency, and he talks about all sorts of things with him now. Hearty, bluff, gray-haired, ruddy, he was once Washington bureau chief for *The Los Angeles Times,* and he is shrewd and accurate in assessing how the press will respond to whatever the President does. He has a mischievous look in his eye as he hands the President a strip of teletype, saying, "You'll be happy to see that Martha Mitchell is against you."

The President reads and laughs. "That's a cheery note at eight in the morning," he says.

Hartmann hands him another item — some not-so-cheery news about conservative Republicans; and an announcement that the Senate is planning to recess for Easter in just ten days — which allows a very short time for the struggles over taxes and Cambodian aid.

He tells the President that a delegation from the Gridiron Club — "the Privy Council of the Press" — seeks an audience with him to present a formal invitation to this year's dinner.

He gives the President a speech Ford had made at William and Mary, as possible background for an interview he is to have later in the day with the editors of *Fortune,* on the development of American institutions.

Then Hartmann says that Jack Stiles, a Grand Rapids newspaperman who collaborated with Ford on *Portrait of the Assassin,* a book that was a by-product of Ford's service on the Warren Commission, wants some information from the President's personal files.

Now I have a moment of seeing the President as an author, with the look on his face of one who may have a deal in the works.

THE AUTHOR: M-G-M contacted me about taking *Portrait* and making a documentary of it. Buchen turned them down. Then M-G-M contacted Jack, and he went to California for a day or so. They want to make three two-hour documentaries, using *Portrait* as a theme. Our book took the testimony of witnesses from the report, and it backed up the commission's finding that Oswald did it alone. Simon and Schuster's thinking of republishing it. Jack wants to find out how the radio and television rights stand. With all these charges of assassination plots against Castro and everything, there may be some interest. I still think the way we used the witnesses' testimony was: Number One *(the forefinger rises to the count),* more readable than the report and than the other books that were critical. . . .

The President does not get beyond Number One.

8:35 A.M. The senior staff meeting is apparently lasting somewhat longer than usual this morning, and Rumsfeld's deputy, Richard Cheney, fills in for him while he is delayed.

Right away, Cheney brings up a sticky item. In his first State-of-the-Union Message, in January, urging "energy independence," the President asked Congress to authorize full-scale commercial development of the naval petroleum reserve at Elk Hills, California. Out of the blue, a few days later, without having notified the Administration, the Standard Oil Company of California announced its intention of pulling its drilling rigs out of Elk Hills in order to avoid possible criticism of its role there. (Elk Hills was one of the reserves involved in the Teapot Dome scandal of 1923.) The Navy, Cheney says, has not yet found a new operator and he raises the question whether the reserve should be transferred from Navy to Interior Department control.

FORD: I'm more interested in getting action, getting production, getting oil, than I am in what agency runs the place. On my next trip West I want to go out there and see first-hand what Elk Hills looks like. I'm disturbed nothing's happening there. I'd like to get some action. We're interested in substance, not jurisdiction!

8:50 A.M. Donald Rumsfeld, who comes in now, is by far the most equal of the theoretically equal top members of Mr. Ford's staff. He is also, at forty-two, the youngest of them. His gift is for organization. He is the only member of the staff frequenting the Oval Office in whose eye I think I can see, now and then, behind his fashionable "aviator" glasses with their delicate black rims, a glint that seems to say, "That big leather chair on the other side of the desk looks comfortable. I wonder if it would fit me." He is bright, jealous, crafty and fiercely combative; he once captained the Princeton wrestling team. He served four terms in Congress, representing the wealthy North Shore above Chicago, and his voting record was almost identical with Gerald Ford's. He is a Nixon holdover — campaigned for him in '66, ran the Office of Economic Opportunity for him awhile, and in 1970 entered the White House as his Counselor and Director of his Cost of Living Council. To Rumsfeld's credit, he eventually was given the shudders by Haldeman and Ehrlichman, and he had himself shot out as far away from them as he could be — to Brussels, as Ambassador to NATO. President Ford called him home from there. His active hands move as if blown by every gust in his mind — always shaping, shaping, grasping bits of form out of the chaos of power.

Now, taking over from Cheney, he reviews the senior staff meeting and helps the President plan the rest of the day.

9:07 A.M. As Jack Marsh is about to enter the Oval Office, someone hands him an urgent cable for the President's eyes, Marsh reads it. He says to Terry O'Donnell, "Get General Scowcroft. The President's going to want to ask him some questions about this." He enters and hands the paper to the President. It is from Ambassador Frank Carlucci in Lisbon, and it informs the President of an uprising against the Portuguese Government by airforce units. Snowcroft is soon at attention before the big desk.

FORD (*unflapped*): Do we have any information that their air force has been unhappy?
SCOWCROFT: Not particularly, as a whole. Two or three weeks ago there were some rumors of a possible coup, primarily, it was thought, in armed forces guarding —
FORD: Any philosophical differences between the air-force group and other army units?
SCOWCROFT: Not that we know of. As a practical matter, it would be difficult for the air force to mount a coup.
FORD: Keep me posted, Brent.
SCOWCROFT: I will, Mr. President.
FORD: I'm glad we've got Frank Carlucci over there. He's a good man. Any further word from Henry?
SCOWCROFT: Yes, sir. I'll bring it in later. From Turkey. Not particularly encouraging. (*He leaves.*)

John O. Marsh, Jr., who is forty-eight, and who, as Counselor, is in over-all charge of the President's relations with Congress and with various sectors of the public, including businessmen, women, minorities and consumers, has a way of pointing at a photograph over the mantel in his office of his farm in the Virginia hills and, with a slanting look just above and off to one side of his interlocutor's forehead, saying, "That's my little shanty in Strasburg. I'm just a country lawyer." Roughly translated, this means: "Watch out, my friend — take a good grip on your credit cards." Jack Marsh was in Congress with Gerald Ford — as a Byrd Democrat. Now calling himself an independent, he is ideologically much the most conservative man in the inner circle on the staff (in the 90th Congress, Gerald Ford voted 63 percent of the time with the so-called conservative coalition of Republicans and Southern Democrats; Marsh voted with the coalition 98 percent of the time), yet he seems personally the most sensitive and humane man in the group.

MARSH: Did you see that they've got this $6-billion bill up there to create jobs? They apparently put it together quietly in committee. . . .

By now I have noticed that whereas the Nixon insiders used the word "they" when speaking of hostile forces, the press, demonstrators, enemies, all who were considered threatening, this Administration uses it exclusively for a single, solid and frustrating entity — the Democratic majority in Congress.

FORD: Let's get some more information on the bill. . . .
MARSH: I've been talking with some folks from Chrysler, and they feel there's maybe too much bad news about the economy coming out of here. They were talking about boat shows. They've been doing real well, selling lots and lots of big craft. Sales are down on the blue-collar lines, the small boats, but they're real happy over-all. Chrysler boat sales are up and auto sales are down. Maybe we ought to take hold of some signs. . . .

Now Marsh brings up a sensitive matter. *The Washington Star-News* has carried a story that Representative John Rhodes, the man who succeeded Gerald Ford as Minority Leader of the House and an old friend of his, has announced that House Republicans are going to develop a legislative program of their own, separate from the President's. He has been quoted to the effect that "the days Republicans can get elected on somebody else's coattails are gone, gone forever."

MARSH: I'm not that upset about it, Mr. President. . . .
The President's face is a mask. I can see no surprise, no hurt, no anger.

9:20 A.M. The Nessen group comes in.

NESSEN: I had a big go-round on the C.I.A. in yesterday's briefing. I'd like to ask you this: What are your personal views on the use of assassination?

Here I do see a moment's flash of the Truman style. Mr. Ford's answer is an immediate reflex.

FORD (*leaning forward, striking the edge of the desk repeatedly with a fore-finger*): I've been assured it's not going on, and I don't want it to go on.

Nessen gives a full account of the ferocity of the questioning in yesterday's briefing. The range of allegations, he says, is widening, to the point of speculation that the C.I.A. may have been involved in one of the Kennedy assassinations, or both. What is he to say about all these things?

A long discussion ensues, about who is, or should be, checking out allegations of past plots by the C.I.A. The question is not settled here; it will be taken forward.

And I have seen one way in which policy is spurred, if not engendered.

The Rhodes embarrassment is discussed. Rumsfeld bitterly says he thinks the Republicans on the Hill have been watching the President slide in the polls and "are trying to put some light between them and you. Wait till the polls go up again: then they'll come running."

FORD: John's all right. I don't worry about him.

HARTMANN: It's like when I was writing papers for the Republican Policy Committee — remember, Mr. President? — and we called them Constructive Republican Alternative Proposals. It didn't take those clever Democrat lads long to find out what the initials spelled.

Hearing this, I suddenly remember the parentheses marking deleted expletives marching like an army of ants across the Nixon transcripts, and I realize that I have yet to hear — except in Hartmann's acronym, to cheer the President up — a single four-letter word in this room.

Max L. Friedersdorf, Assistant to the President for Legislative Affairs, gives a report on how the President's request for $222 million in emergency aid for Cambodia stands in a Senate Foreign Relations subcommittee and in a House Foreign Affairs subcommittee, and how the dickering on the tax-cut bill is coming along in the House Ways and Means Committee. Friedersdorf, a tall blond Hoosier, a former newspaperman, is in complete command of his material; he has preliminary counts on how the votes will go in various committees. The President, thoroughly at home with Congressional give-and-take, talks zestfully, predicting how this man and that man will finally come down. He names some who are dead set against him; he speaks their first names with fondness.

The prospects are bleak. It is hard to understand why the President, who has made so much of the need for this aid, is not upset.

10:50 A.M. The President receives a young lady who has been designated Maid of Cotton for 1975. This stunt is a replica of yesterday's reception of Miss America, except that it has more crassly commercial overtones.

At his press briefing a few minutes later, Ron Nessen tells the mediamen about the visit to the Oval Room of the Maid of Cotton, who in real life is Miss Kathryn Tenkhoff, of Sikeston, Missouri.

NESSEN: Secretary Butz also attended the meeting.

Q: Did Butz come over just for that?

NESSEN: Cotton is his area of responsibility.

Q: How much cotton do they grow in Missouri?

NESSEN: They grow cotton queens in Missouri. They grow cotton somewhere else.

11:01 A.M. The first sharp shock of the week is in store for me.

Assembled in the Cabinet Room are all the Administration's big guns on the economy and energy; the President himself; Vice President Nelson Rockefeller; Secretary of the Treasury William Simon; the President's Cabinet-rank Assistant for Economic Affairs, William Seidman; the new Secretary of Labor, John Dunlop; James Lynn of the Office of Management and Budget; Chairman Alan Greenspan of the Council of Economic Advisers; Chairman Frank Zarb of the Energy Resources Council; Dr. Burns of the Fed; Rumsfeld, Hartmann, Scowcroft and some staff assistants.

The President asks Secretary Simon for a report on the status of the tax-rebate bill.

SIMON: Mr. President, we're attempting to keep this to a temporary, one-shot thing. As you know, the House has proposed a $21.3-billion rebate using more or less our method, but lowering the income allowance. No one in his right mind believes that when they get going on this it'll be temporary. On the Senate bill, I went up and testified before the Senate Finance Committee, and I guess a ball-park figure of where they'll come out would be $25 billion, and you can bet your hat the House won't be able to resist matching those goodies. . . .

FORD: Any chance of lifting the $200 ceiling on individual rebates?

SIMON: There's a fair shot of getting $500. Mr. President, this whole deal of theirs is more of a welfare thing than anything else. They're making the asumption that low-income people should get more than their share of the giveaway. It's just a welfare thing, Mr. President.

FORD: Let me ask you this: I have two sons who worked last summer and earned about $1,500 each. Would they get $100 rebate?

SIMON: In my judgment, absolutely.

FORD: That's ridiculous.

SIMON: If they're typical of young people who work in the summertime —

FORD: It's ridiculous.

SIMON: I couldn't agree more, Mr. President.

SEIDMAN: Essentially it gives them back their Social Security tax.

SIMON: That's exactly what it does.

HARTMANN: But if they go out and spend it —

FORD: They'll spend it, all right! (*Laughter.*)

A little later:

FORD: What's going on about the oil-depletion allowance?

SIMON: I think they're cutting a deal up there right now. . . .

FORD (*after more discussion*): Our position should be that we do not want a Christmas-tree bill, with a whole lot of favors and gifts attached to it, and we've got to attack the whole issue of including cutting out the oil-depletion allowance in the tax-stimulus bill.

This was the first time I had seen the President and the Vice President in the same room. They now face each other on opposite sides of the center of the long Cabinet table. The President, as usual, is still, controlled, imperturbable. The Vice President, by contrast, is as active as a two-month-old kitten. He slumps, shoots bolt upright, leans to one side, then to the other, whispers, nods when he agrees, shakes his head when he differs. Now he speaks up.

ROCKEFELLER: Is it too late to propose an excess-profits tax on the oil companies with an allowance for plow-back?

SIMON: It is, sir. We've proposed a windfall-profits tax in preference to that.

FORD: I'm not sure I understand the difference between a windfall and an excess-profits tax.

SIMON: Sir, the windfall tax aims like a rifle at crude oil, as opposed to an excess-profits tax, which would cut across the whole range of an extremely complex system of profit calculation.

GREENSPAN: Trying to audit through the profits system of the multinationals would lead you into a hopeless maze.

The Vice President subsides like a balloon with the air escaping.

FORD: The main thing is to attach as few amendments as possible to the tax bill, so as to get the stimulus as soon as we can. . . .

The meeting lasts for an hour and fifteen minutes and goes into great detail on issues that are quite technical: an intention to impose countervailing duties on European Community dairy products; proposed Export–Import Bank financing of liquefied natural-gas facilities abroad; negotiations with Chairman Albert Ullman of the House Ways and Means Committee on the energy bill, and what to do about "their" $5.9-billion Emergency Employment Appropriations Act.

Mr. Rockefeller with belling tones interrupts the Ex-Im discussion with a warning that supertankers carrying liquefied gas are extremely dangerous. If one blew up in an American port, he says, the whole city would go up. He paints a vivid picture of urban devastation.

The President's interventions are minor, until the discussion of the Democrats' big bill to provide jobs. Here his only interest is in keeping spending down. He proposes the preparation, as quickly as possible, of "an updated scoreboard" on the budget, reflecting Congressional proposals to spend more and more, and Congressional refusals to rescind or defer spending already authorized. He stresses more than once the need to dramatize "their" additions to the deficit.

Why am I shocked? Because in this discussion I have seen a first glimpse of another side of the man who has been so considerate, so open and so kind to me as an individual — what seems a deep, hard, rigid side. Talking here, he has seemed a million miles away from many Americans who have been hardworking people all their lives and are now feeling the cruel pinch of hard times. What is it in him? Is it an inability to extend compassion far beyond the faces directly in view? Is it a failure of imagination? Is it something obdurate he was born with, alongside the energy and serenity he was born with?

12:16 P.M. He takes Rockefeller in to the Oval Office with him. To my regret, I am not invited to join them — I would have loved to see the Immovable Object and the Irresistible Force collide.

I gather they talk about two things. First, the Domestic Council. This body, originally conceived as a planning unit in the Executive, devolved under Nixon and Ehrlichman into an operational clearinghouse that kept things moving. Ford and his staff early saw a need to restore its predictive function, because it was obvious that the President was not by nature a planner. Ford had had a long habit of juggling a multiplicity of problems in the Congress that demanded instant attention; everything was always on a day-to-day basis. And he succeeded to the Presidency, as his Counsel Philip Buchen puts it, "under a tyranny of urgency." And much as he would have liked to emulate Truman, he lacked Truman's sense of history —

lacked a feel for how a decision would look five — or fifty — years hence. The thought was that Rockefeller, having put a Commission on Critical Choices to work after he resigned from the Governorship of New York, might bring a planning competence to the council. Ford appointed James M. Cannon, long a political adviser to Rockefeller, as director of the council, and the two men talk now about the early stages of Cannon's and the council's work.

Second, the C.I.A. Who should investigate?

12:35 P.M. The President calls in Alan Greenspan to fill him in on the conversation yesterday with Dr. Burns. Alan Greenspan is a devotee of Ayn Rand (*The Fountainhead, Atlas Shrugged*), the Objectivist philosopher, and, like her, he advocates pure *laissez-faire* capitalism and "rational selfishness."

12:46 P.M. General Scowcroft goes in for two minutes — presumably with the latest word from Dr. Kissinger.

12:48 P.M. Mr. Ford receives Frank Stanton, former vice chairman of the board of CBS, who for a year and a half has chaired a panel, set up jointly by the U.S. Advisory Commission on Information and the U.S. Advisory Commission on International Education and Cultural Affairs, reviewing the operations of the U.S. Information Agency, the Voice of America and the Bureau of Cultural Affairs of the Department of State.

Before each appointment, the President is given what is formally called a briefing paper; informally, a talking paper. It has three parts: a statement of the purpose of the appointment, background and "talking points" — actual language the President might appropriately use.

In this instance, Mr. Ford has been given the following talking points:

"(1) I understand that your panel has addressed some of the long-standing issues. . . . These activities play an important role. . . .

"(2) There have been a number of proposals in recent years for restructuring our information and cultural activities. . . ."

Mr. Stanton is then to be given a chance to make his recommendations — which, in the event, are that U.S.I.A's information functions be transferred to the State Department, that the long-range cultural functions of U.S.I.A. and State be combined within State and that the Voice of America be set up as an independent entity under a Government-and-public board.

"(3) The scope of your study and its recommendations are very impressive. I will want to have it studied very carefully. . . .

"(4) Thank you for your efforts. . . . You have made a most needed and timely contribution."

Actually, the exchange is far freer and a little less grammatical than this, but, all the same, it's the way it goes.

1:10 P.M. The President retires for lunch. I join him for a few minutes in his two-room hideaway. One room is a small study, the walls of which are covered with mementos, including a huge Presidential seal which is actually a rug, hooked for the President in Grand Rapids by his half-sister-in-law, Mrs. Richard Ford; in one corner there is a luxurious stuffed-leather Barca-lounger, into which the President occasionally settles to read.

His lunch is served on a tray on a small table beside a desk in the other room.

Day in and day out, Mr. Ford eats exactly the same lunch — a ball of cottage cheese, over which he pours a small pitcherful of A-1 Sauce, a sliced onion or a quartered tomato, and a small helping of butter-pecan ice cream.

"Eating and sleeping," he says to me, "are a waste of time."

I tell him that it has appeared to me that he likes being President.

"I do," he says. "It's mainly the challenge, John. I always have enjoyed facing up to problems; it's always been a sort of way of life with me — and you certainly have them here. I really enjoy getting up every morning, looking at the schedule, seeing what the problems are. I don't long for the end of the day."

2:03 P.M. Secretary of Defense James Schlesinger and General Scowcroft are closeted with the President, to report on the deteriorating situations in Cambodia and Vietnam. After about half an hour, I am admitted.

They are talking about G.I. Bill education, which the President apparently wants to cut back, or perhaps cut out altogether. The tall, rugged-looking Secretary holds the line as well as he can.

FORD: You do get into a paradoxical situation. You have an all-volunteer service, but these benefits give an incentive to get out.
SCHLESINGER: They give an incentive to get in, sir. But many will stay. We're attracting a different sort of person.
FORD: Ever thought of offering a greater educational opportunity if they stay in?
SCHLESINGER: We do some of that now, Mr. President, but we're going to cut back on it. English grammar but not basket weaving, for which they've gotten credit in the past.
FORD: There are things I can do to cut off certain benefits. But we'll have to go to Congress sooner or later. There has to come a time when we end the so-called Vietnam war and all its extras.
SCHLESINGER: We'll get up an options paper on the whole thing.

The two now discuss several other subjects — officers' pay, certain personnel decisions, Thailand, Diego Garcia, Turkey.

Suddenly the President leans forward, and with a vigor far surpassing any I have previously seen him show, his voice rising almost to a shout, his forefinger pounding on the edge of the desk, he adjures the Secretary to get the Navy going on the Elk Hills petroleum reserve.

FORD: Get up there and get the legislation, or we're going to give that whole deal to Interior. Tell 'em to get off their cushions up there at the Navy. The Navy damn well better get moving. I want you to get action. It strikes me the Navy likes the cushy little deal they've got out there. I'm going to go and see Elk Hills, and when I come back I'm going to be one of the few people who's actually seen the place, and I'm going to be in a position to tell 'em what's what. Now you get going.

SCHLESINGER (*to his Commander in Chief*): Yes, sir.

3:08 P.M. Rumsfeld, Cheney and William N. Walker, Director of the Presidential Personnel Office, come in to talk about some prospective appointments.

4:20 P.M. Marsh, Cheney, Cabinet Secretary James Connor and Dr. Robert Goldwin enter to warm Mr. Ford up for the *Fortune* interview. Dr. Goldwin has recently been appointed a consultant, with a mission of bringing intellectuals in to see the President. So far, he has exposed Ford to people like Irving Kristol, of the Department of Urban Values, New York University; Gertrude Himmelfarb, historian, of City College, New York; Thomas Sowell, an eminent black economist, of U.C.L.A.; Herbert Storing, a political scientist, of the University of Chicago; and Edward Banfield, an urban specialist, of the University of Pennsylvania.

In preparation for this meeting, Dr. Goldwin has provided Mr. Ford with the *Encyclopedia of American History,* edited by Richard B. Morris *et al.,* and the *Encyclopedia of American Facts and Dates,* edited by Gorton Carruth, with certain pages tabbed. Mr. Ford has done his homework. There is a meandering conversation on history — one which Mr. Truman would never have needed; or, had he heard it, would have called just too damned highfalutin.

4:55 P.M. *Fortune* editors in. Goes pretty well, Mr. Ford reports afterward.

5:40 P.M. Marsh, Friedersdorf, Cannon, Cheney, Lynn, Lynn's O.M.B. deputy, Paul O'Neill, and a couple of other staff members meet with the President to discuss the possibility of sending a message to Congress on a consumer-protection bill.

Once again, as the group reviews a long options paper, I hear in the President's comments the distant, hard-edged, negative voice I heard this morning in the economy–energy meeting.

FORD: Is a consumer-protection bill in any form a violation of our new policy of limited spending?

LYNN: You're going to get a new law, no matter what you put in this. It's almost a certainty they'll have a law.

FORD: Then you get a question: Is it wise for me to go with a message?

LYNN: Well — to get out in front with the consumer. . . .

FORD: On page two, we ought to hold this for further study. . . . I'd be very hesitant about establishing a consumer-representative office in every department. Your agency head is going to lose control. . . . We ought to get better titles for things. The Democrats come up with titles like Model Cities, and we come up with the Ocean Dumping Act. . . . (*Considerably later, after discussion of nineteen of twenty-four options:*) I must say, on the basis of what we've been talking about, I can't see justification for sending up a message on consumer protection. . . .

In the end, Marsh suggests that at a Cabinet meeting the President might "mandate the departments to concern themselves with consumer considerations." The President adds that he might then also write letters to the chairmen of the appropriate committees, on the need for certain reforms in the regulatory agencies.

So much for the faraway consumer.

6:55 P.M. Rumsfeld and Cheney come in together for the evening cleanup. At one point:

RUMSFELD: This is just something to think about. It occurred to me after our meeting this morning with Ron [Nessen] that began as a session where he could get guidance from you, and then the Congressional side came in, so Max [Friedersdorf] could get guidance, then other voices were added, so that now it has become a kind of senior staff meeting. This morning it was scheduled for fifteen minutes and lasted an hour.

FORD: This morning the circumstances were rather special.

RUMSFELD: That's true. That's true. But what I'm wondering is whether there shouldn't be a regular senior staff meeting in place of that. And whether we shouldn't get in a somewhat different cast of characters — Jim Lynn, Brent, Jack, Bob. It's fine for Ron to come to you and get your position on things, beyond which he wouldn't go.

FORD: As long as he could get some input from you and others besides myself —

RUMSFELD: Sure. He does that all day every day. . . . Maybe the senior staff meeting should be followed by a smaller group in here with you.

CHENEY: Or perhaps you should preside over the senior staff group.

FORD: Always remembering that I get more out of a meeting with several people than just one.

RUMSFELD: I'm just thinking of the most efficient use of your time.

FORD: Why don't you think it through and come up with a plan?

7:20 P.M. Mr. Ford leaves for the residence. Today he spent four minutes less in his office than yesterday.

SECTION C. THE PRESIDENT, THE CONGRESS, AND ENERGY POLICY

EDITED BY JOHN BRIGHAM AND LARRY PRESTON

In assessing Gerald Ford's performance in December of 1975, eight months after his week observing the President, John Hersey noted Ford's "conviction that the threat to his tenure comes from the right, from Ronald Reagon." Hersey believed that this perception had "wiped out any hope there may have been ... that his early undertakings to work with Congress in a spirit of compromise might move him toward the center."[1] In the following materials, the President's role in policy formation has been traced from early speeches, through confrontation with Congress, to ultimate compromise. Presidential statements on energy and related congressional activities from late in 1974 to the end of 1975 show that his policy initiatives had roots lying well within the framework set by his predecessor. Ford's policy, like Nixon's, had always been favorable to the "right," and it was largely due to congressional resistance on this very sensitive domestic issue, and a perception that it hurt him in the area of the country where his support from party leaders was strongest, that the President came to believe the Reagan threat was no longer insurmountable.

In setting the framework for discussion of energy and functioning as an initiator, the President was able to minimize, postpone, and rationalize hardships resulting from his policies. There were elements of the plan which worked to minimize this reaction. The response to energy as a policy issue, built by President Ford on an inherited foundation, bridged the domestic and foreign policy field. It has traditionally been to the President's advantage to treat issues as matters of "foreign"

[1] *The New York Times Magazine*, December 28, 1975, p. 39.

policy because the country has been predisposed to grant him greater freedom in this area. But energy is clearly an important domestic issue as well and, as such, in 1975, it was an issue handled with attention to the domestic political situation, particularly a primary challenge from a very conservative opponent.

When Gerald Ford became the President of the United States on 9 August 1974, he inherited the Nixon energy policy. Referred to as "Project Independence," the Nixon plan had been proposed in response to the sense of crisis following the escalation of oil prices in the fall of 1973. The underlying interpretation of the crisis assumed that Arab policy rather than that of the American oil cartel was responsible. Nixon thus called for energy independence for the United States by 1980, issued a number of executive orders emphasizing conservation of existing supplies, and requested cutbacks in the use of oil. President Ford's first major statement on oil policy fixed the blame on the oil Producing and Exporting Countries (OPEC) and linked energy policy to America's sovereign independence and world peace. Although accepting a framework that raised a specter of struggle with foreign powers, President Ford also realized that the key to increased production from American corporations was higher prices. The challenge was to get this unpopular solution accepted by the Congress and the American electorate immediately prior to an election year. The following public statements reveal this debate.

Speaking at the Ninth World Energy Conference in Detroit on 23 September 1974, Ford stated his belief that:[1]

> Sovereign nations try to avoid dependence on other nations that exploit their own resources to the detriment of others. Sovereign nations cannot allow their policies to be dictated, or their fate decided, by artificial rigging and distortion of world commodity markets.
>
> ... We recognize the desires of the producers to earn a fair price for their oil as a means of helping to develop their own economies. But exorbitant prices can only distort the world economy, run the risk of worldwide depression and threaten the breakdown of world order and safety.
>
> It is difficult to discuss the energy problem without lapsing into doomsday language. The danger is clear. It is severe. I am nevertheless optimistic. The advantages of cooperation are as visible as the dangers of confrontation. And that gives me hope as well as optimism.

Speculation concerning the possibility of American military actions

---

[1]As reported in *The New York Times*, 24 September 1974, p. 12.

against OPEC followed the speech. Secretary of Defense James R. Schlesinger issued a guarded denial that any military actions were being considered. But, in waving the flag, the President had also waved the "big stick."

Following the application of "diplomatic" pressure, Ford turned to the domestic aspects of energy independence. In his Presidential Address on the Economy to a Joint Session of the Congress on 8 October 1974, Ford asserted that:

> One-third of our oil — 17 percent of America's total energy — now comes from foreign sources that we cannot control, at high cartel prices costing you and me $16 billion — $16 billion more than just a year ago.
>
> The primary solution has to be at home. If you have forgotten the shortages of last winter, most Americans have not.
>
> Priority legislation — action, I should say — to increase energy supply here at home requires the following:
>
> One, long-sought deregulation of natural gas supplies,
>
> Number two, responsible use of our Naval petroleum reserves in California and Alaska,
>
> Number three, amendments to the Clean Air Act; and
>
> Four, passage of surface mining legislation to ensure an adequate supply with commonsense environmental protection.
>
> Now, if all of these steps fail to meet our current energy-saving goals, I will not hesitate to ask for tougher measures.

Ford's plan to stress the increase of domestic supplies over the alternative of energy conservation was challenged by the findings of a Ford Foundation "Energy Project," which was released on 17 October 1974. The conflict between increasing supply and conservation is said to have led to an administrative shake-up announced on 29 October 1974. Dr. John Sawhill was ousted as Federal Energy Administrator in a move interpreted by many as having been initiated by Secretary of the Interior Morton, under pressure from oil company lobbyists. Sawhill had long advocated energy conservation and increasing fuel excise taxes as a means to reduce energy dependence, while Morton faithfully advocated the attempt to increase production. The new administrator and his chief assistant both had oil industry backgrounds. Frank Zarb, Sawhill's successor, had previously been connected with the oil industry as a management trainee with the Cities Service Company for four years. Melvin Conant, the assistant, left a position at Exxon to be a member of the Ford Administration.

The persistent theme in Ford's energy campaign would be the charge that America's energy capacity was directly related to her ability to carry out a leadership role in the "free world." The first indication of Ford's policy came on 3 December 1974, in an address to the American Conference on Trade. Speaking in support of passage of the Trade Reform Act, Ford claimed that "the central issue of trade reform is the close interrelationship between the domestic economy" and "economic international relations."

The phrases "national destiny" and "national security" were used again in the President's Address to the nation on 13 January 1975. In this address, Ford outlined the energy and economic proposals that he would deliver to the Congress in his State of the Union message two days later. The plan was a marked contrast to his previous attempt to solve the energy issue through development of new supplies. In recognizing the necessity of gaining approval for his proposals from a Democratic Congress, Ford proposed a "more comprehensive program of energy conservation taxes on oil and natural gas" and referred to his program as "my national energy conservation plan."[1]

Americans are no longer in full control of their own national destiny, when that destiny depends on uncertain foreign fuel at high prices fixed by others. Higher energy costs compound both inflation and recession, and dependence on others for future energy supplies is intolerable to our national security.

This plan requires personal sacrifice. But if we all pitch in, we will meet our goal of reducing foreign oil imports by one million barrels a day by the end of this year and by two million barrels before the end of 1977. The energy conservation measures I have outlined tonight will be supplemented by use of Presidential powers to limit oil imports as necessary to fully achieve these goals.

By 1985 — 10 years from now — the United States will be invulnerable to foreign energy disruptions or oil embargoes such as we experienced last year. Of course, our domestic needs come first. But our gains in energy independence will be fully coordinated with our friends abroad. Our efforts should prompt similar action by our allies.

If Congress speedily enacts this national energy program, there will be no need for compulsory rationing or long waiting lines at the service station. Yes, gasoline prices will go up, though not as much as with a 20-cent-a-gallon tax. Furthermore, the burden of the conservation taxes on oil will be shared by all petroleum users, not just motorists.

---

[1]President's Address to the Nation, 13 January 1975. *Weekly Compilation*, vol. 11, no. 3, p. 41.

The following article from *The New York Times* of January 15, 1975, summarizes the response to the President's proposals from a number of groups.[1]

Reaction to the Proposals

Some Congressional Democrats agreed with the Administration's proposal to cut taxes, but some said low- and middle-income groups should derive more benefits. Some members of Congress, particularly from New England, were critical of proposed oil tariffs.

Business and financial executives, as well as economists and labor leaders, gave the President's economic program a lukewarm reception. Some applauded the program, but many saw the pump-priming as inflationary and said they were worried about large Federal deficits.

Utility and petrochemical industry officials reacted angrily to the energy program, and real estate owners and developers were critical as well. Oil companies reacted blandly, while economists said the program would have an inflationary effect.

Auto executives said they were pleased with the package since it contained most of the proposals they had been advocating to save energy and turn the economy around. Some seemed reassured that they would not have to bear the full burden of energy conservation.

Consumers in a dozen cities said they would use their tax rebates to pay off old bills, for savings, or to buy something luxurious. Many felt that higher gasoline and oil prices would cancel out the one-shot bonanza, however.

In his State of the Union Message to Congress on 15 January 1975, Ford presented his "comprehensive energy plan." He stressed that his executive measures were only interim ones until Congress devised a compromise plan of its own.

The Economic disruptions we and others are experiencing stems in part from the fact that the world price of petroleum has quadrupled in the last year. But, in all honesty, we cannot put all of the blame on the oil exporting nations. We, the United States, are not blameless. Our growing dependence upon foreign sources has been adding to our vulnerability for years and years. And we did nothing to prepare ourselves for such an event as the embargo of 1973.

I am proposing a program which will begin to restore our country's surplus capacity in total energy. In this way, we will be able to assure ourselves reliable and adequate energy and help foster a new world energy stability for other major consuming nations.

But this nation and, in fact, the world must face the prospect of energy

[1]*The New York Times*, January 15, 1975. © 1975 by The New York Times Company. Reprinted by permission.

difficulties between now and 1985. This program will impose burdens on all of us with the aim of reducing our consumption of energy and increasing our production. Great attention has been paid to the considerations of fairness, and I can assure you that the burdens will not fall more harshly on those less able to bear them.

I am recommending a plan to make us invulnerable to cutoffs of foreign oil. It will require sacrifices. But it — and this is most important — it will work.

I have set the following national energy goals to assure that our future is as secure and as productive as our past:

First, we must reduce oil imports by one million barrels per day by the end of this year and by two million barrels per day by the end of 1977.

Second, we must end vulnerability to economic disruption by foreign suppliers by 1985.

Third, we must develop our energy technology and resources so that the United States has the ability to supply a significant share of the energy needs of the free world by the end of this century.

To attain these objectives, we need immediate action [on] our imports. Unfortunately, in the short-term there are only a limited number of actions which can increase domestic supply. I will press for all of them.

I urge quick action on the necessary legislation to allow commercial production at the Elk Hills, Calif., Naval Petroleum Reserve. In order that we make greater use of domestic coal resources, I am submitting amendments to the Energy Supply and Environmental Coordination Act which will greatly increase the number of power plants that can be promptly converted to coal.

Obviously, voluntary conservation continues to be essential, but tougher programs are needed — and needed now. Therefore, I am using Presidential powers to raise the fee on all imported crude oil and petroleum products.

Crude oil fee levels will be increased $1 per barrel on Feb. 1, by $2 per barrel on March 1 and by $3 per barrel on April 1. I will take action to reduce undue hardship on any geographical region.

The foregoing are interim administration actions. They will be rescinded when the broader but necessary legislation is enacted.

To that end, I am requesting the Congress to act within 90 days on a more comprehensive energy tax program. It includes:

• Excise taxes and import fees totaling $2 per barrel on product imports and on all crude oil.

• Deregulation of new natural gas and enactment of a natural gas excise tax.

• I plan to take Presidential initiative to decontrol the price of domestic crude oil on April 1.

• I urge the Congress to enact a windfall profits tax by that date to ensure that oil producers do not profit unduly.

The sooner Congress acts, the more effective the oil conservation program will be and the quicker the Federal revenues can be returned to our people.

I am prepared to use Presidential authority to limit imports, as necessary, to guarantee success.

I want you to know that before deciding on my energy conservation program, I considered rationing and higher gasoline taxes as alternatives. In my judgment, neither would achieve the desired results and both would produce unacceptable inequities.

A massive program must be initiated to increase energy supply, to cut demand and provide new stand-by emergency programs to achieve the independence we want by 1983.

The largest part of increased oil production must come from our new frontier areas on the outer continental shelf and from the Naval Petroleum Reserve No. 4 in Alaska. It is the intent of this Administration to move ahead with exploration, leasing and production on those frontier areas of the outer continental shelf where the environmental risks are acceptable.

Use of our most abundant domestic resource — coal — is severely limited. We must strike a reasonable compromise on environmental concerns with coal. I am submitting clean air amendments which will allow greater coal use without sacrificing clean air goals.

I vetoed the strip-mining legislation passed by the last Congress. With appropriate changes, I will sign a revised version when it comes to the White House.

I am proposing a number of actions to energize our nuclear power program. I will submit legislation to expedite nuclear leasing and the rapid selection of sites.

In recent months, utilities have canceled or postponed over 60 percent of planned nuclear expansion and 30 percent of planned additions to non-nuclear capacity.

Financing problems for that industry are worsening. I am therefore recommending that the one-year investment tax credit of 12 percent be extended an additional two years to specifically speed the construction of power plants that do not use natural gas or oil. I am also submitting proposals for selective reform of state utility commission regulations.

To provide the critical stability for our domestic energy production in the face of world price uncertainty, I will request legislation to authorize and require tariffs, import quotas or price floors to protect our energy prices at levels which will achieve energy independence.

Increasing energy supplies is not enough. We must take additional steps to cut long-term consumption. I therefore propose to the Congress:

• Legislation to make thermal efficiency standards mandatory for all new buildings in the United States.

• A new tax credit of up to $150 for those homeowners who install insulation equipment.

• The establishment of an energy conservation program to help low-income families purchase insulation supplies.

• Legislation to modify and defer automotive pollution standards for five years which will enable us to improve new automobile gas mileage by 40 percent by 1980.

These proposals and actions, cumulatively, can reduce our dependence on foreign energy supplies to three to five million barrels per day by 1985.

To make the United States invulnerable to foreign disruption, I propose stand-by emergency legislation and a strategic storage program of one billion barrels of oil for domestic needs and 300 million barrels for national defense purposes.

I will ask for the funds needed for energy research and development activities. I have established a goal of one million barrels of synthetic fuels and shale oil production per day by 1985 together with an incentive program to achieve it.

I have a very deep belief in America's capabilities. Within the next 10 years, my program envisions:

- 200 major nuclear power plants.
- 250 major new coal mines.
- 150 major coal-fired power plants.
- 30 major new refineries.
- 20 major new synthetic fuel plants.
- The drilling of many thousands of new oil wells.
- The insulation of 18 million homes.
- And the manufacturing and the sale of millions of new automobiles, trucks and buses that use much less fuel.

. . .

The whole world is watching to see how we respond.

A resurgent American economy would do more to restore the confidence of the world in its own future than anything else we can do. The program that this Congress passes can demonstrate to the world that we have started to put our own house in order. If we can show that this nation is able and willing to help other nations meet the common challenge, it can demonstrate that the United States will fulfill its responsibility as a leader among nations.

Quite frankly, at stake is the future of the industrialized democracies, which have perceived their destiny in common and sustained it in common for 30 years.

The Democrats in Congress of course responded before the whole world, and they may have been thinking more of their reelection in the next year. That was certainly not wide of the mark for Senator Henry Jackson, whose Senate committee was crucial to the development of legislation dealing with natural resources. Jackson's committee staff prepared the following response.

ECONOMIC ANALYSIS OF PRESIDENT FORD'S
ENERGY PROGRAM

Summary

The short-term impact on the economy of the President's energy proposals is tremendous. The cost of energy will rise in one year by over $40
billion, an amount greater than the steep increase initiated during the Arab
embargo. The impact will be absorbed by an economy already facing recession and double digit inflation. Costs to low- and middle-income households will soak up 5 to 10 percent of before-tax income under either of the
programs which the President has proposed: the one he can implement
independent of Congress or the program which he has asked Congress
to enact.

Both proposals have as their goal the reduction of energy consumption
through a broad increase in energy prices which is being applied without
regard for the degree of flexibility available to consumers to initiate conservation in the short run. The removal of energy prices from control in-
sures that the price of all energy consumed in the United States will be
affected directly by OPEC pricing policies.

Over the long run the impact of higher prices could be absorbed in normal economic growth and consumers would be able to adjust gradually to
signals which slowly rising prices would send by choosing not to consume
energy and by increasing the efficiency of use for the energy which they
do consume. The present administration proposal attempts to achieve
long-term energy goals in the short run, and in doing so, threatens the
quality of life of the large number of families for whom added energy
costs and energy induced inflation mean substantially reduced purchasing
power.

A number of economists feel that an increase in basic energy costs of
$1.00 is transformed, as it "ripples" through the economy, into $1.50 to
$2.00 in increased consumer costs. Thus, under this hypothesis, the ul-
timate cost of $30 billion annually which the administration itself ascribes
to its program would be transformed into $45 to $60 billion by the time it

SOURCE: From *Economic Analysis of President Ford's Energy Program*, a staff
analysis prepared by Arlon Tussing, Chief Economist, 2nd Benjamin Cooper,
Professional Staff Member, at the request of Senator Henry Jackson, Chairman,
Committee on Interior and Insular Affairs, pursuant to Senate Resolution 45,
the National Fuels and Energy Policy Study, February 4, 1975. Reprinted in
Economic Impact of President Ford's Energy Program, Ser. 94–6 (92–96).

reaches consumers. The analysis which follows does not include any estimate of ripple effects. Only a direct dollar-for-dollar passthrough of energy
costs is assumed. The operation of a ripple effect would therefore increase
each cost estimate which follows by at least 50 percent.

Program To Be Implemented By Executive Order

The energy pricing proposals announced in the State of the Union message which (1) can be implemented by the President without any additional
grant of authority by the Congress and (2) do not require congressional
approval, would cost the U.S. consumers an additional $33.5 billion on an
annual basis. This cost includes (1) direct increases in the price of petroleum which result from Presidential action, and (2) induced increases in
the prices of alternate fuels which compete, at the margin, with imported
and uncontrolled oil.

Impact of Ford Energy Program on Consumers in Various Income Groups

Precise estimation of the detailed impact of the energy program proposed
by the administration is complicated . . . by the absence of reliable data
describing the consumption of energy at the household level in American
society. Calculations using average figures for the country as a whole ignore
significant regional differences in energy use, such as the relatively heavy
dependence of New England on imported fuel oil for electricity generation
and home heating, the widespread use of unregulated natural gas in gas-
producing States and the importance of relatively cheap hydroelectric power
in the Northwest. Thus, national averages often substantially obscure cata-
strophic regional impacts of specific events or policies affecting energy.

When the average impact of a policy nationally is as large as that of the
administration's present energy pricing proposals, truly substantial regional
dislocations and other cost impacts are bound to occur. Thus, the figures
quoted below will often significantly underestimate impacts in places where
dependence on oil and unregulated natural gas is heavy.

Any projection of additional costs to U.S. consumers from the administration program depends on a variety of assumptions including those regarding levels of production, pricing decisions by sellers of alternate fuels,
and the flexibility of contracts between producers and consumers. Moreover, the added costs to be expected in 1975 are surely less than those
which will be imposed in later years as the producers free themselves from
long-term agreements negotiated at pre-1974 prices, and dislocation costs

and markups in excess of dollar-for-dollar fuel cost passthrough are reflected in prices to consumers.

Estimates of the annual impact of acceptance of the administration's program range from $40 billion to over $60 billion as the ultimate cost. An administration spokesman's estimate of $55 billion was quoted by the UPI wire service on January 14, 1975.

None of these estimates include the effect of a further price increase by the OPEC cartel in the future in response to the U.S. import tariff. Each such dollar per barrel increase is estimated to add approximately $8 billion more to the annual energy bill for U.S. consumers.

These energy costs, whether they amount to $40 billion per year, $50 billion per year or, ultimately, much more, represent nothing less than a major escalation in the basic cost of all fossil fuels consumed in the United States. This escalation, moreover, is entirely comparable to the shock received only a year ago from OPEC; the major difference is that this second major quantum jump in the cost of energy for consumers arrives at a time when the United States economy is in a deepening recession.

The annual cost of 850 gallons of gasoline — 16 gallons per week — could increase from $85 to $120. The price of 8,000 kilowatt-hours of electricity would increase by $40 on the average and as much as $80 in areas heavily dependent on oil and unregulated natural gas. These increases, contoured to the price of fuels and electricity purchased directly by households total to approximately $250 which administration representatives have indicated is the average cost of their program to American households. However, this estimate is a clear misrepresentation of the real impact of the program on the American household. Using the total number of households in the United States, approximately 70 million, the total cost of the program, derived from this administration estimate amounts to only $17.5 billion, much less than the other administration estimates of the total cost. Thus, $250 is only a third of the real cost of the program to an average American family. The difference is that this estimate includes only direct purchases of fuels and electricity by households. The additional impact of energy costs because of their passthrough in the price of all goods and services dependent on energy, is nearly three times as large as the direct purchases of fuels and electricity by households. These costs all reach the consumer; no one else pays them. Indirect energy costs arise from the increased prices for every item which must be transported before it is sold: food, clothing, construction materials, manufactured goods. Indirect energy costs arise from increases in the price of basic materials which are produced with a large energy input: glass, steel, cement, aluminum, petrochemicals.

Thus, the impact on the average American family of the administration energy pricing program is not $250 per year; it is at least three times that figure. This projection is an average for all families. Yet not all families consume the same amount of energy, nor do they possess similar abilities to pay for it. A study carried out by the Washington Center for Metropolitan studies for the Ford Foundation's energy policy project estimated direct and indirect energy use in families in different income categories for the year ending June 1975 . . . .

. . . For a poor family, approximately $125 in increased costs for direct energy purchases corresponds to nearly $340 in increased costs when purchases of nonfuel goods and services are accounted for. For middle-income families, $200 to $250 in increased costs for direct purchases of fuels and electricity become $500 to $700 in total cost increases per family when all purchases are considered. For well-off families the total cost will be in excess of the average cost.

. . . The poor must find extra cash to pay for a third as much energy as the well off, yet they must find this cash in an income which is on the average, only [a] 6th to a 10th as large. Thus, the basic requirements for food, shelter, heat, transportation, and essential clothing and manufactured goods place a floor on energy requirements which does not respect relative ability to pay. When basic energy prices increase, the burden falls much more heavily in proportion to ability to pay on the poor.

. . . Added energy costs which the President's program would provide for will reduce the purchasing of the poor by over 11 percent while for the well off, only 3 percent of income will be affected.

On 23 January, President Ford signed Proclamation 4341, which put into effect the first phase of his oil fee plan to discourage importation and consumption. The legality of the action was based on a section of the Trade Expansion Act of 1962, which purportedly gave the President the power to dictate tariffs when, on the advice of the Secretary of the Treasury, he felt that the continued importation of certain products threatened to "impair the national security." The proclamation stated, in part:

Whereas the Director of the Office of Civil and Defense Mobilization found pursuant to Section 2 of the Act of July 1, 1954, as amended (19 U.S.C. 1352a), "that crude oil and the principal crude oil derivatives and products are being imported in such quantities and under such circumstances as to threaten to impair the national security";

Whereas, pursuant to Section 232 of the Trade Expansion Act of 1962, as amended (19 U.S.C. 1862), the Secretary of the Treasury having made an appropriate investigation to determine the effects on the national security of imports of crude oil and the principal crude oil derivatives and products and having considered the matters required by him to be considered by the Trade Expansion Act of 1962, as amended, has reported the findings of his investigation and has advised me that crude oil, the principal crude oil derivative and products, and related products derived from natural gas and coal tar, are being imported in such quantities and under such circumstances as to threaten to impair the national security and has recommended that I take action to reduce such imports;

. . .

Whereas, I judge it necessary and consistent with the national security to further discourage importation into the United States of petroleum, petroleum products, and related products, in such quantities or under such circumstances as to threaten to impair the national security; to create conditions favorable to domestic crude oil production needed for projected national security requirements; and to increase the capacity of domestic refineries and petrochemical plants to meet such requirements; and to encourage the development of other sources of energy; and

Whereas, in order to achieve the above objectives, I determine that a supplemental fee should be imposed on all imports of petroleum and petroleum products, and that certain other changes in the existing license fee system be made;

Now, therefore, I, Gerald R. Ford, President of the United States of America, acting under and by virtue of the authority vested in me by the Constitution and the laws of the United States, including Section 232 of the Trade Expansion Act of 1962, as amended, do hereby proclaim that, effective as of February 1, 1975, a new system of oil import fees is instituted, and accordingly, Proclamation No. 3279, as amended, is hereby further amended as follows:

Section 1. Subparagraph (1) of paragraph (a) of section 3 is amended to read as follows:

Sec. 3(a)(1). Effective February 1, 1975, the Administrator shall issue allocations and licenses subject to fees, on imports of crude oil, unfinished oils, and finished products. Such licenses shall require, among other appropriate provisions, that:

(i) with respect to imports of crude oil and natural gas products, over and above the levels of imports established in Section 2 of this Proclamation, such fees shall be $0.21 per barrel;

(ii) with respect to imports of motor gasoline, unfinished oils, and all other finished products (except ethane, propane, butanes, and asphalt), over and above the levels of imports established in Section 2 of this Proclamation, such fees shall be $0.63 per barrel;

(iii) with respect to imports of crude oil, natural gas products, unfinished oils, and all other finished products (except ethane, propane, butanes, and asphalt) entered into the customs territory of the United States on or after February 1, 1975, there shall be a supplemental fee per barrel, of $1.00, rising to $2.00 on imports entered on or after March 1, 1975, and to $3.00 on imports entered on or after April 1, 1975.

. . .

In Witness Whereof, I have hereunto set my hand this twenty-third day of January, in the year of our Lord nineteen hundred seventy-five, and of the Independence of the United States of America the one hundred and ninety-ninth.

Gerald R. Ford

With the signing of this executive proclamation, Ford challenged Congress to devise its own comprehensive measure or pass his plan substantially intact. Following a meeting with northeastern state governors on 23 January, Ford was questioned by reporters. His responses reflected what seemed to be almost an obsession to prod Congress to act, particularly when he persisted in answering successive questions with the same general answer:[1]

Q: Mr. President, you spoke recently of compromise with Congress, not quibbling over details. When Congress — some of the Democratic Congressmen asked for you to delay your proclamation, you refused to delay it. Is that compromise?

THE PRESIDENT: The Congress is in session. The Congress has an opportunity to act on my program or produce their own, and if the Congress produces an equitable, comprehensive plan, of course I will consider it. But the time for action is now. We have diddled and dawdled long enough. We have to have an energy program in this country, and the only way I know to get it is to take the action that I took, which has, incidentally, produced more action within the last 10 days on energy than I have seen in the last 2 or 3 years.

Q: Do you think the Congress is going to be fast in acting on this program?

THE PRESIDENT: All I can say is the Congress can act fast, and I hope they do.

. . .

Q: Mr. President, are you at all concerned that the Governors do not seem to have been convinced when they left here?

THE PRESIDENT: Well, there is an honest difference of opinion. I respect their views, and I trust they respect mine.

[1]*Weekly Compilation*, vol. 11, no. 4, pp. 86–88.

Q: If this becomes a nationwide reaction, what hope is there for progress?

THE PRESIDENT: Well, the Congress has the opportunity to act. The Congress is in session, and the Congress can act on my plan or if they have an alternative plan that is action and equitable, then the Congress has carried out its function. But the Congress right now has the responsibility to act affirmatively.

Q: The Governor of Maine says that you seem to be isolated and listening to just your own aides on this issue.

THE PRESIDENT: I looked at a number of volumes of alternative proposals, a number of options. I analyzed the various options. And after a thorough study and a great deal of consultation, I have put together a comprehensive plan.

Now, what we need as an alternative, if they don't like this, is something as comprehensive, as equitable. And I hope the Congress will take the initiative.

Q: Mr. President, you have indicated a willingness to compromise?

THE PRESIDENT: I have indicated a willingness to compromise, but the Congress has to act in order to have any compromise.

Later that same day, in a televised NBC news interview with John Chancellor and Tom Brokaw, Ford again chastised Congress, reaffirmed his belief in acting decisively, and amended his earlier "self-sufficiency" goal to state that by 1985 the United States should be importing about 10 percent of its needs as compared to the 37 percent it imported in early 1975.

Actions taken by both the President and the Democratic leadership from March until the passage of the Omnibus Energy Bill in December of 1975 added to the confusion caused by the seeming inconsistency between Administration statements that high OPEC prices for oil were threatening the industrial democracies and the Administration's tariff on imported oil. It was a period of stalemate between the executive and the legislature. In early March, the major Democratic proposal was delivered on the floor of the House by Representative Al Ullman of Oregon. Though it was considered by many Democrats to be harsh, the Ullman plan was actually favored by Treasury Secretary Simon and Energy Administrator Zarb over an earlier plan of the House and Senate leadership. The plan differed significantly from the Ford program in its call for institution of steep gas taxes, taxation of "gas-guzzling" automobiles, adoption of an allocation system, and a five- to eight-year decontrol program.

On the same day that Ullman revealed his proposal, Zarb revealed that the Administration and the Ways and Means Committee had achieved "60% agreement" on a compromise program. An article by Edward Cowan in the 18 March 1975 issue of the *New York Times* reported Zarb's statement as "calculated indirect support" for the Ullman plan. However, according to Zarb, the compromise did not extend to Ullman's gas tax proposals. Zarb also suggested that the President had abandoned his goal of cutting oil imports in 1975 by 1 million barrels a day and from then on would concentrate on his 1977 target cut of 2 million.

Ford noted the progress made by the Democratic Congress in remarks following his veto of H.R. 1767. The bill would have suspended the President's authority to impose fees on imported oil for a period of 90 days. At the same time, however, Ford made a gesture of cooperation by signing Proclamation 4355, which postponed the March and April fee hikes in order to give Congress the opportunity to iron out details in its plan. In part he stated:

Last Friday, the majority leaders of the Senate and House asked me to delay scheduled increases in the import fees on foreign oil for 60 days while they work out the specifics of an energy policy they have jointly produced. Their policy blueprint differs considerably from my energy program as well as from the energy legislation now being considered by the House Committee on Ways and Means.

I welcome such initiative in the Congress and agree to a deferral until May 1, 1975. The important thing is that the Congress is finally moving on our urgent national energy problem. I am, therefore, amending my proclamation to postpone the effect of the scheduled increases for two months while holding firm to the principles I have stated. It is also my intention not to submit a plan for decontrol of old domestic oil before May 1.

I hope the House and Senate will have agreed to a workable and comprehensive national energy legislation.

But we must use every day of those two months to develop and adopt an energy program. Also, I seek a legislative climate for immediate action on the tax reductions I have requested. It is my fervent wish that we can now move from points of conflict to areas of agreement.

I will do nothing to delay the speedy enactment by the Congress of straight-forward income tax cuts and credits by the end of this month.

Under present conditions, any delay in rebating dollars to consumers and letting businessmen and farmers expand, modernize and create more jobs is intolerable.

I do not believe the Congress will endanger the future of all Americans. I am confident that the legislative branch will work with me in the Nation's highest interests.

What we need now is a simple tax cut and then a comprehensive energy plan to end our dependence on foreign oil.

What we *don't* need is a time-wasting *test* of strength between the Congress and the President. What we *do* need is a *show* of strength that the United States government can act decisively and with dispatch.

GERALD R. FORD
The White House,
March 4, 1975

In addition to this gesture, Ford signed the tax-cut bill which repealed the 22 percent oil and gas depletion allowance on 29 March 1975. However, a close reading of the bill revealed many loopholes, exemptions, and gradual measures that tended to lessen its impact.

Despite these actions by the President, the stalemate continued through March and April. In a letter to the Speaker of the House and the President of the Senate, Ford expressed his disappointment in Congress' failure to have passed energy legislation by that time. The two-year phase out of price controls mentioned in the letter was later described by Zarb as an Administration concession to Congress, despite the fact that congressional leaders were talking about a minimum five-year phase out period. In part, the letter stated:

April 30, 1975

Dear Mr. Speaker: (Dear Mr. President:)

Three and one-half months have passed since I presented the Nation and the Congress with a comprehensive program to achieve energy independence by 1985. Although the policy I put forth was not an easy solution, it was, and remains today, the only comprehensive and workable national energy program . . . .

I am hopeful that the weeks ahead can result in agreement between the Congress and the Administration. I believe it can if we are willing to work diligently, honestly, and more rapidly. But I am concerned about the possibility of the Congress passing politically popular legislation which will not only fail to meet our energy needs but which could create serious economic problems for the Nation. From my many years in the Congress, I know how easy it is to become embroiled in endless debate over tough decisions. I also know how easy it is for the Congress to enact legislation full of rhetoric and high sounding purpose, but short of substance. That must *not* happen in this case.

Neither the House nor the Senate has passed one significant energy measure acceptable to the Administration in these past few months. Hence, I must be a realist — since the time before final legislation will be on my desk is very long. I understand that in many ways the timing and substance is beyond the control of the individual committee chairmen. Yet, postponement of action on my part is not the answer. I am, therefore, taking these administration actions at this time:

First, I have directed the Federal Energy Administrator to implement a program to steadily phase out price controls on old oil over two years, starting June 1, 1975. . . .

Second, I will again defer the second dollar import fee on crude oil and the $.60 per barrel fee on imported petroleum products in order to continue the spirit of compromise with the Congress. However, I will be forced to impose the higher fees in 30 days, or sooner, if the House and Senate fail to move rapidly on the type of comprehensive legislation which is necessary to resolve our critical energy situation. Such legislation must not embody punitive tax measures or mandated, artificial shortages, which could have significant economic impact and be an unwarranted intrusion on individual freedom of choice.

. . . To the extent comprehensive and effective legislation is passed by the Congress, I stand ready to approve it. What I cannot do is stand by as more time passes and our import vulnerability grows. If this happens, I will not hesitate to impose the higher import fees. Meantime, my administrative actions must fill the gap in this endeavor. The country can afford no less.

Sincerely,
GERALD R. FORD

On 27 May 1975, Ford attacked Congress' "do-nothing" approach in a nationally televised address. He seemed to be moving toward his old position of seeking a solution through increased domestic supply rather than conservation. His decontrol proposal, his request for a plowback incentive for exploration, and his criticism of congressional concentration on conservation measures such as the gas tax all suggested this new shift in emphasis.[1]

Good evening.

Last January 15, I went before your Senators and Representatives in

[1]*Weekly Compilation*, vol. 11, no. 22, pp. 563–565.

Congress with a comprehensive plan to make our country independent of foreign sources of energy by 1985. Such a program was long overdue. We have become increasingly at the mercy of others for the fuel on which our entire economy runs.

· · ·

I asked the Congress in January to enact this urgent 10-year program for energy independence within 90 days, that is, by mid-April.

In the meantime, to get things going, I said I would use the standby Presidential authority granted by the Congress to reduce our use of foreign petroleum by raising import fees on each barrel of crude oil by one dollar on February 1, another dollar on March 1, and a third on April 1.

As soon as Congress acted on my comprehensive energy program, I promised to take off these import fees. I imposed the first dollar on oil imports February 1, making appropriate exemptions for hardship situations.

Now, what did the Congress do in February about energy? Congress did nothing — nothing, that is, except rush through legislation suspending for 90 days my authority to impose any import fees on foreign oil. Congress needed time, they said.

· · ·

What did the Congress do in March? What did the Congress do in April about energy? Congress did nothing.

In fairness, I must say there were diligent efforts by some Members — Democrats as well as Republicans — to fashion meaningful energy legislation in their subcommittees and committees. My administration worked very hard with them to bring a real energy independence bill to a vote. At the end of April, the deadline set by the Congressional leaders themselves, I deferred for still another 30 days, the second one dollar fee on imported oil. Even then, I still hoped for positive Congressional action.

So, what has the Congress done in May about energy? Congress did nothing and went home for a 10-day recess.

February, March, April, May — as of now, the Congress has done nothing positive to end our energy dependence.

On the contrary, it has taken two negative actions: The first an attempt to prevent the President from doing anything on his own, the second, to pass a strip mining bill which would reduce domestic coal production instead of increasing it, put thousands of people out of work, needlessly increase the cost of energy to consumers, raise electric bills for many, and compel us to import more foreign oil, not less.

I was forced to veto this anti-energy bill last week because I will not be responsible for taking one step backward on energy when the Congress will not take one step forward on energy.

The Congress has concentrated its attention on conservation measures such as a higher gasoline tax. The Congress has done little or nothing to stimulate production of new energy sources here at home.

· · ·

Four months are already lost. The Congress has acted only negatively. I must now do what I can do as President.

First, I will impose an additional one dollar import fee on foreign crude oil and 60 cents on refined products, effective June 1. I gave the Congress its 60 days plus an extra 30 days to do something — but nothing has been done since January. Higher fees will further discourage the consumption of imported fuel and may generate some constructive action when the Congress comes back.

Second, as I directed on April 30, the Federal Energy Administration has completed public hearings on decontrol of old domestic oil. I will submit a decontrol plan to Congress shortly after it reconvenes. Along with it, I will urge the Congress to pass a windfall profits tax with a plowback provision.

These two measures would prevent unfair gains by oil companies from decontrol prices, furnish a substantial incentive to increase domestic energy production, and encourage conservation.

. . .

The sudden fourfold increase in foreign oil prices and the 1973 embargo helped to throw us into this recession. We are on our way out of this recession. Another oil embargo could throw us back. We cannot continue to depend on the price and supply whims of others. The Congress cannot drift, dawdle, and debate forever with America's future.

I need your help to energize this Congress into comprehensive action. I will continue to press for my January program, which is still the only total energy program there is.

I cannot sit here idly while nothing is done. We must get on with the job right now.

Thank you and good night.

Despite the hard line adopted in this speech, a 23 July 1975 interview with reporters from the *New York Times* showed Ford more tolerant of the difficulties of securing passage of any legislation in Congress.[1]

QUESTION: You are a man of Congress, and when you came into office, into this office, you said that you wanted to have a good marriage with the Congress. It seems now that there is a separation or even a divorce impending, particularly on the energy question.

Why is it that you and the Congress can't agree on what is best in the energy problem?

THE PRESIDENT: One of the basic problems, as most members of Congress who are knowledgeable would agree, is that a President or an Administration can pull everything together in one place and put a comprehensive

[1]*New York Times*, 25 July 1975, p. 10. © 1975 by The New York Times Company. Reprinted by permission.

program together and submit it as a package. With a problem as broad-based and diverse as energy, with many things that have to be done on taxation, conservation and a whole variety of things, controls to some extent — when you send the package up, it goes to about six or eight committees up there on each side of the Hill.

I have met with the leaders, Democratic and Republican, and they recognize that this is almost an insoluble problem. They can't get any committee in both bodies that has jurisdiction to tackle the problem as broad-based as this. Each committee has its historical jurisdiction and doesn't want to give it up to another committee. That is one of the fundamental problems we find in trying to come to an agreement in this area.

The other, or another problem, is there are parochial regional differences. The people in Texas and Louisiana, Democrats or Republicans, have one philosophy. It doesn't bear a Democratic or Republican label.

Then you go up to New England. I got castigated on one of the TV shows the other night by one of my good friends, Sil Conte [Republican Representative of Massachusetts]. That is a parochial geographical problem.

Committee and Regional Problems

So you have committee problems, you have regional problems, plus a number of other problems, but those are ones that affect the Congress.

So to try and get agreement, you don't know who to deal with and if you deal with one group on one problem you have to deal with another group on another problem.

On 9 September, 1975, President Ford vetoed Senate Bill 1849, which would have extended price controls for another six months. He gave the following reasons and proceeded to grant further extensions:[1]

I have today vetoed S. 1849 which would have extended for 6 months price controls on domestic oil. So there is no question in the minds of the American people and the Congress, let me tell you why I have taken this action:
- first, to save American jobs;
- second, to protect our future economic stability and our national security;
- third, to assure that this Nation, after months and months of delay, achieves a comprehensive national energy program for future independence from foreign suppliers.

. . .

If I signed this bill continuing controls, America's start on the road to energy independence could be delayed indefinitely. I am well aware of the

[1]*Weekly Compilation*, vol. 11, no. 37, pp. 974–975.

reluctance of Members of the Congress to face up to such a very difficult problem just as an election campaign is getting underway.

For more than 8 months, I have tried to get the Members of this Congress moving on a solution to this urgent problem of national energy independence. My latest effort at a compromise with the Congress has resulted in nothing more than this proposed 6-month extension of the existing law, which is no answer at all to a program of energy independence for the United States.

. . .

During the 4 years that Federal control programs have been in operation, controls which Members of Congress now want to extend, the cost of energy to American consumers has soared, and our dependence on foreign oil has doubled. Still Congress refuses to enact a national energy program.

If this veto is sustained, I would accept a 45-day extension of controls to provide time to work with the leaders of the Congress who have again assured me they will seek an acceptable compromise during this period. If all efforts at compromise fail, I will act to ensure an orderly transition from government controls to the free market.

On 27 September 1975, OPEC announced an increase of 10 percent on the price of exported oil. Ford's response was:[1]

In my State of the Union Message in January, I warned the Members of Congress that we would become more and more vulnerable to oil price increases imposed on us by other people in other countries unless the Congress acted quickly to approve my program to free America from its dependence on foreign oil suppliers. And today's action by OPEC demonstrates vividly that my warning was accurate.

The American people should realize that Congress has refused to take any step to reduce our vulnerability to such whims of the OPEC oil cartel. So long as Congress refuses to enact a program which will allow America to produce its own energy with its own workers and to set its own prices, we will find ourselves increasingly vulnerable to OPEC.

. . .

Until Congress acts constructively, we will continue to lose American dollars and American jobs to foreign energy producers. I hope that today's OPEC action will finally get the message through to the Members of Congress that we cannot afford to remain vulnerable and without an energy policy.

On 29 September 1975, President Ford signed H.R. 9524 into law, extending the Emergency Petroleum Allocation Act from 31 August to 15 November. He pushed for adoption of his programs and ap-

[1] *Weekly Compilation*, vol. 11, no. 40, p. 1181.

peared to have come full circle tactically by renewing his original call for increasing domestic supply.[1]

I am today signing H.R. 9524, a bill extending until November 15 the Emergency Petroleum Allocation Act, which expired on August 31.

This extension of controls on domestic petroleum for 47 days carries out my part of an understanding with the leaders of the House and Senate and will provide more time for the Congress to act on a sound and mutually acceptable plan for phased decontrol or, alternatively, to pass the emergency legislation necessary to cushion the effect of immediate decontrol on certain elements of our domestic economy.

On 14 November, Congress approved a one-month extension of price controls. It was the second such extension, but Ford signed it in order to give the Democratic staff time to finalize technical points on the final energy measure with Administration representatives. There was still some doubt about whether Ford would sign the final measure. In the interim, a Gallup Poll taken from 21 to 24 November and released on 12 December showed that Ronald Reagan had overtaken Ford as a preferred Republican candidate for President in 1976. Reagan had announced that if he were President, he would not hesitate to veto the congressional energy bill. On 22 December 1975, President Ford reluctantly signed the Energy Policy and Conservation Act, thus ending a year-long fight over energy policy.

With due consideration for political expediency, the act postponed the price rise until well after the 1976 elections. Some of the provisions were reduction in the average price of domestic crude oil by $1 a barrel with a provision that after 1977 Congress may halt any fuel price increases above the inflation rate; decontrol of prices at the end of 40 months, with Congress having the option to vote new price control bills. Other major provisions established mandatory gasoline mileage standards, increasing to 27.5 miles per gallon by 1985; set efficiency standards for appliances; instituted a policy of developing strategic petroleum reserves; authorized the President to develop contingency plans for energy emergencies, which could include fuel rationing; and provided funds to guarantee loans for coal operators investing in new mines.

A comparison of the President's energy proposals as outlined in the State of the Union message in January 1975 with the provisions of

[1]Ibid., pp. 1182–83.

the final plan signed into law in December indicate the policy result of the bargaining process. The decontrol provision was postponed 40 months with congressional limits placed on Presidential actions in the interim. The immediate price rollback was contrary to the President's earlier support for a "free market." The Government Accounting Office was empowered to audit the records of the oil companies. The President admitted that a 100 million barrel a day saving by the end of 1975 was unobtainable. Even when weighed against congressional compliance with the proposals for a strategic oil reserve and relaxation of environmental standards, the final plan indicated the power wielded by Congress. When Gerald Ford tried to link his energy proposals to national defense and national honor, he failed to arouse public concern and anxiety along this dimension. The public and the Congress, who had finally disentangled themselves from the Vietnam situation, seemed far more sensitive to the domestic challenges of inflation and unemployment than to foreign threats. The President's choice was between (1) vetoing the bill because it failed to provide the decontrol of prices that both he and his major challenger for the Republican Presidential nomination advocated and (2) signing the bill in order to prevent fuel costs from soaring as the primary elections got under way. The decision to take the second alternative seems to have been based largely on political considerations.

Figures on oil resources available in March 1976 suggest the failure of this policy to stimulate a movement toward energy independence in the period immediately following the enactment of energy legislation in December 1975. Not only were total imports up, but the share of these constituted by imports from the Arab countries, which had been around 37 percent in 1974, was up to 39 percent by early 1976. Although Americans seemed to be conserving on their use of fuel, the country's reliance on imported oil continued to grow. The Federal Energy Administration maintained its commitment to independence, which it hoped to stimulate by full decontrol of prices, a lessening of environmental safeguards, and subsidies. Although a Congress controlled by the opposition party is very cautious on such sensitive matters, neither the Congress nor the President seemed willing to risk responsibility for shortages following another embargo.

Such a stalemate might indeed shift the burden of responsibility for the crisis back on the oil companies. If the issue remains dormant and shortages do not return, neither the President nor the Congress seems

Public Law 94-163
94th Congress, S. 622
December 22, 1975

An Act

To increase domestic energy supplies and availability; to restrain energy demand; to prepare for energy emergencies; and for other purposes.

Be it enacted by the Senate and House of Representatives of the United States of America in Congress assembled, That this Act may be cited as the "Energy Policy and Conservation Act".

Energy
Policy and
Conservation
Act.
42 USC 6201
note.

TABLE OF CONTENTS

Sec. 2. Statement of purposes.
Sec. 3. Definitions.

TITLE I—MATTERS RELATED TO DOMESTIC SUPPLY AVAILABILITY

PART A—DOMESTIC SUPPLY

Sec. 101. Coal conversion.
Sec. 102. Incentives to develop underground coal mines.
Sec. 103. Domestic use of energy supplies and related materials and equipment.
Sec. 104. Materials allocation.
Sec. 105. Prohibition of certain lease bidding arrangements.
Sec. 106. Production of oil or gas at the maximum efficient rate and temporary emergency production rate.

PART B—STRATEGIC PETROLEUM RESERVE

Sec. 151. Declaration of policy.
Sec. 152. Definitions.
Sec. 153. Strategic Petroleum Reserve Office.
Sec. 154. Strategic Petroleum Reserve.
Sec. 155. Early Storage Reserve.
Sec. 156. Industrial Petroleum Reserve.
Sec. 157. Regional Petroleum Reserve.
Sec. 158. Other storage reserves.
Sec. 159. Review by Congress and implementation.
Sec. 160. Petroleum products for storage in the Reserve.
Sec. 161. Drawdown and distribution of the Reserve.
Sec. 162. Coordination with import quota system.
Sec. 163. Disclosure, inspection, investigation.
Sec. 164. Naval petroleum reserves study.
Sec. 165. Annual reports.
Sec. 166. Authorization of appropriations.

TITLE II—STANDBY ENERGY AUTHORITIES

PART A—GENERAL EMERGENCY AUTHORITIES

Sec. 201. Conditions of exercise of energy conservation and rationing authorities.
Sec. 202. Energy conservation contingency plans.
Sec. 203. Rationing contingency plan.

PART B—AUTHORITIES WITH RESPECT TO INTERNATIONAL ENERGY PROGRAM

Sec. 251. International oil allocation.
Sec. 252. International voluntary agreements.
Sec. 253. Advisory committees.
Sec. 254. Exchange of information.
Sec. 255. Relationship of this title to the international energy agreement.

89 STAT. 871

42 USC 6201.

Sec. 2. The purposes of this Act are—

(1) to grant specific standby authority to the President, subject to congressional review, to impose rationing, to reduce demand for energy through the implementation of energy conservation plans, and to fulfill obligations of the United States under the international energy program;

(2) to provide for the creation of a Strategic Petroleum Reserve capable of reducing the impact of severe energy supply interruptions;

(3) to increase the supply of fossil fuels in the United States, through price incentives and production requirements;

(4) to conserve energy supplies through energy conservation programs, and, where necessary, the regulation of certain energy uses;

(5) to provide for improved energy efficiency of motor vehicles, major appliances, and certain other consumer products;

(6) to reduce the demand for petroleum products and natural gas through programs designed to provide greater availability and use of this Nation's abundant coal resources; and

(7) to provide a means for verification of energy data to assure the reliability of energy data.

DEFINITIONS

42 USC 6202.

Sec. 3. As used in this Act:

(1) The term "Administrator" means the Administrator of the Federal Energy Administration.

(2) The term "person" includes (A) any individual, (B) any corporation, company, association, firm, partnership, society, trust, joint venture, or joint stock company, and (C) the government and any agency of the United States or any State or political subdivision thereof.

(3) The term "petroleum product" means crude oil, residual fuel oil, or any refined petroleum product (including any natural liquid and any natural gas liquid product).

(4) The term "State" means a State, the District of Columbia, Puerto Rico, or any territory or possession of the United States.

(5) The term "United States" when used in the geographical sense means all of the States and the Outer Continental Shelf.

(6) The term "Outer Continental Shelf" has the same meaning as such term has under section 2 of the Outer Continental Shelf Lands Act (43 U.S.C. 1331).

(7) The term "international energy program" means the Agreement on an International Energy Program, signed by the United States on November 18, 1974, including (A) the annex entitled "Emergency Reserves", (B) any amendment to such Agreement which includes another nation as a party to such Agreement, and (C) any technical or clerical amendment to such Agreement.

(8) The term "severe energy supply interruption" means a national energy supply shortage which the President determines—

(A) is, or is likely to be, of significant scope and duration, and of an emergency nature;

(B) may cause major adverse impact on national safety or the national economy; and

(C) results, or is likely to result, from an interruption in the supply of imported petroleum products, or from sabotage or an act of God.

likely to face the issue as they were forced to in 1974–1975. If short-ages do return, and the issue again becomes a formidable one on the "policy agenda," its resolution will no doubt again be a function of who is held responsible. If the policies of the oil producing countries are seen as the cause, high prices to stimulate domestic production are more likely to be tolerated than if the American oil companies are held responsible for the shortages. In the latter case, there may again be support for controls on these very independent sources of power.

FURTHER READING FOR CHAPTER 3

Barber, Benjamin, *The Presidential Character* (Englewood Cliffs, N.J.: Prentice-Hall, 1972). A major effort to delineate the role of personality as an influence in the conduct of the office of President of the United States.

Cronin, Thomas E., *The State of the Presidency* (Boston: Little, Brown and Company, 1975). A post-Watergate assessment linking the person, the office, and the public to an explanation of the Presidency.

Oppenheimer, Bruce, *Oil in Congress* (Lexington, Mass.: Lexington Books, 1974). Discusses the pressures on Congress and the rules, procedures, and processes within which national oil policy is worked out.

Chapter 4 Agency and Advice

The Determinants of National Economic Policy

JOHN BRIGHAM AND
KENNETH M. DOLBEARE, EDITORS

The ideas of economists and political philosophers, both when they are right and when they are wrong, are more powerful than is commonly understood. . . . Practical men, who believe themselves to be quite exempt from any intellectual influences, are usually the slaves of some defunct economist. Madmen in authority, who hear voices in the air, are distilling their frenzy from some academic scribbler of a few years back.

— John Maynard Keynes[1]

Keynes recognized the power that experts in general and economists in particular have in determining what the public addresses, what it can accomplish, and what means are appropriate. Indeed, Keynes' own theories are the ones that have come to dominate national thinking in matters of economic policy. His work in the 1930s was influential in fostering a belief that government policy could stabilize the national economy. This work stimulated the development of economic indicators by which the experts claim to be able to assess the nature of the economy. Consequently, the role of experts has come to be crucial in understanding how economic policy is made and, to an even greater extent, in understanding the policy alternatives considered realistic.

Government officials have always been confident that America's political institutions could be a positive force in economic matters. The

[1]*The General Theory of Employment, Interest and Money* (New York: Harcourt, Brace, and Co., 1936), p. 383.

amount of government involvement in the economy and its beneficiaries has differed from the Revolution to the present, but involvement has been a characteristic of American politics in spite of the rhetoric of a free market. Ever since the issues of inflation and full employment have been identified and their relationship has been understood, they have generated considerable debate. Following the Depression and World War II, the nation embraced a program of monitoring and trying to influence economic trends. Institutions were established to explain the economy and to inform governmental officials about policy implications. This chapter focuses on those institutions and on the current debate over the economic planning activity of the federal government.

As a result of the Keynesian tradition, governmental attention to stable economic growth has been directed at monetary policy and fiscal policy. Those concepts dominate the institutional response to economic problems by determining the way in which officials see the choices available. Monetary policy deals with the amount of money in circulation and the credit available in the nation. The government's influence in this area derives from its control over the amount of money printed and the cost of making loans; those factors in turn affect the level of economic activity. Fiscal policy, on the other hand, refers to government policy on taxing and spending. These areas have both program implications and economic significance. The government influences the economy by adjusting taxing and spending to economic conditions. The two considerations appear in discussions of national economic policy as issues related to price stability/inflation on the one hand and employment/unemployment on the other. The outcome of policy depends on which issues have the greatest effect on decision makers. Policy makers feel the effects through pressure from constituent groups. Businessmen and those on fixed incomes are more likely to be adversely affected by inflation than workers who may be cut back by slowdowns in the economy and who risk the loss of employment. The areas are interrelated in that efforts to slow down inflation have traditionally been thought to increase unemployment, while efforts to increase employment are often considered inflationary. The balance is worked out through actions of government agencies with power to determine monetary policy and with reference to expert advice on the appropriate fiscal policies.

John Maynard Keynes has influenced practical men not simply by the categories in which they think about economics but also in the institutions and agencies that administer their policies. This influence is evident in proposals to establish more powerful economic controls. The Depression and the striking way in which a national mobilization for war revived the economy no doubt assisted Keynesian ideas toward their significant measure of acceptance. In facing the crisis potential of de-escalation from military mobilization, government officials established a number of agencies to supervise the economy. The frame of reference was Keynesian, and the mode of implementation was expert advisers.

The present debate concerns the degree of involvement that the government will have and the side of the conceptual balance on which it will put its weight. The first section of this chapter deals with two institutions that have been particularly significant in national economic policy. One of the institutions, the Federal Reserve Board, is largely autonomous and reflects the interests of its member banks and their assessment of the policies to be followed. The other institution is the Council of Economic Advisers, which is, as its name implies, an advisory body that depends for its influence on the policy maker's desire for the information and ideas that it dispenses. Study of these institutions shows how policy has been made and lays the foundation for examining both the proposals to extend economic planning and the mechanisms that the proponents of planning desire to institute.

SECTION A. DETERMINING ECONOMIC POLICY

Since World War II, national policy on economic matters has been influenced by government agencies operating behind the scene. Their influence is in the information they provide and sometimes in the technical choices they are empowered to make. These choices often have an unrecognized policy significance. In order to see the sorts of mechanisms and practices that have determined the political policy choices that have become the subject of debate over economic planning, it is appropriate to look at the operation of the Federal Reserve Board (the "Fed") and the Council of Economic Advisers (the CEA). The Fed, as a public/private body, manipulates the amount of money and credit in the economy. This institution sets the pace of economic growth and investment. The CEA provides the data and the interpretations that are the key to the taxing and spending power used by the government to influence the economy. Where policy is directed to a highly technical field, as in economic affairs, agencies such as the Fed and the CEA play a critical role.

THE FUNCTIONS OF THE FEDERAL RESERVE

The Federal Reserve was instituted in 1913 as a central banking agency. At that time, the congressional mandate that set up the institution apparently did not foresee that the board would come to influence the economy to the extent that it has. It has, however, become a major instrument in economic stabilization with influence on employment and growth that surpasses its simple banking functions. The Federal Reserve is less dependent on Congress than institutions like the President's Cabinet. It does not depend on appropriations and is thus freed from the most frequently used tool of congressional administrative supervision. The terms of office for members of the board also insulate it from legislative intrusion.

The Federal Reserve System is administered by a board of governors known as the Federal Reserve Board. This board is composed of seven members appointed by the President with consent of the Senate. The members of the board serve for 14 years. Beneath the board is the Federal Open Market Committee, which is composed of all board members plus five of the presidents of the 12 Federal Reserve Banks. The Reserve banks are administered by a Board of Directors, which consists of nine persons, six of whom are elected by the member commercial banks of the district in which they operate and three of whom are appointed by the Federal Reserve Board in Washington. For all practical purposes, the Chairman of the Federal Reserve Board *is* the board's policy arm. He meets regularly with the other policy advisers, the Secretary of the Treasury, and the Council of Economic Advisers, is the spokesman for the system in front of Congress, and is the person representing this vast banking network to the public. The chairman has a fixed four-year term that does not coincide with that of the

President of the United States. He is also chairman of the Federal Open Market Committee.

One of the major tools through which the board sets monetary policy is the "rediscount rate." It is the rate of interest charged by the Federal Reserve Banks to their member bank borrowers on loans. The authority to determine this rate is shared by the Reserve Bank Boards of Directors and the Federal Reserve Board. The board also sets reserve requirement levels for the member banks, while the Federal Open Market Committee sets policy on the open market operations in securities of the federal government. Partially because of the weakness of the Nixon Presidency in its last year, but also because of its own independence, the Federal Reserve carried the major effort of the federal government to fight inflation in 1974. At that time, the growth of money in circulation was held down and interest rates were pushed to the highest levels ever recorded in the United States. These steps were undertaken in an effort to control the extent to which dollars were able to buy less and less.

The Federal Reserve system had been left out of the push for coordinated planning and centralized economic authority after World War II. It is only mentioned once in a very comprehensive presentation of the struggle behind the institutionalization of the Employment Act of 1946.[1] Relying on its public/private status, the board has been able to maintain its independence. But the policies of the Federal Reserve must be part of any comprehensive planning that is to succeed; thus, it is useful to examine some of the explanations and descriptions of how the Reserve operates before turning to the congressional initiative that is supposed to provide comprehensive planning.

The board has not been without critics — and how seriously these critics are taken seems to depend on the extent of prosperity at the time. When the economy is weak, the country gets a closer look at the Fed. Such is the aura of the specialist surrounding the Federal Reserve that this institution may be able to get itself exempted from "Sunshine" laws, which would open other government agencies to public view. The attempts to influence policy of the Fed have also come from congressional desire for centralized control over the economy. The materials included in this chapter amplify the activities of

[1]Stephen K. Bailey, *Congress Makes A Law* (New York: Vintage Books, 1950), p. 6.

the Federal Reserve and provide a basis for evaluating the debate over greater public control of the board.

There are other significant institutional influences and responsibilities that bear on monetary policy. The President monitors wage and price increases through the Council on Wage and Price Stability, an agency formed by President Ford in 1974. Additionally, regulatory agencies, such as the Civil Aeronautics Board and the Federal Trade Commission, monitor requests for rate increases. These agencies, although subject to criticism for dominance by the interests that they are supposed to regulate, have nothing that approaches the independence and the special relationship to its clients that is characteristic of the Federal Reserve Board. Although not originally created to exercise the predominance in the area of monetary policy that it has come to wield, the board — through its semiprivate status, its institutional setup, and its expertise — is now the preeminent agent in the creation of monetary policy.

THE FEDERAL RESERVE EXPLAINS ITSELF

A national "summit" conference on inflation was held in the fall of 1974. It was called by President Ford only a month after he assumed office to provide a forum for economists to discuss the nation's economic problems. Although the country had been "fighting inflation" for some time, there was little confidence that the government knew what it was doing. At this time, the country seemed to be slipping deeper into recession. That the conference was called to consider inflation and not unemployment is an indication of the new administration's major concern with regard to the tradeoff discussed previously. Many of the conferees addressed themselves to the tight money policies of the Federal Reserve; in his rebuttal, Arthur Burns, Chairman of the Federal Reserve Board, indicated how the Fed has approached monetary policy. One of the most striking things about the testimony is that Burns, unlike the other economists at the panel, is not giving advice; rather, he is telling the nation what the Fed has done, is doing, and plans to do. The Federal Reserve, he explains, has been successful in holding back the growth of money and credit. He calls on those who make "fiscal" policy to "emphasize surpluses instead of deficits" and thereby join with the Fed in its efforts.

COMMENTS BY ARTHUR BURNS ON THE ROLE OF THE FEDERAL RESERVE SYSTEM

Now, the job of the Federal Reserve System is not to be popular. Our job is to see to it, to use all of our energy, all of the ability and knowledge that we can muster, to help to protect the jobs of American workers and the integrity of their money.

Now, in doing our job we operate in an environment that is made by others, by the Congress, by trade unions, by business firms, by the general public. Now, there are facts of life that the Federal Reserve Board must take account of if it is to serve the public with good conscience; the Federal Reserve has to make some hard decisions if only because hard decisions are being avoided by others. I want to call your attention to some hard facts of life.

We are in the midst of an inflation which has been gathering force over the past decade and this inflation has now reached a stage where it is endangering our economic and political future. As a result of this inflation, first of all, our nation's capacity to produce has suffered a setback. Despite sluggish economic conditions for some months now, shortages of materials, components, parts, and equipment remain acute in many of our essential industries.

Secondly, as a result of inflation, consumer purchasing power is being eroded. During the past year, the take-home pay of the typical worker has declined from four to five percent in what it will buy.

In the third place, as a result of the inflation, the real value of the savings deposits, pension reserves, and life insurance policies of the American public has diminished.

Fourth, as a result of the inflation, corporate profits derived from domestic operations have eroded, a fact that is concealed by accounting techniques that were devised originally for inflation-free times.

Fifth, as a result of the inflation, financial markets have been experiencing strains and stresses. Interest rates have soared. Some financial and industrial firms have found it more difficult to refund maturing debt or to raise needed funds in the money and capital markets. The savings flow to thrift institutions has sharply diminished and stock prices have been badly depressed.

SOURCE: Arthur Burns, Chairman of the Federal Reserve Board, delivered these comments during the 1974 Conference on Inflation Sept. 27–28. Reprinted from Transcript issued by the Office of the President (Washington, D.C.: U.S. Government Printing Office, 1975), pp. 30–33.

In short, as a result of the inflation, much of the planning that American business firms and households customarily do has been upset and the driving force of economic expansion has been blunted.

It should not be surprising, therefore, that the physical performance of the economy has stagnated in recent months, and that unemployment is now larger than it was last fall. We cannot realistically expect a resurgence of economic activity until confidence in our nation's economy is restored. The most important requirement for rebuilding confidence, I believe, is hard evidence that we are making progress in checking the disease of inflation.

Now, in view of the protracted character, the growing intensity of inflation, the Federal Reserve has been striving for some time to hold down the growth of money and credit.

Now, I received a good deal of advice this morning, all of which suggested that the monetary spigot should be opened up, let the money supply expand more rapidly so that interest rates could come down. If that advice were followed, the inflation would become much more intense and interest rates, as they always do, would go higher and higher and be a good deal above their present level.

Rapid monetary expansion in the present inflationary environment would add fuel to the fires of inflation and thus worsen our economic troubles.

Now we at the Federal Reserve have tried to apply the monetary breaks firmly enough to get results, but we have also been mindful of the need to allow the supply of money and credit to keep expanding moderately.

The overall supply of money and credit has continued to grow this year but at a slower pace than before.

However, the demand for money and credit has been much greater than the supply. As a result of the huge demand for borrowed funds, credit markets have become tight and interest rates have risen to an . . . [extraordinarily] high level.

These high interest rates have imposed a heavy burden on businesses and families across the nation. Home building in particular has been hard hit by the developments in the money market. Soaring interests rates, outflows of deposits from thrift institutions, and the consequent decline in availability of mortgage credit have greatly aggravated the condition of the homebuilding industry, which was already suffering from sharply rising construction costs, from erosion in the purchasing power of the consumer incomes, and from the overbuilding of the last two years.

It may now be, however, that tensions in financial markets are beginning to ease. With continued moderation in current demands for goods and services, shortages and imbalances in our factories and shops are diminishing.

The Federal Reserve in recent months has been successful, as I have already suggested, in limiting the growth of money and credit to reasonably appropriate dimensions.

We have, therefore, been able recently to take actions that have reduced somewhat the pressures exerted on the banking system. Short-term market interest rates have responded to this relaxation and have declined from their early July peaks.

Long-term market interest rates have stabilized, albeit at very high levels, and they can surely be expected to fall back once some progress is made in curbing inflation.

Mortgage interest rates and other institutionally determined rates traditionally lag behind market rates, and they, too, will respond to progress in curbing inflation.

The recent movements of interest rates are encouraging, but we cannot count on any very substantial reduction until borrowers and lenders in the market are convinced that the Federal Reserve is no longer pursuing a lonely struggle against inflation.

Monetary policy is much too blunt an instrument to be relied upon exclusively in what needs to be a national crusade to bring inflation under control.

It is of vital importance that fiscal policy actively join in the battle. Frugality in public expenditures and a budget that is tilted toward surpluses instead of deficits can make an enormous contribution to curbing inflation and to lowering interest rates.

A policy of monitoring wages and prices but relying on voluntary cooperation can also play a modest, but useful, role in curbing inflationary excesses.

I am hopeful that the newly established Council on Wage and Price Stability will help to point the way to anti-inflationary conduct on the part of business, labor, and the consuming public alike.

Programs that seek to enlarge our nation's productive capacity and to intensify the forces of competition can be very helpful in combating inflation over a longer period of time.

In this connection let me stress the need to devise effective measures for improving the productivity of our labor force which has been lagging badly of late.

The rationale behind the Fed's operation and the procedures for carrying out the activity of the board, as well as its insulation from political pressure, are explained in the following remarks by board member Holland. The deep involvement of the board in economic policy making, in spite of its claim to expertise and its insulation, are the primary matters revealed by this selection. Autonomous authority demands both this sort of scientific rationale and the protection provided by an independent mechanism for making decisions.

MONETARY POLICY AS A "SOCIAL SCIENCE"

ROBERT C. HOLLAND

... Monetary policy falls into that category of knowledge labeled "social science." When I was student on campus, professors of the physical sciences were self-assured enough to use the term, "social science," as an occasionally satirical expression, being quick to point out its vagueness, imprecision, and lack of empirically validated theories. The basic reason for such imperfections, of course, is that the social sciences deal with people, and people simply are not as precise, as predictable, or as rational as machinery . . . .

Monetary theory has made great strides in the last three decades. Much of that advance has been based on abstractions, statistical and theoretical. Implicit in the equations and models that populate current monetary literature is a kind of idealization of the people involved — both the people who make policy and the people who are affected by it. Careful econometric analysis of past experience has done much to improve our ability to perceive underlying tendencies in aggregate economic behavior, but it has also tended to play down the variability of individual instances around those tendencies.

Those variations are people-caused. They are inevitable in the world in which we live. If they are not recognized and taken account of, more than theories will be disrupted.

... The Federal Reserve is insulated from short-run pressures to change its policy by a variety of protective arrangements, some provided deliberately by law and others resulting from the very indirect effects of its operations.

Source: Robert C. Holland, a member of the Board of Governors of the Federal Reserve System, delivered this talk at the Distinguished Lecture Series of the Ohio State University, 20 February 1975. The selection was obtained from the Federal Reserve Board, Washington, D.C.

This protection permits monetary policy to pursue even a course with highly unpopular side effects for some period of time. Often it can be essential for the Federal Reserve to do just that, for some of the good effects of a policy — such as slowing down price increases — can materialize only with considerable lags, while the intervening adjustment period can bring such unpopular consequences as high interest rates and curtailed availability of loans.

Over the longer run, however, I think it is crucial for the public to come to accept the basic objectives at which a particular monetary policy is aimed, and to develop some appreciation that policy is working to achieve those objectives. To state the converse, I doubt that the Federal Reserve could or would pursue a very unpopular set of fundamental objectives year after year.

If there are changes in public attitudes toward the relative merits of various basic economic objectives, then the feasible scope for monetary policy is shifted correspondingly. For example, it seems clear to me that public concern over inflation has mounted within the last two years, both absolutely and relative to the importance attached to other economic objectives such as full employment. Consequently, I believe it has been both possible and proper for monetary policy to have placed greater emphasis on fighting inflation during much of this interval. I hope and expect that the longer-run benefits of that policy emphasis will accrue to the American people for years to come. Now, of course, recessionary forces have developed in the economy that are being resisted by appropriately eased monetary conditions, but it will be important to carry through this latter task in ways that do not create a new wave of inflation.

THE CONGRESS AND THE FEDERAL RESERVE

The fears of Congress with regard to the actions of the Federal Reserve Board are evident in a confrontation between Congress and Board Chairman Arthur Burns, reported in the *Wall Street Journal*. It is obvious from the article that the lawmakers have considerable difficulty even finding out what the Fed is up to, much less influencing its policies. That situation is revealed in an instance in the continuing struggle between the board and the Chairman of the House Banking and Currency Committee. Congressional action in 1975 is a vivid example of the frustrations of the lawmakers with the independence of the Federal Reserve Board.

BURNS TELLS CONGRESS FED HASN'T SHIFTED TO DELIBERATELY TIGHTER MONETARY POLICY

By a *Wall Street Journal Staff Reporter*

Washington — Arthur Burns tried to convince Congress yesterday that the Federal Reserve isn't really tightening its monetary policy amid some lawmakers' fears that rising interest rates might kill any economic upturn.

The Federal Reserve Board chairman conceded that the Fed's recent moves to check an "explosion" in the nation's money supply had increased short-term interest rates, but he insisted the Fed hasn't switched to a policy of deliberately pushing up borrowing costs. He defended the Fed actions as a "signal" that the nation's central bank won't tolerate an excessive growth in the money stock, which might produce a new wave of inflation. The money supply is money in circulation plus demand, or checking, accounts in banks.

Mr. Burns' appearance before the House Banking Committee produced expressions of concern from Congressmen over rising interest rates — and demands for more information on the Fed's economic goals, which Mr. Burns rejected. The committee's chairman, Henry Reuss (D., Wis.), urged the Fed to "cease and desist" from any actions that would cause rising interest rates, which he said could prevent a recovery from the steep recession.

REBOUND OF "AVERAGE INTENSITY"

The economy is just beginning a recovery, Mr. Burns told the panel. He predicted the upturn would be of "average intensity," compared with previous rebounds from recessions, and would reduce the nation's unemployment rate to 7.5% of the work force or less within the next year. The nation's jobless rate was 8.6% in June.

The Fed chairman made it clear he is at least as concerned about inflation as unemployment. "Economic recovery is apparently beginning at a time when the rate of inflation, while lower than a year ago, is still well above a tolerable pace," he testified. The June jump in consumer prices, to a 9.6% annual rate, "is a warning that the menace of inflation is still very much with us," he said adding that more "bad news" on inflation is likely soon because wholesale food prices are climbing this month.

Mr. Burns' testimony before the panel was his first since Congress enacted a resolution requiring the Fed chairman to report quarterly on monetary policy. He spent much of his time explaining that the Fed hasn't altered its basic policy recently but has acted to offset a temporary bulge in the money supply, causing interest rates to rise.

REAFFIRMATION OF TARGET

Mr. Burns said that in mid-June the Federal Reserve's policy-making Open Market Committee reaffirmed its target to seek 5%–7.5% growth over the next year in the money supply. The 12-member policy panel "as yet sees no reason to alter the general course of monetary policy," Mr. Burns declared.

Confusion over the Fed's policy may have been triggered by recent developments, he said. As the Treasury paid out billions of dollars of tax rebates and Social Security bonuses in May and June, the money stock swelled at a 14.5% annual rate in those two months, Mr. Burns explained. The jump was "larger than we expected and very much larger than we desired."

To offset this bulge, the Fed acted to return the growth of the money stock "to the moderate path desired," Mr. Burns said. He didn't explain the actions, but they generally were steps designed to draw reserves out of the banking system. These steps, the Fed chairman conceded, "have left their mark" on short-term interest rates, which have been rising since mid-June after falling sharply earlier this year.

Rep. Reuss charged that letting interest rates rise just as the nation was trying to escape the recession "is simply the wrong thing to do." But Mr. Burns strongly defended the Fed's actions.

DEFENSE OF POLICY

"We were faced with an explosion" in the money market, Mr. Burns said. If the Reserve hadn't reacted, "this would have confirmed the fears of the financial and business community that the Fed is unleashing a major new wave of inflation" by allowing the money supply to swell too rapidly, he declared.

But Mr. Burns warned lawmakers they shouldn't conclude "that we are embarked on any policy to raise interest rates." He said, "That is in no sense our policy." The Fed's recent actions were just a "signal" that it won't let the money stock grow at an inflationary rate, he said.

After Rep. Reuss complained that the Reserve System had allowed the interest rate on federal funds — excess reserves banks lend one another — to exceed 6.5% Wednesday, Mr. Burns suggested that that fee wasn't a good gauge of Fed intentions. "Go back to Tuesday if you want a representative reading of rates," Mr. Burns suggested. The average effective rate on federal funds that day was 6.1%.

On the economic outlook, Mr. Burns said he is "reasonably confident" that a business upturn "will develop soon, if it isn't already under way."

The jobless rate historically has fallen 1.5 to two percentage points in the first year of economic recovery, Mr. Burns said. "I anticipate we will have a recovery of average intensity, or perhaps better," he said. Because ... the June jobless rate fell sharply due to a statistical quirk, Mr. Burns said he figures the actual unemployment rate currently is agout 9%, and he looks for a decline to about 7.5% by mid-1976.

The official turned aside repeated requests from panel members for specific Fed forecasts of the levels of unemployment, production, inflation and interest rates likely to be produced by its present monetary policy. "The projections made by our staff turn out to be wrong very frequently," Mr. Burns said, declaring it would be "very unwise" to divulge such internal "working papers."

Rep. Reuss asked the Fed chief to supply the data "on a confidential basis" to the committee, but Mr. Burns responded that he doubts it would "remain confidential very long." The official also rejected a suggestion that one or two Congressmen be allowed to sit in on a meeting of the Federal Open Market Committee. He replied heatedly, "Either you want an independent monetary authority, or you don't. Congress is informed fully."

Criticism of the Autonomy of the Federal Reserve Board

For nearly three decades, Congressman Wright Patman carried on a running battle with the Federal Reserve. Even from his powerful committee chairmanship, Patman was only able to snipe at the Fed throughout most of this period. However, the combined effects of an exhilarated Congress and the most severe recession since the 1930s led to the following policy statement from Patman with regard to the Federal Reserve.[1]

Mr. Speaker, the House of Representatives is currently considering a Department of Defense appropriation bill totalling $90.3 billion.

This $90.3 billion is to provide for the defense of all the citizens of the United States. And no one would deny the importance of this budget.

And yet, Mr. Speaker, every penny in this budget went through the congressional appropriations process. That is, hearings were held on the

[1]Reprinted from the *Congressional Record*, October 1, 1975.

individual items, changes were made, some deletions were made, some additions were made and Congress, in line with the Constitution, worked its will on the budget for this most important department of our Government.

On the other hand we have an agency — the Federal Reserve System — holding a portfolio of $93 billion — a figure the same size as the Defense Department budget — in its Open Market Committee at the New York Federal Reserve Bank on which Congress has never worked its will.

The Federal Reserve does not come to the Congress for this money and it earns nearly $6 billion annually in interest on these U.S. Government securities out of which it takes its expenses and returns what it pleases to the U.S. Treasury. No congressional committee scrutinizes the Federal Reserve's budget: no congressional committee makes additions or deletions — in short, Congress does not have a word to say about this part of the Federal Government.

Now why is it that the Defense Department which is providing for the common defense of all Americans has to come to Congress and defend its budget while the Federal Reserve — which affects the economic well-being of all Americans — does not?

Why does the Congress, year after year, continue to let the Federal Reserve build up its portfolio of holdings of U.S. Government securities — from $62 billion at year-end 1970 to $93 billion today — without demanding an accounting?

Why does the Congress, year after year, continue to let the operating expenses at the Federal Reserve increase — the operating expenses of the Federal Reserve have increased 70 percent since 1970 — without demanding an explanation of the necessity of these increases?

If we demand a line by line justification and explanation from the Department of Defense on their very important budget of $90.3 billion, the very least the Congress can do is make the Federal Reserve account for its portfolio of $93 billion in Government bonds.

House Concurrent Resolution 133

The House Concurrent Resolution printed below was passed in March 1975 and expresses Congress' approach to the matter of the autonomy of the Federal Reserve Board regarding monetary policy. The final resolution is a watered-down version in which the Fed gives up very little autonomy. It may indeed be more revealing for the amount of autonomy it leaves untouched than for the inroads it makes on the independence of the board. Since its formation, the board has been insulated from political control by the lengths of its members' terms, the ties it has to its member banks, and its ability to generate its own sources of revenue from the 85 billion dollars in investments over which it has authority. The fact that congressional intervention in the manner of H. Con. Res. 133 is quite rare indicates something of the sensitivity of Congress to this tradition of autonomy.

94TH CONGRESS 1ST SESSION: H. CON. RES. 133
[REPORT NO. 94–38]
IN THE SENATE OF THE UNITED STATES:
MARCH 5, 1975; MARCH 17, 1975

March 5, 1975: Referred to the Committee on Banking, Housing and Urban Affairs

March 17 (legislative day, March 12), 1975: Reported by Mr. Proxmire, with amendments

March 17 (legislative day, March 12), 1975: Considered, amended, and agreed to; preamble agreed to; title amended

CONCURRENT RESOLUTION

Referring to the conduct of monetary policy.

Whereas article I, section 8, of the Constitution provides that Congress shall have the money power; namely, " . . . to coin money and regulate the value thereof";

Whereas Congress established the Federal Reserve Board as its agent, and delegated to its agent the day-to-day responsibility for managing the money supply;

Whereas the United States economy is now suffering from excessively high unemployment and a decline in production and the gross national product, together with inflation;

Whereas the substantial budget deficit anticipated during fiscal years 1975 and 1976 could result in substantially higher interest rates and a reduced supply of mortgage credit in the absence of reasonable growth in the monetary and credit aggregates; and

Whereas Congress has received expert evidence that the economy's performance is affected by changes in the rate of growth of the monetary and credit aggregates: Now, therefore, be it

Resolved by the House of Representatives (the Senate concurring), That it is the sense of Congress that the Board of Governors of the Federal Reserve System and the Federal Open Market Committee —

(1) pursue policies in the first half of 1975 so as to encourage expansion in the monetary and credit aggregates appropriate to facilitating prompt economic recovery; and

(2) maintain long-run growth of the monetary and credit aggregates commensurate with the economy's long-run potential to increase production, so as to promote effectively the goals of maximum employment, stable prices, and moderate long-term interest rates.

Pursuant to this resolution, and taking into account the international flows of funds and conditions in the international money and credit markets, the Board of Governors shall consult with Congress at semiannual hearings before the Committee on Banking, Housing and Urban Affairs of the Senate and the Committee on Banking, Currency and Housing of the House of Representatives about the Board of Governors' and the Federal Open Market Committee's objectives and plans with respect to the ranges of growth or diminution of monetary and credit aggregates in the upcoming twelve months. Nothing in this resolution shall be interpreted to require that such ranges of growth or diminution be achieved if the Board of Governors and Open Market Committee determine that they cannot or should not be achieved because of changing conditions.

Passed the House of Representatives March 4, 1975.

Attest:

W. Pat Jennings,
Clerk

THE ROLE OF ECONOMIC ADVISERS

Outside the sphere of the Federal Reserve Board and with regard to the whole economic picture, the President has been the central figure in economic matters. Since 1946, he has had at his disposal the advice and forecasts of a group of economists. In that the President's Council of Economic Advisers is similar to the sort of institutional setup envisioned by the planning legislation presented later, in Section B, it merits substantial attention. A number of other persons, however, share the Executive Office and the President's official ear on economic matters.

The President has recently appointed an Assistant for Economic Affairs who coordinates the economic information flowing in and out of the White House. This position has, at times, played an important policy making role, depending on the person holding the job and his relation to the President. In 1974, President Ford's assistant, L. William Seidman, directed the national economic "summit" on inflation.

The Secretary of the Treasury, as head of the executive department most directly involved with the economy, has traditionally had a significant effect on an administration's economic policy. There have been suggestions that a Cabinet-level economic post ought to be established. Unless that is done the position of Secretary of the Treasury will remain important in economic affairs, as it has been since Alexander Hamilton occupied that post. The position has been filled in recent years by men who have influenced national affairs in other important posts. Arthur Burns went from Treasury to the Federal Reserve Board, and William E. Simon came from the important energy post in the midst of the crises of 1973 to the Treasury.

In addition, the President is also close to the Office of Management and Budget (OMB), which works from the White House. OMB Director Roy Ash, a holdover from the Nixon Administration, was credited with diverting the President's attention from monetary or anti-inflation policy to the fiscal initiatives directed toward full or fuller employment. This course led to the budget deficits and tax cuts in 1974–1975 that were to stimulate the economy and put people back to work. During the Nixon Administration, the OMB was created out of the Bureau of the Budget, which had traditionally prepared the budget and coordinated governmental evaluation of expenditures and cuts. The Nixon OMB served an active policy role. President Ford promised to change its orientation from defending policy choices to simply preparing the budget. But the OMB has a critical function in translating various policy preferences of the President into a national budget. It remains partly up to the Director of OMB to determine how great a policy role to play.

Soon after he took office, President Ford set up an Economic Policy Board to advise him on the economic aspects of the decisions that he would have to make. The board met every weekday morning through 1975 and early 1976 and formed a central clearinghouse for Presidential policy on all economic and financial matters. The board was chaired by the Secretary of the Treasury and included the President's Assistant for Economic Affairs, the Chairman of the Council of Economic Advisors, the Secretary of Labor, the Secretary of Commerce, the Head of the Office of Management and Budget, and the Director of the Council on International Economic Policy.

The game of adviser and agency identification can be overplayed, but the degree to which these various agencies have institutionalized responsibilities and the reliance of policy makers on their expertise indicates their importance in determining the outcome of economic policy. Even where they do not have direct policy making responsibilities, as is the case with the CEA, their advisory role is often quite important.

The major advisory agency on economic matters was the result of failure to establish a legal obligation, a national commitment, to full employment. The Council of Economic Advisers was created by the Employment Act of 1946. The proponents of the Employment Act had hoped to guarantee full employment in America through a government obligation. The act did not, however, get that far, and instead of full employment, it promised the following:

... It is the continuing policy and responsibility of the Federal Government to use all practical means consistent with its needs and obligations and other essential considerations of national policy with the assistance and cooperation of industry, agriculture, labor, and State and local governments, to coordinate and utilize all its plans, functions, and resources for the purpose of creating and maintaining, in a manner calculated to foster and promote free competitive enterprise and the general welfare, conditions under which there will be afforded useful employment, for those able, willing, and seeking to work, and to promote maximum employment, production, and purchasing power.

In order to provide this coordination, the act set up the CEA with responsibility for evaluating the economic programs of the government and for gathering economic information and making special studies at the President's request. In creating the CEA, the act substituted an advisory for a policy making body.

The council has collected much of the data through which the state of the economy is interpreted and it has given considerable advice. Its importance has, however, been dependent on the reception of its advice by the President. Each year the council reports to the President on its activities. The report delivered in February 1975 covers activities for the preceding year. It contained the following information.

1975 ANNUAL REPORT OF THE COUNCIL OF ECONOMIC ADVISERS

RESPONSIBILITIES OF THE COUNCIL

The principal directive of the Employment Act is that the Federal Government "use all practicable means consistent with its needs and obligations ... for the purpose of creating and maintaining ... conditions ... to promote maximum employment, production, and purchasing power."

The basic responsibility of the Council of Economic Advisers is the analysis and interpretation of trends and changes in the economy and the development and evaluation of national economic policies to assist the President in reaching the goals specified in the act. The Council prepares regular reports on current economic conditions and forecasts of future economic developments, and its recommendations are an integral part of economic policy making.

The Council also has a responsibility "to appraise the various programs and functions of the Federal Government." The Council thus performs a direct advisory role involving a wide range of economic problems both within the Executive Office of the President and through participation in interagency study groups in which representatives of various departments, agencies, and offices in the executive branch evaluate current programs and consider and develop new ones.

During 1974 the Council and its staff shared in the analysis and examination of many different economic issues incident to the formulating of programs and policies. These included policy issues and proposals regarding agricultural and food policy; measures and programs to support housing construction; a wide range of programs and measures affecting environmental quality; alternative means of dealing with the energy problem; the evaluation of future supplies of strategic materials; exploitation of the resources of the seas; management of the Nation's timber resources; transportation problems and policies; measures to improve the functioning of the labor market and to alleviate the impact of the recession upon the unemployed; proposals for more effective health insurance and income maintenance; and needed improvements in the Government's economic statistics.

International trade and investment problems and policies continued to be

SOURCE: Reprinted from The Annual Report of The Council of Economic Advisers, in Economic Report of the President (Washington, D.C.: U.S. Government Printing Office, 1975), pp. 236–240.

a major concern of the Council, and during 1974 it examined the strains placed upon the world's international trade and financial mechanism by the large capital flows related to oil payments.

Early each year the President submits the *Economic Report of the President* to the Congress as required by the Employment Act. The Council assumes major responsibility for the preparation of this *Report*, which together with the Annual Report of the Council of Economic Advisers reviews the progress of the economy over the past year and outlines the Administration's policies and programs.

The Chairman is a member of the Economic Policy Board, which directs the formulation, coordination, and implementation of economic policy. The Chairman is also a member of the Executive Committee of the Economic Policy Board, which serves as the focal point for economic policy decision making and meets daily to address current issues of economic policy.

The Economic Policy Board operates with a high degree of flexibility, requesting analyses of economic problems and recommendations from the various agencies and departments of the executive branch. The Executive Committee, often augmented by the Chairman of the Board of Governors of the Federal Reserve System, meets regularly with the President to review economic conditions, make recommendations, and discuss possible changes in economic policy.

The review and analysis of the overall performance of the economy is conducted and coordinated through a series of "Troika" working groups, comprising representatives of the Council, the Treasury, and the Office of Management and Budget (OMB). At regular intervals economists from these agencies evaluate recent economic performance and formulate economic forecasts which are then reviewed by a second group, chaired by a Council Member and including the Assistant Secretary of the Treasury for Economic Policy and the Economist for OMB. The analysis and projections are then reviewed and cleared through the Chairman of the Council for presentation and consideration by the Executive Committee, which is chaired by the Secretary of the Treasury and consists of the Chairman of the Council of Economic Advisers, the Director of OMB, the Executive Director of the Council on International Economic Policy, and the Assistant to the President for Economic Affairs, who is the Executive Director of both the Economic Policy Board and its Executive Committee.

The Chairman of the Council is a member of the President's Energy Resources Council, which was formed in October 1974 to formulate and coordinate energy policy. The Chairman is the head of the U.S. delegation to the Economic Policy Committee of the Organization for Economic Cooperation and Development, and he also serves as vice chairman of the Committee. Council Members and staff economists attended meetings of various working parties of the Committee during the year. The Chairman of the Council served as Chairman of the Advisory Committee on the Economic Role of Women, which on April 30, 1974, issued its recommendations for advancing women in industry; the Advisory Committee ended its term in August 1974.

In April Mr. Fellner and several staff economists from the Council visited the Economic Planning Agency for Japan to continue the exchange of information on economic problems and policies that was initiated during 1972. In November the Council was host to a delegation of economists from the Economic Planning Agency.

The Chairman and Council Members appeared before the full Joint Economic Committee (JEC) of the Congress three times during 1974. The JEC, like the Council, was created by the Employment Act of 1946, "to make a continuing study of matters relating to the *Economic Report* and to submit its own report and recommendations to the Congress." On February 7 the Council presented testimony before the JEC on the *Economic Report* and appeared again on July 30 to review economic developments during the first half of 1974. The Chairman presented testimony on September 26 regarding developments during the third quarter. The Council also appeared before the JEC Subcommittee on Consumer Economics on May 10. The Chairman presented testimony on the budget before the Senate Appropriations Committee on February 27 and appeared before the Senate Committee on Commerce and Government Operations on May 9. He also presented testimony before the JEC Subcommittee on Economic Growth on June 12, before the House Budget Committee on September 25, and before the Senate Permanent Subcommittee on Investigations on October 16. Mr. Seevers presented testimony on the Federal budget before the House Committee on Appropriations on February 20 and appeared before the Senate Government Operations Committee on November 26 to discuss regulatory reform.

PUBLIC INFORMATION

The Annual Report of the Council of Economic Advisers, contained in the *Economic Report of the President,* is the main vehicle through which the Council informs the public of its work and its views. It presents a comprehensive review and analysis of economic conditions, forecasts, and projections for the coming year, as well as an explanation of the Administration's economic policy. In recent years about 50,000 copies of the *Economic Report* have been distributed. The Council also assumes primary responsibility for the monthly publication, *Economic Indicators,* which is prepared by the

Council's Statistical Office under the direction of Frances M. James and issued by the Joint Economic Committee with a distribution of about 10,000 copies.

The Council also presents information on and analyses of current economic problems and developments through occasional press briefings, testimony before various congressional committees, and speeches and papers presented by the Chairman and the Members of the Council. The Council answers numerous requests for information from the Congress, the press, and individual citizens, and receives individual visitors as well as business, academic, and other groups as often as is possible without interfering with other duties.

ORGANIZATION AND STAFF OF THE COUNCIL

Office of the Chairman

The Chairman is responsible for communicating the Council's views to the President. This duty is performed both through direct consultation with the President and through regular reports on economic developments. The Chairman also represents the Council at Cabinet meetings, at the Executive Committee of the Economic Policy Board, and at many other formal and informal meetings of Government officials. He also exercises ultimate responsibility for directing the work of the professional staff.

Council Members

The two Council Members directly supervise the work of the staff, are responsible for all subject matter covered by the Council, and represent the Council at numerous meetings, where they assume major responsibility for the Council's involvement. Whenever the Chairman is absent from Washington, one of the Council Members becomes Acting Chairman.

In practice the Chairman and the Council Members work as a team. For operational reasons, however, subject matter is divided informally between the Council Members. Mr. Fellner is responsible for analysis of business conditions, short-term forecasting, and matters related to monetary and fiscal policy; international finance; manpower employment and developments in the labor market; financial markets; housing; health, education, and welfare; taxation; and social security. Mr. Seevers is responsible for the areas encompassing international trade; energy and natural resources; food and agriculture; urban and national growth policy; environmental problems; transportation; regulated industries; and antitrust questions.

Professional Staff

At the end of 1974 the professional staff consisted of 13 senior staff economists, two statisticians, and seven members of the junior research staff.

Supporting Staff

The Administrative Office provides administrative support for the entire Council staff, which includes preparation and analysis of the Council's budget; procurement of equipment and supplies; responding to correspondence and inquiries from the general public; and distribution of Council speeches, reports, and congressional testimony.

CONSENTING TO THE ADVISERS

Nominees to the Council of Economic Advisers must be confirmed by the Senate. As with all nominations where confirmation is required, the Congress holds hearings. It explores the nominee's competence as well as his or her policy preferences. Since it is usually the President's prerogative to choose nominees according to his rather than the Congress' preferences, the investigation of the nominee's stands on the issues is a matter of sounding the nominee out and letting him know the concerns of the Congress. The hearings afford an opportunity to learn what the Congress and the nominee consider to be important in the position. It is evident in the testimony reproduced below that the members of the council have been both advisers and advocates for the administration. There is also an indication of concern about to whom the advisers are responsible. Relations with the Federal Reserve Board and with the Joint Economic Committee of Congress are discussed, and the candidate's interpretation of what constitutes full employment is also explored.

HEARING IN THE UNITED STATES SENATE ON THE NOMINATION OF ALAN GREENSPAN TO BECOME CHAIRMAN OF THE COUNCIL OF ECONOMIC ADVISERS, 29 AUGUST 1974

OPENING STATEMENT BY CLARENCE J. BROWN, REPRESENTATIVE
IN CONGRESS FROM THE STATE OF OHIO

Congressman Brown [of Ohio] ... I appreciate this opportunity to appear before you to express myself on the occasion of the nomination of Alan Greenspan to be the Chairman of the Council of Economic Advisers. I support his nomination because I feel he is probably qualified for the job.

So, rather than take my time and yours to discuss Mr. Greenspan, I should prefer to discuss with you briefly what I feel the Chairman of the Council should be.

After 9 years in Congress, 5 of them on the Joint Economic Committee and many of them observing politics as a newspaperman before becoming involved myself, I feel strongly that an economic adviser on this Council should be a real adviser and not a mouthpiece for the economics collateral to a political policy. And he should not only advise the President but he should advise the Congress and the people of the Nation with the same determination.

Americans are living with the worst inflation of modern times, a domestic economy which is stagnating and a financial system under severe international strain. And American productivity has fallen to new lows in world competition. To get out of the mess we are in, will require the restoration of the American work ethic, the Yankee thrift ethic and some new economic ethics which must also be translated into political ethics.

For example, if America is to maintain her standard of living in the years ahead — let alone sustain our position in an increasingly competitive world economy — it will be necessary to raise staggering amounts of long-term capital to expand the productive capacity in our basic industries which make possible the jobs which fuel American buying power and pay the taxes to finance social progress. With depressed financial markets, low real levels of profit in American industry and record dollar outflows to pay for energy, where will that capital come from?

SOURCE: Hearing Before The Committee on Banking, Housing and Urban Affairs, United States Senate, Ninety-Third Congress (Washington, D.C.: U.S. Government Printing Office, 1974).

I am not asking that the chairman of the economic advisers be a Jeremiah. But I do want him to have the vision for the long range good of our Nation and the courage to call the shots as he sees them. And to be listened to, he must have the reputation to be able to impress other professionally trained economists and the ability to articulate his views in this often esoteric field so that his ideas will be understood and supported by the average citizen for whom our system is supposed to operate. This is particularly important because, if our system is operating properly, most of that motivation which operates it will be coming from the average citizen rather than from the councils of the supposedly omniscient and omnipotent here in the biggest county seat in the world.

The intertwining of politics and economics cannot be unraveled. But the viewpoints of economists and politicians need not be the same. Our economic advisers should address the problems of investors and jobholders, of producers and consumers, of savers and spenders, and leave to politicians the consideration of them as voters. They should not be reluctant to tell it like it is and prescribe the medicine our economy may need from time to time. Politicians are frequently accused of sugarcoating the pill. But if the economists give us sugar pills to start with, the patient may get into serious trouble before anything effective is done.

The Chairman of the Council of Economic Advisers needs to be more than a statistician. He must be a diagnostician. He is not a tout to be supported or rejected for his accuracy at prediction. Rather, he is to preside over the best economic advice our Nation can get at any particular time.

And, Mr. Chairman, we are at a particular time when we need it now. I think we have such a man in Mr. Greenspan — at least I hope so. And if we do, I hope he will resist the powerful temptation to which other economists seem to succumb in Washington and not give up being a professional economist to become an amateur politician.

. . .

THE CHAIRMAN [Sparkman of Alabama]: Dr. Burns and the Federal Reserve Board, I think, have been very much concerned with this problem of inflation.

I think they had hoped that through the control of the money supply they might be able to do something about it. But I notice Dr. Burns was quoted yesterday, I believe, saying that it would probably take 2 years to get control of inflation.

Do you agree with that?

MR. GREENSPAN: Let's say, Mr. Chairman, that I can't disagree with it.

I don't know how we can get a specific time frame. I'm fairly sure it's not less than 1 year, and I'm reasonably certain it does not have to take several years. You also have to determine the time frame in the context of the set policies which are taken.

Two years may be a good guess. If I had to put a number on it, I'd put it slightly less; but we really don't know enough to make that fine a distinction. It's a long time, and there's no alternative.

THE CHAIRMAN: Do you have any comment on the action of the Federal Reserve regarding the money supply?

MR. GREENSPAN: Mr. Chairman, I subscribe to the general policy which the Federal Reserve has embarked upon.

I see it as an attempt to suppress the expansion of the monetary aggregates, to suppress the underlying expansion of credit, which essentially feeds inflationary forces.

I hasten to add, however, that it's a mistake to believe that somehow that's what inflation policy is all about, and that the Federal Reserve is capable, wholly independent of what's happening in the capital areas, to sustain a limited noninflationary money supply growth.

. . .

THE CHAIRMAN: Mr. Greenspan, the Council of Economic Advisors was created under the Full Employment Act of 1946, the Joint Economic Committee of which both Senator Proxmire and I are members was also created under that Act.

And Congressman Brown, who just testified, is a member of that committee, Senator Brock was at one time, but he left.

SENATOR BROCK [of Tennessee]: I left the House.

THE CHAIRMAN: Oh, it was while you were in the House.

I was one of the original members, Wright Patman and I are the only two original members of the Joint Economic Committee, and we were appointed in January, 1947 when it was established.

By the way, the chairman at that time, I know the Republicans will be interested, was a man who served for many years on this committee, Bob Taft, a very able man.

Oh, and this might be of interest, too. When we tried to get the Chairman of the Council of Economic Advisers to come up and testify, they declined. It took us, I believe, 3 or 4 years to get that worked out to the point where they would testify.

Maybe that helped originate the question I asked a while ago if you would appear and testify.

But do you feel that that act has worked well?

MR. GREENSPAN: It's difficult to say, Mr. Chairman, because as you recall, the act specifies the policies which would maximize employment consistent with stable price levels.

Now, I would certainly say that the levels of unemployment on average since the act was initiated, are reasonably good; but I would say that our success in achieving a noninflationary environment, in the context of that original legislation, has been poor.

THE CHAIRMAN: Let me say this: Even though it was called the "Full Employment Act," it was never thought it meant really full.

In fact, as I recall back in those days, the economists used to say if we had unemployment, not more than 3 and 3½ percent, I think it was, that would be satisfying the requirements of the law.

. . .

SENATOR PROXMIRE [of Wisconsin]: Now, Mr. Greenspan, you furnished at my request a client list for Townsend–Greenspan and Co. It's a very impressive list. Do you have any objection to that list being made public?

MR. GREENSPAN: I would prefer that it not be.

SENATOR PROXMIRE: Would you mind if I generalize without referring to specific firms then and certainly to the area of representation?

MR. GREENSPAN: No problem whatever.

SENATOR PROXMIRE: This includes the biggest banks in the country. It includes a number of very large manufacturing firms, including some that are in a very concentrated position in their industry; isn't that correct?

MR. GREENSPAN: Yes, sir.

SENATOR PROXMIRE: I wish you would spell out for us because, as I understand it, you own 99 percent of Townsend-Greenspan, and you would go back to them after your term of service on the Council of Economic Advisers.

Is that correct?

MR. GREENSPAN: Yes, sir.

SENATOR PROXMIRE: Under those circumstances, I think it would be helpful if you would indicate what your service to these firms represent.

You just simply make economic analyses for them. What kind of economic analyses do you make? Do you ever represent them in any way on economic policy before any kind of government agency?

What do you do?

MR. GREENSPAN: No, I made it a general practice, Senator, not to represent them in any way with respect to a particular issue before a governmental agency.

As a consequence of that, I deal largely in economic consulting, both on a macro and on a micro basis. It varies from company to company; but, specifically what it would be, for example, in a major industrial corporation, would be to develop fairly elaborate econometric models of the markets into which these companies sell, endeavoring to try to determine layer upon layer the way the particular industry functions, largely attempting to ferret out where various changes occur, where they are significant and, in a general way, try to determine what type of market forces create the physical volume of sales that these companies can sell.

. . .

SENATOR PROXMIRE: . . . I think your cutting down on Government spending now was wise, trying to reduce the role of the Federal Government was good and necessary and desirable. But many of these views may seem rather harsh, and especially, in the context in which we find ourselves now.

Men in public office find that they are best served when they hear a variety of informed opinion. The worst thing that can happen to them is to become isolated or to hear only the views of their allies and supporters.

I have always believed that a President is best served when he is told the truth and when he gets opinions from competing interests in the economy.

Now, the thing that troubles me most about your appointment — and you're an able man, competent man — is just this point. The people who disagree with your economic philosophy applauded your ability and honesty and competence. The President has surrounded himself by a group of economic advisors who essentially come from the same background of big business.

There is Mr. Ash of Litton, Mr. Rush of Union Carbide, Mr. Simon from Wall Street, and now Mr. Greenspan, a business economist whose clients are among the biggest businesses in the country. You're the four principal men.

One or even two men with such a background ought to be in the Cabinet even of the most liberal and progressive President. But if all of them are from the same background, is the President really getting the best possible advice, a conflict of views and opinions, and a basis on which to make good policy that would serve the whole country? How about that?

Mr. Greenspan: I understand your concern, Senator. It's important to have a broad spectrum of views and, while it's certainly true that I have a consistent economic philosophy, much in line, I would suspect in most instances, with the existing advisory group to the President, I, nonetheless, think that perhaps just because of that it's incumbent upon me as Chairman of Council of Economic Advisers, to search around for an appropriate spectrum of views.

It's quite sterile for people who fundamentally agree with one another to discuss what they think about the world at large, because there is a tendency for one to learn very little from people with whom you agree.

As a consequence of this, I have sought and will continue to seek views which clash — in fact, the more, the better — with my own views. Because the way one learns the truth is by confronting it with opposing views.

Senator Proxmire: What you're telling me is in the present context you wouldn't nominate Alan Greenspan. Not because you're not a very competent man, but because all of the people around the President have the same views.

Mr. Greenspan: Well, Senator, one of the reasons that I was very reluctant to accept, was that my views tend to be quite similar to everybody else's.

I didn't appoint myself, obviously. Having accepted, I accepted only in the context that, while my views are well known, I do and shall attempt to bring the full spectrum of the economics profession's views, which I know quite well, to the President.

. . .

In most instances, I do agree with them; but there are differences.

SENATOR STEVENSON [of Illinois]: Thank you.

Now, getting back to wage and price controls, you have reiterated your opposition.

The question before us is not so much one of wage and price controls as it is to adopt some sort of standby authority, authority to impose wage and price controls or simply keep the broom in the closet.

Arthur Burns has suggested that the Cost of Living Council or some agency be activated to monitor and exercise standby authority. I think he suggested some authority which could at least temporarily defer wage and price increases.

In other words, wage and price controls. Do you agree or disagree with Arthur Burns?

MR. GREENSPAN: Well, I have disagreed with him on the subject, and I must admit that, whenever I disagree with Chairman Burns, I double check my analysis.

Having double checked, I must say I still disagree with him; and the reason is basically this: First of all, wage and price controls per se suppress the symptoms of inflation and ignore the causes. Nor, as is often argued, do they reduce inflation psychology. I know of no evidence which supports the view that wage and price controls do that.

And unless they do that, their value in maintaining a stable noninflationary price level is nil.

If this is the case, as I believe, then what advantage is there in attempting to suppress prices under their equilibrium level? You are distorting and suppressing potential increases in supply, and aggravating inflationary pressures because ultimately they're going to break out and lift prices to a much higher level than you otherwise would have had.

Now, I cannot see any value in a broom if the broom itself doesn't work. I just don't see any reason why one should keep one in the closet. The mere threat that the broom is there and could be taken out and used to swat actually has the potential effect of making people concerned about being locked into a new wage and price control system.

A number of people are going to try to move to anticipate that event, and they will jack up their prices to levels which would not otherwise be sensible for them to do.

If they fear a reimposition of wage and price controls, they might say that while it is in our short-term disinterest, it is in our long-term interest to raise prices now.

· · ·

SENATOR BIDEN [of Delaware]: One of the things that I think is rather encouraging is that everyone I speak to including some of your colleagues tells me you are going to depoliticize the office, which is a welcome thing. You went on to point out, accurately, as have many who have testified before in the 1½ years I have been here, that the choices ultimately come down to political choices, ones which the politicians must make and should be made by Congress on the basis of information presented.

THE INFLUENCE OF ADVICE

The *Phillips curve* represents a theory of the relation between the unemployment rate and the rate of increase in wages and prices. The curve suggests that as wages and prices rise the amount of unemployment will drop. It is on the basis of this relationship that the effect of holding down wages and prices in the fight against inflation is believed to create an increase in the number of persons out of work. The Council of Economic Advisers is responsible for collecting the information on which such theories are built and for interpreting the information for the President. In its 1975 statement, the council presented the theory that the Phillips curve may express an accurate relationship for the short run, but that, over a long period, other factors determine the rate of unemployment. They referred to "frictional" unemployment as a matter of the imperfect match between the jobs available and those seeking work, and "structural" unemployment as relating to groups with persistently high unemployment. This instance offers an example of how the council, by interpreting such matters for the President, exerts its influence.

The President's view is presented in the Economic Report to the Congress. The report for 1976 is reprinted below. To a noticeable degree, this report bears out the influence of the council, and others of a like persuasion whom the President chose to consult. In Ford's interpretation of the relationship between inflation and unemployment, which he considers the "two greatest personal concerns" of Americans, the thrust of the report, contrary to the Phillips curve theory, is to associate "sharply rising prices" directly with increasing unemployment, and the President's answer is to remove government from the market and allow competition to bring down prices.

ECONOMIC REPORT OF PRESIDENT FORD

On January 26th, President Ford submitted to Congress the annual Economic Report. The text of the Report follows. 122 Congressional Record H 286 (H.Doc.No.94–334).

To the Congress of the United States:

As we enter 1976, the American public still confronts its two greatest personal concerns: inflation and unemployment. As valid as those concerns are, we should not let them overshadow the very genuine progress we have made in the past year. The underlying fact about our economy is that it is steadily growing healthier. My policies for 1976 are intended to keep us on that upward path.

A year ago the economy was in the midst of a severe recession with no immediate end in sight. Exceptionally strong inflationary forces were just beginning to abate, and the prospects for containing unemployment were not bright.

It is now clear that we have made notable progress. The sharpest recession in the post-World War II period hit bottom last spring, and a substantial recovery is now under way. There were 85.4 million Americans at work in December, 1.3 million more than during March of 1975. While the rate of unemployment remains far too high, it is slowly moving in the right direction. There have also been appreciable advances in reducing the rate of inflation. The increase in the consumer price index was 7 percent between December 1974 and December 1975, down from a rate of more than 12 percent during the previous 12 months.

. . .

Unfortunately there is no simple formula or single act that will quickly produce full economic health. It has taken many years for excessive stimulation, combined with external shocks like the quintupling of international oil prices, to create the economic difficulties of 1974 and 1975, and it will take several years of sound policies to restore sustained, noninflationary growth. I will not make promises which I know, and you know, cannot be kept. We must restore the strength of the American economy as quickly

SOURCE: *U.S. Code Congressional and Administrative News* (St. Paul, Minn.: West Publishing Co., 1976), pp. 253–256.

as we can; but in so doing we cannot ignore the dangers of refueling inflationary forces, because unchecked inflation makes steady growth and full employment impossible. The events of the past several years have once again convincingly demonstrated that accelerating inflation causes instability and disruptions, increases unemployment, and ultimately precludes real prosperity.

It is often said that we must choose between inflation and unemployment, and that the only way to reduce unemployment is to accept chronic inflation or rigid controls. I reject this view. Inflation and unemployment are not opposites but are related symptoms of an unhealthy economy. The latter months of 1974 illustrate the relationship between inflation and unemployment. Sharply rising prices created a climate of uncertainty and were to blame for part of the massive reduction in the purchasing power of household assets placed in savings accounts and investment securities. In turn, consumers cut back on expenditures; and consequently inventories, already swollen by speculative buying, backed up in distribution channels. By the early months of 1975 there were sharp cutbacks in production and employment. Thus inflation played a significant part in the surge of unemployment, and if we have a new round of inflation it is likely to bring still more unemployment. Chronically high unemployment is an intolerable waste of human resources and entails an unacceptable loss of material production. Clearly, we must attack inflation and unemployment at the same time; our policies must be balanced.

. . .

Success in promoting healthy economic growth and a vigorous private economy depends to a large extent on our eliminating Government policies and institutions which interfere with competition. Traditionally the American system has relied on competition to organize production and to encourage economic progress. The Government, however, has attempted to correct imperfections in competition by regulating prices and the quality of services in many different industries. This attempt has been less than a complete success. Regulation has been useful in curbing the pricing power of certain monopolies and in fostering the growth of new industries, such as air transportation in the 1940s and 1950s. It has also helped to insure compliance with such publicly determined social goals as clean air and safe working conditions. But in several industries, regulation has been used to protect and support the growth of established firms rather than to promote competition.

Over the years, Government regulation has also had many other undesirable effects. Besides reducing competition in many instances, it has also imposed on complying firms enormous burdens, which raise business costs and consumer prices.

Increasing competition from world markets and the need to maintain and improve the standard of living of a growing population require constant improvement of the American market system. For this reason I have asked the Congress to legislate fundamental changes in the laws regulating our railroads, airlines, and trucking firms. The new amendments will free these companies to respond more . . . [flexibly] to market conditions. I have also urged deregulation of the price of natural gas and sought essential pricing flexibility for the oil and electric utilities industries. We will continue to improve all essential protection for public health and safety, trying at the same time not to increase unnecessarily the cost to the public. My object is to achieve a better combination of market competition and responsible Government regulation. The programs I have advanced in recent months have sought such a balance, and I will continue this course in 1976.

Striking a new regulatory balance is likely to entail some economic and social costs during a period of transition, and changes must therefore be phased in carefully. In the long run, however, a revitalized market system will bring significant benefits to the public, including lower prices.

. . .

Of central concern both here and abroad is U. S. energy policy. Without a vigorous and growing industry supplying domestic energy, much of our industrial development in the next 10 years will be uncertain. And unless we can reduce our dependency on Middle East oil, we will not have a sound basis for international cooperation in the development of new fossil fuel and other energy sources.

As an initial step toward greater self-sufficiency, I signed the Energy Policy and Conservation Act in December 1975. I concluded that this act, though deficient in some respects, did provide a vehicle for moving us toward our energy goals. With this mechanism the price of petroleum can be allowed to rise to promote domestic supply and to restrain consumption. At the end of 40 months, under the act, I may remove price controls altogether, and I will utilize the provisions of the act to move toward a free market in petroleum as quickly as is possible and consistent with our larger economic goals. The act offers flexibility, which I have already used to start dismantling price controls and allocation arrangements in fuel markets where no shortages exist. The legislation also establishes a national strategic petroleum reserve which will make our supply of energy secure and give other nations less inducement to impose an oil embargo.

Measures crucial to our energy future still remain to be enacted, however. Natural gas deregulation is now the most pressing of the issues on energy before Congress: shortages grow year by year, while the country waits for more testimony on supply and demand, or waits for extremely expensive new synthetic gas plants to replace the natural gas production choked off by price controls. I urge the Congress to make deregulation of new natural gas one of its first objectives in 1976. The legislation I have proposed in order to assure adequate supplies of fuel for nuclear power plants is also critical. If we are to improve our energy situation, these measures are necessary. They will also reinforce our efforts to remove unnecessary and deleterious Government interference in economic activities where the consumer is adequately protected by market forces.

A year ago I said, "The year 1975 must be the one in which we face our economic problems and start the course toward real solutions." I am pleased with the beginning we have made. The course is a long one, but its benefits for all Americans make the journey worthwhile. The year 1976 must be one in which we will continue our progress toward a better life for all Americans.

Gerald R. Ford
The White House,
January 26, 1976.

SECTION B. THE DEBATE AND THE STRATEGY OF ECONOMIC PLANNING LEGISLATION

This section presents the debate on economic planning stimulated by some important pieces of legislation. According to some members of Congress, the government has not been fulfilling its oversight function adequately, as evidenced in the cycles of inflation and the recurrent recessions and high rates of unemployment. They feel that the solution lies in a national planning mechanism, and they have introduced legislation to create such a mechanism.

Debate over the bills, which propose a formal planning agency at the national level, involves such issues as the degree of coercion (would General Motors be told how many cars to produce?), the degree of success (would business or the public be forced to accept an Edsel?), and the mode of rectifying failure of the government's plans. As Michael Reagan wrote in *The Managed Economy* in 1963:[1] "If government really left the economy alone, there would be no system of

---

[1]Michael Reagan, *The Managed Economy* (New York: Oxford University Press, 1963), p. 159.

competition but Hobbes' war of each against all." Without speculating on what a "natural" state would be, it may be enough to indicate that the government does enforce contracts, protect property, and, through its courts, provide a mechanism for the resolution of conflicts over these and innumerable other activities essential to the conduct of economic affairs in a large and complex society. The foes of government planning seem to object, not to government intervention, but to regulation by government. The fact that such a fundamental issue is still debated in the United States puts advocates of planning on the defensive. The most they seem to hope for is a high level advisory system and a mandate to plan; they are inclined to be pleased if they can slip some of these mechanisms into other legislation; they have indicated that to be able even to talk about the issue at this point will be a victory.

S. 1795, THE BALANCED GROWTH AND ECONOMIC PLANNING ACT OF 1975

Although the planning bill is long, it is reproduced here as an indication of the sort of specifications that lawmakers may include in major legislation. In examining the bill two issues may be kept in mind: (1) What sort of mechanism is being set up? (Who will it relate to and what will the nature and extent of its power be?) (2) What capacities will it have for gathering knowledge and for making recommendations on the substantive matters that it is being set up to deal with? (Can we do this sort of thing given what is known about the nature of government and politics?)

94th CONGRESS, 1st SESSION: S. 1795

IN THE SENATE OF THE UNITED STATES

MAY 21, 1975

Mr. Humphrey (for himself, Mr. Bayh, Mr. Clark, Mr. Eagleton, Mr. Jackson, Mr. Javits, Mr. McGee, Mr. McGovern, and Mr. Nelson) introduced the following bill; which was read twice and referred to the Committee on Government Operations.

A BILL

To amend the Employment Act of 1946 by providing for the development and adoption of a balanced economic growth plan, and for other purposes.

Be it enacted by the Senate and House of Representatives of the United States of America in Congress assembled, That the Employment Act of 1946 is amended by adding at the end thereof the following new title:

"TITLE II — BALANCED GROWTH AND ECONOMIC PLANNING

"SHORT TITLE

"SEC. 201. This title may be cited as the 'Balanced Growth and Economic Planning Act of 1975.'

"FINDINGS

"SEC. 202. (a) The United States is suffering its worst economic decline since the 1930's. The combination of severe inflation and recession has disrupted the Nation's economy and has caused hardship for millions of Americans. Recession and inflation have both revealed basic structural deficiencies in the United States economy and have been intensified by conflicting and erratic short-term economic policies without in many cases providing long-term solutions.

"(b) The failure to develop a long term national economic policy has also created fundamental imbalances in the economy.

"(c) No single Government agency is responsible for acquiring a current detailed view of the national economy and its component interrelationships and the data necessary to maintain such a picture. Without such information, it is not possible adequately to analyze the economy, to anticipate and identify emerging problems, or to advise the President and the Congress about timely and effective action. Government data collection must be better coordinated and systematized and information should be in a form that permits the identification in detailed comparison of major available options.

"(d) Although the Federal Government plays a major role in the Nation's economy, the United States has no single governmental body engaged in the systematic and comprehensive formulation of national economic goals and policies. The formulation of long-term national economic goals, the identification of available and potential labor, capital, and natural resources, and recommendations for policies to reconcile goals and resources would enable the Federal Government to determine and rationalize its own impact on the national economy. These activities would provide assistance to State and local governments and the private sector by permitting action with greater knowledge of the Nation's economic direction.

"(e) The establishment of an agency to recommend to the executive and legislative branches consistent long-range economic goals and priorities, and policies to provide for their realization, would fill a major national need.

"(f) Individual economic security and personal well-being are essential requirements to balanced growth in a free society. The economic decisions of the Federal Government have direct impact on the lives of individual citizens. It is therefore necessary to provide a process of open and democratic planning for the future to enable the citizens of the United States to participate fully in the making of policies affecting the national economy.

"(g) The Congress finds that the formulation of national economic goals, consistent with the Nation's economic resources and the identification of coherent policies to realize those goals are important national requirements which will achieve balanced economic growth and promote the economic well-being of all our citizens.

"PURPOSES

"SEC. 203. The purposes of this title are to:

"(1) Establish an Economic Planning Board in the Executive Office of the President with responsibility for anticipating the Nation's economic needs, measuring available national economic resources, assuring an adequate supply of industrial raw materials and energy, outlining economic goals, and in the light of long-range economic trends and opportunities, for developing a proposed balanced economic growth plan, and recommending policies to achieve the objectives of the plan.

"(2) Provide for the development of a balanced economic growth plan, embodying coherent and realizable long-term economic goals, consistent with the Nation's economic resources and identifying the policies and actions that would be required to attain such goals.

"(3) Provide for the continuing and systematic access by the Economic Planning Board to economic information and data required to prepare, review, and revise the balanced economic growth plan and to evaluate implementation of the plan, and for the general dissemination of such information and data in accordance with this Act to promote widespread, informed and effective public participation in the planning process.

"(4) Provide for appropriate participation by State and local governments and regional organizations, business, labor, consumers, other interested groups, organizations, and private citizens in the development and revision of such plan.

"(5) Provide for congressional review of each proposed balanced economic growth plan and for the approval or disapproval of the plan by concurrent resolution of the Congress.

"(6) Establish procedures whereby the departments and agencies of the Federal Government will contribute to the continued assessment and implementation of the balanced economic growth plan.

"ECONOMIC PLANNING BOARD

"SEC. 204. (a) There is established in the Executive Office of the President an Economic Planning Board (referred to in this title as the 'Board'). The Board shall be composed of three members who shall be appointed by the President, by and with the advice and consent of the Senate. The Board shall be composed of persons of diverse backgrounds and experience. The President shall designate one of the members of the Board as Chairman.

"(b) The Board, shall —

"(1) Prepare and submit to the Council on Economic Planning a proposed balanced economic growth plan, as provided in section 208(a), for approval by the Council;

"(2) seek the active participation by regional, State, and local agencies and instrumentalities and the private sector through public hearings and other appropriate means to insure that the views and proposals of all segments of the economy are taken into account in the formulation of the plan;

"(3) evaluate and measure the achievement of the goals and objectives contained in any approved balanced economic growth plan and report thereon, as provided in section 208(b);

"(4) review major programs and activities of the Federal Government to determine the extent to which such programs or activities are consistent with any approved plan;

"(5) coordinate the long-range planning activities of the departments and agencies of the Federal Government to assure maximum consistency of such activities with the goals and objectives stated in an approved plan; and

"(6) carry out such other functions pertaining to long-term economic planning as the President may direct.

"(c) The Board is authorized —

"(1) to appoint and fix compensation of, such specialists and other experts as may be necessary to carry out the functions of the Board, the Council, or any advisory committee under this title, without regard to the provisions of title 5, United States Code, governing appointments in the competitive service, and without regard to the provisions of chapter 51 and subchapter III of chapter 53 of such title regarding classification and General Schedule pay rates; and subject to all such provisions, to appoint and fix the compensation of such other officers and employees as may be necessary for carrying out such functions;

"(2) to procure temporary and intermittent services to the same extent as is authorized by section 3109 of title 5, United States Code;

"(3) to contract with any public agency or instrumentality or with any person or organization for the performance of services in furtherance of the functions and responsibilities of the Office; and

"(4) hold such hearings at such times and places as he deems advisable, and administer oaths and affirmations to witnesses.

"(d) (1) Section 5313 of title 5, United States Code, is amended by adding at the end thereof the following:

" '(13) Members of the Economic Planning Board.'

"DIVISION OF ECONOMIC INFORMATION

"Sec. 205. (a) There is established in the Board a Division of Economic Information through which the Board is authorized to secure information, data, estimates, and statistics directly from various departments, agencies, and establishments of the executive branch of Government. All such departments, agencies, and establishments shall furnish the Board any available material which it determines to be necessary in the performance of its duties and functions (other than material the disclosure of which would be a violation of law). The Board is also authorized upon agreement with the head of any such department, agency, or establishment, to utilize its services, facilities, and personnel with or without reimbursement, and the head of each such department, agency, or establishment is authorized to provide the Director such services, facilities, and personnel.

"(b) The Board shall carry out a program to insure the dissemination of economic data, statistics, and information in such form and manner as will provide a basis on which State and local governments, private enterprise, and the Federal Government can make informed economic decisions and participate effectively in the planning process carried out under this title.

"(c) (1) The furnishing of any information, data, estimates, or statistics under this title by any person acting independently or pursuant to a requirement established under this title shall not be a violation of or evidence of a violation of any of the antitrust laws of the United States.

"(2) Disclosure of any information, data, estimates, or statistics in violation of any rule or regulation promulgated by the Board or the disclosure of any trade secret or proprietary information or any other information furnished to the Federal Government on a confidential basis by any person in the exercise of functions under this title shall be a violation of section 1905 of title 18, United States Code.

"council on economic planning

"Sec. 206. (a) There is established in the Economic Planning Board a Council on Economic Planning (referred to in this title as the 'Council') which shall consist of —

"(1) the Chairman of the Economic Planning Board, who shall be the Chairman of the Council;

"(2) the Secretary of State;

"(3) the Secretary of the Treasury;

"(4) the Secretary of Defense;

"(5) the Secretary of the Interior;

"(6) the Secretary of Housing and Urban Development;

"(7) the Attorney General;

"(8) the Secretary of Transportation;

"(9) the Secretary of Agriculture;

"(10) the Secretary of Commerce;

"(11) the Secretary of Labor;

"(12) the Secretary of Health, Education, and Welfare;

"(13) the Chairman of the Federal Reserve Board;

"(14) the Chairman of the Council of Economic Advisers;

"(15) the Director of the Office of Management and Budget;

"(16) the Administrator of the Federal Energy Administration; and

"(17) the Chairman of the Advisory Committee on Economic Planning.

"(b) It shall be the function of the Council to review and make such revisions as it deems appropriate in the balanced economic growth plan as submitted by the Board under section 204, and, upon approval of the plan, to transmit the plan to the President, and to review, on a regular basis, progress made in the implementation of the plan. The Council shall adopt such rules for the conduct of its business as it may deem proper.

"advisory committee on economic planning

"Sec. 207. (a) To furnish advice and assistance to the Board in the preparation and review of the plan, there is established an Advisory Committee on Economic Planning which shall consist of —

"(1) four members appointed by the President;

"(2) four members appointed by the Speaker of the House of Representatives; and

"(3) four members appointed by the President of the Senate.

The Committee shall elect a Chairman, and shall meet at the call of the Chairman, but not less than twice a year. The members of the Advisory Committee shall be appointed from among representatives of business, labor, and the public at large, who are competent by virtue of training or experience to furnish advice to the Board on the views and opinions of broad segments of the public in matters involved in the formulation and implementation of the balanced economic growth plan. Each member of the Advisory Committee shall be entitled to be compensated at a rate equal to the per diem equivalent of the rate for an individual occupying a position under level III of the Executive Schedule under section 5314 of title 5, United States Code, when engaged in the actual performance of his duties as such a member, and each member shall be entitled to reimbursement for travel, subsistence, and other necessary expenses incurred in the performance of his duties.

"(b) The Advisory Committee is authorized to establish regional or industry subcommittees to furnish advice and assistance to it in the formulation and implementation of the plan. Any such subcommittee shall consist of at least one member of the Advisory Committee and shall be broadly representative of the particular region or industry, including business, labor, and consumer interests.

"THE BALANCED ECONOMIC GROWTH PLAN

"SEC. 208. (a) Not later than April 1, 1977, and bi-annually thereafter, the President shall transmit to the Congress a proposed long-term balanced economic growth plan prepared by the Board and approved by the Council. The plan shall —

"(1) establish economic objectives for a period to be determined by the Board, paying particular attention to the attainment of the goals of full employment, price stability, balanced economic growth, an equitable distribution of income, the efficient utilization of both private and public resources, balanced regional and urban development, stable international relations, and meeting essential national needs in transportation, energy, agriculture, raw materials, housing, education, public services, and research and development;

"(2) identify the resources required for achieving the economic objectives of the plan by forecasting the level of production and investment by major industrial, agricultural, and other sectors, the levels of State, local, and Federal Government economic activity, and relevant international economic activity, for the duration of the plan; and

"(3) recommend legislative and administrative actions necessary or desirable to achieve the objectives of the plan, including recommendations with respect to money supply growth, the Federal budget, credit needs, interest rates, taxes and subsidies, antitrust and merger policy, changes in industrial structure and regulation, international trade, and other policies and programs of economic significance.

"(b) The President shall submit to the Congress with the proposed plan a report prepared by the Board and approved by the Council. The report shall —

"(1) provide whatever data and analysis are necessary to support the objectives, resource needs, and policy recommendations contained in the plan;

"(2) provide an examination of longer term economic trends beyond the period of the plan and recommend objectives with respect to the goals outlined in subsection (a) (1):

"(3) compare the actual results with respect to matters referred to in subsection (a) since the submission of the previous plan with the projected results of the plan when submitted and indicate (A) the reason for any failure to achieve the objectives of that plan, (B) the steps being taken to achieve the objectives of the previous plan, and (C) any necessary revisions in the plan.

"STATE AND LOCAL PARTICIPATION

"Sec. 209. (a) The Board shall establish procedures to insure widespread consultation with regional, State, and local planning agencies in preparation of the plan.

"(b) At the time of submission of any proposed plan to the Congress, the President shall transmit copies of the plan to the Governor of each State and to other appropriate State and local officials. Within sixty days from the submission by the President to Congress of the proposed plan, the Governor of each State may submit to the Joint Economic Committee a report containing findings and recommendations with respect to the proposed plan. Any such report submitted by a Governor shall include the views and comments of citizens within the State, after public hearings have been held within the State.

"(c) Upon the request of any regional, State, or local planning agency, the Economic Planning Board shall review the plan of such agency to determine its consistency with the plan and recommend changes to bring such plan more fully into conformity with the plan. Funds available to such an agency under section 701 of the Housing Act of 1954 may, in accordance with such regulations as the President may prescribe, be used by such agency for the purpose of making such changes.

"CONGRESSIONAL REVIEW

"Sec. 210. (a) Each proposed balanced economic growth plan shall be referred to the Joint Economic Committee of the Congress. Within sixty days after receipt by the Congress of such proposed plan, each standing committee of the House of Representatives and each standing committee of the Senate and each joint committee of the Congress shall submit to the Joint Economic Committee a report containing its views and recommendations with respect to all matters contained in the plan which relate to matters within the jurisdiction of each such committee. The reports by the Committee on the Budget of the Senate and the Committee on the Budget of the House of Representatives shall contain the recommendations of such committees respecting budget policy for the duration of the plan.

"(b) The Joint Economic Committee shall hold such hearings for the purpose of receiving testimony from Members of Congress, appropriate representatives of Federal departments and agencies, the general public, and interested groups as the committee deems advisable. The committee shall also consider the comments and views on the proposed plan which are received from State and local officials under section 209.

"(c) Not later than one hundred and five days after the submission of a proposed national economic plan to the Congress, the Joint Economic Committee shall report to the House of Representatives and to the Senate a concurrent resolution which shall state in substance that Congress approves or disapproves the proposed plan, in whole or in part, and which may contain such alternatives to, modifications of, or additions to the plan as the committee deems appropriate. The report accompanying such concurrent resolution shall include findings and recommendations of the committee with respect to each of the main recommendations contained in the proposed plan. The Joint Economic Committee may from time to time make such other reports and recommendations to the House and Senate as it deems advisable.

"(d) Not later than one hundred and thirty-five days after submission of a proposed national economic plan to the Congress, the Congress shall act upon a concurrent resolution reported under subsection (c). Upon adoption of any such resolution, a copy thereof, together with a copy of any report or document prepared by any committee of either House or by any joint committee in connection with the consideration by the Congress of the proposed plan shall be transmitted to the President.

"(c) There are hereby authorized to be appropriated to the Joint Economic Committee such sums as may be necessary to enable it to carry out its functions under this section.

"FINAL ADOPTION OF PLAN

"Sec. 211. (a) Upon receipt of a concurrent resolution pursuant to section 208, the President may make such modifications as he deems appropriate in any part of the plan which was disapproved or which was not approved by the Congress, and shall publish a copy of the plan, together with a copy of the concurrent resolution and all reports and documents accompanying such resolution, except that, if the concurrent resolution disapproved the entire proposed plan, the President shall revise the plan and resubmit it to the Congress not later than thirty days after the receipt of the concurrent resolution. Not later than thirty days after receipt of a revised plan under the preceding sentence, the Congress shall, by concurrent resolution, approve or disapprove, in whole or in part, the revised plan.

"(b) The President directly, or acting through the Board, may not take any action under section 212, and the Board may not take any action under such section, with respect to any part of the plan which has not been approved or which has been disapproved by the Congress.

"EXECUTIVE BRANCH IMPLEMENTATION OF THE PLAN

"Sec. 212. (a) The President, with the assistance of the Board, shall take appropriate actions to insure that the departments and agencies of the executive branch will carry out their programs and activities in such a manner as to further the objectives of the plan, and to encourage State and local governments and the private sector to carry out their programs and activities in such a manner as to further the objectives of the plan.

"(b) Whenever the Board determines that any department or agency of the Federal Government has submitted any budget request to the President or the Congress, or proposed any legislation, rule, or regulation, or undertaken any other activity which may have a significant effect on the achievement of the goals and objectives contained in an approved balanced economic growth plan, the Board may require the head of such department or agency to submit a detailed statement to the Board assessing the consistency of the proposed budget, legislation, rule, regulation, or other action, with the plan, together with the reasons for any significant departure from such goals and objectives.

"DIVISION OF BALANCED GROWTH AND ECONOMIC PLANNING

"Sec. 213. (a) There is established within the Congressional Budget Office a Division of Balanced Growth and Economic Planning (hereinafter referred to as the 'Division') to perform long-term economic analysis. The Division shall be headed by a Deputy Director who shall perform his duties under the supervision of the Director of the Congressional Budget Office and shall perform such other duties as may be assigned to him by the Director. Such Deputy Director shall be appointed in the same manner, serve for the same period, and receive the same compensation as the Deputy Director provided for in section 201 of the Congressional Budget Act of 1974.

"(b) It shall be the responsibility of the Division to assist the Joint Economic Committee in the discharge of its duties under this Act and to provide —

"(1) information with respect to long-term economic trends, national goals, resource availability, and the economic policies necessary to achieve balanced long-term economic growth,

"(2) information necessary for the preparation of the report and concurrent resolution identified in section 210 (d), and

"(3) such related information as the committee may request.

"(c) At the request of any other committee of the House of Representatives or the Senate, or any joint committee of Congress, the Division shall provide to such committee or joint committee the information necessary to fulfill their responsibilities under section 208 (a).

"AUTHORIZATION

"Sec. 214. There are authorized to be appropriated such sums as may be necessary to carry out the provisions of this title."

RELATION TO THE COUNCIL OF ECONOMIC ADVISERS

Sec. 2. It shall be the duty of the Council of Economic Advisers to make an analysis of the relationship between the economic report and the plan. The analysis of the Council shall be included in the economic report transmitted to Congress.

ECONOMIC INFORMATION

Sec. 3. At the time of the presentation of the first balanced economic growth plan to Congress, the Division of Economic Information of the Economic Planning Board, at the direction of and with the approval of the Board, shall transmit to the Congress a report on economic data, statistics, and information, which shall contain the following:

(1) A review, carried out in conjunction with other departments and agencies of the Federal Government, of the activities, methods, and purposes of the information and statistical gathering, collation, analysis, and presentation functions of the Federal Government.

(2) An analysis of the existing information and statistical systems, and the economic data required under section 204 of this Act.

(3) Recommendations for the improvement or modification in the standards, methods, and systems of statistics and information gathering.

(4) Recommendations for such additional authority as may be necessary to obtain data not available under section 204 of this Act.

THE DEBATE ON PLANNING

Debate on a far-reaching piece of legislation like S. 1795 is not simply a theoretical exercise. It is conducted with reference to various views of the political world, and the discussion is carried forward by recognizable interest groups who perceive their lives will be affected if the ideas are put into practice. There are various arenas for this sort of debate; each has a different audience and approaches the matter differently. A specialized magazine like *Challenge* reaches an audience interested in economic matters, while a newspaper article will present the information to a much larger and more diverse audience. An address to a chamber of commerce or an article in a magazine of opinion like *The Progressive* reaches people likely to have different views of the proper activities of government. Differences in approach, in response to the varied audiences, are evident in the following presentations.

THE FEAR OF PLANNING

FROM THE EDITOR

"Frankly," said I to my barber, "I am afraid of economic planning."

My barber is the most literate person I know. No matter how early I arrive for a haircut, he has already read every word of *The New York Times.*

"But monsieur," he replied, since he is French, "you are a businessman. It is not becoming to a businessman to be afraid of planning." He picked up the *Management Review* and leafed through its pages.

"Read this ad," he said, jabbing a finger at a headline. " 'Any organization that doesn't plan for its future isn't likely to have one.' That is what a corporate planning service has to say. Businessmen will agree. Family heads will agree. The Joint Chiefs of Staff will agree. The Mafia will agree. But suggest that the President and the Congress of the United States plan, and you are in trouble."

He fastened the apron around my neck. "Everyone knows that businesses have to be run by people; but the economy, mon Dieu! the economy runs itself."

I muttered something about the invisible hand as the scissors clicked around my head.

"The will to believe in miracles: what a wonder! Long ago nature was generous; workers were obliging; and the economy was small and simple. Those days are gone, monsieur, gone. We must plan. But first we must cast out fear."

"Fear, yes, fear," I said as I sank into the chair. "I fear that planning means the end of something we all cherish — the free market system."

"You say this to a Frenchman? To me, the only French barber in America? We French have been planning for thirty years. Do we not still have a free market system? Our planning tries to make the market work well. You Americans are very practical. Maybe you will do better than the French.

"Let us try to be sensible," he continued, applying lather to my neck. "Suppose the Congress and the President — perhaps Mr. Ford's successor — decided in a general way how to spend our national income between now and the year 2000. So much for consumption; so much for investment; so much for housing, mass transit, health care, energy, and research. Then suppose the economists told them what kinds of incentives and controls would be necessary, not to destroy the market, but to guide it. Is this a terrible thing?"

"But Pierre," I interjected, "the economy is an intricate web. A vague idea of how all the strands tie together will not do."

"True," he replied, stropping his razor. "Planning will require a much more intimate knowledge of the economy than we now have. Summary figures of gross national product, employment and price levels will not do. Detailed information about the transactions between one industry and another will be required. It will take a big staff to get the information and it will take a lot of money.

"But what is the alternative? We have no means at present, none at all, neither automatic nor deliberate, to see to it that the structure of the economy will be as we wish it in ten or twenty years. How many cars, trains, trucks, ships and planes will we have by the year 2000? How much energy will we have to run them? Do not tell me that the commuter and the shipper will decide such matters. Am I to believe that the auto industry grew; roads were built; railroads declined; blacks moved from the rural South to the urban North; the middle class fled to the suburbs; Lake Erie was polluted; energy-using metal containers replaced returnable bottles; indestructible synthetic fibers replaced biodegradable cottons and woolens; and multinational corporations exported jobs to Hong Kong and Korea because the public wanted it that way? Sacre bleu! You Americans will believe anything."

This remark was accompanied by a savage slash at my right sideburn. I began to perspire. It seemed best to concede a point. "Let us admit that planning might help the market satisfy our needs a little better than it does now. Still I do not want to go down a road that will destroy private enterprise and end in socialism and dictatorship," said I as firmly as circumstances permitted.

"My dear sir," replied Pierre, temperately shaping my left sideburn, "if planners wish to sleep nights, they will not try to meddle in the millions of decisions made by businessmen every day. Instead, they will use gentle inducements like taxes and capital regulations to persuade management to play the game according to the rules.

"As for socialism, that is up to the public. But if I were a capitalist wanting to preserve the status quo, I would lobby for planning. Planning means an orderly economy. Planning means cooperation. Planning means more confidence in the future. Planning means less anxiety among workers. That is how I would see it if I were a capitalist.

"On the other hand, if I were a socialist wanting to change the status quo, I would still lobby for planning. Planning means a national debate about the future of the country. Planning means an open discussion about the allocation of resources and the distribution of income. Planning means making our economic goals explicit. Clearly, the public — so the socialist should reason — will be horrified to learn what objectives Big Business pursues and will want to change them. May the better arguments win."

I felt my fears ebbing away as the pleasant sensation of the electric massager spread throughout my shoulders. "Dictatorship?" Pierre mused. "Authoritarian governments engage in authoritarian planning. Democratic governments engage in democratic planning. Sleep in peace. Plans are subject to change at the next election."

"Must I swallow five-year plans, too?" I ventured. "They are so rigid."

"Plans are not plans without deadlines," came the ineluctable reply, as my hair was parted, the clock ticked away and the next customer finished *Playboy* and started to fidget. "Take it from Peter F. Drucker: 'What do we have to do now to attain our objectives tomorrow?' 'Tomorrow' for me means cutting a head of hair in fifteen minutes. For a town planner it means building a new town in ten years. For a planner of mass transit it means constructing a national transportation system in twenty-five years. Plans are schedules, not straightjackets. If the unforseen happens, if crops fail, if oil supplies are cut off, how much better is it to have a plan that can be adjusted than to have no plan at all."

"But," said I, as I rose from the chair, dug in my pocket for $3.50 and put on my jacket, "when planners make mistakes, heaven help us. They will be bigger mistakes."

"Bigger than what?" asked the astonished Pierre. "Here we are without planning, enjoying the worst shortages, the biggest inflation, and the deepest recession in forty years. Can planners do worse?

"My dear friend," concluded my friendly barber, walking to the door with his arm over my shoulders, "once fear is cast out, planning will become irresistibly appealing to the human sense of order, logic and purposefulness. Think what a tribute it is to the persuasive talents of the economics profession that people have been convinced against all the testimony of their senses that the economy plans itself. Sadly, miracles happen only in economic theory, not in the workaday world. When fear stops, the illusion of the miracle will end. Then planning will not only become irresistible; it will become respectable."

MES
[Myron E. Sharpe]

A PLANNED ECONOMY IN THE U.S.?

JACK FRIEDMAN

With the unemployment rate approaching 9 per cent and inflation at a similar level Americans are very critical of the way in which national economic decisions are being made.

The general belief is that policymakers do not anticipate upcoming problems and that current economic policy is determined by the timing of the next election. Under these conditions, it is felt, the winner of the 1976 Presidential race may well be determined largely by the state of the economy and by a candidate's image as an economic problem solver.

Democratic and Republican Presidential candidates alike, then, are searching for politically appealing economic proposals which are general in nature and do not commit them to definite programs. One of the most appealing will be national economic planning.

Leonard Woodcock, head of the United Automobile Workers Union, puts the case this way: "We live in a large, complex, technological society in which planlessness means massive dislocations. It is a crime to allow millions of workers to lose their jobs because we refuse to plan."

Although widely practiced in Western Europe, planning was for years associated here with Communist central planning alone. It has not been

Mr. Friedman is a management consultant for Arthur D. Little, Inc.
SOURCE: From *The New York Times*, May 18, 1975. © 1975 by The New York Times Company. Reprinted by permission.

attempted in the United States in peacetime since the National Resources Planning Board of the New Deal days.

A change in thinking has recently occurred. America's economic turmoil during the last decade has created a new open-mindedness throughout the United States, even among businessmen, toward the idea of national planning.

Just last week Senators Hubert H. Humphrey, Democrat of Minnesota, and Jacob K. Javits, Republican of New York, introduced the first bill that would establish national planning here, creating a Federal agency, the Economic Planning Board. The legislation has had the backing of a private group including Nobel Prize-winning economist Wassily Leontief, Robert V. Roosa, partner in Brown Brothers, Harriman, and Mr. Woodcock.

But economic planning is an idea that is not well understood in the United States. As John Dunlop, Secretary of Labor, observes, "It's hard to discuss planning because almost nobody knows what it means."

In a basic sense, planning simply means thinking ahead to prepare for the future.

Short-term economic thinking goes on continuously throughout the Federal Government. Such activity is fragmented. It usually focuses on specific issues such as highway construction or agricultural price supports. Often the objectives and implementation of different programs conflict.

The new Senate and House Budget Committees provide a Congressional overview of spending levels and priorities instead of the usual piecemeal approach. Their activity is a step toward planning.

In contrast, the Humphrey–Javits bill would establish comprehensive planning, with consideration of the economy as a whole or major sectors of it over a long period of time. A plan might include projections of gross national product, investment, employment, prices, government spending, taxes and other factors. When imbalances between national needs and resources are identified, specific actions could be taken to correct them.

According to this concept, the plan, covering six years, would be a guiding document for the executive branch. It would be revised and extended every two years. The President would submit it for congressional approval through a joint resolution. New appropriations or laws needed to implement the plan would require legislative authorization.

The first step in establishing United States planning would be to improve data collection, analysis and forecasting capabilities. The incompleteness and decentralization until recently of data gathering on energy is cited as an example of the general weakness of current collection methods.

While improved forecasting is widely supported as an objective, many experts are skeptical about its feasibility based on recent experience.

William Fellner, who recently served on the President's Council of economic Advisors, has observed, "The success of long-term forecasting to date has been quite limited."

Until the results of forecasting are widely accepted, the resistance to using them to guide policy will be powerful.

Many businessmen, labor leaders and economists see national planning as helping industry and government anticipate problems and design long-term programs. They want a plan to be tied to the formulation of government monetary, fiscal and spending policies.

This approach contrasts to planning involving direct controls over the private sector such as preferential credit allocations or price and wage controls.

James Balog, chairman of the Wall Street firm of William D. Witter, Inc., argues, "We wouldn't run our families the way we run the economy. We try to have a boom during an election year at the price of recessions in between. Corporations plan and the government should, too. Planning could help us look beyond the next election."

Henry Ford 2d, chairman of the Ford Motor Company, speaks out frequently in favor of planning, as long as it does not lead to new Federal controls.

Mr. Ford believes that the shortages in the supply of metals and other materials seen in 1973 and 1974 could have been anticipated if there had been planning. Secretary Dunlop has already begun to warn that prosperity after the current recession will be cut short unless Federal officials begin to deal now with likely industrial capacity bottlenecks.

Despite the support for planning without direct controls, there is fear that it could create momentum toward such controls, fears that spur often violent opposition.

Walter Wriston, chairman of the First National City Bank, believes that the Leontief group "is pressing for a program designed to destroy the free-market system and with it our personal liberty. National economic planning would be delegated to bureaucrats who like all regulators would then require arbitary power to enforce each decision."

Conservative Senator James Buckley of New York agrees: "The economic efficiency which comes from the free-market system is the key to satisfying human needs. Planning will systematically inhibit industry's ability to respond to the wishes of individuals."

Eli Shapiro, chairman of the finance committee at the Travelers Corporation, asks: "How do you keep planners, who believe that they have a better vision of the future than anyone else, from eventually trying to run the private sector as a self-appointed elite?"

On the other hand, many believe that planning does not necessarily lead to elitism or strong government controls. "The fear of controls is exaggerated," says Prof. Paul Samuelson of the Massachusetts Institute of Technology, a winner of the Nobel Prize in economics.

Interestingly enough, many conservatives tend to envision the planning elite as being dominated by liberal economists and professors who want to move toward more government spending and control. Many liberals, meanwhile, fear that the elite would be dominated by conservative business interests which would use planning to suppress economic reform and to support big business.

Kenneth Arrow, a Nobel Prize-winning economist at Harvard, speculates, "If the economic stakes in planning were ever high enough, business interests would try to use planning to maintain the status quo. They would be tempted to corrupt the system for their own advantage."

Thus basic questions must be asked: What is the purpose of planning and whose values will predominate? Should we plan for greater material growth or for qualitative change in American life such as improved urban living and environmental protection?

George Meany, head of the American Federation of Labor and Congress of Industrial Organizations, argues:

"We need long-range economic planning and priorities to minimize unforeseen major developments and reduce the degree to which American society has stumbled and fumbled along in the past few years," he says. "As an example, the United States was not prepared for the urban crisis of the 1960's — which could have been foreseen by sensible long-range economic planning in the 1950's."

Almost all non-Communist countries do attempt some form of planning. Cooperation of the private sector is not legally mandatory, but powerful government inducements usually exist, most notably preferential credit allocations. France, Great Britain and Japan are distinctive examples.

France has the best known system, called "indicative planning." It is called that because it indicates where the economy and government policies will be heading but does not coerce industry into fulfilling plan objectives. The lessened uncertainty which results is intended to aid businessmen in evaluating their long-term investments.

Bruce Scott and John McArthur, professors at the Harvard Business School, reached a very different conclusion, however, after a three-year analysis of French planning.

According to Professor Scott, currently a trustee of the Penn Central, "France's Ministry of Finance as well as industry executives generally disregard the plans. When the Government allocates credit or intervenes in the private sector, which occurs often, it isn't done with the plan in mind."

The fact that plans often become simply academic documents is a common complaint among economists. Nevertheless, many of them believe that the process of creating a plan in itself can be of great value, drawing all interested groups into a national dialogue on long-term priorities and programs.

British planning began during World War II. The Labor Party, with its ambitious program of nationalization, extended it into the peacetime years.

But plans of the Conservative and Labor Parties alike have been continually revised and then dropped as rapidly changing international economic conditions forced the adoption of numerous short-term economic policies.

The current Labor Government has proposed the concept of a "planning agreement," under which a company would make pledges regarding investment and employment for the following three years and in conjunction the Government would promise to maintain a certain level of financial assistance.

In Japan, industrial associations and government agencies meet to project future growth of key industries and investment priorities. Government policies are defined and coordinated as a result of this informal process as well as through the formal five-year plans which the Economic Planning Agency creates.

Business cooperation is not mandatory, the Government uses credit policies and informal "administrative guidance" to induce cooperation. Many Western executives believe that Japan has the most-planned economy in the world and that it has been quite successful despite the nation's pollution and urbanization problems.

Norway and Sweden are cited by Professor Leontief as successful examples of planning. He particularly admires their data collection, coordination and analysis activity.

But the professor believes that "America cannot import a planning system from abroad. Countries differ in their planning methods because the countries themselves differ. We should want and expect a distinctive American style."

Many other countries have parliamentary systems involving a unified executive and legislative majority. In contrast, the United States has a check-and-balance system with divisions between the President and Congress; among Federal, state, and local governments, and among agencies within the same Administration. This may protect against excesses by planners and politicians. On the other hand, some argue that such institutional fragmentation would obstruct agreement on a plan and prevent continuity and coordination in its execution.

At this time Congress, the Administration, the business sector and labor are increasingly receptive to planning — if it does not lead to government control over industry. Sentiment is growing in the United States for more long-term, coordinated government approaches to economic problems. And this is the substance of planning.

THE EMPTY PROMISE OF THE PLANNER: PRIVATE ENTERPRISE OR NATIONAL ECONOMIC PLANNING?

THOMAS A. MURPHY

The present thrust toward national economic planning is no textbook exercise. It is a pending bill — S1795 — introduced last month into the United States Senate by Senators Hubert Humphrey and Jacob Javits, and compared by them in importance to the Employment Act of 1946 and the Budget Act of 1974.

Proposals such as these concern me as a businessman. While I marvel at the overriding strength of free-market forces, I also appreciate how fragile and subtle are their workings. I know, on the one hand, that the American practice of free enterprise has, over more than two hundred years, lifted our way of life to a level beyond even the dreaming of the vast majority of the world's people. But I know as well that, like a living thing, our economic system is dangerously vulnerable. It is dependent upon a myriad of intensely personal decisions made every day in a million marketplaces by people who themselves are largely unknowing of the system and often distrustful of its operation. Too many people, unfortunately, have come to accept the benefits of free enterprise as flowing automatically to America as God-given rights. They do not see these benefits as results earned by hard work and sacrifice — and which must continue to be earned to be preserved.

Critics of free-market economics are as old as the idea of America itself, and as young as this year's freshmen. Nevertheless, their criticisms, given new topicality by recession and new audiences by our communication media, foster widespread public suspicion that our economic system — free enterprise, competitive capitalism, call it what you will — is no longer adequate for our times.

Their continuing attack on America's ability to make a market-directed economy work for the benefit of its people has profound implications. The

SOURCE: Thomas A. Murphy, Chairman of the Board, General Motors Corporation; talk delivered before the Greater Detroit Chamber of Commerce, Detroit, Mich. Reprinted from *Vital Speeches of the Day*, 41, No. 19 (15 July 1975), pp. 591–594.

alternative they suggest, national economic planning, strikes directly at the very foundation of free enterprise: at individual freedom, at the authority of the American public to direct, to determine, and to decide for itself. The calls for economic planning, well-meaning as some of them may be, are nevertheless rooted in a distrust of economic democracy, in a reluctance to leave decision-making in the hands of the people, in an unwillingness to let the public choose in a free market the kinds of products it wants and needs.

Professor Irving Kristol of New York University astutely describes the free market's current critics as "a new class," but the inheritors of an attitude towards capitalism which has flourished among intellectuals for more than 150 years. This attitude, he writes, "is basically suspicious of, and hostile to, the market precisely because the market is so vulgarly democratic .... responsive to the common appetites, preferences, and aspirations of common people. The 'new class' — intelligent, educated, energetic — has little respect for such a commonplace civilization."

Unfortunately, the idea of national economic planning seems to have wide appeal. People usually respond sympathetically to the word planning, as in "planning a vacation," or "planning retirement." The meaning there is "to prepare for" — and, as every Boy Scout knows, to be prepared is good. But "planning" to the advocates of economic planning means more than preparation: it means an organized effort to direct, to control, to allocate the resources of a society — not according to the desires of freely-acting men and women — but instead to allocate resources in order to create a society according to the ideal of — guess who — the planners themselves.

A case in point: the public preference in automobiles. Some Americans — a great many in fact — like or need full-size cars. They are not merely an affluent few who are willing and able to pay a higher price and accept a penalty in gas mileage for the extra room, extra comfort, and extra security. Many American families need a car that has enough room to accommodate a family of five or more and their luggage on a vacation trip, for example. More than a luxury, it is a necessity which for many can only be met by a used car. However, because so many people do use these cars, certain consequences result throughout society. So some advocates of planning would like to take the decision on the size of cars out of the free marketplace. They want to intervene in the decision-making process in order to produce a result in closer conformance to the society of their ideal, not necessarily the common ideal of common people.

The critical question is: who's going to do the planning? The advocates of national economic planning are unwilling to leave decisions in the free market. So we can be sure any national economic planning will be done by members of this new class, these idealistic, energetic, articulate people who have certain ideas about the kind of civilization they wish to live in. And who would make all the rest of the people conform to their ideas as well!

In that context, the word planning means power. That is precisely what it means, and precisely what the new class has in mind — power for them. It means that they will decide what our society should look like ten years from now, or fifteen years from now. Should they make mistakes, and should their plans not work so well — so what? As far as these people are concerned, every failure in planning helps to establish the necessity of planning. Obviously what is more logical to correct the mistakes in planning than more planning, more comprehensive planning, more intensive planning.

When we talk about national economic planning, we are not engaging in some trivial little disagreement on economics. We are discussing a basic, secular change in our liberal capitalist society: a change in decision making, a turn away from the individual's economic freedom.

Surprisingly, the disparagement of our system comes from those who should be best able to see the contrast between our country and others, between the diverse riches of freedom and dreary poverty of planned economies. To all who would substitute national economic planning for the free market, the system in which free people freely decide the best use of resources, I say consider only this: what we define as the poverty level in America is the average family income in Russia.

In the current issue of *The Reader's Digest*, former Governor Reagan of California tells how we could match Russia's record after more than half a century, of its five-year plans. "We'd have to cut our paychecks back by more than 80 percent; move 33 million workers back to the farm; destroy 59 million television sets; tear up 14 of every 15 miles of highway; junk 19 of every 20 automobiles; tear up two thirds of our railroad track; knock down 70 percent of our houses and rip out nine out of every ten telephones. Then all we have to do is find a capitalist country to sell us wheat on credit to keep us from starving!" Then, as Governor Reagan reminds us, we would be on a par with Russia.

As a businessman — an American businessman — I am concerned about the slide toward economic regimentation in the United States. I stand with those who believe that economic freedom is indivisible from our other freedoms. It would be tragic if by our indifference we were to allow the Bicentennial Era to become the twilight of America's freedom — the freedom that has given America its national greatness.

Fundamentally, there are only two ways to organize economic activity — either through voluntary cooperation or by means of coercion; that is, by freedom or by force. All societies are mixtures of these two forms. At one end of the scale are the command societies where economic activity is centrally directed by government planners. The world has too many examples of these. At the other extreme are unfettered free-market economies, or what is known as capitalism. America, thankfully, remains the best example, having been founded and having prospered into the earth's wealthiest and freest country on the principles of private enterprise which are consistent with our national dedication to other freedoms — of worship, of the press, of thought, and of individual economic choice.

Over time, however, we in America have drifted farther and farther away from a free-market, consumer-choice economy and more and more toward a centrally planned or command society. Each new national problem or world crisis has been used to justify an increase in the government's power to manage and control the economy. In 1929, government spending was 10 percent of our Gross National Product. Today it accounts for 32 percent — about a third of our GNP. Our economy, as it stands now, is to a high degree mixed — and mixed up as well.

One question with mixed economies is that when problems develop — and there will always be problems — what do you do to the mix? The critics of a free market have a ready answer: private enterprise is the problem; more government is the solution.

When I hear such assertions, I'm reminded of the scientist who decided to study the reflex actions of a flea. He found a healthy six-legged specimen. After much effort, he succeeded in getting the flea to hop over his thumb at the command "jump." The scientist decided to alter his experiment. He snipped off two of the flea's legs, shouted "jump," and the flea still hurdled his thumb. He then removed two more legs. The flea, tottering now, still managed to get over the thumb. The scientist then snipped off the last two legs, and shouted "jump." But — aha — the flea did not move. The scientist went to his desk and wrote up his findings as follows: "When you remove the legs of a flea, it becomes deaf."

Like this scientist, the advocates of national economic planning, after cutting the legs out from under capitalism, claim that it is the free-market system which has failed. They do not acknowledge the part that their very own remedies have played in reducing our well-being. Free enterprise, the victim, is termed the villain of the piece; and the prescription is to increase the dosage which has laid him low.

BALANCED GROWTH AND ECONOMIC PLANNING ACT OF 1975

REMARKS BY SENATOR JACOB JAVITS

. . . Mr. President, when Senator Humphrey and I introduced the balanced growth and economic planning bill last month, I said that I viewed this as the opening of a great national debate on the American economy and its future. I am greatly pleased by the tremendous response that this bill has received. We had expected that there would be substantial interest in the bill, but even we had not expected the outpouring of editorial comment and in-depth analysis of economic planning.

This is precisely the sort of response that rekindles one's faith in the political process and its ability to generate ideas and reach out to gather inspiration from the American people. In fact, it is this sort of response that the planning bill seeks to engender and systematize with regard to national economic objectives. In the process of this debate, it is inevitable that there will be misinformation and misunderstandings, deliberate and unintentional, about the type of economic planning we have in mind and the specifics of our bill. It is important to set the record straight at this point so that an accumulation of misunderstandings and false labels, such as "garden variety socialism" to quote the *Wall Street Journal*, does not weigh down the bill and prevent a fair consideration on its merits.

. . .

For example, Leif Olson, vice president of First National City Bank, managed to drag in a quote from Premier Kosygin of the U.S.S.R., in his testimony on economic planning, even though he admits that there is absolutely nothing in our legislation that requires the private sector to conform to the plan.

Similarly, in a *Wall Street Journal* editorial of June 17, on the planning bill, the editorial writer manages to pin a label of "garden variety socialism" on the bill — a term which would surely puzzle Marx or Lenin — while simultaneously admitting that there is nothing in the bill calling for the Government control over — let alone takeover — of the means of production, the standard measure of socialism as a policy.

. . .

Although Senator Humphrey and I have both repeatedly stated that our planning bill is neither mandatory nor self-operative and has nothing what-

SOURCE: Reprinted from the *Congressional Record*, June 25, 1975, p. S11506.

soever to do with the centralized planning of socialist states which set production targets and worker and consumer norms — I find it necessary to keep repeating those denials. Because economic planning is a novel concept to Americans, the first inclination in some is to think of the socialist model. Planning must be an integral part of the Soviet economy, because there it is true that planning supplants the free market. However, even the Soviets have learned that it is necessary to subject some portions of their economy to a limited free market system if their plants are not to spew out millions of unwanted left shoes.

On the other hand, Americans are probably less acquainted with economic planning in France and the Scandinavian countries, where there is substantial evidence that it has had a salutory effect on their economies. A recent article on Sweden in the *Wall Street Journal* makes it clear that although Sweden is a welfare state in spending, it has managed to encourage capital investment, saving, and productivity much more successfully than either Great Britain or the United States. This is achieved by providing business with a relatively stable economic climate — in contrast to our on-again off-again approach as for example in our handling of the investment tax credit in the United States — and by providing Swedish corporations with generous incentives. The result is that in 1972 Sweden collected 3.9 percent of its tax revenue from company income taxes while the comparable figure for the United States was 11.2 percent. The Swedish example makes clear a point I have repeatedly stressed — that planning is a neutral tool that adapts to the character of the country. This simple truth should allay fears that we are introducing a socialist device, at the same time that it tempers our expectations that planning will solve every problem in this society.

There are a number of arguments made against Government economic planning and I will try to list these arguments and deal with them. It should be clear from what I said previously that certain arguments rest upon the assumption that our planning bill intends to supplant the free market. Hence, I state once more that our planning bill will only set economic objectives and determine what resources are available to meet them. Yet, even if we set aside this basic misconception relating to displacing the free market, we must nevertheless deal with arguments against any type of planning.

First, it is argued that economic planning is inconsistent with less Government regulation and interference with the economy.

This argument, best illustrated by Walter Wriston's article in *Newsweek*, assumes that the inevitable direction of Government planners is to substitute their judgment for individual judgments. However, it is clear that our bill grants no such powers to planners even if it were their inclination.

As I have stated previously, opponents of planning do not seem to want to believe that it can be a force for improving competition or abolishing outdated government regulation.

But more important there is good evidence that planners do not necessarily have a proclivity toward police state behavior. As an example, the *Wall Street Journal* of June 18, 1975, contained a very interesting article by Timothy D. Schellhardt, on the success of the tiny Council on Wage and Price Stability in forcing other Government agencies to examine the economic impact of their rules and regulations on business and consumers. When one recalls the hew and cry raised in Congress by conservative forces and the business community when the Council on Wage and Price Stability was established, it is interesting to find that its actions have drawn praise from the business community. This is once again an example of the business community's often negative approach to government initiative only to discover later that these were actually in their interest. Just as business has discovered that the Council on Wage and Price Stability can be a flexible tool to make the operation of Government more efficient, it is just possible that they may discover the same thing about an Economic Planning Board.

. . .

Second, the free market, while not perfect, is the best system available and should not be interfered with — so goes the second argument.

In the first place, I have already stated that our bill does not in any fashion supplant the free market. However, no one seriously believes that is the intention of our bill.

The real fear is that planning means the Government will intervene more frequently and systematically in the economy. Without planning the Government will follow its consistently inconsistent course of limited intervention — in certain areas and times, especially hard times, but without a systematic approach.

. . .

The prime consideration, of course, is the fact that we wish to keep the great majority of our population in private employment as the surest guarantee of political freedom. Side by side with this development has been the development of new concepts of technology, marketing, and financing. In today's world many corporations are as big as nations. In many cases they are impervious to normal market pressures of a free enterprise economy. They are sometimes able to increase prices while demand declines. They are frequently able to frustrate demand or create artificial demand for given products.

. . .

As I have said before, government is more involved in our economy because it is more complex, because we face environmental and resource limitations for the first time, and because social objectives are pursued more vigorously. None of these constraints will vanish in the absence of planning. We cannot turn the clock back to the agrarian society of open spaces, and clean air and water, at the time of our independence. Our greatness as a nation has rested on our ability continually to interpret our Constitution while clinging to fundamental values to meet changing circumstances. We are not true to ourselves if we pretend that 18th century economic solutions are adequate to today's world. To follow such [an] antiquated path will cause ever increasing numbers of Americans to become misfits in the economic system, and thus cause their economic powerlessness to vent its frustration in the political nihilism. Let those who would have us blunder through our own and the world's complex economic system look to and be responsible for the consequences of their acts.

. . . A third, and related argument, is that planning seeks to substitute government choice by planners for individual decisions. The implicit assumption in this argument is that people are now free to make a vast variety of meaningful choices.

I wish first to challenge the assumption. It is undoubtedly true that people have major choices among trivia, such as the types of razor blades they wish to use. They can also choose from among a vast assortment of deodorants, hair sprays, frozen foods, tires, shoes, and various other items. It is beneficial to be able to choose among these items, and as we are reminded ad nauseum the Russians are not fortunate enough to be able to make such choices. What is lost in the obfuscation on this issue is that the Swedes can make the same choices, but also get a national health care scheme, and a safer environment.

There are more fundamental choices than the trivial ones — in employment, housing, education, and leisure time use. Americans are fortunate in the great scope of freedom in these significant areas, but let us not get carried away as to what freedom means in certain contexts. Before the JEC hearings on planning last week the witness was incensed because the Government imposed a minimum wage which he said:

Prevents the young and the unskilled from exercising the fundamental freedoms of negotiating for a job on their own terms.

This is known as freedom for employers to control the job market for their benefit, but I do not think you will find many teenagers or unskilled workers who would be enthusiastic about this freedom.

. . .

Fourth, one school of thought finds planning perfectly acceptable for corporations, but quite unacceptable for Government. The reason for this, as stated by the *Wall Street Journal*, is:

Unlike corporate planning, which generally leads to decisions with an eye to maximizing efficiency and profits, government economic planning is dictated by political goals that are often inimical to efficiency.

. . . It is correct that political goals sometimes may be inimical to efficiency but efficiency is neither the exclusive property of private enterprise nor necessarily the highest virtue in our society — ours is not yet a corporate state.

It just may be that one source of our current economic problems is too great concern with "efficiency" in Government. In the name of efficiency millions of Americans could be consigned to the scrap heap of endemic unemployment in order to try to shave some fractions off inflation. Even if the trade-off works, our society has larger, more humane goals than efficiency alone.

It is likely that the development of a plan under our bill will require political compromise, and that is altogether proper. That is after all what the political system is about — to articulate and set in a legal framework the goals and means to achieve those for the society. Economic policies, to be accepted politically, must serve social ends, not vice versa.

. . .

Fifth, a final argument made against planning is that recent government economic policy does not give one great confidence in the ability of government to be farsighted. A corollary is that if the plan and the economy began to diverge, the Government would be tempted to enforce the plan rather than change it.

In many ways, this is the most difficult argument of all because of the erratic nature of our economic policy in the last decade. Economic planning will introduce no magic stability into this decision-making arena, and will only be worthwhile if it is used wisely.

However, one can think of many examples of how it might have been used in recent years to avert poor decisions. Even then it requires a political will to act on better information. As examples, the devaluation of the dollar and the imposition of wage and price controls on domestic sales in 1971 caused an unexpected and very substantial outflow of basic materials and food from the United States, contributing to shortages at home and ultimately to higher prices. The Economic Planning Board might have pointed out the interconnection between the two.

Our agricultural policies have been extremely short-sighted and ill-planned. Everyone knows of the Russian grain deal, but perhaps we have forgotten the freeze on meat prices, which led to meat shortages, or the slaughter of calves when feed grain prices shot up beyond the ability of farmers to make a profit on raising calves. And, acreage restrictions continued long after shortage of grain was well known.

. . .

Planning can give us a road map of where we are going. It cannot force us to choose the road we take. But it helps the driver to know whether the road is paved or bumpy — the same can be said of the alternatives the Economic Planning Board will present.

Our hope is that the planning bill will introduce a longer term view in Government economic policy. Since the plan is only a tool, and since our bill calls for revisions of the plan every 2 years, it is our clear intention that we will change the plan with circumstances rather than vice versa.

I have tried to present what I see as the five main arguments against Government economic planning, and my answers to these arguments. In the course of doing this, I have made several arguments in favor of economic planning as embodied in the balanced growth and economic planning bill . . . .

WHO WILL PLAN THE PLANNED ECONOMY?

JAMES R. CROTTY AND RAFORD BODDY

Four months have passed since President Ford announced his ten-point economic program to a joint session of Congress. The program was dismissed by most commentators at the time as unimaginative, inconsistent, and ineffectual. *The Wall Street Journal* characterized it as "biting the marshmallow."

This was hardly an appropriate characterization for the *real* program chosen by the Ford Administration to deal with the crisis — a long, deep, and potentially disastrous recession. While Ford was unveiling his marshmallow before Congress, the Government's monetary authorities were continuing the severe restriction of money and credit begun in the spring of 1974, while on the fiscal side, the Federal budget would have been in surplus for more than a year if high employment had prevailed.

The *real* Ford program is working — with a vengeance. The take-home pay of the average worker, adjusted for inflation, is more than 5 per cent lower than it was a year ago. The unemployment rate has been rising since October 1973, and recently began a dizzying ascent; it is now generally agreed that it will top 8 per cent some time this year. The inflation-adjusted

James R. Crotty and Raford Boddy are economists on the faculties, respectively, of the University of Massachusetts and the American University in Washington, D.C. Both are members of the Union for Radical Political Economics.

SOURCE: *The Progressive* (February 1975). Reprinted by permission from *The Progressive*, 408 West Gorham Street, Madison, Wisconsin 53703. Copyright © 1975, The Progressive, Inc.

value of the gross national product has been declining for more than a year. There is no hard evidence of an upturn in sight.

The Administration has made it clear that it intends to take any steps necessary to restore order to the economy. If the recessionary policy does not work, even stronger means are available, as we will note later in this article. What may not be as clear is our understanding of how we got into this mess. What is the nature of the crisis which has brought us to this chaotic and dangerous juncture in American and world history?

The roots of the current crisis are not to be found in poor world grain harvests, nor in the diabolical machinations of some Harvard-trained sheiks, nor in the profligacy with which Arthur Burns handled the money supply until last year — though food, oil, and money problems have had their effect. Rather, the crisis has evolved out of the basic institutions of American capitalism and the changing position of the United States in the world capitalist system during the past quarter century. That is, the roots of the current crisis lie in the fundamentally unstable nature of the capitalist growth process — instability which, though relatively dormant at the height of American imperialist power, resurfaced during the past decade when the United States fought to maintain its declining international hegemony.

By its very nature, a capitalist market economy develops through sporadic phases of hectic expansion followed by periods of recession or even depression. The contradictions in our system are such that balanced, full-employment growth cannot be sustained. When an economic expansion reaches the stage of relatively full employment, a series of distortions and imbalances develops which destroys the basis for the continuation of that expansion. For example, increased worker demands at full employment result in higher wage rates and a lower rate of growth of productivity. Inflation accelerates, but not by enough to prevent profit margins from starting to decline. Corporations are forced to turn increasingly to external sources in order to finance investment in plant, equipment, and inventories. Debt thus accumulates just when interest rates are highest. Moreover, serious balance of trade problems develop as the rising price of U.S. products retards exports, and, aided by strong aggregate U.S. demand, stimulates imports.

Eventually, of course, lower profits lead to cutbacks in production and investment and thus, before long, to the end of the expansion. The Government also reacts to these developments, particularly to the decline in profits and the problems in the international sector. With the critical exception of the late 1960s, the Government has reinforced the recessionary pressures developing in the private sector by restricting the supply of money and credit, and by tightening its own budget. Thus, the expansion turns into its opposite — recession.

It is the economic function of the recession to correct the imbalances of the previous expansion and thereby create the preconditions for a new one. By robbing millions of people of their jobs, and threatening the jobs of millions of others, recessions reduce worker demands and end the rise of labor costs. They eventually rebuild profit margins and stabilize prices. During recessions inventories are cut, loans are repaid, corporate liquidity positions improve, and the deterioration in the balance of payments position is reversed. All the statements of Keynesian economists to the contrary notwithstanding, *recessions are inevitable in the unplanned economy of the United States* because they perform an essential function for which no adequate substitute has *thus far* been available.

The adoption in the postwar period of Keynesian approaches to managing the economy has not changed this basic characteristic of the system, nor has the continued monopolization and concentration of market power in the hands of the major corporations lessened the potential for economic instability. Until recently these factors did moderate the fluctuations of the business cycle, but they managed to do so under what now appears to have been a set of unusually favorable conditions — conditions which are no longer in effect.

From the end of World War II until the early 1960s, the United States was the unchallenged leader of world capitalism and the dominant military, political, and economic power. The economic strength of China and the Soviet Union could not compare with that of the United States, and American foreign policy was built on this fact. Western Europe and Japan, on the other hand, began the period with devastated economies; they were almost completely dependent on the United States for imports, particularly capital goods.

In the world of the 1950s, the United States could pour hundreds of billions of dollars into its military machine, waste countless billions on consumer gadgetry and planned obsolescence, and still dominate world trade, accumulate a huge corporate empire in the developed world, and maintain control of the vast natural resources of the underdeveloped world.

The world of the 1950s is gone forever. (See Sidney Lens, "Running Out of Everything," in the October 1974 issue of *The Progressive*.) American political power is now constrained by a strong Soviet Union; its economic supremacy has been challenged by Western Europe and Japan, and its assured supply of cheap raw materials has disappeared. The economic chaos we are witnessing is the re-emergence of the basic instability of our economic system — a re-emergence triggered by the desperate attempts of the United States to maintain its status as the unchallenged leader of world capitalism in the face of the erosion of its power monopoly.

The changing status of American imperialism has had its greatest effect on the economy through the Indochina war, though its impact would eventually have been felt even if that war had not been fought. The outpouring of military expenditures on Vietnam between 1965 and 1968 came on top of an economic expansion which had about run its course. But American imperialism demanded the pursuit of victory in Vietnam, so the Johnson Administration chose to overheat the economy through 1968 by accelerating military spending while taking no effective steps to reduce private spending. The prolongation of the U.S. expansion created, in turn, an environment in which the export-oriented economies of Japan and West Germany could sustain expansions.

In other words, in order to protect the worldwide empire of the multinational corporations, the U.S. Government, by extending the expansion many years beyond its "natural life," created a situation in which the distortions, pressures, and imbalances in the capitalist economies were magnified to proportions which could only be eliminated by an unusually long and severe recession.

The incoming Nixon Administration did engineer a recession by the end of 1969, but it only lasted five or six quarters — clearly not long enough to restore balance to the economy. The Administration was forced to abandon restrictive policies in 1970 because their continuation would have resulted in an unemployment rate too high to be reduced to a politically acceptable level for the 1972 election; because corporate profits, squeezed first by five years of full-employment wage pressure and then by the initial impact of the recession, were in need of immediate relief, and because the debt and liquidity problems of many corporations and banks were too severe to respond to the usual medicine.

By 1971 the economy was clearly in crisis. Falling U.S. interest rates had triggered huge short-term capital outflows and our trade surplus had completely eroded, leading to an explosion in the U.S. payments deficit. The international monetary system was drowning in a flood of U.S. dollars. These dollars in turn were bloating the money supplies of Japan and Europe, causing both inflation and demand-induced economic expansions.

The attempt to shore up the failing U.S. empire through the war in Vietnam can thus be said to have had several important repercussions: First, by prolonging the American economic expansion for three or four years, it left the system vulnerable to its fundamental instability. Second, by laying the foundation for a decade-long expansion in the world capitalist system, it led to a world-wide commodity or raw-material inflation. Third, by accelerating the relative decline in U.S. power, it created the preconditions for the political and economic revolt of the Third World raw-material suppliers, most significantly the exporters of oil. Fourth, it led to the introduction of Government economic controls through Nixon's New Economic Policy, thus signaling the end of the postwar "miracle" of the Keynesian revolution.

The increases in oil and food prices are of relatively recent origin and cannot be held responsible either for domestic inflation or for international financial crisis. But they have seriously exacerbated the existing crisis, and clearly must be taken into account.

The most important cause of the food crisis is the accelerated, worldwide growth in the demand for food which evolved from the sustained world economic boom of the last decade. The food crisis cannot be understood in isolation from the entire set of economic forces. There were bad harvests in 1972, but these were more than compensated for by the good harvests of 1973. The average rate of growth of the world's food supply has not declined over this period. It is the growth of demand which has accelerated, leading to higher prices.

The staggering increase in food prices in the United States has the peculiar characteristic of being deliberately supported by the U.S. Government. In an attempt to protect its international financial strength, the Government embarked on a "great agricultural export drive." One reason the dollar was devalued was to make U.S. food exports more competitive in world markets. Further, the wage–price controls of 1971–1974 fostered the export of agricultural commodities. Raw agricultural products were exempt from controls, as were wood exports. Profit margins on exported food products were thus higher than profit margins on food sold domestically. And wage controls in the face of skyrocketing food prices meant that American workers could not afford their usual share of agricultural production.

The export drive succeeded; agricultural exports rose from an average of $5 billion per year in the late 1960s to $9.4 billion in 1972 and $17.5 billion in 1973.

Even in the case of oil prices, the declining world power of the United States has played a role. So long as this country enjoyed a virtual monopoly on economic, political, and military power, it could depend on a supply of cheap raw materials. Because of our weakened international position, however, it was impossible to prevent the oil producing countries from quadrupling the price of crude oil in the fall of 1973. Despite the recent saber-rattling rhetoric from Washington, the U.S. Government has been forced to exercise caution in its attempts to discipline the oil producing nations and reduce the price of imported crude.

What are the likely prospects for the future? There is no easy way out of the current crisis of inflation and falling real wages. In the twisted logic of capitalist development, the current crisis requires a prolonged recession as well as the possible imposition of wage and price controls.

The price of dampening world-wide inflationary pressure will be high, but no one really knows how much unemployment, idle capacity, and other waste it will take to win the fight against inflation. Unfortunately, there is little reason for optimism. The recession of 1969–70 was too short, and thus failed to restore balance to the economy. The Ford Administration certainly does not intend to repeat that mistake. The White House noted, in a fact sheet distributed with Ford's October 8 speech on the economy, that "twice within the past decade, in 1967 and in 1971–72, we let an opportunity to regain price stability slip through our grasp." Apparently, then, the present recession will have to be deeper and more widespread than any previous postwar recession if it is to overcome the forces of inflation.

But can the recession be contained within reasonable bounds without deteriorating into a major economic depression? Several considerations indicate that the current crisis is easily the most serious since World War II. The relative prosperity of the entire postwar era in America has been built on the foundation of U.S. imperialism, and the long expansion of the 1960s and early 1970s was dependent on an incredible accumulation of corporate and family debt.

The declining international position of the United States has received much comment, and now the debt and liquidity position of the U.S. economy are in the spotlight. As *Business Week* put it in a special issue on the "Debt Economy," "The United States is leveraged as never before. There is nearly $8 of debt per $1 of money supply, more than double the figure of twenty years ago. Corporate debt amounts to more than fifteen times after-tax profits, compared with under eight times in 1955. Household debt amounts to 93 per cent of disposable income, compared with 65 per cent in 1955. U.S. banks have lent billions overseas through Euro-currency markets that did not even exist in 1955."

Faced with profit levels which have probably peaked and will surely decline as the recession rolls into high gear, debt-ridden corporations will find it increasingly difficult to meet their fixed-interest obligations. A snowballing of bankruptcies could follow the failure of a few giant corporations. The inability of unemployed workers to maintain payment on their debt would only aggravate the problem.

Astounding as it may seem, even some *countries* seem in danger of bankruptcy under the tremendous pressure of mounting bills for oil imports. Italy, at the moment, is the most likely candidate. In addition to its debt to the International Monetary Fund and the central banks of other countries, Italy has borrowed $10 billion in the past few years from private international sources. Default on these massive debts would reverberate throughout the capitalist system — to what eventual effect no one is sure. Nor is it possible to forecast with any accuracy the political, economic, and financial impact of the massive accumulation of petrodollars by the oil producing countries.

Moreover, Western Europe and Japan can no longer serve as a buffer to mitigate the impacts of a U.S. recession. They, too, are experiencing rising unemployment and falling output, bringing pressure on U.S. export markets just as our recession is pressuring *their* exports. To make matters worse, this recession-induced decline in world exports is occurring at a time when most capitalist countries have huge balance-of-payments deficits toward the oil producing countries. These deficits, coupled with declining exports, might lead to export–import controls, controls on long-term capital movements, or competitive devaluations.

With the weakening of American hegemony, it is no longer certain that the United States can organize and discipline its competitors in order to generate an orderly treatment of the deficit problem. The American defeat in Vietnam and the breakdown of international monetary arrangements in August 1971 have had serious consequences for the world capitalist economic order. And the political strains emerging in Greece, Great Britain, Italy, Portugal, Japan, and France — not to mention the United States — make it even more difficult to count on economic cooperation, as opposed to competition, in dealing with mounting economic and political dislocations. This growing economic instability is fostering political instability which threatens capitalist governments throughout the Western world.

Because American capitalists no longer have the political and economic strength to control their allies, they may turn to a strategy of exploiting the existing economic and political instability. Although the decline in American power and the coming of age of Germany and Japan were the factors that permitted the oil producing nations to impose dramatic price increases, the most damaging effects of higher oil prices have not been felt by the United States. Rather, the economies of Japan and Western Europe were, at least temporarily, most severely pummeled. Furthermore, since Japan and Western Europe are much more immediately dependent on their export sectors than the United States, the prospect of severe world-wide recession poses a more direct threat to them than it does to the United States.

Paradoxically, then, the combination of high oil prices and world recession constitutes the situation in which the strength of the United States relative to its allies is greatest, because of their dependence on oil imports and world markets. It has thus become possible for a U.S. recession, needed for domestic purposes, to be turned into a weapon to be used against both the oil producers and our economic rivals.

If, as recent statements by high-level American officials seem to indicate, the U.S. oil strategy is to "break" the oil producers and eventually reduce energy prices, then a huge reduction in the world demand for oil is essential. One way to guarantee such a decline in world oil demand is to have a long, deep, world-wide recession. Indeed, the mere threat of such a recession may be enough to pressure Germany, Japan, and even France into participating in a subservient way in U.S.-designed and dominated international economic and political tactics in the oil conflict. Maximizing the threat of world recession may, therefore, be attractive to those concerned with the maintenance of the American empire.

But this would be a dangerous gambit because the American corporate elite clearly has fewer means at its disposal for controlling the dynamics of a world-wide recession than it has with respect to a domestic one. And the political implications of an out-of-control world depression must be sobering indeed to corporate and Government leaders.

All of these strains and uncertainties make it increasingly likely that the managers of the American system will seek new tools and policies to cope with the economic and political crisis. The contradictions inherent in the attempt to "solve" the current multidimensional economic crisis through the exclusive use of orthodox monetary and fiscal tools seem overwhelming.

If the Government is unwilling to risk a depression, it could choose to postpone the day of reckoning by imposing mandatory wage and price controls. Although wage–price controls are generally thought of as a mechanism used to control inflation during an economic expansion, they have attracted increased interest in the face of projections of an 8 per cent unemployment rate *and* a 10 per cent rise in the hourly wage rate this year. Wage controls might handle part of the job of the recession by reducing the rate of wage increase.

But these controls are themselves contradictory. The experience in Western Europe and the United States with temporary or on–off aggregate wage–price controls indicates that a repetition of such controls as Nixon's Phases I through IV can only promote increased instability in the system. For one thing, wage and price decisions are themselves affected by the removal of controls or the anticipation of their introduction. Under these conditions, temporary controls simply reallocate inflation over time, they do not eliminate it. Moreover, controls eventually lead to surpluses and shortages because they suppress market forces which, however socially irrational, have their own internal coherence in our system. This is perhaps best seen in the confused decision to freeze the price of meat and poultry in the summer of 1973, a decision that led to the withdrawal of these foods from the market, and a subsequent mammoth increase in food prices in August 1973.

In light of these considerations, more permanent and extensive controls than we had from 1971 to 1974 appear to be required. The Democratic Party, at its miniconvention in Kansas City in December, called for "an across-the-board system of economic controls, including prices, wages, executive compensation, profits and rents." Leonard Silk reported in *The New York Times* that some leading Democrats were "moving to support a program that would put far more stress on economic planning as a means of directing industrial investment to meet critical needs. . . ." We assume that there has been serious private discussion among the corporate elite on the same topic. And, since it is recognized that the use of planning by Japan, Germany, Sweden, and France contributed heavily to their superior economic performance in the 1960s and early 1970s, there are long-run as well as short-run forces pressuring the United States toward a planning imperative.

A move toward planning, it should be clear, would have profound economic and political implications. Government policy will directly determine the share of total income going to capital as opposed to labor, and perhaps the distribution of labor income among workers as well. This alone might produce considerable conflict, since organized labor could be expected to fight for its share of production. But there would be more to permanent controls than the setting of wages and prices. They could require Government-directed allocation of raw materials and credit, a detailed system of tax credits and subsidies, anti-strike or even anti-collective-bargaining legislation, and administratively coordinated investment strategies among firms and industries.

The planning process eventually will require detailed management of the economy and of people. This can obviously lead to serious political conflict. In short, controls may not deliver us from our current crisis, but may instead create a new one, overtly political in nature.

The development of detailed economic planning within the present array of political forces in the United States will undoubtedly mean corporate control of the planning process, just as the introduction of Federal regulatory agencies has historically meant control by and for the regulated industries. It is, therefore, more important now than ever before that the political balance of power be changed and the power of the corporate elite broken. What we need now is a democratic, socialist, national political organization to defend the interests of the majority of the American people against the fundamentally antagonistic interests of the corporations and the super-rich who own and control them.

Because the problems we face are derivatives of our capitalist institutions, neither the Republican nor the Democratic Party offers real hope to the working people of this country. These parties are committed to existing power relations, and dominated by corporate money and capitalist ideology. Democratic party reformers may wish to return to the corporate liberalism of the 1950s and 1960s, but if the arguments presented here are correct, there can be no turning back.

It seems clear that over the long run the only permanent solution to the economic instability and insecurity which derive from the monopoly, inequality, and imperialism of modern capitalism is to build a democratic, socialist society. A nationwide socialist organization will be necessary to defend ourselves in the short run and to aid us in the task of developing an egalitarian society wherein production is for use rather than profit, and decisions are collectively made by workers, not bosses.

THE EDUCATIONAL PROCESS AND LEGISLATIVE STRATEGY

As Senator Javits noted, S. 1795 was introduced to stimulate debate. A good deal of the stimulus is of course a result of the fact that the document is a bill, an idea that has taken at least the first step on the road to institutionalization. But if that idea is to progress along that road there needs to be a push, and there were indications by early 1976 that the proponents of the bill were not going to push for the whole package but were willing to pursue a longer term strategy of discussion and piecemeal introduction of portions of the scheme.

Remarks by Hubert H. Humphrey on Legislative Strategy

Q: What do you think the chances are for the acceptance of this kind of program? Will we turn to planning some time in the dim future, or will the present Congress start looking in this direction? Will planning develop piecemeal, or will the organizational structure, as outlined in your bill, be enacted at one stroke?

A: The truth is that we are approaching it piecemeal. We have a piece of it in the Budget Reform Act. We have a piece of it in the National Commission on Supplies and Shortages. Part of it exists in the General Accounting Office in some of its analysis. There's more of it in the Office of Management and Budget. The Joint Economic Committee is spending more time at it. It's an idea whose time is coming. And like most things in this country, it will come because of distress. If we get into serious enough economic trouble, we'll start to take a good look, not only at how we tax people and at what kind of Social Security benefits we give, but at the structure of government and at the structure of our economic system.[1]

Indeed, the influence of the planning formulation developed in

[1]Hubert H. Humphrey, "Planning Economic Policy," *Challenge*, March–April 1975, p. 23. Copyright © 1975 by International Arts and Sciences Press, Inc. Reprinted by permission of International Arts and Sciences Press, Inc.

S. 1795 can be seen in S. 50, the Full Employment and Balanced
Growth Act of 1976, a major piece of legislation introduced simultaneously by Senator Humphrey and Congressman Gus Hawkins. A
portion of a summary of the bill prepared by the Library of Congress
and reprinted from the *Digest of Public General Bills and Resolutions*
indicates this strategy. The bill also contains a provision for incorporat-
ing the Federal Reserve in the planning process and recognizes the Fed
as an important factor in economic policy making.

S. 50: A Summary of the Full Employment and Balanced Growth Act of 1976

S. 50 — FULL EMPLOYMENT AND BALANCED GROWTH ACT OF 1976

SUMMARY AND SECTION-BY-SECTION ANALYSIS

Summary

The Full Employment and Balanced Growth Act of 1976 establishes the
right of all adult Americans able, willing, and seeking to work to opportunities for useful paid employment at fair rates of compensation. To support that right, the act commits the U.S. Government to fundamental
reform in the management of the economy so that full employment and
balanced economic growth are achieved and sustained. This includes the
creation of a permanent institutional framework within which the President,
the Federal Reserve Board, and the Congress are systematically encouraged
to develop and establish the economic goals and policies necessary to provide productive employment for all adult Americans, as well as the mandating of specific employment programs to achieve the goal of 3 percent
unemployment as promptly as possible, but within not more than 4 years
after the date of the enactment of this act.

SEC. 103—ECONOMIC GOALS AND THE ECONOMIC REPORT OF THE PRESIDENT.

The Employment Act of 1946 is amended to require the President in each
annual Economic Report to recommend numerical goals for employment,
production, and purchasing power, as well as policies to support these goals

and achieve balanced growth and full employment of the Nation's human and capital resources as promptly as possible.

. . .

SEC. 104—FULL EMPLOYMENT AND BALANCED GROWTH PLAN.

The Employment Act of 1946 is amended to establish a process of long-range economic planning, through the Council of Economic Advisers, to analyze developing economic conditions, to recommend long-term goals for full employment, production, and purchasing power, and to propose priority policies and programs to achieve such goals and to meet national needs. A long-term full employment goal is set at 3 percent adult unemployment, to be attained as promptly as possible, but within not more than 4 years after the date of the enactment of this act.

. . .

SEC. 106—FISCAL AND MONETARY POLICIES.

The Employment Act of 1946 is amended to require that monetary and fiscal policies be utilized in the optimum manner necessary to achieve full employment and balanced growth, including the requirement that the President determine the extent to which fiscal policy can be relied upon to achieve our economic goals and priorities, so that it becomes possible to estimate what supplementary job creation and anti-inflation policies must be utilized to achieve the objectives of this act.

This section also requires the Federal Reserve Board to make an independent report to the President and Congress, in conjunction with each Economic Report, identifying the extent to which the Federal Reserve will support the economic goals recommended in the President's Economic Report and, if the Federal Reserve Board does not support such goals, to provide a full justification of why and to what extent its policies will differ from those recommended by the President. If the President determines that the Board's policies are inconsistent with proposed economic goals and priorities, the President shall make recommendations to the Board and Congress to insure closer conformity with the purposes of this act.

. . .

SEC. 108—COUNCIL OF ECONOMIC ADVISERS.

The Employment Act of 1946 is amended to establish a 12-member pri-nomic Advisers to prepare the Full Employment and Balanced Growth Plan, to consult with the Advisory Committee, and to meet other requirements under this act.

SEC. 109—ADVISORY COMMITTEE ON FULL EMPLOYMENT AND BALANCED GROWTH.

The Employment Act of 1946 is amended to establish a 12-member private Advisory Committee on Full Employment and Balanced Growth to advise and assist the Council of Economic Advisors on matters relating to the Economic Report and this act. The members of the committee shall be appointed proportionately by the President, the Speaker of the House of Representatives, and the President pro tempore of the Senate in a manner broadly representative of the Public.

. . .

SEC. 202—COUNTERCYCLICAL EMPLOYMENT POLICIES.

This section requires the development and submission by the President, within 90 days of the enactment of this act, of a coherent and flexible countercyclical program to reduce high unemployment arising from cyclical movements in the economy. This comprehensive program shall include, as appropriate, public service employment, standby public works, antirecession grants for State and local governments, skill training in both the public and private sectors, and other programs. Moreover, this program shall be automatically implemented during periods of high unemployment, allocate employment assistance to areas of highest unemployment, provide for a well-balanced combination of job creation and related activities in both the private and public sectors, and incorporate transitional mechanisms to aid individuals in returning to regular employment as the economy recovers.

SEC. 203—COORDINATION WITH STATE AND LOCAL GOVERNMENTS AND PRIVATE SECTOR ECONOMIC ACTIVITY.

This section requires the development of policies that facilitate harmonious economic action between the Federal Government, regions, States, localities and the private sector. As a primary effort to achieve these ends, the President is required to submit legislation, within 90 days of the enactment of this act, creating a permanent, countercyclical grant program that will serve to stabilize State and local budgets during periods of recession and high unemployment. This program shall be automatically implemented when the national unemployment exceeds a specified level and distribute its funds to those areas of most serious unemployment.

. . .

Title III — Policies and Procedures for Congressional Review

SEC. 301—STATEMENT OF PURPOSE.

This title establishes procedures for congressional review and action with respect to the annual economic goals in the Economic Report, the Full Employment and Balanced Growth Plan, the report of the Board of Governors of the Federal Reserve System, and the other policies and provisions of this act. This title also establishes a Division of Full Employment and Balanced Growth within the Congressional Budget Office to assist the Congress in meeting its responsibilities under this act.

Legislation and Education: The Prospects for Economic Planning

Will Congress pass a bill like the Equal Opportunity Employment Act? I'm not sure. But I know that in order to get something done, you have to start educating people. I proposed Medicare fifteen years before it was adopted, and I proposed the Civil Rights Act fifteen years before it was adopted. I proposed the Peace Corps five years before it was adopted. I proposed the Arms Control Agency five years before it was adopted. But I kept at it. I am the original author of the Food Stamp plan in Congress. It covered only six counties when it started, but we got the seed planted. Even if we could pass the Equal Opportunity Employment Act of 1975, I'm sure that the administration would veto it, and I know we wouldn't have the votes to override the veto. But that does not deter me. I think that we've got to offer hope to the American people. I believe that we've got to educate the public to understand that costs are not merely what the government spends, but costs are also what happens to individuals within the social-economic structure, and to the total economic fabric.[1]

The preceding remarks by Senator Hubert Humphrey were made in an interview published in *Challenge* magazine. Senator Humphrey emphasizes the educational process implicit in new proposals. There was no effort to bring S. 1795 to a vote in 1975, but as Senator Javits indicated, it generated considerable discussion. The educational process is tied to legislative strategy. In S. 50, as introduced in 1976, the instruments of planning, modified and toned down, reappear as important additions to an amended version of the Equal Opportunity Employment Act of 1975, introduced in 1974 itself as an amendment to the Employment Act of 1946. It was the 1946 Act that created the

[1]Hubert H. Humphrey, "Planning Economic Policy," *Challenge*, March–April 1975, p. 27. Copyright © 1975 by International Arts and Sciences Press, Inc. Reprinted by permission of International Arts and Sciences Press, Inc.

Council of Economic Advisers and the Economic Report of the President. The planning mechanism in S. 50 relies heavily on these familiar forms. During the Presidential election of 1976, S. 50 (known as the Humphrey-Hawkins Bill) became a measure of commitment to fighting unemployment. It generated much discussion but did not come up for a vote in Congress.

FURTHER READINGS FOR CHAPTER 4

Bailey, Stephen Kemp, *Congress Makes a Law: The Story Behind the Employment Act of 1946* (New York: Vintage Books, 1950). Not only considers the process of making a law in depth but also gives the background on economic policy making, to which the planning bill is linked.

Reagan, Michael D., *The Managed Economy* (New York: Oxford University Press, 1963). Ties political theory, private power, and the role of government into the formulation of economic policy.

Flash, Edward S., Jr., *Economic Advice and Presidential Leadership* (New York: Columbia University Press, 1965). Examines the relation of the Council of Economic Advisers to the President and to the fiscal–monetary "citadels" such as the Federal Reserve Board and the Joint Economic Committee of Congress.

Greenberg, Edward S., *Serving the Few: Corporate Capitalism and the Bias of Government Policy* (New York: John Wiley & Sons, 1974). Traces government intervention in the economy and twentieth-century institutional reforms to the needs of corporate capitalism.

Chapter 5 Bureaucracy

Formulating and Implementing
National Indian Policy

LINDA MEDCALF, EDITOR

Most government policy has an identifiable effect on people's lives. Security from military attack, the availability of gasoline, and a right to choose to have an abortion are all a result of policies examined in previous chapters. Certain agencies, however, have been given a more pervasive role in the formulation and implementation of policies that directly affect the capacity of some Americans to enjoy fully the benefits of citizenship. The operation of these agencies reveals the effects of bureaucracy. Agencies like the Veterans Administration, the Social Security Administration, and the Bureau of Indian Affairs are large; the policy makers are distant from the clients; and, most important, the clients have been among the least powerful in the society. Through the delegation of authority to implement policies for particular groups, these agencies exercise a comprehensive power over the clients within their spheres.

Originally characterized as simply a body of officials appointed to carry out a specialized function, usually by means of fixed rules and some degree of hierarchical organization, bureaucracy has come to signify unwieldiness and the absence of initiative and flexibility. Almost all large organizations have bureaucratic features, and examples of indifference, rule mongering, and excessive complexity can be found throughout government. However, where the specialized function is one that encompasses a significant segment of citizens' lives, the way policy is implemented becomes as important as the substance of the policy. The bureaucracies that serve and regulate the powerless have a special feature that increases their importance for those interested in understanding the impact of policy impact. In no other sphere does the dependency become so great and the frustration caused by governmental indifference so severe as when government influence is exercised over the lives of those who are relatively powerless.

This sort of relationship is most characteristic in the realm of health and welfare. In such cases, the democratic idea is reversed, and the government rather than the citizen becomes sovereign. Indian policy is a unique example of this situation in that it evolves from the clash of two distinct national cultures, but the dependency established between the Bureau of Indian Affairs and the American Indian is similar to that reported by Frances Fox Piven and Richard A. Cloward in *Regulating the Poor: The Function of Public Welfare.*

In addition, the Bureau of Indian Affairs (BIA) is an excellent example of an agency plagued by problems in the implementation of policies for a population that it sometimes does not seem to understand. The BIA was moved from the War Department to the Department of the Interior in 1846, when it became "trustee" of Indian lands and tribes, making it the oldest bureau in existence. Although policies have changed, the agency continues with remnants of former policies embedded in its structure. This problem, only heightened by time, plagues all service agencies. Policies intended to improve clientele benefits may also be warped during implementation. The BIA demonstrates this characteristic, and it reveals how the competing interests in a society are a determinant of policy. The Bureau is supervised by the Secretary of the Interior, who also has responsibility for the utilization of the vast natural resources of the federal government. Exploitation of these resources has been one of the most significant influences on the welfare of American Indians.

Overseeing the Bureau are not only the internal changeable executive appointments, but also House and Senate committees. Budgeting is an ongoing problem of preparation, presentation, and justification. Maintenance of the agency usually comes first. Funding for specific programs that might aid the clientele is always in competition for a share of the limited funds for all service agencies. This process places the Bureau in the position of advocating programs for the Indians in order to justify its own existence, while also encouraging (even requiring) the "we know best" syndrome, resulting in a paternalistic attitude (at best) of the Bureau toward "its" Indians.

The staff of any bureau — that is, those who develop policies and programs for a bureau's clientele — is almost entirely composed of executive and administrative governmental officials, who are terribly aware of the needs and functions of others, like them, in the political arena. This situation, at best, results in a tendency for them to identify with the government's problems rather than with the problems of the agencies' clientele, making it difficult for an agency to endorse its clientele's needs wholeheartedly, and rendering the agency wishy-washy. At worst, conflicts of interest can emerge for the official who is supposedly an Indian advocate but who also understands, for example, the need of the oil industry for new lands.

There is a built-in ambivalence in American service agencies. Although it is now recognized that the American capitalist system necessitates welfare programs, the ideology of the self-sufficient individual is strong and deeply embedded. Thus, although aid is *recognized* as required, it is never really *believed* to be consistent with the ideal. The ideological emphasis turns "need" into a shameful position and, in the case of the BIA at least, the ambivalence is often compounded by racism. The history of the BIA reveals a determined effort to *mold* Indians into self-sufficient individuals through the use of policies that encourage dependency; thus each successive effort of the Bureau further contributes to the impossibility of self-sufficiency for the Indians. And then, as the clients become more dependent upon aid, the agency becomes more determined to turn them loose. As indirect policies increase the number of clients and their spectrum of needs, the agency responds with tightened standards and practices for accepting clients. Such an underlying ideology and the regulations and behavior it encourages result in a schizophrenic agency, one that offers aid while simultaneously degrading the individual who accepts it.

The problem of physical survival also creates a genuine dilemma — for both the agency and its clients. For a bureau to exist, it must have clients. In order for the Indians to survive, they must have the Bureau. It is a strange Catch-22 typical of all service bureaucracies. Both the agency and the clients are locked into a system that makes such bureaucracies necessary; but, if the agency were abolished, the clients would risk losing even the slight protection afforded by it, as difficult and degrading as that aid might be. And, in spite of the agency's rhetoric about its intention to work itself out of a job by helping all its clients become self-sufficient, its internal imperative (and American ideological acceptance) works to maintain the clientele in bondage. Thus, its existence is also assured. Thus, mutual distrust between the clientele and the Bureau is accompanied by recognized mutual need.

The selections in this chapter were chosen to pose some of the dilemmas and problems inherent in American service agencies. The BIA has managed to encompass all the attributes that such agencies in the American system possess, to one degree or another. Section A begins with an account of the history of the Bureau. It documents the place of the BIA as a creature of national Indian policy. Section B presents statements from those charged with carrying out the government's Indian policy and the client's response, indicating some of the specific problems they encounter. Section C presents the plight of individuals as a result of the twin plagues of bureaucracy — dependence and indifference. The Indian response has been an increasingly vociferous refusal to accept such treatment passively.

SECTION A. HISTORY OF THE POLICY MAKING PROCESS

The first selection, "Federal Indian Policies," traces the development of national policy regarding the Indian people and the concomitant development of the Bureau of Indian Affairs. Since this material was prepared and distributed by the BIA itself, it presents that history in a manner that is extremely favorable to the Bureau. However, it does not take much imagination to read between the lines for an understanding of the pressures exerted by groups *other than the Indians* that shaped national policy toward the Indians. As the story progresses, it becomes clear that the "benevolent" intentions written into legislative preambles somehow resulted in destruction of Indian lives and culture when the enacted policy was pursued. This *seeming* contradiction between stated purpose and bureaucratic practice is a prevalent one, not confined to the BIA[1] — only, perhaps, more obvious here.

[1]See Murray Edelman, *The Symbolic Uses of Politics* (Urbana, Ill.: University of Illinois Press, 1967).

The selection also provides clues to present-day problems through careful examination of the assumptions behind past policies. Often terms such as "civilized" and "self-sufficient" and "competent" obscure ideological biases through the uncritical acceptance of the definition of the term and the positive attributes associated with it. In other words, even the "benevolent" intentions may contain destructive tendencies. They only *appear* benevolent to those who accept the underlying assumptions—for example, that "progress" and "self-sufficiency" are suitable and proper goals. Such key assumptions, past and present, permeate bureaucratic structure and policy. They make real *change* in policy toward the Indians difficult.

The short selection following the history illustrates the bind in which the situation just described puts the Indians. What should be their "service and support agency" often is their oppressor. On the other hand, the BIA is one of the few groups that, at the very least, must ensure Indian survival. Without a client to serve and support, there would be no reason for the Bureau to exist. The bedrock of survival binds agency and client together — but it is often a very strained relationship and, as noted above, one that results in schizophrenic policy formation and implementation.

FEDERAL INDIAN POLICIES: FROM THE COLONIAL PERIOD THROUGH THE EARLY 1970's

Our country's first administrator of Federal Indian policies, Henry Knox, said at the time of his appointment as a Cabinet officer in George Washington's Administration:

> That the civilization of the Indians would be an operation of complicated difficulty; that it would require the highest knowledge of the human character and a steady perseverance in a wise system for a series of years, cannot be doubted. But to deny that, under a course of favorable circumstances, it could be accomplished, is to suppose the human character under the influence of such stubborn habits as to be incapable of melioration or change.

In the early colonial period the Indians represented a strong balance of power between the forces of Spain, France, and England and were therefore treated as sovereign nations until the issue of North American domination was settled.

Source: Publication of the Bureau of Indian Affairs, United States Department of the Interior, Washington, D.C., 1975.

Until 1755, the individual English colonies had no coordinated policies on Indian affairs. During that year the British developed an Indian policy designed to: (1) protect the Indians from opportunistic traders and speculators; (2) negotiate boundary lines by treaties; (3) enlist the Indians on the side of the British in the French and Indian War; and (4) exercise as much control as possible over the fur trade.

King George III in 1763 proclaimed: "The several nations or tribes of nations, with whom we are connected, should not be molested or disturbed in the possession of such parts of our dominions and territories, as, not having been ceded to, or purchased by us, are reserved to them, or any of them, as hunting grounds."

The proclamation by King George III defined the "Indian country" to be administered by two superintendents, one north and one south, and set aside "reserved lands" for the Indians. The two superintendents took on the role of diplomatic agents negotiating with the various tribes by means of a series of treaties.

The leadership of Benjamin Franklin is of historical importance to the development of this and subsequent periods of Indian affairs. He proposed, at the Albany Congress of 1754, that all colonial Indian affairs be centrally administered. The Franklin plan was a forerunner of later centrally administered British Indian policy under the two superintendents and of centralized Indian policy under the new American Government.

The outbreak of hostilities between the Americans and the British in April, 1775, pitted tribe against tribe and produced strenuous efforts for Indian alliances by both colonial and imperial governments. The young American revolutionary government attempted to win the friendship of the Indians through treaties. But most of the tribes supported George III, and even tribal neutrality was counted a success by the colonists.

The Continental Congress, in one of its first actions, named a Committee on Indian Affairs in 1775. This committee produced a report a month later which prompted the Congress to set up "three departments of Indians" — the Northern, Middle, and Southern. The Congress continued many of the policies of Colonial times as well as creating new ones. Included among the outstanding Americans serving as commissioners of the Indian Departments were Benjamin Franklin and Patrick Henry in the Middle Department, and General Philip Schuyler in the Northern Department.

The Indian Commissioners were given authority "to treat with the Indians . . . in order to preserve peace and friendship with them and to prevent their taking part in the present commotions." The first negotiation was with the Six Nations (Mohawk, Oneida, Onondaga, Cayuga, Seneca, and Tuscarora) in July, 1775, and called for employment of two blacksmiths among the Indians and the opening of trade.

The first of 370 Indian treaties to be concluded during the next century was with the Delawares on September 17, 1778. This treaty held out the possibility that an Indian state might later be established as one of the states in the new country. This idea reappeared many times as an ultimate goal for Indian policy, without substantial result.

During the Revolutionary War, the Indian commissioners acted primarily as diplomatic agents, negotiating with various Indian tribes to gain their allegiance. Their work was kept under the authority of the Congress until a year after the war ended.

THE BEGINNING OF FORCED REMOVAL

In 1784 the Congress of the Confederation placed the administration of Indian affairs within the War Department, with the Secretary of War directed to place armed militia at the disposal of the Indian commissioners "for negotiating treaties with the Indians."

The Northwest Ordinance of 1787 was important in establishing the framework for settlement beyond the Alleghenies and in shaping Indian policy. It provided that:

> The utmost good faith shall always be observed toward the Indians: their land and property shall never be taken from them without their consent: and in their property, rights and liberty, they shall never be invaded or disturbed unless in just and lawful wars authorized by Congress; but laws founded in justice and humanity shall from time to time be made for preventing wrongs done to them, and for preserving peace and friendship with them.

Over the next 50 years, the new Nation and its government grew stronger. Laws regulating the trade between whites and Indians were added to the books, and a network of Indian agents and sub-agents was established following a report relating to military administration of trade practices with Indians. The report called for legislation "to ensure faithful disbursement of public money" and to enforce "prompt settlement of accounts."

In 1824, Secretary of War John C. Calhoun had begun to tie together all Federal Indian activities under an Indian Affairs Agency. He saw the Federal role as providing for: (1) appropriations for tribal annuities to be made to tribes for lands they had lost; (2) examination of Indian claims relating to trade laws; (3) bookkeeping; (4) correspondence with Indian superintendents and agents; and (5) administration of a fund for the civilization of Indians.

Meanwhile the systematic forced removal of Indian groups from the choice eastern lands to the western wilderness across the Mississippi had begun. Nearly all the Cherokees in the lower Appalachian area were driven across the mountains to settle in the Indian Territory. This territory, carved from the Louisiana Purchase, was created by President Thomas Jefferson, who expressed the hope that the removal of Indian groups from heavily settled eastern regions would contribute to their advancement.

The "removal" policy had been precipitated by activity in the late 1820's within the State of Georgia. The Cherokee Tribe in that State, a highly advanced civilization, had adopted an Indian constitution, modeled after the U.S. Constitution. The Georgia Legislature then nullified the Cherokee Constitution: appeals made by the Cherokees eventually resulted in a U.S. Supreme Court decision nullifying Georgia's action.

Chief Justice John Marshall's decision recognized that earlier Congresses had passed laws "which treat (Indians) as nations" and "as distinct political communities, having territorial boundaries."

The Indian Removal Act of 1830 established procedures for voluntary exchange of eastern Indian lands for new western acreage that was to be held by the tribes under perpetual guaranty from the Federal Government.

In 1834 Congress gave regular and permanent status to the Indian Affairs office and it began carrying out President Andrew Jackson's directive to remove all Indians living east of the Mississippi River to new western lands. These removal policies relied more on military force than diplomatic treaty.

The Five Civilized Tribes — Cherokees, Chickasaws, Choctaws, Creeks, and Seminoles — were pressured by negotiations and threat of force to move westward to the new Indian Territory. Although some members of these Tribes resisted, most became established in the new lands and were among the first citizens of Oklahoma when statehood was proclaimed.

Other Indian tribes from the northeast and Great Lakes regions also were subjected to the removal policies. Removal was justified by the Federal Government as a means of protecting the Indians from repeated encroachment of eastern white settlers. The Government policy bitterly divided the country — in the Congress, among the religious groups, in the press, and among Indians themselves.

"In the consummation of this grand and sacred object rests the sole chance of averting Indian annihilation," argued Commissioner of Indian Affairs Elbert Herring, in 1832.

Another Indian Commissioner, George Manypenny, 1854, urged the abandonment of the removal policy.

"By alternate persuasion and force," Manypenny said, "some of these tribes have been removed, step by step, from mountains to valley, and from river to plain, until they have been pushed half-way across the continent. They can go no further. On the ground they now occupy, the crisis must be met, and their future determined.

"Many of those people who sympathized with the plight of the survivors of Eastern tribes who were now settled west of the Mississippi, thought they were doing these people a good turn by removing them from civilization's path until they could acquire the skills and knowledge necessary for assimilation."

THE START OF INDIAN EDUCATION PROGRAMS

A number of separate treaties with Indian tribes had set the precedent for placing responsibility for Indian education in the hands of the Government. One of the first of these treaties was with the Oneidas, Stockbridges, and Tuscaroras in 1794. Two years earlier the famed Seneca Chief, Cornplanter, visited President Washington, asking the Government to "teach our children to read and write and our women to spin and weave." A Federal directive to provide the "blessings of civilization" to Indians through treaties was issued in that year.

A "civilization fund" was contained in a law passed by Congress in 1819 which appropriated $10,000 annually to provide elementary educational services to Indians. All funds provided by this act were channeled through religious and mission groups for the education of Indians. The Federal Government and the private mission groups combined later in the 1840's to launch the first Indian boarding school system. Not until 1860 was the first non-mission Federal Indian school started. (Congressional Acts of 1896, 1897, and 1917 eventually established that no further Federal funds for education could go to sectarian schools.)

CIVIL ADMINISTRATION BEGINS IN MID-CENTURY

Repeated efforts were made in the Jacksonian period to regularize Federal Indian administration through legislation. The War Department's head of Indian Affairs reported in 1828, that there were "fruitful sources of complaint" due to the lack of an organized system. In 1834 Congress passed a Trade and Intercourse Act setting up an Office of Indian Affairs, and modernizing trade practices as the result of a report in 1829 by two experienced Indian affairs specialists, Lewis Cass and William Clark.

Both Clark (of Lewis and Clark Expedition fame) and Cass had been territorial governors in Indian country for many years and Clark also had been superintendent of Indian affairs at St. Louis. Case was to become Secretary of War in 1831. Their report called for new legislation "to ensure a faithful disbursement of the public money" and "to enforce a strict accountability and a prompt settlement of accounts."

Noting the increased lands to be supervised by a still-growing United States, and the need for establishing peaceable relations with the Indians, Treasury Secretary Robert J. Walker voiced the sentiment of many who advocated transfer of the Bureau of Indian Affairs from the War Department to a new Department, soon to take shape as the Department of the Interior.

Walker said: "The duties now performed by the Commissioner of Indian Affairs are most numerous and important, and must be vastly increased with the great number of tribes scattered over Texas, Oregon, New Mexico and California, and with the interesting progress of so many of the tribes in Christianity, knowledge, and civilization. These duties do not necessarily appertain to war, but to peace, and to our domestic relations with those tribes placed by the Constitution under the charge of this Government."

By 1849, with creation of the Department of the Interior, the Bureau of Indian Affairs passed from military to civil control. Its work consisted of attempts at "civilizing" the Indian people by training them for farming or trades. In 1862, Secretary of the Interior Caleb Smith recommended a "radical change in the mode of treatment of Indians" to regard them as "wards" of the Government. Consequently, the Bureau's efforts were often in conflict with military policy and it sometimes became the uneasy and unhappy buffer between the Indians and the U.S. Army.

THE CALL FOR PEACE

The removal policy had succeeded in large measure with the Five Civilized Tribes because they envisioned an Indian nation, fully sovereign and federated. But many of the Plains Indians resisted all military moves to relocate them. They possessed the white man's horse and gun and fought bitterly against further encroachments on their lands and their way of life.

Tensions grew between Indians and whites in the western territories in the late 1850's and throughout the 1860's, as the railroads began moving west, culminating in a series of Indian "uprisings" and a Congressional demand that peace prevail in Indian country. After the Civil War, Congress authorized establishment of an Indian Peace Commission, comprising four civilians and three military leaders including Indian Commissioner Nathanel G. Taylor and General William Tecumseh Sherman.

Peace Commission field trips had disclosed considerable corruption among Indian agents. Its report of 1867 stated: "The records are abundant to show that agents have pocketed the funds appropriated by the Government and driven the Indians to starvation." It blamed Indian agent corruption or incompetence for creating Indian incidents, notably the 1862 Sioux uprising in Minnesota.

Two separate actions were taken by the Federal Government to produce reforms in Indian policy. In 1869 a Board of Indian Commissioners was named and charged by Congress with the responsibility for advising the Secretary of the Interior on matters relating to Indian affairs. President Grant at the same time requested religious organizations to nominate Indian agency superintendents. The Board of Indian Commissioners, lacking any policy-making authority, was continued until 1933, when it was abandoned by President Franklin D. Roosevelt's executive order; nominating of Indian Bureau agents by religious groups was discontinued a few years after it was begun.

In 1867 and 1868 the Indian Peace Commission negotiated the last of 370 Indian treaties. These required tribes of the Upper Great Plains, the Southwest, and the Northwest to settle on various reservations in the West. The last treaty, signed with the Nez Perce of Oregon on August 12, 1868, removed the tribe to a new reservation in Idaho.

The U.S. Congress, on March 3, 1871, finished the Indian treaty period with a clause tacked to a Congressional appropriation for the Yankton Indians: ".... hereafter no Indian nation or tribe within the territory of the United States shall be acknowledged or recognized as an independent nation, tribe, or power with whom the United States shall contract by treaty."

Ironically, it was a mixed-blood Seneca Indian, Eli S. Parker, said to be the grandson of the warrior Red Jacket, who presided over the Indian Bureau when the last chapter in the history of treaty-making was written. Parker was a professional engineer, recognized authority on the Iroquois League and personal secretary to General Ulysses S. Grant in the Civil War.

THE RESERVATION SYSTEM

Twenty years of intermittent warfare followed the signing of the last Indian treaty before the last of the Western Indians were moved to reservations. Geronimo's surrender in the Southwest in 1886 and the battle of Wounded Knee in South Dakota in 1890 followed numerous Federal military victories in the southwest, Dakotas and Oregon, and marked the end of serious resistance to relocation policies.

The reservation system brought a new set of woes to the Indians, as the Government pressured them into relinquishing customs and culture.

Chieftainship, which had been encouraged since Colonial days as a means of tribal control, was not attacked directly. Instead, chiefs were bypassed while law and order was delegated to tribal police forces and Courts of Indian Offenses. The result was a gradual breakdown of tradition upon which the Indian had always leaned heavily, with nothing to replace it.

Native religions were discouraged, some ceremonies forbidden, and Christian misionaries encouraged. Particularly vicious were the attacks upon Indian "prophets" which culminated in the battle of Wounded Knee in 1890.

Commissioner Francis Walker (1871–73) set the tone of the "forced reservation" period, which lasted until 1887, stating that, when the reservation system began, "it was expressly declared that the Indians should be made as comfortable on, and uncomfortable off, their reservations as it was within the power of the Government to make them; that such of them as went right should be protected and fed, and such as went wrong should be harassed and scourged without intermission."

Those Indians who "went wrong" — such as the Apaches under Cochise in the early 1870's, the Sioux led by Crazy Horse and Sitting Bull in the mid-1870's, and the Nez Perce with Chief Joseph a short while later—were "harassed and scourged without intermission," conquered eventually and returned to reservations.

Those Indians who "went right," were, as Walker promised, "protected and fed" through a new practice of furnishing daily food rations and clothing to Indians, instituted as a by-product of the Indian peace treaties of the late 1860's and continued by the Indian Bureau until well into the 1920's.

The rations practice was the forerunner of special aids for Indians which continue to this day. The giving of rations was defended by Commissioner Walker:

Can any principle of national morality be dearer than that when the expansion and development of a civilized race involve the rapid destruction of the only means of subsistence possessed by members of a less fortunate race, the higher is bound as a simple right to provide for the lower some substitute for the means of subsistence which it has destroyed? That substitute is, of course, best realized, not by systematic gratuities of food and clothing continued beyond a present emergency, but by directing these people to new pursuits which shall be consistent with the progress of civilization upon the continent.

There were contrary views, too. Indian Agent V. T. McGillicuddy, on the Pine Ridge Reservation in South Dakota, later commented: "What reason or inducement can be advanced why an Indian should go to work and earn his own living by the sweat of his brow, when an indulgent Government furnishes him more than he wants to eat and clothes him for nothing?"

The "wardship" approach prevailed, with the pace set by Secretary of the Interior Caleb Smith. Education for farming and trades became a goal.

A start in providing health services to Indians had come in 1832 through funds authorized by Congress for smallpox vaccination of certain tribes.

By the 1870's health services had expanded to include medical doctors on various reservations in an effort to combat the ravages of disease that were taking a heavy toll of the Indian population.

As the 19th Century came to a close, steps had been taken to launch programs of education and land resource development. Two vocational schools — Haskell Institute in Kansas and Chilocco Indian School in Oklahoma — opened in 1884; and five years later a broader education program was instituted at the Carlisle School in Pennsylvania.

On the land development side, some tribal groups were encouraged to enter into livestock grazing, although these enterprises were not highly successful among the nomadic groups, and overgrazing and loss of stock were common. Some irrigation of Indian lands was attempted — as early as 1876 on the Colorado River Reservation in Arizona — but this project was later abandoned. Even into the 20th Century, irrigation and conservation measures on Indian lands lagged behind the national efforts as a whole.

THE LAND ALLOTMENT PERIOD — 1887–1934

All of these Indian programs, the initial phases of the broad "civilizing" process, came at the height of a long Indian Bureau and Congressional push for helping Indians to become "self-supporting" by allowing the Indian lands to be subdivided to individual Indians through what is known as allotment in severalty — or individual ownership of small pieces of land.

Dating back to 1633, when the General Court of Massachusetts Colony provided for Indians to receive "allotments amongst the English," there had been slowly growing advocacy of an allotment policy for Indians.

It was in the 1850's that the Federal Government reached its peak in Indian land title extinguishment and began to spell out more clearly in the next 30 years a growing preference for the allotment policy which at last was approved by Congress in 1887.

"In no former equal period of our history have so many treaties been made, or such vast accession of land obtained," Commissioner George Manypenny said in 1857. Through 52 separate treaties from 1853 to 1857 a total of 174 million acres of Indian land was acquired by the United States Government. Many allotments of land were provided through treaty to individual Indians, and for the next 30 years each succeeding Commissioner of Indian Affairs (except Francis A. Walker in the 1870's) favored the policy of subdividing the large tribal-held lands into small pieces owned individually.

The Indian Allotment Act, introduced in Congress by Senator Henry L. Dawes of Massachusetts, was passed in 1887. Its intent was to assimilate the Indian by giving him individual ownership of land, as opposed to the collective land use and possession practiced by most Indian groups. Under the plan, small pieces of tribal land — from 40 to 160 acres — would be allotted to Indian families or individuals. Within 25 years, in a manner similar to that of the Homestead Act, the Indian, if adjudged "competent," would be given the land to use as he saw fit and would also acquire full citizenship status. However, before the 25 years had elapsed, the Burke Act (1906) permitted those Indians adjudged "competent" to acquire ownership at once.

The result of nearly 50 years of the allotment policy was to reduce the Indian land holdings from over 140 million acres in 1886 to under 50 million acres in 1934. Thousands of Indians receiving these allotments sold them to non-Indians who had the financial means and business abilities to develop the lands.

This sale or rental of land tended to increase the Indian's dependence upon Government support. In many cases rental income was too small or sale funds soon exhausted and the Indian was forced to turn back to the Government for assistance. In addition, the demands of this newly imposed civilization were often contrary to Indian culture and created psychological conflicts that still persist.

In the first decade of the 20th Century the Bureau of Indian Affairs embarked on further land development programs — in establishing services of conservation, reclamation and forestry — all designed to complement execution of the allotment policy.

THE ROAD TO CITIZENSHIP

The determination of Indian "competency" was carried out as part of Federal Indian policy well into the 1920's, and was highlighted by a 1917 "Declaration of Policy" by Commissioner Cato Sells and Interior Secretary Franklin Lane, which stated: "The time has come for discontinuing guardianship over all competent Indians and giving even closer attention to the incompetents that they more speedily achieve competency."

To determine whether an Indian is "as competent to transact his own business as the average white man," a practice of issuing "certification of competency" was established, and a network of "competency commissions" was created.

This approach was hailed by Commissioner Sells as indicating that "the competent Indian will no longer be treated as half ward and half citizen." Because of the growing number of Indians who obtained citizenship through allotment and because of a national appreciation for the record of Indian volunteers in World War I, the Indian Bureau began a push for full Indian citizenship. In 1924, Congress passed the Indian Citizenship Act, granting citizenship to all Indians who had not previously acquired it.

THE ATTACK ON THE ALLOTMENT SYSTEM

Increasing public agitation for reforms in the administration of Indian affairs led Interior Secretary Hubert Work in 1926 to request the Institute of Government Research (the Brookings Institution) to study the Federal Indian policies. He asked for recommendations that would "embrace the education, industrial, social and medical activities maintained among the Indians, their property rights, and their general economic conditions." An institute staff headed by Lewis Meriam produced the lengthy document in 1928 to be known as the Meriam Report which called for these basic Indian policy reforms:

1. "Establishment of a professional and scientific Division of Planning and Development to hasten agricultural advances, vocational guidance, job placement, and other aspects of economic development on the reservations."
2. "A material strengthening of the school and reservation forces that are in direct contact with the Indians and are responsible for developing and improving their economic and social condition through education in the broadest sense of the word" by deemphasizing the boarding school practice of taking children out of their tribal environment and accelerating development of a day school system on the reservations.
3. "Maximum practical decentralization of authority" from the central office to the local agency offices, plus better salaries for Indian Bureau personnel and enlisting more Indians into career Indian administration.

Of the allotment law, the Meriam Report charged:

When the Government adopted the policy of individual ownership of land on the reservations, the expectation was that the Indians would become farmers. Part of the plan was to instruct and aid them in agriculture, but this vital part was not pressed with vigor and intelligence. It almost seems as if the Government assumed that some magic in individual ownership of property would in itself prove an educational civilizing factor, but unfortunately this policy has for the most part operated in the opposite direction. Individual ownership in many instances permitted Indians to sell their allotments and to live for a time on the unearned income resulting from the sale. Individual ownership brought promptly all the details of inheritance, and frequently the sale of the property of the deceased Indians to whites so that the estate could be divided among the heirs. To the heirs the sale brought further unearned income, thereby lessening the necessity of self support.

The report also proposed that Indians be permitted leasing rights in order to add enough land to their own allotments to make an efficient farm or ranch. This policy would counteract the easier tendency to lease these same lands to whites, a policy which deterred active land management by Indians. Furthermore, leasing to whites "gave the Indians unearned income to permit the continuance of a life of idleness," the study concluded.

INDIAN REORGANIZATION PERIOD — 1934 TO 1961

The Congress responded to the Meriam Report with passage of reform legislation in 1934 — the Indian Reorganization Act (Wheeler–Howard Act).

It brought a halt to the process of allotment, prohibited unrestricted sales of Indian land, and provided for acquisition of additional lands by tribes and individuals. It created a foundation for tribal economic self-sufficiency by the establishment of constitutional tribal governments, the extension of credit from Federal funds, the fostering of tribal enterprises, and the institution of modern conservation and resource development practices. The keynote became cooperation between Indian tribes and the Federal Government to achieve change without forcing it.

The new Commissioner of Indian Affairs, John Collier, said of the Act:

While the Wheeler–Howard Act marks a decisive shift of direction of American Indian policy, and endeavors to give the Indians not only a broad measure of economic assistance but also those "national rights of man" mentioned by President Roosevelt in his letter of endorsement sent to Congress, it stops far short of the ultimate goal. It is merely a beginning in the process of liberating and rejuvenating a subjugated and exploited race living in the midst of an aggressive civilization far ahead, materially speaking, of its own.

From the perspective of two decades later, the Committee on Organization of the Executive Branch of Government (Hoover Commission) summarized the impact of the Meriam Report and the resulting 1934 Indian Reorganization Act as follows:

In the years immediately following the Meriam Report there was marked progress in professionalizing the Indian Service through better personnel, improved methods, and higher professional standards. Indian education was modernized and a stronger and better coordinated economic program got underway. In the 1930's these activities were carried forward vigorously. The Indian Reorganization Act (IRA) has given further impetus to the economic program by authorizing enlargement of Indian lands, extending the lending function, and establishing a policy of scientific range and forest management.

The IRA also paved the way for revival of tribal organization, and establishment of tribal law.

Aside from the Wheeler–Howard Act, other significant Indian legislation of the 1930's included the Johnson–O'Malley Act of 1934 and the creation in 1935 of an Indian Arts and Crafts Board within the Department of the Interior.

The Johnson–O'Malley Act provided Federal educational funds to assist States and local districts, and brought about an expansion of the practice of educating Indian children in the public school system. The Arts and Crafts Board revived interest in native crafts as a means of livelihood for Indian people.

The Indian Extension Service program began providing modern technical assistance to Indians in the fields of conservation, irrigation, grazing and dry-farming. An Indian credit program was launched with a revolving loan fund.

But the big development of the whole period was the start of tribal self-government, with several hundred reservation tribal groups determining by popular vote to govern themselves in a democratic manner with modern constitutions. Today's tribal council form of Indian government largely stems from this Act, although a number of Indian tribes had maintained constitutional self-government prior to 1934, and still others rejected the self-governing feature contained in the Indian Reorganization Act.

EFFECTS OF WORLD WAR II

World War II, to a great extent, changed both the Indian way of life and Federal Indian policy directions. Nearly 70,000 Indian men and women left reservations for the first time to go into military service and defense industries. The Indian record in both instances was widely praised.

The war produced both new skills and a greater degree of cultural sophistication than had ever before been achieved by large numbers of Indians. But it also brought post-war demands for assistance in Indian vocational training and relocation, for expanded education and for reservation economic development.

The post-war period brought on the "area office" system of decentralized Indian Bureau administration. Many development projects — roads, irrigation and building construction — were resumed in 1946, after being stalled during the war.

The fifteen-year post-war period also saw: (1) greatly increased programs to aid education of the Nation's largest tribe, the Navajos (a study in 1947 showed that nearly 75 percent of all Navajo children were not in school); (2) a ten-year economic development and rehabilitation fund for the Navajos and Hopis to bring much needed capital investment to this poverty-stricken region of the southwest; (3) development of Federal Indian programs of employment assistance, including vocational training and on-the-job training to Indian workers; (4) a start on Indian adult education for those Indians who had missed the elementary education now being expanded for their children; and (5) the beginnings of an Indian industrial development program to encourage private business and industry to locate in Indian areas.

ESTABLISHMENT OF INDIAN CLAIMS COMMISSION

The Indian Claims Commission was created in 1946 to permit Indians to file suits against the Government. The Commission received a total of 852 claims in 370 petitions entered during the five years allowed for filing. Any "identifiable" groups of Indians within the United States or Alaska — then still a territory — could take their claims to this Commission. It was empowered to hear and adjudicate suits arising from claims in law or equity: tort claims; claims based on fraud, duress, unconscionable consideration, mutual or lateral mistake; claims based upon fair and honorable dealings not recognized by existing rules or law or equity; or claims based on the taking of land without payment of the agreed compensation.

Commissioner Collier and others hoped the settlement of claims would enable the Indians to become socially and economically assimilated into the fabric of American life. By November 1969, about one-half of the claims had been adjudicated, and settlements exceeding $305 million made. Although in some instances the judgments resulted in a per capita distribution of funds, many tribal awards have remained largely intact with the money "programmed" for community and economic development.

Congress has directed the Commission to complete the task of hearing and determining the claims before it by April 10, 1972.

NEW TRENDS OF THE 1950's

Revival of pressures for Federal termination of trusteeship responsibilities occurred with the Hoover Commission's recommendation that programs be developed to terminate "the trust status of Indian lands."

Among members of the Hoover Commission's committee on Indian affairs was John Nichols, who became Indian Affairs Commissioner in 1949.

House Concurrent Resolution 108 of the 83rd Congress in 1953 led to passage in the next few years of a number of termination bills. Introduced by Representative William H. Harrison of Wyoming and by Senator Arthur V. Watkins of Utah (who later became Chairman of the Indian Claims Commission), the termination resolution read in part:

It is the policy of Congress, as rapidly as possible, to make the Indians within the territorial limits of the United States subject to the same laws and entitled to the same privileges and responsibilities as are applicable to other citizens of the United States, and to end their status as wards of the United States, and to grant them all the rights and prerogatives pertaining to American citizenship . . . .

On June 17, 1954 the Menominees of Wisconsin became the first tribe slated for termination of Federal trusteeship. The tribe had a large investment in forest lands and tribal sawmill. The Menominee Reservation was to be fully removed from Federal trust status on December 31, 1958, although later Congressional Acts delayed final termination until April 30, 1961.

Other tribes "terminated" by law in this period were the Klamaths and Western Oregon Indians; four small bands in Utah; the Alabama–Coushattas of Texas; the Ponca Tribe of Nebraska; the Uintah and Ouray Ute Mixed Bloods of Utah; the Wyandottes, Ottawas, and Peorias of Oklahoma. Termination proceedings have been moving on a piecemeal basis under legislation passed in 1958 for the Indian rancherias throughout the State of California.

Strong opposition to termination from among some Indian tribes and others led to a statement by Interior Secretary Fred Seaton, who declared in 1958: "It would be incredible, even criminal, to send any Indian tribe out into the mainstream of American life until and unless the educational level of that tribe was one which was equal to the responsibilities which it was shouldering."

The 1950's produced several other important new legislative directions affecting Indian policy:

1. Indian lands in three States and part of two others were brought under State civil and criminal jurisdiction by an Act of August 1953;
2. The prohibition was lifted against the sale of alcoholic beverages to Indians outside Indian country and a local option system was established within reservations, also in 1953;
3. The Division of Indian Health was transferred effective July 1, 1955, from the Bureau of Indian Affairs to the U.S. Public Health Service. Notable progress has subsequently been made in reducing the Indian infant mortality rate, lengthening the Indian life span, and curtailing the severity of many illnesses.

The record in Federal–Indian relations over two decades was summarized in the late 1950's by the noted anthropologist and Pulitzer Prize winning author, the late Oliver LaFarge, as follows:

The progress has been great, and it has been spotty. You cannot make over a race in 25 years, despite what the allotment theorists believed. It takes more than one generation to make the jump from a home in which no English is spoken, where the very sight of a white man is a rarity, where the thinking is the same as it was 300 years ago, to full competence in our alien and complex way of life. If, while the Indians are struggling desperately to make the great adjustment, the last remnants of their land base are lost to them; if, as they fear, the Indian Reorganization Act will be junked some day, their struggle will be hopeless. It is the Government's responsibility to enable [Indians] to keep and use what they already have, to allow them an ordinary choice, and not the flat alternatives of migrate or starve.

NEW DIRECTION IN THE 1960's

A "New Trail" for Indians leading to equal citizenship rights and benefits, maximum self-sufficiency, and full participation in American life, became the keynote for administration of the programs for the Bureau of Indian Affairs after the close of fiscal year 1961.

This keynote was provided in a report to the Secretary of the Interior Stewart L. Udall, by a special task force on Indian affairs, which he appointed in February 1961.

To move toward the accomplishments of these goals, the task force recommended less emphasis on the purely custodial functions of the Bureau, greater concentration of time, energy, and funds on fostering fuller development of both the human and natural resources on Indian reservations.

Probably the most important single recommendation was a shift in program emphasis away from termination of Federal trust relationship.

This was coupled, however, with a recommendation that eligibility for special services be withdrawn from Indians with substantial incomes and superior educational experience who are as competent as most non-Indians to look after their own affairs.

An administrative reorganization was accomplished — not only in Washington but in area offices and agencies — combining in one new Division of Economic Development all operating units directly concerned with economic development. The resources functions of the Bureau were brought into closer relationship with the industrial development work and the revolving credit program. In the Washington office, the new division also included a program planning staff and a specialist in housing. In later years, the housing activity was transferred to the Division of Community Services.

A program to improve Indian housing, a product of the 1960's, opened up Indian reservations to the financial assistance already available through Federal housing agencies to non-reservation areas. Indian tribes established local housing authorities as a first step in qualifying for Federal housing assistance under the programs of the Department of Housing and Urban Development (HUD). The Indian housing program is slowly and steadily gaining a foothold on the reservations.

To alleviate Indian unemployment, the Bureau also increased attention to job opportunities, through expanded programs in adult vocational training, voluntary relocation of Indians for employment in urban centers, industrial development on or near the reservations, and increased use of Indian labor by the Bureau on needed work in road maintenance and construction, repair and maintenance of buildings, and construction of buildings and utilities, all of which provided the Indians valuable construction training. Projects launched under the 1963 Accelerated Public Works Program on nearly 100 reservations provided useful work for thousands of tribal members and contributed importantly to the protection and development of Indian timber stands and other physical resources.

The declaration of war on poverty, first enunciated by President Johnson in his State of the Union message to the Congress in January 1964, was followed by his assurances to tribal leaders that Indian poverty was to be a major target. The Bureau of Indian Affairs was fully committed in the battle to drive poverty from American Indian reservation communities. Education and economic development were the major fronts in the war on poverty.

This period saw substantial progress in involvement of other agencies of the Federal Government in providing meaningful programs among the Indian people. They included the Departments of Labor; Commerce; Health, Education, and Welfare; Housing and Urban Development; and Office of Economic Opportunity.

The programs for the disadvantaged under the Economic Opportunity Act of 1964 have provided the Indians an opportunity to participate in and control their own programs. The heaviest activities have been in programs for community action and youth training.

The Bureau, together with other Federal agencies launched selected Indian reservation programs to step-up the pace on the economic development process on 39 Indian reservations and waged a concentrated effort to stimulate economic and social change for Indians.

In 1966, the Indian people were in the forefront of public attention. That year, Robert L. Bennett, an Oneida Indian, was appointed Commissioner for the Bureau of Indian Affairs. The people-oriented approach was apparent in the stated policy of Commissioner Bennett. He espoused greater Indian involvement in decision-making and program execution. A new era of Federal-Indian relations was emerging with the Bureau taking the form of a coordinating and advisory agency, rather than the sole primary agency concerned with development of the human and economic resources of Indian communities.

. . .

A historic special message on goals and programs of the American Indians was sent to the Congress by President Johnson in March of 1968, which proposed "a new goal — a goal that ends the old debate about termination of Indian programs and stresses self-determination, a goal that erases old attitudes of paternalism and promotes partnership and self-help." The message continued: "Our goal must be: A standard of living for Indians equal to that of the country as a whole, freedom of choice — an opportunity to remain in their homeland, if they choose, without surrendering their dignity, and an opportunity to move to the towns and cities of America if they choose, equipped with skills to live in equality and dignity: full participation in the life of modern America, with a full share of economic opportunity and social justice."

Indian involvement in decision-making was made an integral part of policy planning by the issuance of an Executive Order which established a National Council on Indian Opportunity to review Federal programs for the American Indians, make broad policy recommendations, and to ensure that programs reflect the needs and desires of the Indian people, including those who live in urban areas. The Vice President was appointed as Chairman and council members include a cross-section of Indian leaders and high Government officials.

The President's message and the Senate pronouncement in Senate Concurrent Resolutions 11 of the 90th Congress, clearly enunciated for the first time since 1953, a declaration of purpose toward the American Indians and the Alaska Natives. These pronouncements also took affirmative action to reverse the unilateral termination policies since House Concurrent Resolution 108 of 1953.

PRESIDENT NIXON REAFFIRMS SPECIAL RELATIONSHIP

In August 1969 President Nixon appointed Louis R. Bruce, an Indian of Sioux-Mohawk descent, the new Commissioner of Indian Affairs. Mr. Bruce was the third Indian to be appointed Commissioner since the Bureau of Indian Affairs was established in 1824. With the approval of the President, Commissioner Bruce subsequently announced a realignment of the top management positions at the BIA central office and appointed a new executive staff, composed of 14 Indians, one Alaska Native, and four non-Indians, more Indians than ever before in Bureau history to hold management positions.

A series of occupations of Federal land surplus to the immediate needs of the Government by American Indians began with the occupation of Alcatraz in San Francisco Bay in 1969. June 11, 1971 — 19 months later — U.S. Marshals removed 15 Indians from the island. Indians had been negotiating with Government officials on plans to convert the island to an Indian cultural center. However, the Golden Gate National Recreation Act of October 27, 1972 established the approximately 34,200 acre Golden Gate National Recreation Area that now includes the island.

Other occupations have included that of the Nike missile site at Chicago, which Indians held June 14 to July 1, 1971 in a protest over a lack of suitable housing, and Mount Rushmore, June 6, 1971 when about 40 Indians set up a camp and demanded that the Federal Government honor the Sioux Treaty of Fort Laramie (1869) which they said gave them the right to all land in South Dakota west of the Missouri River.

President Nixon's special Message to the Congress on July 8, 1970 regarding Indian affairs established future Federal Indian policy. Along with more specific proposals for legislation, the message affirmed the historic relationship between the Federal Government and Indian communities, guaranteed that it would not be abridged without Indian consent, and proposed that Indian communities be allowed to take over control and operation of Federally-funded Indian programs when they chose to do so. The President added, "It is long past the time that the Indian policies of the Federal Government began to recognize and build upon the capacities and insights of the Indian people .... the time has come to break decisively with the past and to create the conditions for a new era in which the Indian future is determined by Indian acts and Indian decisions."

In his message, President Nixon called for self-determination for Indian people without the threat of termination of the trust relationship over Indian lands and the services guaranteed to Indian people along with this relationship. While President Nixon's message is the second delivered by the President of the United States, it is the first to be implemented by legislation. Among his recommendations, the President asked for:

• A new Concurrent Resolution that would "renounce, repudiate and repeal" the termination policy outlined in HCR 108 of the 83rd Congress;

• Support for voluntary Indian control of Indian programs with the necessary technical assistance from the Government to facilitate transfers of responsibilities;

• Restoration of the sacred lands near Blue Lake to the Indians of Taos Pueblo;

• Support for Indian communities to take over Indian schools, to establish Indian school boards, to receive funds and to contract for the operation of schools;

• Economic development legislation through the "Indian Financing Act of 1970" to enable Indian leaders to arrange for the development and use of natural resources;

• Improved government efforts to deliver services needed to assist Indians living in urban centers;

• The establishment of an Indian Trust Counsel Authority "to assure independent legal representation for the Indians natural resource rights" and to avoid conflicts of interest within government agencies;

• The creation of a new office within the Department of the Interior — Assistant Secretary for Indian and Territorial Affairs.

The first of the President's recommendations to become law was the act restoring Blue Lake and the 48,000 acres of surrounding land to the Taos Pueblo Indians of New Mexico. This act is significant because it returns lands to an Indian tribe that had been taken and used for other purposes. Former practice had been to make cash settlements alone in compensation for land taken.

In keeping with the President's recommendations and proposals for legislation, Commissioner Bruce and his Indian executive team announced five policy goals in November 1970 to guide the Bureau in its new administration of Indian affairs:

• Transformation of the BIA from a management to a service organization;

• Reaffirmation of the trust status of Indian land;

• Making the BIA Area Offices fully responsive to the Indian people they serve;

• Providing tribes with the option of taking over any or all BIA Program functions with the understanding that the Bureau will provide assistance or reassume control if requested to do so;

• Working with Indian organizations to become a strong advocate of urban Indian interests.

BIA SERVICE AND SUPPORT AGENCY

In its new role as a service and support rather than a management organization, the BIA encouraged and assisted tribes in their assumption of program operations. The Zuni Tribe of New Mexico assumed the responsibility for directing BIA activities at the pueblo in May 1970. Almost a year later, the BIA signed a contract with the Miccosukee Tribe of Florida empowering it to administer BIA programs on the reservation, including all education and social operations. BIA field technicians and administrators are working directly with these two Indian groups to assist with the development and implementation of programs to meet the expressed and particular needs of the two Native American communities.

The recent emergence of a strong and positive attitude on the part of Indian people that they can and will have better lives has become historically important. Indians of all ages, representing all tribes, are undertaking unprecedented efforts to overcome the problems confronting them. Evidence of this new attitude is apparent in the establishment of the National Tribal Chairmen's Association (NTCA), a new organization of elected tribal chairmen. Created in April 1971, NTCA set up a 15-member commission to advise the BIA on national Indian policy. Through this group, reservation Indians can present a single, united voice in shaping the future of Indian affairs.

NTCA is not the only voice being heard at the decision-making levels in Indian affairs. As the urban Indian population has gained in numbers, other Indian organizations such as the National Congress of American Indians and the American Indian Movement have been instrumental in bringing recognition to the Indians in off-reservation communities.

Since World War II, when thousands of Indians left the reservations for military service or for wartime jobs, a steady off reservation movement has been taking place. This was given an additional boost in the early 1950's with the initiation of the BIA Employment Assistance Program which assisted Indians in locating permanent employment in non-reservation areas. The urban Indian movement of the 1950's and 1960's has resulted in an estimated 350,000 Indians living off the reservations today.

In his message to the Congress on national Indian policy, President Nixon pointed out that although the "BIA's responsibility does not extend to Indians who have left the reservation", this fact is "not always clearly understood. As a result of this misconception, Indians living in urban areas have often lost out on the opportunity to participate in other programs designed for disadvantaged groups." President Nixon directed the Office of Economic Opportunity (OEO) to lead efforts to help urban Indian leaders work toward solutions to their problems.

OEO announced in May 1971 that it had joined with the Departments of Health, Education, and Welfare (HEW), Housing and Urban Development (HUD), and Labor to create a Model Urban Indian Center Program to provide special assistance to the growing urban Indian population. Federal grants totaling some $880,000 were used to upgrade Indian centers in Los Angeles, Minneapolis, Gallup, and Fairbanks, and to establish a central research technical assistance and coordinating offce in New York City.

As a result of experience gained in various tribal, State and Federal programs there is presently a trained and educated Indian leadership available to staff management positions at levels where decisions are made regarding Indian affairs. Indian leaders are working in government agencies having programs that serve Indians both on and off the reservations. The Indian desk concept, after experimentation and successful operation in OEO, has been extended to the Departments of Commerce, Labor, Agriculture, Justice, HUD, and HEW. In 1974, HEW became the lead agency for programs to help urban Indians.

The Alaska Native Claims Settlement Act was signed into law December 18, 1971. This brought about the largest cession of land to a group of Native Americans in the history of the United States — one-twelfth of Alaska. This transfer of jurisdiction from Federal to Native hands — for 95 percent of Alaska belongs to Uncle Sam— began early in 1974. Concurrently, as land is put into Native hands, the United States Government and the State of Alaska will contribute $962,500,000 to Alaska Natives through the Alaska Native Fund.

Commissioner Bruce welcomed 1972 by announcing plans for a massive redirection of the BIA's programs. This included helping Indians toward self-determination by reservation development plans, redirection of the BIA employment assistance program, resources protection, reservation roads improvements, and increased tribal control over Indian education.

The five-point program includes a reversal of a 15-year-old policy of training Indians to work in urban areas off the reservations. The primary objective of the new strategy was to encourage the development of totally viable Indian economies on reservations.

"Developing Indian economies does not mean merely locating non-Indian industry close to or on the reservations so that these corporations can enjoy a cheap labor supply. It means the development of truly Indian economic systems so that a dollar once earned by an Indian citizen can be spent and kept moving throughout an Indian economy, thus developing that economy and making a maximum impact upon that community. . . . I want to see Indian economies where dollars move from Indian hand to Indian hand and are not drained out by those non-Indian cities that develop and grow and feed upon Indian reservations," stated Commissioner Bruce.

. . .

The Bureau of Indian Affairs building in Washington, D.C. was occupied by Indians representing the Trail of Broken Treaties Caravan from late afternoon November 2 through the evening of November 8, 1972. The occupying group made certain demands of the Federal Government which, in turn, said it would not consider until artifacts and documents taken in the protest were returned.

Following the protest, the resignation of Louis R. Bruce was accepted by President Nixon and Marvin L. Franklin, an enrolled member of the Iowa Indian Tribe of Oklahoma, was named Assistant to the Secretary for Indian Affairs, a new position in the Interior Department. Franklin became senior official for Indian affairs within Interior with direct responsibility for all Department programs concerning Indian and Alaska Native people on an interim basis, reporting directly to the Secretary.

Shortly after he took command, a $2.5 million supplemental appropriation made it possible for some 3,000 Indian youths to receive scholarship money from the Bureau, making a record 14,000 students who had received such money during the current school year.

A 71-day siege of the village of Wounded Knee on the Oglala Sioux reservation near Pine Ridge, South Dakota, began February 27, 1973 when nearly 200 members of the American Indian Movement (AIM) and its supporters took control. Members of AIM, the Oglala Sioux elders and Sioux people who supported the occupiers of Wounded Knee charged the elected tribal chairman at Pine Ridge with running a corrupt reservation government and called for repeal of the Indian Reorganization Act of 1934 which drastically altered the power base of most of the traditional leaders.

. . .

[On] August 13, 1973, an Office of Indian Rights within the Department of Justice was formed. It has the responsibility of enforcing Federal statutes regarding the civil rights of American Indians, primarily Title II of the 1968 Civil Rights Act, commonly known as the Indian Bill of Rights.

The American Indian National Bank was dedicated November 15, 1973, in Washington, D.C. Unique among the Nation's financial institutions, it is wholly Indian owned and operated. The concept that led to creation of the bank took form in the early '60's. The vision was for an institution with the financial services, counseling, and planning ability necessary to free the American Indian from the isolation of an economic island that meant higher unemployment, inadequate housing, and a smaller share of economic independence.

Morris Thompson, an Athabascan Indian and native of the State of Alaska, became Commissioner of Indian Affairs December 3, 1973. [On] December 22, 1973, the President signed into law an act restoring the Menominee Indians of Wisconsin to Federal services. Candidates for the Menominee Restoration Committee were nominated January 19. Menominee land will not be put into trust until 1975, but when it is the resulting reservation will be the largest in Wisconsin.

. . .

Thompson immediately stabilized the organizational structure for the Central Office by appointing five directors, four of whom are Indian.

The issue of Indian preference was clarified by the Supreme Court — which found that the Bureau of Indian Affairs must follow Indian preference in initial hiring and promotion. Thompson's appointments have been made in the light of this decision.

A thorough understanding of the Indian's bind, described in the following selection, "Our Brother's Keeper," is essential to any valid delineation of the nature of the complex bureaucratic relationship that exists between the Indians and the Bureau of Indian affairs. That relationship is a primary determinant of the policy making process, and it further influences the impact of national policy on the clientele. The Indians need the Bureau if they are to maintain their racial and cultural identity. Yet the BIA has often been the agent of national policy to terminate the special status of Indians and throw them into the "melting pot." This is an ambivalent position, for both the Indians and the Bureau. As a result, Indians have been reluctant to criticize the Bureau, and policy initiatives have flowed from the top, from the government in Washington.

OUR BROTHER'S KEEPER

The Indian tolerates his present impotent and unjust status in his relations with the Federal Government because he sees the Bureau of Indian Affairs as the lesser of two evils. The BIA is all he has, and every promise to replace it with something better has been broken.

Those new to Indian problems and enraged by the conduct of the BIA, and even those long acquainted with the Bureau's impenetrable bureaucracy, often reach an obvious conclusion: why not just do away with the Bureau and, in the words of a U.S. Senator, "free" the Indians?

The easy answer is the wrong answer, and the Indian knows it better than anyone else. Those who would abolish the Bureau to "help" the Indian will find as their most vehement opponent the Indian himself. He knows that he must, even at the cost of his liberty, preserve the Bureau — because the Bureau and only the Bureau stands between the Indian and extinction as a racial and cultural entity. Only the Bureau stands between the Indian and total, unilateral renunciation of all federal treaty obligations. The Bureau has been and the Bureau remains the special protector of the Indian and his champion, at times, against predatory interests. The Bureau and the solemn promises of the Federal Government are symbolically synonymous in the mind of the Indian. To destroy one is to destroy both.

The Bureau has done a terrible job; it has compromised the Indian time and again; it has permitted, tolerated, even assisted in the erosion of Indian rights and the whittling away of the Indian land base. Still, to the Indian, it is *his*. In the light of wisdom gained from long years of bitter experience, the Indian knows that a threat to the Bureau, an attack on the Bureau or any change in its structure is to be resisted as a threat to his own survival. . . .

. . . Those who try to make changes in the Bureau will find themselves met with substantial opposition from Indians. . . . Indians can and often do criticize the Bureau, but they do not necessarily regard the non-Indian

Source: Reprinted from *The Citizen's Advocate* (October 1969).

critic as an ally. They know that criticism can play directly into the hands of their worst enemies — those who wish to end the special relationship which exists between the Indian and the Federal Government.

Even the truth is to be resisted, if it is a truth which can endanger their protector, the Bureau. The Bureau plays upon this fear to stimulate Indians, and particularly tribal leaders, to attack and deny any report which seeks to tell the truth — although the same Indians privately will admit the truth of the charges, and even cite examples.

The Indian not only tolerates the injustice of the system; he helps insulate it from scrutiny and criticism, because history has convinced him that an attack on the Bureau will lead to the destruction of his special status as an Indian, and to the death of his people.

SECTION B. PRESENT POLICIES
AND PROBLEMS

The organizational chart on page 306 points toward some of the problems in the formation and implementation of Indian policy. Indians are only one interest under the Interior umbrella and Interior is one department within the executive branch. Other agencies within this single bureaucracy may and do have conflicting interests. For example, energy needs, national parks and forests, and Indian reservations all require land, but for different and conflicting uses. The national policy to be developed for land use sets bureaus and their clientele, internal to the Department of Interior, against each other. Any national policy comes from the "political" branches, the President and Congress, through the Secretary, through the Commissioner of Indian Affairs, and down through the hierarchy, until it reaches the Indian. The vestiges of past policies influence through old assumptions and continuing civil service personnel. What looks like a line of command on a chart is very hard to implement in practice.

This section consists of policy statements from prominent officials up and down the chart, juxtaposed with the clientele's complaints and questions. It is important to keep in mind past events as they echo through present-day positions. Again, in most cases, personal intentions as stated cannot be faulted and do not mislead deliberately. But they exist in an environment dominated by national and competing and "more powerful" interests. Additionally, distrust (not without rea-

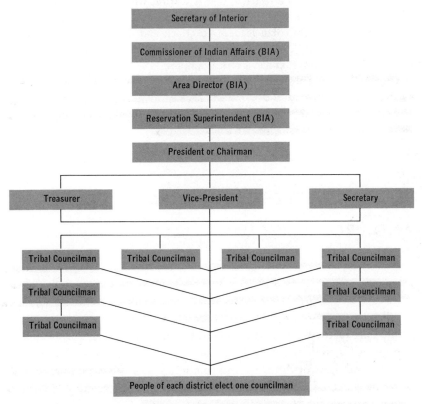

TRIBAL GOVERNMENT TODAY

(Under Indian Reorganization Act of 1934)

'No act of tribal government except taxation of tribal members
can be performed without express approval of the BIA'

- Secretary of Interior
- Commissioner of Indian Affairs (BIA)
- Area Director (BIA)
- Reservation Superintendent (BIA)
- President or Chairman
- Treasurer
- Vice-President
- Secretary
- Tribal Councilman
- People of each district elect one councilman

"Tribal Government Today" from *The Road to Wounded Knee* by Robert Burnette and John Koster; copyright © 1974 by Robert Burnette. Reprinted by permission of Bantam Books, Inc.

son) pervades the relationship between the Indian client, the Bureau of Indian Affairs, the Interior Department, and so on. Present policies, criticism, and the relationship between policy intentions and activities must be understood within this broad climate. The following selections bring the preceding ones up to date and illustrate the difficulties in policy making and implementation, even when all concerned are given the benefit of the doubt and the best of intentions are acknowledged.

GOOD INTENTIONS

The problem with bureaucratic policy making often lies not in the intentions of those at the top but rather in the ability (or inability) of a large and distant agency to carry out those intentions. The promise and expectation that accompanies the appointment of a new agency head is often evident in the remarks made during hearings on his nomination. By reviewing the activities of the agency following such an appointment, it is possible to compare these promises with the resulting policies, as they affect and are experienced by the clientele. A selection from the hearings on the nomination of a new Commissioner of Indian Affairs is here followed by an articulation of some of the ensuing difficulties the Indians have had with the bureau headed by that Commissioner.

NOMINATION OF MORRIS THOMPSON TO BE COMMISSIONER OF THE BUREAU OF INDIAN AFFAIRS

U.S. SENATE COMMITTEE ON INTERIOR AND INSULAR AFFAIRS

WEDNESDAY, NOVEMBER 14, 1973

STATEMENT OF HON. HENRY M. JACKSON, A U.S. SENATOR FROM
THE STATE OF WASHINGTON

The purpose of the meeting today is to consider the nomination of Mr. Morris Thompson of Tanana, Alaska, to be Commissioner of Indian Affairs.

Although he is a relatively young man, Mr. Thompson brings a rich background in public service experience to this challenging and difficult post.

In addition to his academic and professional qualifications, Mr. Thompson is an Athabascan Indian and understands the needs, hopes, and aspirations of Indian people across the land.

SOURCE: Hearing Before the Committee on Interior and Insular Affairs, United States Senate, Ninety-Third Congress (Washington, D.C.: U.S. Government Printing Office, 1973).

If his nomination is approved by the committee and confirmed by the Senate, Mr. Thompson will assume leadership of the Bureau of Indian Affairs at a time when it has just undergone one of the most critical periods in its long, sometimes stormy history.

Because the Bureau is statutorily charged with fulfilling the Federal Government's unique trust responsibilities to Indian people, the agency is required to make numerous decisions affecting the property and lives of Indian people, both now and in the future.

These decisions are often considered unpopular by the Indians and general public and result in sharp, public attacks directed against the Bureau.

Two major disruptions have occurred in the Indian field during the past year which further complicate the role of the Bureau of Indian Affairs.

In early November 1972, the Bureau headquarters building was occupied by the participants of the Trail of Broken Treaties who later inflicted considerable damage to the physical property, records, and equipment.

More recently, the symbolic community at Wounded Knee, S. Dak., was occupied by Indian people and before a peaceful negotiation was arrived at, considerable damage was brought to the community and most unfortunately two Indian people died as a direct result of this confrontation.

These episodes taken together, in my view, represent the culmination of decades of Indian resentment, bitterness, and rage over the general state of Indian affairs.

. . . Former Commissioner Bruce resigned from his post effective January 20, 1973, and although the administration endeavored to provide interim leadership to the Bureau, the record speaks for itself.

Employee morale has fallen to a new low. The organizational structure of the Bureau has come under attack from congressional and tribal leaders.

In short, I question whether the Bureau is meeting its minimum responsibilities to the Indian community. The ultimate losers in this situation are the Indian people themselves who are striving so desperately toward a resolution of the serious social and economic problems affecting their reservations and communities.

But rather than belabor the past and all that is wrong with the Bureau, I would suggest to the nominee, Mr. Thompson, that he has before him an opportunity to make a valuable contribution to his own people, to the Federal Government, and to the general public of this Nation.

But to do so he must devise the means and methods to marshal the Bureau's financial and personnel resources in such a way that it may again become a functioning agency in the Indian field.

I consider this initial step essential if employee morale is to be improved and if the Indian community is to regain any degree of confidence in the ability of this organization to assist them in their efforts to improve living conditions throughout Indian country.

Further, I believe the Bureau's organizational structure must be stabilized in order to utilize new tools which Congress has or will hopefully approve for use by the Bureau in the Indian field.

Let me cite a couple of examples. S. 1016, the judgment authorization bill, has been approved by Congress and is now Public Law 93–134.

This new law authorizes a speedier method for processing judgment awards made to Indian tribes so that the distribution of funds may be made more promptly for the benefit of the recipient of the award.

Under this law the distribution will be made on the basis of an administrative action with Congress maintaining an oversight responsibility on the total process.

The Bureau by necessity must play a key role in implementing the provisions of this new statute. In the area of Indian financing, self-determination and education, key bills are moving forward in both the Senate and the House and I am confident that new laws in these important areas will soon be enacted.

To put it more bluntly, unless the Bureau's house is brought into order, I cannot possibly envision how they will be able to assume additional responsibilities in the future, all of which are designed to assist the Indian people.

In addition to potential new responsibilities brought about by legislation, I believe that the new Commissioner and the Bureau must be prepared to play an ever increasing role as an advocate in representing Indian interests before other Federal departments and agencies whose programs and services hold potential for improving the lifestyle of the Indian people.

I believe the time has arrived when we must face reality and recognize that because of limitations in both authority and finance, the Bureau cannot possibly begin to cope with the wide range of social and economic conditions affecting the Indian community.

There are, however, other programs and resources available throughout government to assist citizens in need and certainly the first citizens of this Nation should share in these benefits.

There are two important areas currently under litigation which the new Commissioner will be required to follow closely. These are in the area of Indian preference for employment and the extent to which the Bureau of Indian Affairs and the Indian Health Service should extend their special services to Indian people residing beyond federally recognized reservations and other Indian communities.

Depending on the final court decisions in these areas, it may be necessary for the new Commissioner to redefine the important roles of the Bureau.

In conclusion, . . . I am hopeful that Mr. Thompson will provide this committee and the Indian community, through this official hearing record, with a clear statement of his basic philosophy on Indian affairs; his stand on the key issues of the day; his vision of the Bureau playing a constructive rather than destructive role in Indian affairs; and finally, his intention to involve the Indian community itself so that the rank and file tribal members, as well as their leaders, become true participants in an effort geared toward real progress.

. . .

STATEMENT OF MORRIS THOMPSON, NOMINEE FOR THE
POSITION OF COMMISSIONER OF INDIAN AFFAIRS

I accept this nomination with the full knowledge of the tremendous responsibility entrusted in this position and this Bureau. I accept this responsibility because of the concern for American Indians demonstrated by this administration, this Congress and the American public. Not only has concern been expressed but much needed action is now being taken that I am confident will lead to real progress in the next several years. I feel that I can contribute to this progress.

The biographical information you have been provided indicates the various positions I have held. What it doesn't provide is my personal philosophy on Indian affairs. This statement and the exchange we will have in this hearing hopefully will provide you and the Indian people a better understanding of what to expect from the Bureau of Indian Affairs under my direction. American Indians have a right to expect an effective and efficient Bureau of Indian Affairs. They have a right to expect that the money appropriated by Congress for Indians is spent wisely and that each dollar directly or indirectly benefits Indians at the local and individual level.

Indian people have a right to determine what the Indian priorities will be and how they are to be met. In addition, if the Indians so desire, and at their own initiative, Indians have a right to direct and administer programs developed for them.

The President recognized these rights and therefore established a policy of self-determination for Indians, without the threat of termination of the trust responsibility. I believe in this policy, and as Commissioner will insure that meaningful Indian involvement is an integral part of all Bureau operations.

The right of Indians to expect an efficient and responsive Bureau is very important. It is unfortunate, however, that in recent months concern with reorganization and realinement appears to have been elevated to a high mission status. Even more unfortunate is that this high concern for organizational changes has somewhat diverted valuable resources and attention from what should be the Bureau's top priorities.

Under my leadership, the Bureau's top priorities will be meeting our trust responsibilities, the delivery of meaningful services, and the achievement of greater Indian self-determination. I hope to do this by providing strong leadership and applying sound management practices to the Bureau's operations.

Within the Department of the Interior, the Secretary establishes all major policies, including those involving Indian affairs. Secretary Morton has given me assurance that I will work closely with him in developing policies on Indian affairs. He has also assured me that I will have the freedom to select my key staff. These assurances are essential to any new Commissioner.

One distinct advantage today, however, is the fact that the Commissioner will report directly to the Secretary.

The ability to select a key staff is also a distinct advantage. The Bureau has several key vacancies both at the central office and field levels which offer an unusual opportunity to develop a well balanced staff. In my selection of key staff I will be seeking not only technical competence and proven ability, but more importantly, I will be looking for people with a deep personal commitment and understanding of Indian problems. Hopefully, this process can be accomplished in a timely manner.

Although we have a tremendous responsibility, I recognize that the Bureau of Indian Affairs is not the total answer to all the problems facing Indians today.

Other Federal agencies and State and local governments also have Indian concerns and responsibilities. It is not only desirable but essential that we work together more closely to take advantage of each other's resources and thinking which hopefully will minimize duplication and maximize total delivery of services. I will make a concerted effort to establish and maintain this needed cooperation.

Of high importance is cooperation between the Congress and the Bureau. I have been following with great interest the progress being made with Indian legislation by this Congress. This progress is more than encouraging in that it demonstrates Congress' understanding of Indians and its sincere desire to provide much needed laws to meet today's needs.

I am extremely hopeful that you will be successful in enacting the Indian legislation before you in the near future. Once enacted, we will be able to more effectively deal with the Indian crises along with the many other foreign and domestic crises facing our country today.

I know that you will want my personal views on many issues facing the Bureau today. Rather than anticipating your specific concerns and attempting to expand on my views in this statement, I will reserve most of my comments for direct response to your questions. You and the Indian people, however, have a right to know what priorities I feel are important in Indian affairs.

If I left with you the impression earlier that I am unconcerned about the organizational structure of the Bureau, this was not my intent. My real intent was to place this concern in its proper perspective. Reorganizations and realinements are administrative problems rather than concerns.

My primary objective is to insure that whatever form the organization happens to be in now, or whatever form it may take in the future, that it be as effective and responsive as possible. If major changes are warranted, these will be taken at my initiation and under my direction. No major changes will be implemented, however, without full Indian involvement.

The most immediate concern is in filling our key positions and becoming fully operational again.

In addition to my concerns for the organization and developing cooperation among the administration, this Congress, and State and local governments, I feel very strongly that our efforts must be consistent with the expressed desires of Indian people.

From my experience in Indian affairs I have developed a tremendous respect and confidence in the Indian leadership throughout this country. The quality of this leadership is demonstrated by numerous examples of outstanding tribal government management, a total commitment to the development of both human and natural resources, and the ability to maintain progress without sacrificing Indian culture. What is most impressive is the unwavering faith Indians have in Indians, that given the opportunity Indians can and will solve Indian problems.

Indian tribes must have the opportunity to develop their tribal governments. Resources must be made available to the tribes for this purpose. If assistance is desired, this must be provided without paternalism. Developing effective tribal governments will be a major step toward true Indian self-determination.

The threat of termination has been a major barrier to the development of Indian resources, enterprises, and governments in recent years. Whether real or imagined, the feeling existed that any success might be used as justification for terminating the Federal Government's trust relationship. One of my major priorities will be to overcome this fear.

Basic to the role of the BIA is assuring the fulfillment of the Federal Government's trust and treaty responsibilities to Indian people and their resources. I intend to work closely with Indian people and the solicitor to better define these responsibilities and see to it that the BIA fully discharges its responsibilities.

Of the many programs developed and administered for the benefit of Indians today, none is more important than Indian education. The American taxpayers are investing millions of dollars in the education of Indian youth. Indian people and all Americans have a right to expect that the best education program possible is being provided to Indians.

It is not enough to say that we are meeting minimum standards of education, or that we are providing an adequate level of education, or that we are doing our best under the circumstances. We must establish the highest standards possible and insure that those standards are met. We must utilize the most modern education techniques available and also develop new ones. We must provide the best materials, equipment, and facilities available. Finally, we must insure that our teachers are not only of the highest caliber available but also that they be personally committed and sensitive to Indian needs. In short, we must be sure that each dollar appropriated for Indian education is spent wisely, whether through Bureau-operated systems or through other systems.

I recognize and respect congressional responsibility to establish Indian policy. I also recognize and respect the oversight responsibility of the Congress to insure that the congressional intent is met. As Commissioner, I look forward to work[ing] very closely with the Congress, the Secretary, and the Indian people in establishing national Indian policy. Once these policies are established, I pledge to carry them out to the best of my ability . . . .

THE PERCEPTION OF INACTION

Three articles collected from a leading Indian newspaper during the period after Morris Thompson assumed office as Commissioner of Indian Affairs relate the Indian struggle with the Bureau over promises dealing with water rights, the arts, and education. The emphasis is on delay and inaction on the issues where the agency has promised more than it has been able to produce.

COLORADO RIVER TRIBES CHARGE BIA DELAYS: WATER RIGHTS ISSUE

RUPERT COSTO

Phoenix, Arizona — An emergency meeting of the Confederation of Indian Tribes of the Lower Colorado River has exposed the Bureau of Indian Affairs' handling of tribal business as "a real runaround, filled with delaying tactics, well calculated to put the tribes completely out of existence."

This was the consenus of tribal leaders who attended the meeting.

The Confederation is comprised of these five tribal groups: Quechan, Cocopah, Colorado River Tribes, Fort Mojave, and Chemehuevi.

Without exception, each of the tribes has experienced delaying tactics and a failure to protect their rights. The Quechan have been claiming 40,000 acres of land which is theirs. Nothing has been done about it and they are left to flounder with the prospect of finally losing their claim.

The Cocopah desperately need irrigation so that they can develop their economy. This has been promised for years, and the project has been approved, but nothing has been done.

The Colorado River Tribes have a project which is years old, and has been approved. The work has started, but it is far from completion and is floundering in a sea of paperwork.

The Fort Mojave Indians have a claim for the use of their valuable swampland. Nothing has been done.

The Chemehuevi have been working and consulting for a sewer line on their reservation. They are shuttled from one bureaucrat to another, with paper work flying in all directions. But there is no evidence that this work is in progress.

Some of the projects are as much as one hundred years old. The tribal representatives are forced to fly from their reservations to the capitol many times a year, with little result. "We are treated like a yo-yo ball, tossed from one office to another, but we aren't getting anywhere," said Lou Barrackman, of Fort Mojave Indian Reservation.

The meeting was unanimous in condemning the Central Arizona Project, which is now under way. Water is to be drawn from the surrounding reservations to feed this huge monster, stated one spokesman. "But there is no water to put into it," said Joe Miguel, chairman of the Confederation. Miguel is Quechan, who have been subjected to the same delaying tactics as the others.

Evidence was submitted by experts such as William H. Veeder, showing vast over-appropriation of water.

"We want to work; we need to put our people to work," said Barrackman, "but how can we do this, with the lack of support and the delaying tactics of the BIA. Something has got to give, and we are going to see to it that it does."

A resolution passed by the meeting requested a fund of $250,000 with which the tribes can make an inventory of their irrigable acreage (which has never been done), and a clear statement of their rights to their waters.

BIA NOW CHARGED WITH FOOT-DRAGGING, INDECISION BY INDIAN REGENTS COUNCIL

JEANNETTE HENRY

Albuquerque, N.M. — Foot-dragging, indecision, and a failure to respond to Indian needs in education as the Indians see them, is the essence of charges against the Bureau of Indian Affairs by Mr. John C. Rainer, Sr., chairman of the Native American Council of Regents, Institute of American Indian Arts in Sante Fe.

According to Rainer, "Over the past six years, repeated efforts have been made by the Institute of American Indian Arts, to obtain upper management decisions from the BIA that would allow the Institute to develop from an effective but naturally limited secondary school into a major cultural institution."

Meetings with high echelon BIA officials have been held, but they have reached no decisions, "as to the critical major issues confronting the institute," Rainer stated.

"Commitments has been made from time to time by the BIA, that major policy decisions spelling out the future of the Institute would be handed down," Rainer asserted. "But," he said, "no such commitments have yet been made."

BUREAUCRATIC NONACTION

A litany of bureaucratic indecision was spelled out by Rainer, revealing these facts:

In 1969, the Congressional Subcommittee on Indian Education recommended that "The Institute of American Indian Arts at Santa Fe, N.M., should be raised to the level of a four-year college, supported by the BIA."

In 1972, the BIA conducted an evaluation of the transitional position of the school, the Evaluation Division recommending that "It should be the goal of the Institute of American Indian Arts to develop a four-year college with emphasis on the Indian arts and cultural studies."

In August, 1973, Associated Council members of Haskell Indian Junior College, Southwestern Polytechnic Institute and the Institute of American Indian Arts met with a representative of the Secretary's office to express concern about the programs of all three higher education institutions controlled by the BIA. Action was promised, but there was none.

PROMISES, PROMISES

On August 1, 1974, following a meeting wth Dr. Clennon Sockey, newly appointed director of Indian education, the Council of Regents passed a resolution informing the Commissioner of Indian Affairs, that, if decisions were not immediately forthcoming regarding the future of the Institute, they would have no choice but to seek direct assistance from the Congress.

If necessary, the Regents would ask for a major audit of the Office of the Commissioner in the failure of the Bureau as to the handling of the school's problems, the resolution stated.

Furthermore, the resolution asserted the Regents would "launch legal proceedings against the BIA, if that became necessary."

The BIA has agreed to the Institute's aspirations to become more professionally structured. It contracted with the Rhode Island School of Design to assist the Institute in a move to a college-level, structured institution.

The Rhode Island School has not been fully compensated for their services during the last fiscal year, Rainer charged. This liaison position, so necessary for current student accreditation and for final accreditation, is now in jeopardy.

BIA "NO HELP" IN EDUCATION, TESTIMONY SAYS

Washington, D.C. — Dr. Clennon E. Sockey, Choctow, BIA director of education programs, testified recently before Indian Education Oversight hearing that the BIA education contracting program from 1969 to the present is "not the most impressive record."

Chairman Senator Edward Kennedy (D.–Mass.), Subcommittee on Administrative Practices and Procedures, sponsor of many Indian education hearings, called the BIA record "not a commendable kind of experience," adding "there is a substantial body of opinion that rather than helping these communities . . . in too many instances the attitude of the BIA has been one of obstructionism."

SOURCE: Reprinted from *Wassaja*, 2, No. 9 (October–November 1974). Copyright © 1974 by The American Indian Historical Society. All rights reserved.

Upon questioning by Kennedy, Dr. Sockey stated that of the 200 Indian communities having BIA education programs, only 29 have direct control. While in 1969 four schools had BIA contracts to run their schools, in 1974, there were only a total of thirteen. In addition, sixteen tribes have contracts for administering Johnson–O'Malley funds and fifteen administer the higher education assistance programs.

Sockey stated that in the future "We will be contacting some 100 schools and affording 50 of them the opportunity to select their own system of management for the operation of their schools."

He added that the BIA has developed a training package "designed to help a school board, staff, students, parents, tribal leaders to assess their school's programs and needs to understand the management options available for operating that school."

The various options mentioned were: operation under BIA management; becoming part of a tribal school system; operating with local community control under contract; or achieving public school status.

Kennedy's response to the plan of offering 50 tribes the chance to take over their schools was "that means four more years — you have 200 schools and so it will take four more years before they get a chance to get an option." Dr. Sockey then stated that other schools could "make requests for contracting purposes."

It was further revealed that one-half of the 29 school contracts had not yet been renegotiated and signed for the new school year, although those schools can continue operations under the old contracts and still receive BIA funding, according to BIA sources.

In discussing the new Johnson–O'Malley regulations agreed upon in August, Dr. Sockey mentioned that although eligibility for assistance is broadened by eliminating the Indian-owned, tax-exempt land requirement, it is still limited to Indians living on or near reservations.

(Indian groups involved in formulating the new regulations with BIA officials had pressed for eligibility of all Indians regardless of their residence. This was rejected by the BIA, however, although the other "red regs" were accepted in the new regulations.)

Sockey spoke of a study being made by the Bureau education office to identify the students needing aid who are not receiving it, and to ascertain what the cost would be to extend JOM funding to them.

"We possibly might see the necessity of recommending legislation for strengthening the JOM program," Sockey added, which would make JOM funds available to all Indians.

In discussing the current BIA reduction-in-force program now under way, Kennedy said that Indians are the ones who lose their jobs in a reorganization and added, "meanwhile you have vacancies in the central office that are unfilled. Why doesn't it make sense to close down these vacancies rather than have Indian educators lose their jobs?"

Dr. Sockey replied that the one vacancy in Washington is a GS–15 and that those professional Indian educators who have been moved out of education are not at the GS-15 level and cannot qualify under U.S. Civil Service regulations.

Also testifying was Will Antell, White Earth Chippewa, chairman of the National Advisory Council on Indian Education. He was accompanied by Clarence Skye, Sioux, NACIE council members, and Dwight A. Billedeaux, Blackfeet, NACIE executive director.

Discussing the 1972 Indian Education Act, Antell testified that the U. S. Office of Education never requested increased funds for Part A of the Act for fiscal year '75. Consequently, if the number of school districts being funded increased as anticipated, the per capita payment for each child would drop from $112 to $75 in the 1974–75 period.

Antell said that the executive branch has never accepted the Indian Education Act, and reminded the subcommittee that a court order had been necessary in order to release impounded funds for the Act.

Antell added that a deputy commissioner of Indian education still had not been approved by the Office of Education, although the NACIE submitted a list of nominees in October 1973, as required by the Indian Education Act, from which a deputy commissioner was to be chosen.

According to Antell, Dr. John Ottina, acting commissioner of education, informed him in January, 1974, that he had submitted the names of both Dr. William G. Demmert, Jr. and Earl J. Barlow, to the U. S. Civil Service Commission, for consideration for the post of deputy commissioner of Indian education.

However, it was later revealed that Ottina's statement was incorrect. A letter from Joseph Udomahof of the Civil Service Commission to Dwight Billedeaux, NACIE executive director, explained that in March, 1974, only the name of Earl Barlow was submitted by HEW and then, for reasons which are unclear, HEW requested that the submission of Barlow's name be returned to them without action.

In May, 1974, the agency then submitted the name of Demmert. Also in May, Ottina told Billedeaux and Antell that Demmert's name was rejected by the Civil Service Commission on the basis of his present grade level, insufficient department training, lack of experience.

Antell further asserted, "The Commissioner, his associates and key policy makers are not Indians and it is this echelon who tend to discount the importance of NACIE," he said. "Are we a Presidential Council or something else?" he questioned.

"The Office of Management and Budget's recent decisions have further restricted NACIE; our staff members are now under Civil Service and assigned as staff members to the Office of Education. The budget allotted for our council is now within the agency and we cannot spend these resources without going through several stages, which sometimes takes several weeks.

"They make final decisions whether our council will meet, where we will meet, and a whole host of other decisions which we feel we should be making. It seems to be another blatant attempt to control the council and its acts," he said.

Clarence Skye commented, "I feel the Office of Education is making us a rubber stamp organization," and added that the council was considering a lawsuit against the Office of Education.

Senator Kennedy asked Antell to develop a list of grievances that could be taken to the Commissioner of Education for discussing.

BUREAUCRATIC RESPONSIBILITY AND CONFLICTS OF INTEREST

The nomination of Thomas Kleppe to be Secretary of the Interior and Kent Frizzell to be Undersecretary in the fall of 1975 generated probing questions from members of Congress and representatives of Indian groups. The transcripts of these hearings show various aspects of the problem of establishing bureaucratic responsibility and the various conflicts that have arisen in the Department of the Interior as a result of the multitude of interests that it serves.

In the following material, Senator Fannin presses nominee Kleppe on the extent to which he will support the BIA and the tribal councils in their administration of the reservations. The difficulty Kleppe has in responding is at once understandable and symptomatic of the maze of bureaucratic power. Mr. Tonasket's remarks on the role of the secretary make more explicit some of the problems of bureaucratic responsibility and also raise the issue of conflict of interests that derive from some of the multiple orientations of the Department of the Interior.

The more specific exchanges that came out during the Frizzell hearings give a detailed account of manipulation of the bureaucratic maze by those at the top, at least from the perspective of those affected. The cases mentioned are instances where Indian interests have been subverted in favor of others in the American system who have greater access to the Bureau and to departmental policy makers.

HEARINGS BEFORE THE COMMITTEE ON INTERIOR AND
INSULAR AFFAIRS OF THE UNITED STATES SENATE ON THE
NOMINATION OF THOMAS S. KLEPPE TO BECOME
SECRETARY OF THE INTERIOR, SEPTEMBER 23 AND 25, 1975

SENATOR FANNIN: . . . Mr. Kleppe, as you know, my State of Arizona has 44 percent of its land under Federal ownership, and 27 percent being owned by the first Americans.

So we are very much involved with the Department of Interior. Indecision has created great problems in the State of Arizona over the years. I could point back to some of them, such as the Hopi–Navajo land dispute, because there was not a decision made by the Department of Interior or the BIA.

We have a conflict and I was very pleased that you have made it very specific that you are willing to make decisions. You brought out that this has been a part of your work in the SBA.

I praise you for that. You feel that you will be able to make decisions on these conflicting matters that will be coming before you?

MR. KLEPPE: Senator Fannin, from a personal point of view, I look at myself as a decision maker. I am not a procrastinator. If there is one thing I like to do it is to get going.

But I do not like to leave that wide open at that point, because of so many factors that become involved, particularly in these controversial issues.

SENATOR ABOUREZK: Mr. Kleppe, I guess you know that the Bureau of Indian Affairs, which is in the Interior Department, has almost unfettered jurisdiction over the Indian tribes in this country through the 1934 Indian Reorganization Act.

They have what you would call open-ended authorization to run Indian affairs about the way they want to. Each Indian tribe has a different condition and a different problem under which they either suffer or live.

In South Dakota right now, especially at the Pine Ridge Indian Reservation, we have probably more than our share of difficulties with regard to Indian militancy, with regard to what the tribe itself either does or does not do to deal with that militancy.

In line with that, the U.S. marshals and Justice Department recently proposed a system by which law enforcement would be brought back to some kind of normal level on Pine Ridge for about a year's time.

Are you familiar with that?

Mr. Kleppe: To some degree, Senator, yes.

Senator Abourezk: What it would do is to try to train Indian police, using marshals as a supervisory force, a training force out there, just long enough to restore things to normal.

As you know, the murder rate on the Pine Ridge Reservation is six times higher than that of Chicago ... [although] 100 FBI agents on the reservation have cut down the murder rate somewhat this year.

So far the Bureau of Indian Affairs, in typical fashion, I might say, has refused to go along with the marshal's plan. I suspect the reason they have refused to is because they see that as an invasion of their own empire.

They do not want that to happen, no matter what happens to the Indians out there. Second, I know, also, that the tribal council which was set up under the 1934 Indian Reorganization Act has been almost completely ignored by the tribal chairman of the Pine Ridge Reservation.

He makes decisions through himself alone or through the executive committee. The Bureau of Indian Affairs, which is under Interior and would be under your jurisdiction if you are confirmed, has gone along with the chairman and ignored the tribal council's decisions, which has resulted in the great political turmoil and violence that has occurred on the Pine Ridge Reservation.

With all that background, my question to you is this: do you intend to make sure that the Bureau of Indian Affairs stays out of tribal — internal tribal politics to the extent that they will allow the Indian people, through their council, to make decisions, rather than going along with what the chairman wants?

Mr. Kleppe: Senator Abourezk, it seems to me that the question of self-determination, which is what you are talking about, the tribal council, vis-a-vis the BIA, ought to be given all the opportunity to work itself out that can possibly be provided.

Senator Abourezk: What does that mean in terms of my question?

Mr. Kleppe: That means specifically — what I am saying is — the tribal council ought to have more voice in the affairs of the reservation.

Senator Abourezk: More voice —

Mr. Kleppe: More voice. This is a backing away, not a relinquishing of any of the authority of BIA, but a backing away of the administration of the affairs of the tribes on the Pine Ridge Reservation.

That is a general statement, but it provides an answer to your question, I believe. I did not know the details of all the things you recite about the murders and the difficulties and the situation at Pine Ridge.

But this question of self-determination has two sides to it, from what I am able to learn. You have some tribes who like to have more authority in running their affairs. You have others concerned about it because of losing some control — losing some support that they might otherwise get from the Federal Government through the BIA.

So it works both ways, depending on the local situation. If that condition exists in Pine Ridge, where the tribal council — and you have a dichotomy, apparently, between the council and the chairman, so I had better stay out of that because I just do not know enough about it.

But where you have the tribal council wanting to make more decisions from the standpoint of the affairs of the tribe, I think that would be a proper policy that I would support from the standpoint of the activities of the BIA in that given area.

SENATOR ABOUREZK: Even if you believe in that, would you enforce that belief on the BIA?

MR. KLEPPE: I would certainly attempt to give that a go, yes.

SENATOR ABOUREZK: They work for you, of course.

MR. KLEPPE: Yes.

STATEMENT OF MEL TONASKET, NATIONAL CONFERENCE OF AMERICAN INDIANS

I am Mel Tonasket, President, National Congress of American Indians. As President of an organization composed of numerous Indian Nations, Tribes, and people, I wish to say this to Mr. Thomas S. Kleppe, whose nomination is before the Congress for confirmation as the Secretary of the Interior:

American Indian people and the Nation as a whole desperately need a man of integrity who can bring to the Department of the Interior the credibility which for many years has been meager, if not non-existent.

It is our fondest hope that Mr. Kleppe will step forward and firmly announce that he will act expeditiously to prove that he is honest; that he is competent; that he is reliable; and, being honest, competent, and reliable, he will restore to the Secretary's Office the power and the credibility, and that in lieu of long-winded diatribes on Indian affairs, he will act as the Chief Agent of the Trustee United States for and on behalf of all Indian people, and not for the special interests which have established for their own benefit the policies and practices of the Interior Department in regard to Indian (a) water, (b) coal, (c) timber, (d) fish and all matters pertaining to Indian natural resources.

To accomplish those things Mr. Thomas S. Kleppe must recognize at the outset this fact — that within the Interior and Justice Departments this pattern is now and for a long time past, has been adhered to within Interior's grossly inept bureaucracy:

1. There has been oppression of all Indian Tribes and peoples by the inept bureaucracy through the undercutting of tribal leadership and its inherent power of self-government;

2. The bureaucratic activities have as their single objective the self-preservation of that bureaucracy and the tight controls by it of all aspects of Indian life and property;

3. The bureaucracy raids Indian property and the Treasury of the United States for non-Indian purposes and projects to the irreparable damage of the Indian Tribes and people;

4. The bureaucracy within the Interior and Justice Departments perverts laws which are favorable to the Indian people and by twisting those laws, benefits non-Indian users and projects.

Failure of the Interior Department to fulfill its function as the principal agency of the Trustee United States for the Indian Tribes and people, can be attributed to many factors. A principal reason for that failure is this:

Due to their shameful conflicts of interest the Attorneys in the Solicitor's Office of the Department of the Interior and the Attorneys in the Department of Justice are now and for many years past have been usurping administrative powers and perverting the law in furtherance of non-Indian interests to the irreparable damage of Indian people.

I am now so gravely concerned over the conduct of the Attorneys in both the Interior and Justice Departments in regard to Indian matters, that I have presented the issues to Attorney General Levi. . . .

. . .

Undoubtedly the greatest problem confronting Mr. Kleppe is the fact that he will be the chief administrator of the Bureau of Reclamation which is the single greatest enemy of the Indian people in the United States. How can the Secretary of the Interior perform his functions as the principal agent of the Trustee United States for the Indian people and at the same time administer the Bureau of Reclamation which at this moment and for many years in the past has raided Indian land and water rights for its powerful political backers who are the land and water speculators in the West?

My concern is this, and I pledge my own best efforts and those of the National Congress of American Indians to achieve a very necessary end:

The new Secretary of the Interior must insist that the Indian people be given the full benefit of the laws respecting the performance by the United States Trustee. In performing for the Indians the Secretary and his staff must exercise the highest degree of care, diligence and skill when acting for the Indians. The Secretary of the Interior must, moreover, force his lawyers in the Solicitor's Office to act *for* the Indians, not against them as so frequently has happened. Lawyers in the Justice Department must, moreover, rely upon the very formidable body of law that supports the Indian rights and the Indian power of self-government. If Mr. Kleppe follows that course he will at least take steps in the right direction and the Indian people will support him, I believe.

HEARINGS ON THE NOMINATION OF DALE KENT FRIZZELL[1]
TO BE UNDERSECRETARY OF THE DEPARTMENT OF THE
INTERIOR, OCTOBER 22, 1975

MR. FRIZZELL: . . . As has been indicated, this is the second occasion on which I have had the pleasure of appearing before this committee as a nominee for a position at the Department of the Interior. In 1973 when I was the nominee to become Solicitor, as a result of my having been Assistant Attorney General for Lands and Natural Resources at the Department of Justice, I was generally aware of the great challenge facing the Department.

Now having been Interior's Solicitor for 2½ years, as well as Acting Secretary on numerous occasions, I am hopefully aware of the responsibility of the Office of the Under Secretary. I welcome the new challenge presented by this opportunity, and I am indeed honored to be here today.

In my first few weeks as Solicitor, many issues were brought to my attention, some of which had been pending in the Department for years. I determined early on that, if at all possible, I was not going to take the easy way out by deferring decisions. Instead, where I felt matters were ready to be resolved, I've called them as I saw them, according to my best judgment. My record will show that I have acted on many of the issues, and that I have made every effort to hear all parties before making a decision.

My past personal association and communication with members of this committee and other Members of Congress have been of great assistance to me in this regard. If confirmed, I intend to continue in the same vein.

I do not pretend to have the answers to all of the problems and controversies that center upon the many important missions of the Department of the Interior. Nor do I think that these problems and controversies are insolvable. What I do believe is that the road to meeting the issues requires fairness and imagination in an effort to strike a delicate and equitable balance between what usually are legitimate but opposing concerns.

Interior is a guardian of the public domain — a domain replete with various uses that includes vast natural parks, recreation areas, large water and power facilities, Indian reservations, millions of acres of grazing lands, large wildlife refuges and wilderness areas, and great deposits of mineral wealth. Sometimes these uses conflict, and one use must be chosen to the

[1]Mr. Frizzell signed the documents, on behalf of the United States, ending the Wounded Knee occupation. Subsequent to the Indians' surrender, the promises were broken.

exclusion or alteration of another. The goal is to strike the proper balance.

The Department's conduct of management responsibility for this country's natural resources can make a difference in whether we yield to pressure from a foreign cartel — or become energy independent. The Department's actions can affect whether our country remains "America the Beautiful" — or becomes an environmental disaster. With our responsibility to the Indian people, Department decisions can influence the honoring of our treaties and other commitments, or result in unresponsiveness and unaccountability toward the forgotten first Americans.

My role as Interior's Chief Legal Adviser has been professional in nature and clothed with the usual precepts of the legal practitioner. The Under Secretary's role is broader in scope, and legal parameters are but a few of many considerations affecting the day-to-day decision process. I realize that the President and the Secretary must set the overall policy and guidance for the Department. It would be my role to be supportive as Under Secretary.

My pledge to you, if confirmed, will be to do my best to assist Secretary Kleppe in making sure that the appropriate facts are sought out, and examined fairly and objectively, thereby making and implementing the decisions which must be made — decisions which vitally affect all Americans.

THE CHAIRMAN: Thank you, Mr. Frizzell. I appreciate having your general comments. As you know, concern has been expressed by Members of Congress over the lack of responsiveness of some executive branch officials in agreeing to appear and testify at committee hearings. The question I ask is this: Can you assure the committee of your own intention to maintain open, free, and responsive communication with the committee and see that your subordinates do likewise?

MR. FRIZZELL: Without hesitation or mental reservation, Mr. Chairman.

THE CHAIRMAN: Thank you. Will you be available after reasonable notice to appear before this committee and other congressional committees to present Departmental and administration positions on pending legislation and to respond to committee questions on such matters as the committee might be looking into or investigating?

MR. FRIZZELL: At any and all appropriate times.

THE CHAIRMAN: I think that is a clear and forthright response. In accordance with the committee's rule, you have provided the committee a sworn confidential statement of your present financial condition. For the public record I would want to ask you whether you are aware of any personal holding or investment that could constitute a conflict of interest or which could create the appearance of a conflict of interest should you be confirmed as Under Secretary?

MR. FRIZZELL: None whatsoever, Mr. Chairman.

THE CHAIRMAN: While your financial statement has been given to the committee in confidence, would you have any problem in making that statement public or if the committee desired to do so?

Mr. Frizzell: Not at all.   . . .

STATEMENT OF MEL TONASKET, PRESIDENT, NATIONAL CONGRESS
OF AMERICAN INDIANS

Mr. Tonasket: Mr. Chairman and members of the committee, I am Mel Tonasket, president of the National Congress of American Indians. Sharing this panel with me are Sam Cagey, acting chairman of the Lummi Business Council, Ed Cline, Omaha tribal chairman, and Ted Risingsun, Northern Cheyenne Tribal Council member. We thank you for the opportunity to appear before this committee and to address ourselves to the nomination of Kent Frizzell as Under Secretary of the Interior Department.

At the confirmation hearing for Interior Secretary Kleppe, I presented to this committee what may be characterized as a petition on behalf of the American Indian people, in which I asked for fairness to and honesty with Indian people. I asked that Secretary Kleppe administer Indian affairs within the scope of the broad and favorable body of law which establishes the Interior Secretary as the principal agent of the United States, trustee for the Indian people. I asked that the Secretary perform his functions and uphold his duty and require that his staff perform their functions and uphold their duties with the highest degree of care, skill, and diligence. I asked that the Secretary bring new blood into the Department and select his support staff with caution, avoiding those bureaucrats whose paternalistic attitudes turn our legal battles into full-scale wars at a time when we are fighting through the courts for our very existence.

The importance of support staff within the Department is clearly witnessed in the Office of the Solicitor where there is a documentable and lengthy history of suppression of Indian rights and seizure of Indian property. For much of this year Kent Frizzell, as Interior Solicitor and Acting Secretary, has borne the responsibility of running the entire Department, has devoted little time to Indian affairs and has relied upon the recommendations of his chief administrative assistants. Many of those recommendations have been anti-Indian in nature and in fact. It is my fear that many of those same ill-advisers will be raised to higher levels of authority along with Mr. Frizzell, whose responsibility it was to oversee all activities within the Solicitor's Office.

Before I go on, I would like to add that it is very difficult for the tribes to testify here today, whether we testify for or against Mr. Frizzell. Normally, if you look at the past testimonies that the tribes present on confirmation hearings, we take a middle-of-the-road position and we ask questions. Because most of the people that we have been asked to give testimony on are people who have not really been involved with Indian affairs and Indian decisions. This is one instance where it is different. There are going to be some recommendations made.

I would like to assure this committee and the chairman that the questions we have are questions on facts, of law, and actions. For myself, I have made it a point to stay out of personalities and to deal only with facts of law and actions that have happened to our tribes throughout this country. In recent months, intimidations of that Office by the Justice Department appear to have increased, resulting in hasty decisions and extreme actions vigorously protested by the tribes involved. There also appears to have been a complete usurpation on the part of that Office of certain administrative authorities of the Commissioner of Indian Affairs, a Presidential appointee and chief line officer for Indians. One example of both points is the Blackbird Bend case, a boundary dispute in which the Omaha Tribe, with concurrence of the Commissioner's Office, entered into peaceful possession of Omaha land occupied by non-Indians for 40 years. The Solicitor continually challenged this peaceful possession and, using the excuse of a threat of imminent danger and knowing of the tribe's intent to bring suit to protect their interests, met with Justice Department representatives on a Sunday and agreed to file an unprepared quiet title suit in Federal Court.

This decision was made without the participation or knowledge of the Commissioner and in spite of the tribe's protests against such a suit. I would ask Mr. Frizzell the following: Could you demonstrate for the record that there did exist such a potential for violence that it was necessary to call the secret Sunday meeting and circumvent the authority of the tribe and the Commissioner? Further testimony regarding the Solicitor's actions in this case will be offered by Chairman Cline.

Councilman Risingsun will address the issue of the Solicitor's failure to honor former Secretary Morton's commitment to the Northern Cheyenne Tribe that Interior would defray legal fees involved in court actions surrounding the complex decision on coal leasing. On this issue I would ask Mr. Frizzell the following: (1) Is it not true that the Secretary has authority to honor his commitment and that the tribe qualifies under the two-pronged test contained in the May 30, 1975, Comptroller General's opinion, which states that legal fees may be paid for if Justice Department representation is unavailable and if the tribe is unable to afford the costs? (2) Why was the decision reversed, was there pressure to nullify the commitment and, if so, from what sources(s)? (3) In light of the tribe's experience with the legal fees commitment, to what extent can the Northern Cheyenne rely on the Secretary's commitment to not approve coal development on the reservation without prior approval of the tribe?

I have no need to go beyond the boundaries of my own reservation of the Colville Confederated Tribes to find examples of Mr. Frizzell's disregard of the power and authority of self-government and self-determination inherent in Indian tribes. Because of a vast vacuum on our reservation respecting the administration of our meager water supplies in the internal part of our land, we had developed what I perceived to be, and attorneys agree, the Colville Water Code in an effort to protect one of our most valuable assets. Our authority to exercise our power of internal management was challenged by Mr. Frizzell when he procured from Secretary Morton a declaration that no water code would be approved by anyone in the Interior Department. His staff attacked the efforts on the part of the Colville and Fort Hall Tribes, the Yakimas and others, who desired to perform essential services to their people when the trustee had failed to act; they did so in preservation of an inept, unwieldy and aggressively anti-Indian bureaucracy.

. . . In our water rights case, *United States* v. *Walton*, which involves Colville rights as they relate to the rights of a non-Indian, Walton, Mr. Frizzell's staff has lined up squarely behind the non-Indian, declaring that he has rights as against the tribes and allottees. In this case the Frizzell concept is adhered to, that it is the Interior Secretary who controls and can give water to Walton, to the irreparable damage to the tribes and allottees. I would ask Mr. Frizzell the following: In view of the fact that refusal to approve water codes reinforces the non-Indian position in both Bel Bay and Walton, could you provide an explanation of reasons for continued refusal to approve the codes and the date anticipated for approval?

I am advised that the Crow Tribe is confronted with the dilemma Mr. Frizzell has created for Western Indians by asserting that the Secretary has power to take water from them and to use it for Interior's Reclamation Bureau, and that the Bureau of Reclamation can sell Indian water for industrial purposes. I would ask Mr. Frizzell to point to the statutory authority giving the Secretary such authority. In the event such authority exists, what recourse or appeal do Indians have in this matter? Respecting this and the above interpretations of water law, I would ask: What system of checks and balances can be devised to assure Indian people a fair hearing when Mr. Frizzell is in the position of effectuating administratively the legal concepts he created as Assistant Attorney General, Lands and Natural Resources Division of the Justice Department, and as solicitor?

I am also advised that Mr. Frizzell, in June of 1974 in the case of *Arizona* v. *California*, was prepared to stipulate away the invaluable priorities of the Lower Colorado River Tribes — Mojaves, Colorado River Tribes, Chemehuevi, Fort Yuma and Cocopah — to the Imperial and Palo Verde Irrigation Districts and to the Yuma Federal reclamation project. Senator Jackson, chairman of this committee, moved rapidly to prevent Mr. Frizzell from carrying out that disastrous course and has continued to contact Attorney General Levi, seeking to avoid the consequences of the planned seizure of the Indians' water rights and the subjection of those rights to the inferior rights of the irrigation districts and project. I request that the proposed stipulation in *Arizona* v. *California* be made a part of the record of this hearing, as well as the Colville Water Code, my testimony before this committee during hearings to confirm former Secretary Hathaway and Secretary Kleppe and related data disclosing the treatment of Indian tribes by the Department of Justice and Interior.

SENATOR METCALF: Would you let me comment on this stipulation that has been handed me? It is a rather voluminous document. I would ask that with your cooperation and the help of staff, significant and appropriate excerpts from the document be included in the record and that the entire stipulation be made part of the file so that the record is not too voluminous. We have a printing problem, too, in the committee.

MR. TONASKET: Yes, sir.

SENATOR METCALF: You will meet with Mr. Gerard and decide on appropriate and significant excerpts. The whole package will be incorporated in the file.

MR. TONASKET: Fine.

Related to *Arizona* v. *California* and the Lower Colorado River Tribes is the totally unsatisfactory allocation of Central Arizona project water to the Salt River, Gila River, Ak Chin, Papago and Fort McDowell Tribes, which allocation was participated in by Mr. Frizzell. So important is that allocation that this committee will hold oversight hearings on the issue tomorrow and the next day. Can the nominee provide assurances to the tribes affected by *Arizona* v. *Califorina* and to all Indians that Interior will not place tribes in similar precarious positions by depriving them of the best legal and technical assistance in their assertions of rights over non-Indian assertions?

The details of the solicitor's draft opinion regarding the Quechan title to large portions of the Fort Yuma Reservation and its potential impact upon that tribe's pending case, *Sleepyhollow*, are well known to this committee and are outlined in material already submitted here. I would ask the nominee to explain his reasons for withholding signature of this opinion for so long a time and to give a date anticipated for that signing.

By letter of September 3, 1975, the NCAI made certain inquiries of Mr. Frizzell respecting the Indian Civil Rights Task Force, which appears to have been dismantled prior to completion of products required by law in 1968. To date, we have not received an answer to our questions, and I ask that our letter be placed in the record.

SENATOR METCALF: Without objection, it is so ordered.

MR. TONASKET: We are most concerned about the status of and arrangements for the updating of Cohen's Handbook. It is our hope that Mr. Frizzell will strive to achieve an updated version which meets the highest standards and quality of the original work and to guard against any possibility of repeating the disgraceful and politically motivated 1958 revision.

Finally, I ask that Mr. Frizzell's remarks concerning law enforcement on Indian reservations before the House Appropriations Subcommittee in hearings earlier this year be made a part of this record.

SENATOR METCALF: Without objection, it is so ordered.

MR. TONASKET: Thank you. His statement regarding the inability of Indian people to provide adequate law enforcement on reservations — "I think if you are ever to have law enforcement, the FBI will have to take it over" — is of particular concern to me. I would ask that Mr. Frizzell explain these remarks in more detail. I would also ask that the Under-Secretary-designate answer the following: Does this demonstrated attitude toward Indian management of internal matters and right to self-government have bearing on a vital draft opinion of long standing relating to the jurisdictional rights of Indians, which opinion is favorable to Indian people and which remains in limbo, awaiting Mr. Frizzell's signature? Does this stated attitude also explain why, in many cases, the nominee has delayed actions in cases which call for instant activity and rushed to conclusions where caution is required?

LETTER FROM DALE KENT FRIZZELL (UNITED STATES DEPARTMENT OF THE INTERIOR, OFFICE OF THE SOLICITOR) TO HENRY M. JACKSON (CHAIRMAN, INSULAR AFFAIRS COMMITTEE)

Dear Mr. Chairman:

Pursuant to the request of Senator Metcalf, attached to this letter you will find detailed, written responses to his questions, as well as to those substantive issues raised by Indian witnesses at my confirmation hearing, and numerous questions transmitted to me on October 28 by Forrest Gerard.

However, I believe that the limited testimony before your Committee on Indian matters concerning my record as Solicitor is misleading. Therefore, in addition to my attached responses to specific questions, I want to supplement the hearing record with what I regard to be my positive accomplishments in protecting Indian rights and discharging the trust responsibility of the Department to Indians. I am confident that the Committee will find this to be an overall picture of strong and successful protection of Indian interests.

My first duty as Solicitor was to negotiate an end to the Wounded Knee confrontation. I spent five very sobering weeks on the Pine Ridge Reservation. I returned to my daily tasks in Washington determined that the U.S. Government and, in particular, the Department of the Interior, must devise better ways in which to implement its trust duties to American Indians.

As Solicitor, my responsibilities have included being in charge of an Indian Affairs Division, which counsels the BIA and handles Indian litigation for the Department. For the position of Associate Solicitor to head up that Division, I hired Professor Reid Chambers of UCLA Law School, who had for several years been both a leading scholar in Indian law and a strong advocate for Indian rights as counsel with the Native American Rights Fund in Boulder, Colorado.

I also have substantially increased that Division's personnel. In 1973, the Indian Division had ten attorneys — the same staff it had in the mid-1960s. In two years, I have raised it to 17 attorneys, and we have hired persons with experience in Indian law and organizations that serve Indian people. In addition, we have given this Division the highest ratio of support personnel to attorneys of any division in the Solicitor's Office.

Because I am well aware of the conflict-of-interest that often arises with respect to Indian legal problems, I have strongly supported the creation of an independent Indian Trust Counsel Authority. In the meantime, I directed the Indian Division to vigorously advocate the rights of Indians without regard to the interests of other bureaus within the Department, and to concentrate on the development and prosecution of cases where the United States is suing as a plaintiff to protect such Indian rights. On three occasions where the Department of Justice has been representing other agencies or has been otherwise disinclined to represent the Indians, I have asked Justice to file a "split brief," separately stating the Indian position. In the first two cases, the Indian position was sustained; the third case is still pending.

The result of these changes has been a far stronger protection of Indian rights by Interior than in the years before 1973. We have dramatically increased cases in the water rights, jurisdiction, taxation and hunting and fishing areas. As late as May, 1974, we had only 13 Indian water cases; today, with the recent filing of cases for the Papago, Crow and Northern Cheyenne Tribes, we have 18.

Overall, we have more than doubled the cases in which the United States is suing or participating to protect Indian hunting and fishing rights (from 3 to 7 cases), immunity from state taxation (from 4 to 9 cases), and freedom from state regulation and jurisdiction (from 2 to 10 cases).

Overall, we now have more than 70 cases on file in which the United States is suing as a plaintiff to protect Indian rights. We have participated in 32 Indian cases as plaintiff or "friend of the court" just in the past year.

Of note is the fact that the Department of Justice has established a separate Indian resources section to handle this volume of cases, a move I strongly recommended.

In terms of results, we also have been successful. At our Department's urging, the United States supported the Indian side in all three Indian cases decided by the Supreme Court this past year. We won two: *United States v. Mazurie*, in which the constitutionality of an act of Congress delegating power to tribes to license on-reservation liquor sales was sustained; and *Antoine v. State of Washington*, a decision protecting off-reservation hunting rights of the Colville Tribe confirmed by an agreement ratified by Congress. In addition, I have recommended that the United States support the Indian position in every Indian case now before the Supreme Court, including a case where the Northern Cheyenne Tribe (Mr. Risingsun's Tribe) is claiming ownership of minerals beneath its reservation and a petition for certiorari by the Omaha Tribe (Mr. Cline's Tribe) contesting the state's power to tax the income of tribal members. In lower courts, among our major victories this past year were winning the *United States v. Washington* fishing rights case in the Court of Appeals for the Ninth Circuit and securing reversal — in the Court of Appeals for the Tenth Circuit — of an adverse district court decision dismissing a water rights case filed on behalf of the Southern Ute and Ute Mountain Tribes.

We also are vigorously appealing a decision by the New Mexico federal district court holding that Pueblos have no Winters-type reserved water rights. And I have strongly supported the intervention by the Department in six Federal Power Commission proceedings where we oppose the renewal of licenses to certain private hydroelectric projects that interfere with Indian land or water rights.

The testimony of the four Indian witnesses creates the impression that, when presented with a conflict between an Interior bureau and Indian rights, I have invariably subordinated Indian rights to the needs of the public agency. This is simply not the case. Examples where I have supported the Indian position contrary to the position and interest of other Departmental bureaus are discussed below:

• I strongly recommended a decision by the Secretary that the Chemehuevi Tribe held title to 2,500 acres of land riparian to Lake Havasu in California. The lands in question had previously been administered by the Bureau of Sport Fisheries and Wildlife.

• In June, 1974, I issued an opinion holding that lands taken from Mr. Tonasket's Tribe, the Colvilles, and the Spokane Tribe for the construction of Grand Coulee Dam had not diminished the boundaries of those reservations, that the bed of the original Columbia River remains owned by those tribes, and that the tribes have exclusive hunting, fishing and boating rights on the waters of the Columbia River and Lake Roosevelt behind the Dams within the boundaries of their reservations. This opinion rescinded the authority of the National Park Service to permit non-Indians to hunt and fish on reservation parts of Lake Roosevelt.

· I also issued an opinion holding that a 1930 Bureau of Land Management survey to the "Hay and Wood Reserve" portion of the Fort Mohave Reservation did not follow proper legal guidelines, and reinstating an earlier survey which held that the Fort Mohave Tribe held title to 3,500 acres of land near the Colorado River in California.

· My office has recently signed an opinion holding that lands in dispute between the Quileute Tribe and the National Park Service are within the boundaries of the Quileute Indian Reservation and outside the boundaries of the Olympic National Park in Washington.

· It was upon my recommendation that Secretary Morton cancelled the contract with the irrigation district which for years had diverted water upstream from Pyramid Lake with the support of the Bureau of Reclamation.

· It was also my recommendation that led the Justice Department to file suit against 14,000 non-Indian water users to protect the Pyramid Lake Tribe's water rights.

· I have supported an administrative transfer of national forest lands to the Interior Department to be used as part of the Sierra Blanca Ski area by the Mescalero Tribe.

· I have also supported the rights of Indians to possess eagle and migratory bird feathers.

· I participated extensively both in Secretary Morton's decision which partially granted the petition of the Northern Cheyenne Tribe concerning reservation coal leases and in the renegotiation of the coal leases on the Crow-ceded strip that gave the Crow-Tribe greater control over production decisions and substantially higher royalties.

I do not suggest that I have decided every controversy in favor of the Indians. The testimony before the Committee properly calls to your attention some instances where I have either decided an issue against Indian interests, or where I have been unable yet to complete my review and analysis of a particularly complex question. I believe, however, that my overall record, candidly and objectively assessed, demonstrates strong and successful protection of Indian rights — a more successful series of accomplishments in the Indian area, I frankly believe, than those of any recent Solicitor. If confirmed as Under Secretary, I intend to continue my concern for the vigorous protection of Indian rights exemplified by this record.

> Sincerely yours,
> Kent Frizzell
> Solicitor

The nomination of Kent Frizzell to become Undersecretary of the Interior was reported favorably by the Committee to the Senate. Although the Indians' questions delayed confirmation, there was not sufficient interest in the matter generated by the allegations to prevent confirmation and Kent Frizzell moved up in the Interior hierarchy upon confirmation by the Senate.

SECTION C. MEANWHILE

THE INDIVIDUAL CLIENT

The first two sections were devoted to overall policies and clientele response. They reflected the views and problems of people in administrative, elective, or other official positions. But policy struggles and policies eventually reach individuals who have no "official" status — that is, ordinary human beings. Hints of their influence can be gleaned from the preceding selections; however, this section deals directly with individuals' lives. As was stated in *The Road to Wounded Knee* by Robert Burnette and John Koster:[1]

The self-determination policy and incorporation [under the Indian Reorganization Act] may have freed the tribal chairmen, but the individual Indian still lived under bureaucratic oppression. The landowner could not collect his lease money for more than one year at a time. His lease income went to the U.S. Treasury to be doled out. The unemployment or underemployment rate on most reservations still hovers around 80 percent. U.S. Public Health Service doctors continued to scream at any Indian rash enough to get sick at night or over the weekend. Social workers still controlled the individual Indian's money as if it came out of their own pockets.

The problems the people face are examined in this section. The first group of selections concern Frank's Landing, a very small piece of land occupied by a very small number of Indian people. Their story is a microcosm of the Indian people's relationship with the Bureau of Indian Affairs, as well as with other governmental agencies. As their land and numbers are constantly eroded, both literally and figuratively, the Indians try desperately to move the "trustee" of their land to do something — with little success. The penultimate selection concerns

[1]Robert Burnette and John Koster, *The Road to Wounded Knee* (New York: Bantam Books, 1974), pp. 176–177.

the pain and frustration caused to Indians by bureaucratic service agencies as a person struggles merely to survive. It illustrates the schizophrenia connected with "aid" in the American context — giving with the one hand while degrading with the other. Those who require aid often need several different kinds — food, medicine, housing — and are trapped into actions that maintain this dependency. The final selection, portions of *Traders on the Navajo Reservation: A Report on the Economic Bondage of the Navajo People,* illustrates that technique, accomplished through private enterprise licensed by the BIA for the "benefit" of the Indian.

REPORTS FROM FRANK'S LANDING: A CASE STUDY OF A BUREAUCRATIC RELATIONSHIP

The news articles on Frank's Landing cover a three-year period. The issue is the same throughout the period — getting the BIA to act on a problem. The saga relates the powerlessness of the Indians as a culmination of years of administration from Washington. This particular series of events demonstrates the extent to which current problems can be traced to past actions. The controversy reveals the forced reliance on the methods of "conflict resolution" imposed by the national government on the Indians — resolution through the political process, the BIA, and the courts. Bureaucratic restrictions and procedures are also evident in the Agency's responsibility for tribes rather than individual Indians, as well as in the complications imposed by the number of other agencies with jurisdiction in the area.

FRANK'S LANDING

ELLEN YAROSHEFSKY

The people at Frank's Landing are in Court as often as most people go to the supermarket. Helicopters or small planes fly over their land daily to check out the activities of those at the landing, who's there, how many

SOURCE: From the National Lawyers Guild Law Student Indian Summer Project, Project Report (1973); National Lawyers Guild, Seattle, Wash.

cars are around, is fishing gear being put to use, what's happening at the smoke shop — all evidence of the Government's fear of Indians.

You drive past a sign saying "Federal Property," park near the smoke shop, and walk to the porch where several people sit on rustic, hand-crafted rocking chairs that strike you as an earthy blend of home and environment. Al Bridges, a 45 year old resident of the Landing, greets you and begins to tell stories that give you a feeling of what the struggles are about for those at the Landing. Listening to him calmly relate the brutalities they've encountered to enforce the rights that they, and all Indians, were guaranteed, one recognizes the powerful, special nature of their spirit that enables them to look beyond the unnecessary evils to Mother Earth — the grass, the trees, the roots — the chickens waddling by, the dogs playfully riding children on their backs. The breeze is cool as Al tells the story of the National Guard conducting simulated attacks on Frank's Landing at the nearby Fort Lewis base, training men to shout the names of those at the Landing in their chants of "Kill." (The story was reported in the *Seattle Times* and the Governor was ultimately forced to apologize.) He tells of how the Department of Game, in choosing its officials to confront those at the Landing, asks each applicant "Would you be willing to kill Al Bridges?"

He tells it as if he were talking about a person he's never met. Yet he, and the people at the Landing, have confronted such a situation for years.

Fishing rights were guaranteed to Indians in the 1854 Medicine Creek Treaty as off-reservation fishing rights. Yet these rights, along with numerous other Indian rights, were never honored. In 1963 a Court ruling allowed the Department of Game to intensify crackdowns on Indian fishing; thus confrontation has escalated. The controversy stemmed from a Government action in 1917 condemning 300 acres of Nisqually land because of "war necessity." Billy Frank, after being removed from his original 205 acres, got 6 acres, possessory rights only; the land is on trust by the Federal Government. Billy Frank assumed that his land had the same rights as the reservation land it replaced, including fishing rights. But Washington said the land was under its jurisdiction. Consequently, each year as fishing season begins, the State steps up its patrol of the land, confiscating fishing gear that's never returned, destroying nets and boats, clubbing people, injuring many, constantly putting them in jail. Finally, under the guidance of Hank Adams and due to the death of Valerie Bridges (Billy Frank's granddaughter), the case of state jurisdiction was brought to court. The ruling was that Frank's Landing was Indian country free of State jurisdiction. The harassment has not stopped.

As volumes of legal documents pile up at the Landing, as calls from all over the country come in, the people at the Landing talk about cases and legal terms with a greater knowledge and understanding of the Courts than most lawyers have. Maiselle Bridges, in a voice that bespeaks determination and frustration, says, "What can we do?"

The struggle is not one solely about fishing. It is of dignity and integrity for themselves and for all Indian peoples, from Alcatraz to the Poor People's March, to the Trail of Broken Treaties, to Wounded Knee. The issues are many, the theme is the same: fishing as a constant struggle against the U.S. Government; state intervention with the delivery of cigarettes to their smoke shop; the paternalism of the BIA; and state resistance to the establishment of an Indian hospital that is rightfully Indian owned. The theme is the government's flagrant violation of rights guaranteed to Indians (especially concerning Indian commerce); one broken promise after another; the White Man's disrespect for Indians as a people and for their way of life.

Maiselle Bridges tells stories of Indian hunting, fishing, of Indian religion that give you glimpses into the beauty of the Indian ways. All the while you sit, enraptured by the stories and amazed at the strength of a woman who has seen her 20 year old daughter drown, her family beaten and shot, her people tortured by whites and white culture. Yet, she calmly talks of the need to communicate the truth to whites, for us to tell to our people the facts that the Indians know so well.

Indians have spent $38 million for lawyers since 1961, more money than the Federal government spent on Indians in the first two years of the War on Poverty. Yet the lawyers and the Courts have shown the Indians what white justice is about — pouring dollars into words that solidify power interests.

Frank's Landing people are getting ready to fish again; fishing season begins there toward the end of September. New controversies with old themes are yet to be seen. Legal people with knowledge of what Indian struggles are about, what the Indians want, are essential. We must educate ourselves about the legal issues and be open to being educated by Indians and their way of life.

FRANK'S LANDING FLOODING GIVEN BIA PRIORITY

LARRY CANTIL

The BIA has pledged a "resolute effort" on behalf of the Frank's Landing residents to "carefully explore all possible avenues of assistance" in the fight to find funds to build a dike at the little Nisqually community before the spring flooding.

SOURCE: *Northwest Indian News* (Seattle, Wash.), 4, No. 5 (September 1974).

Stephan Lozar, superintendent of the Western Washington office of the BIA in Everett, said he has contacted by phone the central BIA office in Washington, D.C., about Frank's Landing and assured the community that "a prompt action report will be demanded of them."

The Frank's Landing Indian community is situated close to the banks of the Nisqually River. Erosion in recent years, accelerated by the introduction of diking upriver, has cut a swath 30 yards into the land which is owned by Bill Frank, Sr.

A well house, which is the only source of fresh water on the Nisqually reservation, is presently directly threatened by the eroding riverbank. However, many feel that without an adequate dike, the entire settlement will be swamped during the early spring flooding.

Lozar said the BIA will obtain a legal opinion of the Frank's Landing site which will include an estimate of assistance costs and a list of possible funding sources.

Recently the Corps of Engineers reviewed the Frank's Landing situation but withheld assistance, stating the value of the land (appraised at $18,000) was not enough to warrant the estimated cost of diking, set at $100,000.

The disposition of Bill Frank's Land, which is on a non-tribal "restricted fee" status, has been an obstacle in locating a public agency which is legally responsible for protection of the land.

The BIA is tribal-oriented and cannot easily find funds to aid Indians who own allotted land, Lozar said.

He said that emergency funding has been used for private land assistance in the past and the possibility of these kinds of monies for Frank's Landing will be "exhaustively searched."

AT FRANK'S LANDING

LARRY CANTIL

Frank's Landing has long been a focal point of Indian grievance and unrest illustrating to many people the basic injustices done to Indian people since the coming of the white man.

The struggle for Indian dignity at Frank's Landing has been spotlighted by volumes of legal documents researched by the National Lawyers Guild, the all-Indian staffed Native American Rights Fund, and others, testifying to the overt historic exploitation of these people by white investors which continues in only slightly-veiled fashion today.

Source: *Northwest Indian News* (Seattle, Wash.), 4, No. 5 (September 1974).

Recently, severe riverbank erosion at the Landing has raised a hue and cry for assistance which has all but fallen upon deaf ears. In the scurry to find a legal avenue for aid, the people have tapped the BIA and Corps of Engineers unsuccessfully over several years. Now, with time running out before the winter and spring flooding brings almost sure and final destruction to the community, the people must backtrack, cast a final plea to the Corps, and sit once more in a BIA office discussing possible, if never actual, help from the Bureau.

In his appeal for funding to help build a dike, 96 year-old Bill Frank, Sr., can look back to his childhood to locate a source of his present troubles.

The National Lawyers Guild has prepared a long paper on the history of white intrusion into Puget Sound, which clearly demonstrates seedy land grab policies of early governmental officials and town leaders; the cleverly worded treaties, the casual forgeries of Indian names on legal documents.

The distress among Indian people today, including that which has befallen the residents at Frank's Landing, has at its root the injustice done Indian ancestors by the progenitors of the modern white business establishment.

In the mid and late 1800's, land-hungry white businessmen spun a web of deceitful paperwork which gave license to the industrial plunder of the land and drove the Indian inhabitants into small, ever-decreasing areas of largely unworkable land.

Among the historic precedents unearthed by the lawyers is the odious nature of the Medicine Creek Treaty, whereby the U.S. Government took ownership of the lower Puget Sound area. For $2,500, two acres of land, and a small island, Governor Stevens and his hand-picked Indian "chiefs" executed a treaty chock-full of exploitive avenues, which bound the rest of the Tacoma region over to white corporational enterprise.

Only a united Indian resistance to the "Medicine Creek Death Warrant," as it was popularly described, forced Governor Stevens in 1857 to set aside small parcels of land within each region for Indian use.

The reservation land allotted to the Nisqually tribe was some of the least workable land in that farm-rich area. In shrouded conversation with a Nisqually friend, one of Stevens' aides was quoted as saying:

"He [Stevens] is allotting you Nisquallies the rocky slope over there south of the She-Nah-Nam Creek (Nisqually River), a strip of land no white man would ever want. You can never grow anything there, it's nothing but thick underbrush and rocks."

Nevertheless the Nisqually, who had formerly roamed the She-Nah-Nam Creek at will, fishing and hunting, were now contained within a small area and forced to persevere upon unyielding soil, with limited fishing and hunting rights.

Still, land-greedy investors, not content with the huge chunks of real estate released to them through the Stevens treaties, sought legal methods to obtain reservation land peripheral to the expanding white townships.

Capitalist interests in tribal land were well-served with the passage of the Land Allotment Act of 1887 allowing individual Indians (and often-times their white "guardian" sponsors) to sell segments of land without tribal endorsement.

By 1910, land sales providing room for the development of Tacoma and Seattle cut by half the Indian country in Western Washington.

On the eve of World War I, area planners entertained the idea of beefing up commerce through the construction of a military base somewhere near Tacoma. After arduous lobbying in Washington, D.C., Pierce County was selected as base site for Fort Lewis. Nisqually land, heretofore undesirable to white men, fell under the scrutiny of base planners seeking a large land tract.

The town fathers soon found the adequate legal basis to clear the Nisqually off the land needed for the erection of the fort. Article VI of the Medicine Creek Treaty authorized the President to transfer Indian people to other areas when the "interests of the territory may require it and the welfare of the Indians be promoted."

Using this language to guide them, the government condemned 300 acres of Nisqually land because of "war necessity."

William Frank, after being deposed from his original 205 acres, got six acres. The land that he received is officially termed "restricted fee" land (much like a national park) but doesn't qualify for tribal benefits under federal determination.

Thus the fishing rights at Frank's Landing and concurrently the fight to protect the land from river erosion have been undermined throughout the written record of this region. Although the case in favor of Bill Frank has been well documented, the undoing of a century of legal exploitation is a massive and perplexing chore.

Recently, the BIA has resurrected the Frank's Landing file from its dusty archives and has pledged top priority to bird-dogging the erosion assistance issue clear back to the funding pens in Washington, D.C.

Those close to the matter are skeptical of any possible BIA aid and rightly so, judging from the BIA's performance to date. The Frank's Landing erosion issue was reviewed and tabled by the Bureau years ago.

At any rate, the BIA is the only national agency the community can appeal to for critically important diking assistance.

But in light of the legacy of Indian people in their struggle for survival, they can only frequently awaken their slumbering bureaucratic watchdog, the BIA, point him in the right direction and reservedly hope that he can and will respond to the plaintive cry to drive the most recent wolf from the door.

STRANGE FACES APPEAR ALONG THE NISQUALLY

LARRY CANTIL

The BIA has stepped up measures to combat the serious erosion problem at Frank's Landing along the Nisqually River. Western Washington superintendent Bud Lozar said the issue has received national level attention within the Bureau and possible avenues of assistance have resulted.

A team of researchers dispatched by the BIA has surveyed the erosion plane and has estimated the cost of permanent bank protection, at $87,000.

Although no detailed engineering report was produced, survey director Al Young, an engineer from the Portland BIA office, said the most effective method to prevent continued erosion would be to construct a 1200-foot heavy rock riffraff dike.

The dike would contain the river from a point 600 feet upstream from the property of William Frank, Sr., to a point past the riverbend at the edge of the landing, where the most serious erosion has occurred. Lozar said the BIA presently is attempting to obtain easement rights for the dike construction.

The erosion problem at the small Indian hamlet on the Nisqually River has increased critically in the past few years. The residents of the community, Nisqually and Puyallup Indians, have laid the blame to recent upriver diking by the Corps of Engineers and private enterprise to stabilize the river for capital investment projects. Only 2.5 acres remain of the 6.3 acres granted Frank, Sr., after his original 200 acre allotment was taken by the country to create space for Fort Lewis.

Lozar said a hydrologist from the Phoenix BIA office will be at Nisqually to study the riverbanks upriver to ascertain whether work done there has caused the additional erosion at the Landing.

The hydrologist's investigation, due to begin in early November, will be an important step in the BIA's appeal to the Corps to provide manpower and equipment for the dike, Lozar said.

Speck Waldorf, Asst. Area Director in the Portland BIA office, said proposed congressional legislation charging the Corps with responsibility to non-taxable property, if approved, would mandate Corps assistance for the dike. Waldorf said the BIA legislative liaison office in Washington, D.C., is

SOURCE: *Northwest Indian News* (Seattle, Wash.), 4, No. 6 (November 1974).

closely observing the proposal which is due to come out of Senate committee soon.

FRANK'S LANDING SLIPPING AWAY

LARRY CANTIL AND KAI SYLVA

The erosion of Frank's Landing along the Nisqually River has crept into a condition very near final disaster. While the tiny Nisqually Indian community has spent years demanding and then pleading for federal, state, or BIA help in rebuilding their faltering riverbank, the rushing waters have sliced further into the land. With the recent heavy flooding, the river is virtually at their back doorstep.

Of Bill Frank, Sr.'s original eight acre lot, only one acre remains — with community homes too expensive to move left clinging to the dry earth. Governmental assistance, as has been the case for years, appears to still be bureaucratic miles away.

This year, the Frank's Landing people had asked the Army Corps of Engineers to destroy a wooden breakwater which has been aiding the erosion.

Surprisingly, the U.S. Army agreed to dynamite the breakwater and the Corps concurred with Fort Lewis base to provide trucks and materials to solidify the riverbank along Frank's Landing to prevent further damage.

What followed however was the kind of departmental quagmire which the community has learned to expect from government.

Hounded by congressman Don Bonker's office, Fort Lewis Command Equal Opportunity officer Hank Henderson said that the dynamite would boom and the truckloads of materials would roll as soon as approval from BIA was granted.

Area BIA superintendent Bud Lozar sent a telegram December 10 to post Commander General Warners to expedite the work and pressed Bill Jeffries at the Governors Indian desk into communication with Henderson's Fort Lewis office.

At this point, before any work had started, problems arose. Amy Bell in Don Bonker's office reported that a permit had to be filed with the Dept. of Fisheries, a procedure which could take weeks to fulfill.

Next, the Army confirmed that the trucks were ready but were without gas. Among all the assisting agencies, no funds could be found for gasoline.

SOURCE: *Northwest Indian News* (Seattle, Wash.), 6, No. 1 (January 1976).

Next, an application with Environmental Protection Agency (EPA) became necessary, another long-winded measure. State and Federal applications for emergency services also had to be completed and mailed by Bill Frank, Jr., and, hopefully, eventually granted.

At presstime, while data is scribbled and paper shuffled, the Frank's Landing people are about to lose the last of their land and their homes.

WHO IS GOING TO DO SOMETHING?

ANDY DE LOS ANGELES

If someone does not act soon, Frank's Landing will be lost forever after the spring thaw. Due to glacial activity and heavy rains the Nisqually river has been washing away more and more of Frank's Landing south of Seattle near Olympia.

A Hydraulic Engineer's report submitted by W. M. Borland on January 16, 1975 said there were 3.9 acres left. Frank's Landing has since been reduced to two.

It has been more than a year since the report was submitted to Steven A. Lozar, Superintendent of the Everett agency of the Bureau of Indian Affairs. This year as the landing was losing more of its land, Suzette Mills, a Frank's Landing resident, said she was evacuating and that the river was right underneath her trailer.

"It's not so much that it's going over the banks. My trailer and mom's trailer are in kind of an immediate danger because they're right on top of the river. If that river doesn't go down, my trailer will be in the water by this evening," she said.

Amy Bell of Congressman Don Bonker's office in whose district the area is located, said she was aware of the problems that the landing has been having with river erosion but that she did not know of the current crisis.

By late afternoon, the large shed closest to the river had floated down and rested against the Nisqually bridge.

The next day reporters went to Frank's Landing and surveyed the damage. Billy Frank, Jr., said that at times, the landing was being eroded at the rate of two feet every ten minutes. He also said that although they lost the shed, neither trailer had yet been swept away.

Except for some close friends, there were only a handful of people helping move two trailers and the shrubbery around Maiselle Bridge's trailer.

SOURCE: *Northwest Indian News* (Seattle, Wash.), 5, No. 10 (February 1976).

By that evening the river began to recede. A few stumps that were left in the ground years ago, were the only reason why all of Frank's Landing wasn't eroded away.

The following week *NWIN* began to call various agencies to find out if anyone was going to do anything. The first person contacted was Steven 'Bud' Lozar, Superintendent of the Western Washington Agency of the Bureau of Indian Affairs (BIA) in Everett. His response was that "something should have been done six years ago." Later, in a memorandum directed to the Area Director of the Portland BIA office, Lozar said that the Corps of Engineers informed him that the authority needed to begin work on the Landing would have to be obtained through legislation [of] the U.S. Congress. Billy Frank, Jr., listed two priorities: (1) to effectively and permanently stop the erosion of their land; (2) to reclaim those lands lost to the Nisqually River. Lozar went on to say that he was in support of the Frank family and that he urgently requested the area director's office to make every effort to obtain Federal assistance. Bill Jefferies, Governor Dan Evan's Special Assistant for Indian Affairs, said he needed to obtain more information to help clear up the ownership status of the land and that his office would help coordinate state services with Frank's Landing.

Duke Murray responded from Congressman Bonker's office, saying that Bonker was looking for any existing money because the Nisqually system was declared a flood area years ago.

Thurston County Commissioner Ken Anderson who was at the site when the river began to rise the previous week, said that he would meet with people from Bonker's office to go over the flood area and the Frank's Landing problem.

It appeared that the County Commissioner's office had tried to help Frank's Landing but because of jurisdictional problems, no assistance could really be given except for immediate evacuation. Anderson's office also had been involved with the Army Corps of Engineers and other federal offices and agencies and said he couldn't understand why no one could respond. . . .

At press time, Billy Frank, Jr., had sent out requests to everyone on the congressional delegation for 400 acres of land on the Fort Lewis Reserve. And there has been no response so far.

TWO EXAMPLES OF DEPENDENCY

These last two selections present two different sorts of dependency resulting from policies of the national government and the economic system. The ideology of the free individual in America, developed out of the struggle for dominance of the frontier in which the Indian lived, determines the way in which poverty programs are administered as well as justifying the economic relationships that develop in any segment of the society. The nation may understand the causes of poverty but it seems unwilling or unable to develop a form and supporting rationale for eradicating it. As a result, the policies that are developed have tended to deepen the dependency and necessarily the vulnerability of the powerless to those who are in power.

The relationship between the trader and the Indians is at once unique and, at a symbolic level, characteristic of the dependencies that develop among the powerless. Technically, the traders are regulated by the BIA; however, as long as the traders are both dominant in, and essential to, the Indian economy, the amount of independence and the level of self-sufficiency that the Indian people will be able to develop will be determined by economic facts rather than bureaucratic edicts.

HEARINGS BEFORE THE COMMITTEE ON AGRICULTURE, NINETY-FIRST CONGRESS, FIRST SESSION, OCTOBER 21, 1969

STATEMENT OF MISS LORENE BENNETT, FORT DEFIANCE, ARIZONA, ON BEHALF OF CRASH SURVEY AT CROWNPOINT, NEW MEXICO

MISS BENNETT: I am Lorene Bennett from Fort Defiance, Arizona, having done some work in the Crownpoint, New Mexico area, particularly with the Navajo people in three counties in New Mexico, McKinley County, Sandoval County, and San Juan County. The majority of Navajo Indians who live in this area are receiving assistance from three welfare departments — the tribal welfare, the state welfare, and the Bureau of Indian Affairs welfare.

It seems to me this morning, we are talking about getting people to become self-sufficient. It seems to me that you cannot do this if you are assuming that all people are alike throughout the United States. However, I find this untrue, because in my area, the people of the Navajo Reservation [Tribe] have become too dependent on various agencies in the respect that the agencies are not working to get people to try to do anything better, for the simple reason that I think it is just paternalistic racism on the Navajo Reservation [in the Navajo country]. The people who are working for the welfare in many cases are holding down the Navajo. At the same time, they are screaming that help should not be given to the Navajo. At the same time, they are sitting on these Navajos who can and would like, in many cases, to get self-help.

The Navajos live scattered throughout New Mexico. The roads are in bad condition. In many cases, the roads are dirt roads and in many cases, when it rains or snows, it is impossible to get through.

The food stamp program has only been used in the Sandoval County where 250 Navajos use it. Otherwise, in McKinley and San Juan County, commodities are still being used. We conducted a study and we found that food stamps are being discouraged. When we asked county welfare programs if they had given information regarding food stamps, they said they were not under the food stamp program, therefore, found it irrelevant to give information regarding food stamps. So many people asked in these areas did not know what food stamps were and were totally unaware that such a program existed.

For those people who do know, they are being discouraged daily by the welfare department. They are either told that they can try to get their own funds or that they are being too dependent and that the agencies are being too lenient in helping or even providing such programs.

The majority of the people in Sandoval County who are receiving food stamps switched willingly to food stamps from commodities for the simple reason that in most cases, people are complaining that commodities do not meet their needs. For one thing, certain commodities are not used correctly by the people. . . .

In some cases, it was reported that commodities are used to hold bridges together, such as powdered milk which in most cases, people do not use, and in some cases, they are used to feed animals.

The food stamp program is going to be a big problem if these different counties switch over for the simple reason that traders in certain areas control communities. They are the U.S. Post Office, they are a transportation center, they are an employment center in most cases, and they are general merchants. In one area, a trader uses his private credit to give food stamps. When food stamps are distributed, the trader is harassing the Navajo people to pay the bill, or perhaps he encourages loans for food stamps, whereby 20 to 50 percent interest rate is added on to the loan he gives for the people to buy food stamps. In some cases, the food stamps have been used to pay off credit by the trader.

When brought to the attention of the Sandoval County Welfare Department, they were, according to them, shocked to hear of such incidents, because as far as they knew, there were no problems, which proved to many of us that they were not doing their work, working directly with the people. Up until now, nothing has been done about that situation.

The Senator and the Governor from that state, New Mexico, were notified. We have not had a chance to meet with [them] yet. However, the Governor has discouraged anything [being] done about it. As a matter of fact, a mile from the trading center is a tribally owned land where the people were willing to make the center to have their food stamps distributed. However, because of the trader's political weight as well as the Senator's political weight, we found that the HELP school was discouraged and asked to pull out the invitation. Up to date, nothing has been done about that situation.

The welfare departments are aware of these problems. They are aware of the fact that the traders manipulate welfare checks, that they manipulate food stamps for their own gain. However, they have not done anything about it. I do not think they are that concerned, just so they get the food stamps in the hands of the people. What they do with them is none of their concern from what I gather.

The attitude[s] of the people who work for these welfare agencies are not at all helping. It seems to me like they are constantly worried about the taxpayers' money and, therefore, discourage any kind of assistance for the Navajo. The Navajo takes this for granted. He does not protest because for years, we have been treated in this manner.

Just recently, the welfare rights organizations have been set up in four agencies and people are beginning to get together to ask, what are our rights? We are beginning to question some of the programs such as the food stamps. As I say, there are people who do not know about the food stamps and they are shocked to hear of such an existing program.

In many cases, the Navajo, as I say, is discouraged. There is one incident of a Navajo walking to a welfare office and inquiring about assistance. When the person there saw the Navajo, that she had a beautiful Navajo necklace, why don't you pawn that, he told her. So here is someone asking the Navajo to give up what's the symbol, what's the last dignity or the last pride of a person. These are some of the incidents that happen daily.

Another thing is that there is lack of communication on the part of what programs are available, commodity programs as well as food stamp programs. For one thing, the majority of the welfare workers are Anglos and do not speak Navajo or do not know how to go about relating to the Navajo; therefore, the Navajo is shy to come and speak to the worker.

In many communities, the agencies and different welfare workers, we brought out the fact that there should be more Navajos hired as caseworkers, doing away with the 4-year college requirements or whatever they have, because the majority of the people who do get along, do know some of the problems that exist, do not have 4 years of college. Those that do are drawn away from working with the welfare departments to something else that might provide better pay.

So you see, there is a lack of communication on the reservations. The majority of the people who are working with the welfare departments do have an obnoxious attitude as in one case, a caseworker was very obnoxious when we went up to a trading post to hand out welfare rights leaflets. He commented that we did not like Anglo superiority. So these are some of the caseworkers that do work with the Navajo.

The Navajos usually do not have ready cash, so they would run into a problem with food stamps. As I say, they would have to get loans from the trading posts. In many cases, they will go under the harassment of the trader. Food stamps are known, at least in Sandoval County, where Navajos are receiving food stamps, to provide better foods. The Navajo does have the choice to go to a trading post or to the nearest town to buy vegetables and meats, which they rarely have.

I think when you talk about getting the people, as I think someone mentioned this morning, that someone should contribute, communities should contribute to get something, I think you are dealing with a completely different situation, because I think here you would have to first do away with these kind of attitudes the majority of the workers have there and do away with the attitude the traders have of manipulating the situation to their own political gain.

It would seem to me that some investigation should take place in regard to food stamps for the Navajo as well and in regard to the attitude of the welfare workers with regard to food stamps given to the people. Since the people do not have ready cash on hand, it would be necessary that the food stamps programs should be flexible so that people, whenever they have money, can buy food stamps. It is not always at a certain time that they have money and that certain time being the time when food stamps are distributed.

Also, the majority of people are not working, as I say. They do lack money. As I pointed out earlier, a lot of time, they are on credit and they are in need of money constantly. Because of this, they do not have any money and would have to go to the trader, which binds him to this credit situation. Therefore, I would recommend that the stamps be lower or that some of the people who do not have any income whatsoever get free stamps. I think in many cases, many of these people do have children to provide clothing for and in many cases, they will not have this money to buy food stamps. They would prefer to buy more clothing for their children who go to school during the winter months.

In many cases, many of these people are not eating a balanced diet and many of these children are not eating a balanced diet, except for the time they are in school.

In the commodity program, I would like to point out the fact that in many cases, many of the Navajos do not get what they need, as, for instance, in New Mexico, Navajos receive lima beans, which in many cases, they do not eat, for the simple reason that the pinto beans that are usually given out are given out to the Spanish-Americans in the different counties because they do use pinto beans in a lot of their diet. The Navajos get the leftovers, which is lima beans. In many cases, they do not eat lima beans and do not know how to fix them in many cases, because there is a lack of food demonstration in different areas. For instance, in one area, a woman told me that she did not know how to use many of the foods and they cut up that meat and ate it just that way. In many cases, many of them do not read; therefore, can't read directions on the label, and there is no one to go around to show them how to use these foods creatively.

The commodities, when given out, are taken home by these people. Usually, they weigh a lot and in many cases, many of these people hitch-hike. They do not have trasportation and they live, say, from 20 miles up to 50 miles from the distribution center, so they put them in bags and boxes and stand by the roadside and are lucky if they get a ride. Otherwise, they would have to borrow money from the trader again to buy gas for someone who might have a vehicle. Therefore, he is bound to the trader in that respect, for a high interest rate from the trader.

When asked that the welfare department look into such a situation as providing transportation for people who do not have transportation, the answer from a San Juan County employee was that the Navajos were becoming too independent. However, he failed to even get the Navajos to provide a situation where the Navajos can gain confidence and independence.

People have to wait long periods of time for certification, which involves unnecessary red tape in most cases and in most cases, because of their long wait, which I think is intentional, many people are discouraged and never bother going back and are hardly having a balanced meal. In fact, many of the people who do receive commodities do not have a balanced meal, so you would understand that many of the people who do not receive commodities would have.

After a long wait for certification, if a family does not pick up his commodity 3 consecutive months, he is automatically cut off. In most cases, like during the summer months, families, because they are so desperate in their need of money and because they want to work, go off to migratory labor, off the reservation or outside the state and there they make very little. Because they are working and trying to make what money they can, they are automatically cut off. Upon return, they have to wait for, say a period of 3 months to a year for recertification.

Evaluations sometimes on certifications are based upon the assumed income. As for instance, a grazing permit. Perhaps a family has a grazing permit. They are allowed so many sheep on certain lands. Because of this permit, many of the welfare workers say that they have an assumed income of, say, 20 heads of sheep times $20 and assume that income per year. If this person, if they think this person can make enough money off that sheep, they do not certify him because he is getting some kind of income. But actually, the Navajos do not sell their sheep that much. In fact, maybe one sheep is saved for food per year.

Or else, as I said earlier, a Navajo was asked to give up her jewelry for pawn so she could eat. In other cases, because a certain family went off on migratory labor and bought a vehicle to come back in, the welfare department will refuse to give them assistance because they have a vehicle that is valued at so much.

These are some of the things they use for evaluating. Because the Navajos go through this and take it for granted that this is the way it is supposed to be, they do not protest. The various welfare departments who have been made aware of this, however, have failed to act upon it. These are some of the incidents I found this summer. . . . I would go into more detail on it. However, I have a report here if anybody would like or is interested in getting a copy of one. I would be more than happy to give you a copy.

I would like to comment on another thing. I was also involved in another study conducted by the Southwestern Indian Development in Arizona, who went out to the Navajo Reservation and did a study on the trading post system. A lot of what I brought out is brought out in that report and if you would like a copy, copies will be made available to you.

TRADERS ON THE NAVAJO RESERVATION

HISTORY

The importance of commerce with Indian tribes played so significant a role that the United States Constitution empowered Congress to: "regulate commerce with foreign Nations . . . and with Indian Tribes."[1]

Trading posts on the Navajo Reservation date back to the Treaty of September 9, 1849 between the Navajo Tribe and the United States. This agreement provided no reservations as such, but promised to authorize trading houses to be located in Navajo Territory at the discretion of the government.[2]

SOURCE: From *Traders on the Navajo Reservation,* a pamphlet of the Southwestern Indian Development, pp. 1–6, 26–27.

[1]The Constitution of the United States, Article I, Section 8, Clause 3.

[2]Act of June 30, 1834, ch. 161, Section 2.

In 1865, after a decade of raiding, the Navajos were conquered by a large military force led by Colonel "Kit" Carson. His soldiers swept through Navajo land, slaughtering sheep and horses (99.6% of the sheep and 93.4% of the horses)[3] and laying waste to their fields and orchards. "They were relentlessly pursued, rounded up, and driven to a wretched disease-ridden reservation on the banks of the Rio Pecos, in east-central New Mexico — the infamous Rosque Redondo"[4] — *hwelte*, as the Navajos called it.

There followed four terrible years of imprisonment at Fort Sumner, years which crushed the independence, self-confidence and morale of those who had endured the inhuman treatment of that long walk. Many Navajos did not survive this period because their numbers were depleted by disease and starvation.

The Treaty of 1868 between the Navajo and the United States established a reservation for the *Dine* located in northeastern Arizona and northwestern New Mexico, thus ending the ordeal of Fort Sumner. The first contingent of captive Navajos started the long journey back to their homeland on June 18, 1868.

The Navajos had not only been defeated, but were a demoralized and subjugated people. Thus, the way was opened for the establishment of white trading posts on their reservation.

In contrast to earlier itinerant traders who transported whiskey, rifles, ammunition and trinkets to Indian camps, the trader came among conquered Indians confined to reservations and built his trading post near a dependable water supply.

The trading post became one of the most necessary and influential institutions of reservation life. It was the Anglo trader under the image of the "Great White Father," who preyed upon the needs of the Indian people and thus became an influential figure in the economy of the Navajo Nation.

The Act of August 15, 1876, which is now codified as Section 261 of Title 28, United States Code, provides: "The Commissioner of Indian Affairs shall have the sole power and authority to appoint traders to the Indian tribes and to make such rules and regulations as he may deem just and proper specifying the kind and quantity of goods and the prices at which such goods shall be sold to the Indians."[5] Few of the existing problems and malpractices of the trading post system would exist today if this and other governing statutes and regulations were effectively enforced.

It would seem, taken at face value, that this statute would be sufficient to prevent any malpractices by traders. But there is no sanction to this law.

[3]L. R. Bailer, *The Long Walk* (Los Angeles: Westernlor Press, 1964), pp. 232, 233.
[4]Ibid, p. vii.
[5]19 Stat. 200, U.S.C. Title 25, Section 261.

Even if enforced, how would it be enforced and what would be the penalties? The Navajo Reservation is so vast and isolated that the government and the Bureau of Indian Affairs have had very little contact with the trader and have left him to operate as he wished. As a result, trading statutes and regulations are not enforced and trader practices have become stagnant and uncontrolled, leading to exploitation of the highest magnitude of the Navajo people.

ROLE OF THE TRADER

IN NAVAJO SOCIETY

The trading post has evolved into a multipurpose concern — the reservation trader of today is not merely a general merchant, but has a variety of roles which he is able to manipulate to his personal benefit. He is banker and creditor, pawnbroker, and special claims agent for the Railroad Retirement Board. He purchases Navajo wool, livestock, rugs; has the only telephone for miles around; operates the only gas station; and acts as interpreter for the Navajo in both mail and phone communications with the Anglo world.

Governmental agencies, including the Welfare Department, utilize the trader as an intermediary to contact or confirm facts about Navajo families. He acts, too, as agent between employer and employee in migrant or railroad work. Occasionally, the traders will take it upon themselves to act as law enforcement officers. The trader has, because of these many roles, the power to control the Navajo people in "his" community.

Particularly conducive to the trader's business are the long distances and the remoteness of many trading posts coupled with bad weather and primitive roads making travel to town by the Navajos extremely difficult. There are approximately 1,425 miles of paved roads on the Reservation, while in comparison, the State of West Virginia, comparable in size to the Navajo Reservation, has 32,081[6] miles of road. In the harsh winter months most Reservation roads are practically impassable, leaving the Navajos only the trading post to secure goods and food.

Subsisting on a meager and unpredictable income, the Navajo easily becomes indebted to the trader, who, through a policy known as "credit saturation," encourages his customers to buy goods on book credit up to the amount of known future income. However, once this limit is reached, the trader promptly refuses any further credit, regardless of need.

---

[6]*The World Almanac and Book of Facts*, 1968, Luman H. Long, Ed., New York: (Newspaper Enterprise Assoc., Inc., 1967), p. 573.

As it is common for many Navajos to receive their checks or other income in care of the local trading post, the trader has an accurate method of estimating an individual's income. By withholding the check upon arrival, he can force his clientele to charge at the store, thereby assuring himself of a large portion, if not all, of the check.

The Commissioner of Indian Affairs, as previously stated, has sole authority to license traders and control their practices. Federal and Tribal regulations governing the trading profession are quite explicit, and if taken at face value would appear to be adequate in preventing the existing situation. Yet the reservation trader escapes regulations because there are no clearly defined channels of authority through which enforcement should be made.

There is a dual responsibility atmosphere generated by these regulations. Enforcement, the BIA contends, lies with the Tribe; the Tribe contends it lies with the BIA. "Buck-passing" stifles any progress and in this instance has created apathy and neglect.

The procedure for placing a formal complaint is unclear and ill-defined, especially to the non-English speaking Navajo. One Tribal employee, when asked about such procedure, said that Navajos can use both Chapter representatives and the Trading Committee of the Navajo Tribe to lodge a complaint. History has proven both channels are confusing and ineffective in obtaining results.

In fact, the Trading Post Committee of the Navajo Tribal Council does not understand its responsibilities and has been inactive in the past four years. When active, the authority of this Committee has been used to gain selfish interests of some Committee members, thus nullifying its effectiveness.

If by chance an investigation is begun, it must be routed through so many different agencies, involving so much bureaucratic red tape, that the complainant becomes quickly discouraged by the consistent pattern of referrals. The trader, untouched, continues his exploitation of the Navajo people.

Thus, BIA Area Director Graham Holmes feels confident in stating "In [the] . . . three years I have been here there has been only one minor complaint [to] reach my office . . . . I attend chapter meetings and meet dozens of Navajos every day. All they would have to do to complain about any trader is just mention it to me."[7]

---

[7] "BIA and Tribe Won't Protest," *The Gallup* (N. M.) *Independent*, May 10, 1968, p. 1.

CONCLUSIONS

There are several solutions to some of these questions and problems posed in this report which could effectively combat the monopolistic power of Reservation traders. These will be discussed under separate cover since it was and still is the philosophy of SID that the recommendations should come from the "grass roots" Navajos. Therefore, one of the additional projects this coming summer is to conduct a continuing survey with emphasis on the recommendations of local people directly involved in business with the trader.

In this age of so-called enlightenment and civilization, it is revolting that a group of people should be kept dependent upon a small number of greedy individuals (and intruders) who, due to opportune circumstances, have the chance to relentlessly pursue their own ravenous material advancement at the others' expense.

Admittedly, the institution of the trading post has played an essential part in the development of modern Indian society in its role as mediator between the Navajo and Anglo world, yet this does not give them the unquestioned right to exploit and dominate to the fullest extent those very people who provided their livelihood.

It seems tragic that those that possess wardship powers over us have done virtually nothing since 1886 to prevent or eliminate the unmitigated economic and social monopoly of the trader and increase economic freedom and strength of the Navajo people.

It is apparent that the BIA won't admit its obvious mistakes since it attempts to shove the responsibility of enforcement of the trader regulations onto the Navajo Tribe. The Tribe, in turn, contends that this responsibility lies with the BIA, and further contends that the BIA will not give the authority of enforcement to the Tribe. This rather sad condition is further aggravated by the passing of sanctionless regulations with little or no substantive meaning.

The primary responsibility, nevertheless lies with the Secretary of the Interior, the Commissioner of Indian Affairs, and the BIA — whether they have the intestinal fortitude to admit it is another matter. The voice of the Navajo, through their young, has to be heard and changes made so that the Navajo people would have a clear responsibility to enforce the regulations as recommended by themselves.

As a result of all the foregoing, Indians have become trapped into a relationship with the government and its agencies, especially the Bureau of Indian Affairs, that perpetuates their bondage and puts the government in a position to regulate them as much as to serve their needs. Some never break the bonds. On the other hand, eventually pain and frustration must lead to increasing anger and militance. Indians have fought, in all the ways possible,[1] since the coming of the white man, but the combination of recognition by the media and renewed efforts can be dated somewhere around the late 1960s and early 1970s. Perhaps the taking of Alcatraz in November 1969 was a focal point. Most certainly, the Trail of Broken Treaties (a nationwide caravan of Indian peoples going to Washington, D.C., to dramatize their plight), culminating in the occupation of the BIA's offices in 1972, focused national attention on the American Indian Movement. Numerous sit-ins, takeovers, and so on followed in various places around the country, the most visible being that of Wounded Knee, South Dakota. And, as with other protests, organizations grew in an effort to unite the Indian people in their fight, the most prominent being AIM (the American Indian Movement).

VOICES FROM WOUNDED KNEE, 1973

"We're going to win. Cause the people are standing up, and they're saying, 'no!' and they're saying, 'I don't want this, I don't like this.' With that kind of attitude — this is just the beginning."
— Severt Young Bear

FURTHER READINGS FOR CHAPTER 5

Burnette, Robert, and John Koster, *The Road to Wounded Knee* (New York: Bantam Books, 1974). An essay on the struggles precipitating the Indian takeover of Wounded Knee in 1972.

Piven, Frances Fox, and Richard A. Cloward, *Regulating the Poor: The Function of Public Welfare* (New York: Vintage Books, 1971). The regulatory function of ostensible service agencies.

Schuman, David, *Bureaucracies, Organization and Administration: A Political Primer* (New York: Macmillan, 1976). An original and penetrating examination of the nature of bureaucratic power.

[1]*Chronicles of American Indian Protest*, The Council on Interracial Books for Children, Ed. (Greenwich, Conn.: Fawcett Publications, 1971).

Source: "Voices from Wounded Knee, 1973" published by *Akwesasne Notes*, June 1975.

Chapter 6 Interest Groups and the Governmental Process

Public Policy for the California Coast

JOHN BRIGHAM AND MICHAEL SEMLER,
EDITORS

This chapter reveals how an alliance of citizen groups successfully established a governmental priority. The issue was land-use planning for preservation of the aesthetic and recreational qualities of the California coastal region. The effort to establish this priority utilized the provision in California for popular lawmaking through an "initiative." The materials which follow describe the operation of the institutions charged with carrying out the citizen's mandate and the choices that were made in the final plan for fulfilling the mandated priority. The planning mechanism consisted of a number of regional commissions, which sought to institutionalize the wishes of the citizens through a "Constitution for the Coast" implemented by a statewide commission.

As background to the effort to protect the California coast, it is useful to indicate the ways in which beliefs structure the consideration of public policy. Beliefs operate on the substance of debate, and, in their institutional form, they set the framework for political activity. Knowledge of the shared language, beliefs, and expectations in American society is essential to an understanding of American politics, since political life is shaped and characterized by these traditions. It is widely held that neither ethnic background nor blood makes an American.

Instead, it is the rules delineating the political game that are the essential elements of group political life. The beliefs that serve this function constitute ideologies.

Ideologies are usually acquired in childhood, but they can also be adopted through a concerted effort to assimilate the traditions of a chosen society. Ideologies are important because what people believe and what they accept as appropriate influence the way in which policy is made. In the present case, a group of conservationists advocated an interpretation of the public interest that confronted a basic tenet of America's ideology. Americans have traditionally believed that it is their right to possess land for their own use, to claim the state's support for keeping possession, and to control and manipulate without encumbrance pieces of land acquired according to the procedures stipulated by law. According to the liberal theories that stand as the forerunners of America's political ideology, the right to property emerged from a right to the fruits of one's labor. For generations of Americans, that right has meant that the state will ensure possession of land that one owns. Along with ownership and possession has come the right to use the land with only minimal interference from the state. The proponents of the Coastal Initiative in California significantly expanded the extent to which the state might interfere with the use of land on the coast.

Property rights have never meant that citizens may choose to engage in any sort of conduct on their own land. There have always been important limits to the use of property, but these limits have usually simply meant that one could not engage in illegal practices. In its final plan, the California Coastal Commission linked the limits on use that it set for coastal land to a tradition of limited use, explicitly stating the tradition of limited property rights, especially as applied to social and ecological concerns. The following passage is from the final plan, submitted to the California legislature in December of 1975.

The property rights of a landowner are not absolute. Rights can and do change over time, and the rapid urbanization of the United States during the 20th century has led increasingly to restrictions on the use of private property — restrictions held by the courts to be constitutional. For example, the U.S. Supreme Court held 25 years ago that property owners could not create an enforceable agreement requiring racial discrimination in the future sale of their land. For many years, laws have prohibited the use of property in a way that would result in health hazards or noxious effects on the public at large. And local zoning laws have been upheld by the courts since 1926.

Public attention continues to move away from the individual interests represented by property rights to the common stake that all people have in the earth's limited resources. It has been increasingly recognized that a collective interest exists that demands public decisions consistent with the general welfare. The ecology movement has led to increasing interest in land use consistent with public needs. This movement has sought to increase the limitations placed on individual rights and private property.

The traditional values held by a society become a consideration in whether the interests of a group will gain acceptance; these values are, in fact, one of the centers of political debate. The ecology and conservation movements have often clashed with the values and institutions that traditionally dominate debate on public policy. For environmentalists, land is a common treasure. Seeking to make this view into law, the proponents of the initiative presented a challenge to landowners' expectations about their freedom to dispose of their property. The environmental interests conflicted with the interests of property owners. This conflict of interests, and the fundamental differences in social values that are implicit in it, characterized the electoral struggle over passage of the initiative.

Specific beliefs or values that have established a place in a system of beliefs exist in a complementary relationship with the dominant interests at any given time. Persons of wealth and power rely on acceptance of the sanctity of rights such as those surrounding private property. But, when threatened, even the powerful must organize for effective political action. The alliance behind the Coastal Initiative presented a challenge to some special interests and traditional values. Groups hoping to profit by unrestricted use of coastal land — developers, oil companies, and public utilities — campaigned against the initiative.

In American democratic theory the people are sovereign, but the mechanisms of government operate under a variety of institutional structures rather than by direct access. These structures are the product of past political struggles. The United States Constitution, for instance, was formed as a result of a desire to set up a strong central government to unite the colonies after the American Revolution. The movement for coastal planning in California exemplifies this process of struggle and institutionalization. Like the product of the efforts of the founding fathers, its result is a "constitution," which in this case is directed toward coastal preservation. The passage of the Coastal Initiative portrays the popular institutions. In creating a new planning authority, the citizens of California provided for an institution responsible for the realization of their mandate. Both the permit review process and the formulation of a final plan were to be carried out by means of institutions created especially for those specific goals.

In the United States, the institutional basis of political struggles is characterized by multiple levels of governmental power. This study of coastal planning indicates how shared powers in the federal system operate in a particular situation. The states traditionally retain all the power not delegated to the national government. The localities have the power to conduct their own affairs within the bounds set down by the states. Local governments are legally the creations of the states, and their power is derived from state grants of authority. The states themselves, since they have a legal status that predates the national government's, operate under their own authority except where the national government has become involved. In such situations, the national government is the supreme or sovereign power.

Although state and local power has been eroding in favor of the national government ever since the ratification of the Constitution in 1789, substantial powers remain at those levels of government. The states are responsible for most of the law under which we are governed. The state determines family law, the law for business enterprises, and the rules and regulations governing most areas of human conduct. The criminal law is overwhelmingly state law; until the last few decades, it was almost entirely so. The states delegate the authority they have in these matters to local governments under the provisions for "home rule." Schooling, police and fire protection, and issues related to the development of land have traditionally been local responsibilities (the final reading in this chapter states this last relationship more explicitly).

Restrictions on the use of land have been carried out for the last 50 years through the power to "zone," or determine what sorts of activities are most appropriate in what parts of cities and towns. Most of this regulation has been concerned with conformity to adjacent land uses and with requirements for public improvements such as streets, sewers, and drainage. For the most part, local regulation has placed limits on the use of land only to the extent that these limits serve the interest of both local government and developers in growth. Municipalities get most of their revenue from the property tax. Since development increases property values, it has been in the interest of local government to develop vacant land into a tax-generating resource. Local regulation has also been relatively ineffective because it is focused on a limited area and is, therefore, less likely to be receptive to interests and values that transcend the region. Preservation of the California coastline is such a value.

By the late 1960s, the role of the state and regional institutions in meeting environmental quality and public health goals had begun to grow. The California Coastal Initiative of 1974 was exemplary because it created regional authorities with a mandate to protect the coastline from development. Central to the plan proposed and shepherded through the initiative process was the creation of an agency with regional authority, in order to make a plan that would serve the public interest. Here, the new value — coastal preservation — dictated the necessity for something more than the traditional local government role, since it was believed that localities had not adequately protected this value in the past. The concerns of local government are evident in this statement from the California Association of County Supervisors:

We do not support the creation of new commissions, governments, boards, authorities or what have you to implement land use decisions at a local level. There is more than enough government right now to do the job that needs to be done. Government may need more resources, authority, technology, experience or wisdom; but the people of California do not need more government.

The Coastal Commission chose, in its final plan, to recommend phasing out the regional commissions after the local governments had submitted plans that were consistent with the statewide plan. The state commission would retain the power to review all local decisions. The parties that supported the original proposal were not totally satisfied with the elimination of the regional commissions, as is evident in the report on the preliminary plan by the Planning and Conservation League.

Problems in many different policy areas that have been prominent nationally in the last few years have revealed the inability of existing governments to solve important issues because of jurisdictional limits. In many cases, the solutions that may be appropriate do not fit into the established governmental setup. New York City's government, for instance, claims that the city's tremendous welfare burden is not a local but rather a national responsibility. The debates on busing for racial integration have come to focus on the fact that our governing units often do not have authority to handle the problems that ultimately affect them. Planning for regional needs, and developing policy making capacities consistent with those needs, is apparently becoming a new force in American politics.

But there is a strong tendency in American politics for institutionalization to lead to professionalization. Politicians and planners, like doctors and engineers, have become dependent upon technical knowledge to carry out their function. The professionals in control of this knowledge assume a position which takes power from the rest of the community. While the initial planning process considered here was characterized by a considerable amount of popular participation, the final plan chose to rely on a document and a statewide commission, which will necessarily lead to greater influence of both the professionals and the local politicians. This may be a necessary compromise: to preserve the coast through the representative institutions that already exist. Before too long, there will be evidence of whether this approach works. The chapter is divided into Section A — the struggle for acceptance of a coastal mandate — and Section B — the transformation of that mandate into an institutional structure.

SECTION A. INTERESTS IN CONFLICT

The concern for conservation, like many other political values in American society, has been advanced by groups that become increasingly more organized in order to have a greater influence on policy outcomes. Groups such as the Sierra Club and the Audubon Society have been involved in conservation for generations. But the heightened interest in the movement around 1970 spawned new groups that have grown in influence as a result of public recognition that America's natural and recreational resources are disappearing. The political significance of new groups is dependent on the support that they can generate for their programs. The organization of groups around an issue maximizes the resources, ideas, and energy that may be introduced into a struggle. In the present case, organization was provided by the California Coastal Alliance, which included over 60 groups concerned about the preservation of the coast.

Organizations must work with the tools of policy making available to them. In this case, the emphasis is on the initiative petition. The article by Norman Sanders describes the background for the decision to turn to the initiative, and a newspaper article is included to show the switch from legislative lobbying to the initiative. A discussion of the tradition behind the initiative process and of the practical struggle to get the proposition on the California ballot, in addition to a copy of the initiative, further indicate the nature of the process. Another segment of the article by Sanders — a newspaper account of the campaign contributions and the official ballot statement with its arguments pro and con — reveals the interests and the particular issues in the struggle to enact coastal legislation.

THE NEW TIDE OF COASTAL LEGISLATION

NORMAN SANDERS

The coastal areas of the US are under attack as never before. As our population grows and our per-capita consumption rises, our society places more and more stress upon all our resources. However, it is the very limited area of the coastal zone that bears the brunt of the assault. Oil production, pollution or filling of bays, harbors and estuaries, construction of hotels, apartments, and second homes have all taken their toll. Unfortunately, control over these projects is usually vested in local governments who find it next to impossible to turn down any scheme which will "broaden the tax base."

In the struggle to halt overdevelopment of America's coasts, 1972 was a significant year. On October 28, President Nixon signed the federal Coastal Zone Management Act and on November 7, voters in the states of California and Washington passed coastal initiatives put on the ballot by citizen petition drives. These bills had all been under consideration for years, but by 1972, the problems had become so apparent that the people demanded action.

Increasingly, citizen action is forcing national, state and local governments to coordinate coastal development on a regional basis, planning for the maximum beneficial use of all coastal resources. Government and busi-

SOURCE: *Sierra Club Bulletin*, Vol. 58, No. 2 (February 1973), pp. 10–13.

ness traditionally have cooperated in the hasty exploitation of coastal areas for short-term financial advantage. The battle to change this situation is intense, because the oil, land-development, and utility industries, among others, depend on present loose controls for rapid return on their investments.

The federal Coastal Zone Management Act uses a system of rewards, rather than punishment, to attain proper management of the coastal resource. If the act receives the necessary funds, states will be offered grants to assist in developing a coastal management program. Once that program is established, additional federal money will be available to help administer the program.

Specifically, the states must develop "a comprehensive statement in words, maps, illustrations, or other media of communication, prepared and adopted by the coastal state . . . setting forth objectives, policies, and standards to guide public and private uses of lands and waters in the coastal zone." In addition, legal means must be established to regulate land and water use and control coastal development.

Whether or not the federal act works depends heavily on the willingness of the individual states to come to grips with coastal land-use problems. Many states have yielded to citizen demands to the extent of passing laws to protect coastal wetlands, but basically ignore other lands adjacent to the coast. Such states include Connecticut, Georgia, Maine, Massachusetts, Michigan, New Hampshire, New Jersey, New York, and North Carolina. Delaware has legislation that bans new heavy industry and port facilities from the coastal zone, but does not cover subdivisions, commercial developments or intensive recreational facilities. Hawaii, the first state to institute a statewide land-use program, requires a building permit only within a 20- to 40-foot setback from high tide mark, a zone that environmentalists consider too narrow for effective coastal land-use control.

In 1969, Minnesota passed a law requiring all counties to enact land-use control ordinances for all shorelands in unincorporated areas. The counties administer the act, with the state exercising only limited control. Oregon gives the public unrestricted use of beaches to the vegetation line, but coastal controls inland from that point are only now being considered. Rhode Island passed an act in 1971 establishing a 17-member coastal management council, but the state's quite strict controls covering management of wetlands are offset by weak land-use provisions that do not cover subdivisions, private-home construction, and some types of industrial development. Wisconsin's Water Resources Act is intended to protect the shorelines of inland lakes, and an inventory of Lake Michigan's coast has already been prepared. Observers report, however, that many inadequacies have developed in the enforcement apparatus.

Until November 7, 1972, all the above states had stronger coastal legislation than did California, even though the Sierra Club and other environmental groups had long been too powerful, so the situation had degenerated to the point where only about 263 miles of California's 1,072-mile coastline were legally accessible to the general public. Finally, on election day, the people corrected this situation by passing a coastal protection law themselves, using the initiative process to bypass the foot-dragging legislature.

California's successful Coastal Zone Conservation Act — called Proposition 20 on the ballot — is a direct descendant of the series of bills that environmental organizations had been trying to have passed by the state legislature for several years. Shepherded principally by Assemblyman Alan Sieroty of Beverly Hills and helped along by Sierra Club lobbyist John Zierold and Janet Adams of the Coastal Alliance, the bills had cleared the Assembly only to be stalled repeatedly in hostile Senate committees.

John Berthelson, a reporter for the *Sacramento Bee*, found out why the bills kept dying. A group called the "Committee Opposed to Ecology Issues" had been meeting for several years and had as its main goal the blockage of coastal legislation. The committee consisted of 34 industry lobbyists, including representatives of Southern California Edison Company, Standard Oil, the California Real Estate Association, and various other organizations who benefit financially from poorly controlled coastal land use.

QUALIFYING THE INITIATIVE

In California, voters have an alternative to the legislative process.[1] During the Progressive period, many states instituted a process by which a percentage of the electorate, usually from 5 to 10 percent, can petition to put a proposal on the ballot at the next general election. The process paralleled other reforms, such as the nonpartisan election, woman's suffrage, popular election of Senators, and the recall, in an effort to give the public a check on the activity or inactivity of politicians.

In one form or another, the initiative is in use in 20 states, most of which are in the western part of the country. The Progressive move-

[1]This introductory material was derived largely from an article by Charles M. Price, "The Initiative: A Comparative State Analysis and Reassessment of a Western Phenomenon," *Western Political Quarterly*, Vol. 28, No. 2 (1975), pp. 243–262.

ment swept through the western states soon after many had been admitted to the union, and the early institutionalization seems to have been consistent with the relatively strong interest group activity and weak political parties in states making use of the initiative process. Although the use of the initiative has had its ups and downs, there seems to have recently been a revival of use, especially in California.

COASTLINE CONSERVATIONISTS SWITCH TO INITIATIVE AFTER SENATE UNIT KILLS BILL

RICHARD RODDA

Conservation forces today shifted their muscle to a coastline initiative campaign after a last-minute appeal for legislative help failed.

The Senate Natural Resources and Wildlife Committee late yesterday killed the last of the "tough" coastline regulatory measures in defeating AB 200, Sieroty.

"This, was the legislature's last chance," commented Assemblyman Alan Sieroty, D–Los Angeles, champion of coastline protection efforts. "We will now make every effort to see that the initiative passes."

Initiative Provisions

The measure on the Nov. 7 ballot would create a California Coastal Zone Conservation Commission and six regional commissions. The commissions would establish guidelines and issue permits for residential, commercial and industrial development along the state's 1,000 miles of coastline.

Sieroty said he realized he was "licked" even before yesterday's committee hearing began. "But I felt it was my responsibility to carry this legislation to a conclusion," he added.

The same committee earlier this year defeated a similar measure, SB 100, Grunsky. The vote on AB 200 was a virtual replay of the vote on SB 100....

Nearly Identical

Both the defeated Sieroty and Grunsky bills have provisions almost identical to the initiative measure.

SOURCE: *The Sacramento Bee*, July 25, 1972.

Proponents of the initiative state:

The plan is required because present uncoordinated, piecemeal development is resulting in the permanent loss of irreplaceable coastal zone resources and in a pattern of use which does not properly balance conservation and development needs.

While some cities and counties may have prepared detailed master plans for their own coastal zone lands, no governmental mechanism presently exists for evaluating the effect of such projects on the resources of the entire coastal zone.

Yesterday the forces allied against Sieroty were the same opposing Grunsky: Real estate interests, power companies, subdividers, construction interests and building trades unions.

This is the third consecutive year a Senate committee has rejected coastline proposals embodying the regional concept. SB 860 remains on the floor of the Senate. It would leave coastal regulation up to cities and counties. Conservationists oppose this on the basis [that] local government is susceptible to the pressures of special interests.

Before the voters of the whole state could express their view on the initiative, it had to qualify for a place on the ballot. In the following article, the director of that campaign discusses the effort.

STAGE ONE — SIGNATURE COLLECTION

JANET ADAMS

The qualification process provided new frustrations but much insight into the workings of government. The first step required by law was to obtain a "good government" seal of approval to certify that the proposed initiative was constitutional and fiscally responsible. The determination had to be made by a series of state officials: the Secretary of State, the Attorney General, the Legislative Analyst, and finally the Director of Finance. At last the seal of approval was given and the proposal lurched back down the line, with precious time ticking away for signature-gathering. Under state law, all signatures had to be gathered and validated by 130 days before the election date.

SOURCE: *Syracuse Law Review*, 24, No. 3 (1973), pp. 1034–1036. Janet Adams directed the California Coastal Alliance.

There were no zealots on street corners. Quiet, self-conscious, establishment citizens began to collect the signatures necessary to qualify the coastal proposal as an initiative for election day. The rules were rigid. Signatures of registered voters could only be obtained by a registered voter in the county of residence for both. In many parts of the state, that eliminated a natural — beach crowds. Too many of those people would be out of their county of residence and their signatures would have been invalid. Critics said that it was statistically impossible to collect 16,000 signatures a day for thirty days, get them back to central county headquarters and identify them by precinct number.[1] Alliance leaders knew it could be done.

Precincting! At one point a Southern California group actually sued the county clerk to force *him* to do the precincting. That irresponsible act, if it had not been squashed, could have ruined the entire state campaign. The campaign could not succeed without the cooperation of the county clerks and their staffs, because all signatures submitted to the clerks had to be validated within a twenty day check period.[2] If the county clerks were outraged or antagonized by proponents of the coastal initiative, they might well simply take long coffee breaks for the entire twenty day period. The coastal proposal might never reach the voters. On this and other crises, Alliance leaders were forced to spend time no one had, to soothe fractured feelings and keep overzealous volunteers in line. The overriding aim was to qualify the coastal proposal as an initiative and take it to the voters on election day.

Signature-gathering went on schedule. The numbers grew significant as the burden of precincting hit. The qualification process brought forth heroic efforts on the part of Alliance volunteers. In San Diego, one retired gentleman organized the entire precincting operation and dedicated full time to it.

---

[1]State law required that each signature on an initiative petition be accompanied by the signer's address and precinct number. CAL. ELEC. CODE, Sec. 3511 (West Supp. 1973). Since most voters did not know their precinct numbers, Alliance volunteers had to track down precinct numbers at the offices of the local county clerks. Often a single street would wind through many gerrymandered precincts. It was not impossible, for instance, to track a single Los Angeles street through 30 precincts. Since all California voters could be found in alphabetical order on computer print-outs, it was hardly necessary for precinct numbers to be provided and validated. However, the law required it. Alliance volunteers found the precincting requirement a drain on valuable time and energy which had the effect, if not the design, of making it more difficult to qualify the initiative.

[2]CAL. ELEC. CODE, Sec. 3520(b) (West Supp. 1973) provides: . . . Within 20 days after the filing of such petition in his office the clerk or registrar of voters shall determine from the records of registration what number of qualified voters have signed the petition and if necessary the board of supervisors shall allow the clerk or registrar additional assistance for the purpose of examining the petition. . . . The statute then directs the county clerk or registrar to certify the petitions and transmit them to the Secretary of State for a final determination. *Id.*, Sec. 3520(c).

Where's the beach?

Ridiculous question? Regrettably, no!

In two hundred years the beach of California has shrunk from one thousand sixty two miles to two hundred miles available to the public.

By happenchance two hundred separate entities -- city, county, state and federal governments, agencies and commissions -- regulate the coast of California.

Each time a "special interest" sells a local government one more freeway, a power plant on a spectacular headland, a housing development on an eroding cliff, a non-water related industry, a super sewage outfall, another beach dies. The public interest is scorned.

This is an urgent plea to all Californians -- beachcombers, sunbathers, sailors, surfers, fishermen and sightseeing oldsters -- to join the California Coastal Alliance to create a Coastal Zone Commission that will have the power to stop the destruction of the remaining natural shore.

The California Coastal Alliance
presents this initiative to "Save Our Coast"

Reprinted by permission from the *Syracuse Law Review* (vol. 24, p. 1018) and from the California Coastal Alliance.

In Los Angeles, one remarkable young couple went on leave from their doctoral programs in marine biology to make the initiative drive a success. In Marin County a dynamic biology teacher and chemist pulled a mighty force together. In San Francisco it was a young businessman and his wife. In Santa Clara, Santa Barbara, Santa Cruz, Arcata, San Bernadino, San Luis Obispo, Fresno, Chico and Berkeley, it was the college students, who had registered to vote on campus. Sometimes, the local coordinator was a professor, a member of the League of Women Voters or AAUW, a Park Department employee, or a professional planner — or a surfer or a diver. In Monterey and San Diego it was the Sierra Club working with long-established local coalitions. All the signature collectors were volunteers and all were wonderful. There were 10,000 heroes and heroines to every irritant.

On June 9, 1972, the Alliance filed the signatures with county clerks of forty-seven counties. Of the total collected, twelve percent were invalidated because the signature was illegible, the name had been changed by marriage, or the voter had moved or was not registered. On June 19, the Alliance was informed by the Secretary of State that the coastal initiative had qualified with 418,000 valid signatures. A gargantuan sigh of relief was heard across the state. Election Day lay ahead.

As a part of the formal process, the petition itself is an official document supervised by the state. How it is treated, as the preceding piece indicates, will determine whether conservationists will get over their first hurdle in seeking to circumvent the legislature. The following document is a reproduction of the petition that was carried by members of the Coastal Alliance throughout the state.

INITIATIVE MEASURE TO BE SUBMITTED
DIRECTLY TO THE ELECTORS

COASTAL ZONE CONSERVATION ACT. INITIATIVE. CREATES STATE COASTAL ZONE CONSERVATION COMMISSION AND SIX REGIONAL COMMISSIONS. SETS CRITERIA FOR AND REQUIRES SUBMISSION OF PLAN TO LEGISLATURE FOR PRESERVATION, PROTECTION, RESTORATION AND ENHANCEMENT OF ENVIRONMENT AND ECOLOGY OF COASTAL ZONE, AS DEFINED. ESTABLISHES PERMIT AREA WITHIN COASTAL ZONE AS THE AREA BETWEEN THE SEAWARD LIMITS OF STATE JURISDICTION AND 1000 YARDS LANDWARD FROM THE MEAN HIGH TIDE LINE, SUB-

JECT TO SPECIFIED EXCEPTIONS. PROHIBITS ANY DEVELOPMENT WITHIN PERMIT AREA WITHOUT PERMIT BY STATE OR REGIONAL COMMISSION. PRESCRIBES STANDARDS FOR ISSUANCE OR DENIAL OF PERMITS. ACT TERMINATES AFTER 1976. THIS MEASURE APPROPRIATES FIVE MILLION DOLLARS ($5,000,000) FOR THE PERIOD 1973 TO 1976.

READ INSTRUCTIONS

We need 500,000 signatures by May 15, 1972. Please hurry. Election Officials will check every part of this petition, every name, address and date in order to invalidate improper signatures.

1. You must be a registered voter in the county where you sign or circulate the petition. You may sign your own petition. Ask every potential signer whether he is registered. Don't take signatures of out-of-county persons, refer to nearest area coordinator or give the petition to circulate in own county.

2. Each person must sign name and address as registered. Use complete name when in doubt. Women should not use Miss, Mrs. or Ms. Illegible signatures or addresses cannot be validated. Have the signer print last name as well.

3. Addresses should be printed for clarity. Never use ditto marks, P.O. Boxes, or business addresses.

4. All signatures must be obtained in your presence in a manner which would allow you truthfully to fill out the Declaration of Circulation. Read the Declaration, but,

5. Do not fill it out until you are ready to return the petition. The Declaration is very important. An invalid signature does not invalidate the entire petition, but an invalid Declaration does.

6. Please do not use pencil, felt pens or marking pencils.

7. Make sure the signer fills in the entire date: month, day and year.

8. The First Amendment guarantees you the right to collect signatures for this petition on sidewalks, public streets, and any public areas, such as entry ways and parking lots of shopping centers, as long as you do not interfere with the flow of traffic. (See *Diamond* v. *Bland*, 3 Cal.3rd 653). If you have any difficulty please contact your county coordinator, or if none, the Woodside Office.

9. Please try to return the petition within ten (10) days of the first signature whether or not this petition is completely filled. This will insure a continual flow of signatures for our precincting staff to work on.

10. Return petitions to your county coordinator, or if none, to the Woodside Office, by addressing the blank envelope form below.

11. Circle the number of any signer who would like to carry a petition in pencil. You may sign out a petition to him if you have one, recording his name and address and forwarding it to the Woodside Office.

THE ELECTORAL PROCESS

For the campaign itself, far greater numbers of supporters than had been involved in the signature-gathering stage now had to be mobilized in support of the initiative, which came to be known as Proposition 20 because of its place on the statewide ballot. In this process, the interest group effort moved from the personal process of collecting signatures to the impersonal and public relations–dominated general election campaign. The following selection from Norman Sanders' article recounts some of the important events of that campaign.

The Campaign for Proposition 20

THE NEW TIDE [*continued*]

When a spot on the ballot was assured, the forces that had opposed coastal legislation in Sacramento swung into action to defeat the initiative. The usual coalition of oil companies, developers, utility companies, and others with a vested interest in coastal profits hired the San Francisco political public relations firm of Whitaker and Baxter to conduct a "No on 20" campaign. Whitaker and Baxter was still flushed with its victory in the June primary when it scared California voters into voting against another environmental initiative, Proposition 9, the Clean Environment Act. The firm reported spending $2.4 million of its clients' money on billboards, newspaper ads and saturation radio and television messages, which hammered away at the themes of unemployment, power blackouts, and insect plagues if Proposition 9 passed.

Whitaker and Baxter, promised a similar war chest for Proposition 20, started to work, their main goal being to confuse voters over the actual provisions of the bill. They bought hundreds of billboards and bus posters which screamed: "Don't let them lock up your coast. Vote No on 20" and

SOURCE: Norman Sanders, "The New Tide of Coastal Legislation," *Sierra Club Bulletin*, Vol. 58, No. 2 (February 1973).

"Conservation Yes, Confiscation No. Vote No on 20." Radio and television commercials, with sounds of waves and pictures of unspoiled coastlines, urged voters to preserve the coast by voting against the evil Proposition 20.

To further muddy the issue, Clem Whitaker prompted an acquaintance, Newton Cope, to file a lawsuit alleging that Cope's nightclub on the Sacramento River would be adversely affected by Proposition 20. He and his coplaintiff, who had property on the San Joaquin River, claimed the bill's language was so vague that not only would coastal areas be involved, but vast inland areas along rivers as well. They asked that Proposition 20 be taken off the ballot until the wording had been changed to explain the far-reaching consequences they alleged. A judge hastily signed an order to show cause why Proposition 20 shouldn't be removed from the ballot, a move which newspapers favorable to the "No on 20" camp immediately interpreted as "Proposition 20 Off Ballot" in headlines.

Proposition 20 proponents got their day in court, however, and defused this phony issue. Arguing against the Whitaker and Baxter position were a battery of lawyers from the Sierra Club, the Coastal Alliance, the League of Women Voters, the California secretary of state's office, and other governmental agencies. The judge heard arguments about the true definitions of the coastal zone and the public's right to be allowed to vote on vital issues, and after deliberating overnight, finally decided in favor of the initiative's supporters. Despite their loss in court, the "No on 20" forces kept stating in advertising that the coastal zone extended many miles inland.

Whitaker and Baxter probably lost their campaign through overkill. Even Governor Reagan, longtime foe of coastal legislation, stated that the "No on 20" campaign was misleading. An assembly committee held hearings on the situation, and the media editorialized against the Whitaker and Baxter tactics. Newspapers, television and radio generally favored Proposition 20, in contrast to the earlier Proposition 9 campaign, when they were hostile or neutral. They realized the need for meaningful legislation and couldn't help noting the underdog position of the Proposition 20 proponents.

Supporters of the proposition were short on money, but long on ideas. Whitaker and Baxter couldn't buy the type of coverage that State Senator James Mills generated on his bicycle ride down the coast from San Francisco to San Diego. Senator Mills and his band of cyclists (whose numbers from time to time varied from about 40 to several hundred) were very visible Proposition 20 supporters. The opponents generally kept a very low profile, letting their money talk through Whitaker and Baxter. One exception was a letter urging defeat of the Coastal Initiative sent out by Southern California Edison Company to its millions of customers.

Because of lack of funds, supporters of Proposition 20 waited until the last few days before the election to advertise their position. Whitaker and Baxter had succeeded in confusing the voters, but the proponents had several advantages. For one thing, California law requires that lists of campaign contributions be made public before the election. This information showed who the opposition was and the vast sums they were spending. Whitaker and Baxter's final financial report showed expenditures of over $1,100,000, made up of contributions such as $50,000 apiece from land developers Deane and Deane, Inc., and the Irvine Company. Standard Oil Company gave $30,000, Bechtel Corporation (a major contracting firm) donated $25,000, and the Union Oil Company added $10,000 to the "No on 20" fund.

Proponents used this information to continually point out the opposition of the well-financed corporations to legislation that would benefit the public. A typical effective newspaper advertisement read: "The Sierra Club supports Proposition 20 . . . Signal Oil opposes. You can tell a proposition by the company it keeps." Ads also named other endorsers of the bill, including the League of Women Voters, the California Medical Association, the Federation of Western Outdoor Clubs, the United Auto Workers Union, the American Institute of Architects, Common Cause, the American Association of University Women, and many others.

Sierra Club lawyers persuaded the FCC to order radio and television stations to give proponents free time to offset Whitaker and Baxter's saturation advertising. Doris Day, Charlton Heston, and Lloyd Bridges donated their services to make tapes urging voters to approve Proposition 20. Many candidates for office also urged passage of Proposition 20 in their campaign speeches. On November 7, voters demonstrated that they had seen through the Whitaker and Baxter smokescreen by passing Proposition 20 by a margin of 55 percent to 45 percent.

Opponents of Proposition 20

OPPONENTS OF PROP. 20, SOME FROM EAST, POUR NEARLY $1-MILLION INTO FIGHT

GLADWIN HILL

Los Angeles — Nearly $1–million, some of it from big eastern corporations, has been contributed to defeat a ballot proposition that would establish new controls on the development of California's 1,072–mile coast line.

SOURCE: Gladwin Hill, New York Times National Environmental Correspondent. Courtesy of the New York Times Editorial Research Department. Published in the *Sacramento Bee*, 5 November 1972.

Prominent among the contributors, reported by Secretary of State Edmund G. Brown, Jr., were land development concerns, oil companies, power companies and other concerns interested in coastal development.

The proposition, a citizen originated initiative measure, will be voted on Tuesday.

Drawn up by conservation groups, Proposition 20 calls for the establishment of a zone along the coast running, 1,000 yards inland in which all development would be regulated by a state commission and six regional commissions composed of citizens and representatives of local government.

Much of the coast line is still privately owned, and opponents of the measure in a lavish campaign of television, billboard and newspaper advertising, have denounced it as attempted "confiscation" of property rights.

A law banning industry from a coastal strip was adopted by Delaware this year, and coast line control legislation is pending in New Jersey, among other states.

The Sierra Club, a leading proponent of the control measure, denounced the out-of-state contributors as "investors hoping to cash in on development of California's coast line."

Listed among contributors of $899,223 through Oct. 28, as reported by the opposing organization, Citizens Against the Coastal Initiative, were: Lazard Freres & Co., New York investment bankers, $10,000; Combustion Engineering, Windsor, Conn., $15,000; Realty Holding and Investing Corp., New York, $10,000; Babcock and Wilcox Co., a New York manufacturer of industrial equipment, $15,000; Mortgage Guaranty Insurance Corp., Milwaukee, $10,000; Continental Oil Co., Denver, $5,000; Phillips Petroleum Co., Denver, $5,000; Trans-Land Co., Rosemont, Ill., $2,500; and Tucker Land Co., Phoenix, $5,000.

Charles M. Clusen, assistant conservation director of the Sierra Club, said the total to date of $78,125 in out-of-state contributions "in itself is 20 per cent more than our total contributions."

He said the club had 5,071 contributors who gave an average of $13.20 each, while opponents of the measure listed 277 contributors who gave an average of $3,240 each.

Other contributors to the opposition fund listed were Allis-Chalmers, $10,000; Dart Industries, $13,000; General Electric $25,000; Gulf Oil, $10,000; Pacific Gas & Electric, $251,000; Southern California Edison, $25,000; Southern Pacific Co., $20,000; Standard Oil of California, $30,000; Standard Oil of New Jersey, $25,000; Union Oil, $10,000, and Getty Oil, $5,000.

Official Ballot Summary of the Issues Behind Proposition 20

The following information is the official ballot summary presented to the voters in California in November 1972. It is far more comprehensive than, one suspects, most voters are likely to attempt to handle. The complexity of the implementation of the initiative was the subject of much of the campaign debate. The tendency was often to oversimplify and sometimes conveniently distort the implications of the initiative. The complexity evident here indicates the ample room available for such tactics.

COASTAL ZONE CONSERVATION ACT, INITIATIVE

---

20 COASTAL ZONE CONSERVATION ACT, Initiative. Creates State Coastal Zone Conservation Commission and six regional commissions. Sets criteria for and requires submission of plan to Legislature for preservation, protection, restoration and enhancement of environment and ecology of coastal zone, as defined. Establishes permit area within coastal zone as the area between the seaward limits of state jurisdiction and 1000 yards landward from the mean high tide line, subject to specified exceptions. Prohibits any development within permit area without permit by state or regional commission. Prescribes standards for issuance or denial of permits. Act terminates after 1976. This measure appropriates five million dollars ($5,000,000) for the period 1973 to 1976. Financial impact: Cost to state of $1,250,000 per year plus undeterminable local government administrative costs.

YES

NO

GENERAL ANALYSIS BY THE LEGISLATIVE COUNCIL

A "Yes" vote on this initiative statute is a vote to create the California Coastal Zone Conservation Commission and six regional commissions; to regulate, through permits issued by the regional commissions, development within a portion of the coastal zone (as defined); and to provide for the submission of a Californa Coastal Zone Conservation Plan to the Legislature for its adoption and implementation. The statute would terminate on the 91st day after final adjournment of the 1976 Regular Session of the Legislature.

A "No" vote is a vote against adopting the measure.

For further details, see below.

DETAILED ANALYSIS BY THE LEGISLATIVE COUNSEL

This initiative statute would enact the "California Coastal Zone Conservation Act of 1972." The principal provisions of the act would:

1. Create the California Coastal Zone Conservation Commission and six regional commissions. The regional commissions would be composed of members of the boards of supervisors, city councilmen, and members of regional agencies, plus an equal number of knowledgeable members of the public. The state commission would consist of a representative from each of the regional commissions, plus an equal number of knowledgeable members of the public.

2. Require the state commission to submit to the Legislature, by December 1, 1975, a California Coastal Zone Conservation Plan based on studies of all factors that significantly affect the "coastal zone," generally defined as land and water area extending seaward to the outer limit of the state jurisdiction and inland to the highest elevation of the nearest coastal mountain range.

3. Require each regional commission, in cooperation with appropriate local agencies, to make recommendations to the state commission relevant to the coastal zone plan by April 1, 1975.

4. Beginning February 1, 1973, require a permit from a regional commission for any proposed development (with specified exemptions) within the "permit area," defined, generally, as that portion of the coastal zone lying between the seaward limit of the jurisdiction of the state and 1,000 yards landward from the mean high tide line, subject to various exceptions. Provision is made for appeals to the state commission and to the courts.

5. Define "development" to include the following activities when conducted on land or in or under water:

(a) Placement or erection of any solid material or structure.

(b) Discharge or disposal of any dredged material or of any gaseous, liquid, solid, or thermal waste.

(c) Grading, removing, dredging, mining, or extraction of any materials.

(d) Change in the density or intensity of use of land, including, but not limited to, subdivision of land and lot splits.

(e) Change in the intensity of use of water, ecology related thereto, or access thereto.

(f) Construction, reconstruction, demolition, or alteration of the size of any structure, including any facility of any private, public, or municipal utility.

(g) Removal or logging of major vegetation.

6. Provide criminal penalties for violation of provisions relating to conflict of interest and specify civil fines for violation of other provisions of the act.

In addition, the initiative statute would add provisions to:

1. Require each county and city to transmit to the state commission a copy of each tentative map of any subdivision located in the portion of the coastal zone within its jurisdiction.

2. Appropriate $5,000,000 to the state commission to support it and the regional commissions for the fiscal years 1973 to 1976, inclusive.

3. Terminate the initiative statute on the 91st day after final adjournment of the 1976 Regular Session of the Legislature.

4. Authorize the Legislature, by two-thirds vote, to amend the initiative statute "in order to better achieve the objectives" of the statute.

COST ANALYSIS BY THE LEGISLATIVE ANALYST

This initiative declares that the California coastline is a distinct and valuable resource and it is state policy to preserve, protect and, where possible, restore the natural and scenic resources of the coastal zone for present and succeeding generations. The coastal zone generally includes the land and water area extending seaward about three miles and inland to the highest elevation of the nearest coastal range. In Los Angeles, Orange and San Diego Counties the inland boundary can be no more than five miles.

The initiative would create one state and six regional commissions to:

1. Study the coastal zone and its resources,

2. Prepare a state plan for its orderly, long-range conservation and management, and

3. Regulate development by a permit system while the plan is being prepared.

The commissions begin February 1973. They must adopt the plan by December 1975 and terminate after adjournment of the 1976 Legislature which presumably would establish a permanent commission based on the plan. Commission membership would be balanced between local government officials and state appointed members.

The initiative requires the commission to study a broad range of subjects pertaining to the coastal zone. The final plan must include recommendations on:

1. Ecological planning principles and assumptions for determining suitability and extent of development.
2. Land use.
3. Transportation.
4. Public access.
5. Recreation.
6. Public services and facilities including a powerplant siting study.
7. Ocean mineral and living resources.
8. Maximum desirable population densities.
9. Reservations of land or water for certain uses or prohibited uses.
10. Recommendations for governmental policies, powers and agencies to implement the plan.

The regional commissions, cooperating with local agencies, prepare plan recommendations to the state commission, which shall prepare and adopt the plan for submission to the Governor and Legislature.

During the four years the initiative would be in effect, new developments by any person or state or local agency in the permit area of the coastal zone would be severely restricted. The permit area includes generally the sea and 1,000 yards inland but excluding area under the San Francisco Bay Conservation and Development Commission. Certain urban land areas may also be excluded. No development permit shall be issued unless the regional commission, or the state commission on appeal, has found that the development will not have any substantial adverse environmental or ecological effect and will be consistent with objectives of the initiative which specify orderly, balanced preservation and utilization of coastal zone resources, maintenance of quality of the coastal zone environment, avoidance of irreversible commitments and other stated considerations.

The Legislature may amend the initiative by a two-thirds vote to achieve the objectives of the measure.

The direct state cost is $5 million appropriated to support the commission through 1976 from a fund created in 1971 with $40 million of the one-time revenue from withholding state personal income taxes.

Although staff and funds for the Comprehensive Ocean Area Plan (COAP) are to be transferred to the commission, no funding was provided for COAP in 1972–73.

The state plan must propose reservation of land or water in the coastal zone for certain uses or prohibition of certain uses. The acquisition of such land would probably be necessary but would require additional legislation. However, stringent application of the permit processes could result in unknown damages from inverse condemnation suits on lands not acquired. Oil and gas extraction would probably be restricted, reducing revenues to the state from extraction and possibly resulting in damages for loss of oil production.

The commission may, in its discretion, require a reasonable filing fee to permit applications and the reimbursement of expenses. Therefore, the revenues received depend on fee schedules established by the commission.

Local agencies would have some additional costs assisting the regional commissions in planning and forwarding applications for permits. There are 15 counties within the coastal zone and an estimated 40 cities. The size of their workload would depend largely on the precise location of permit areas as determined by the regional commissions. Deferral of developments along the shoreline would also defer local property revenues.

ARGUMENT IN FAVOR OF PROPOSITION 20

Save California's beaches and coastline for the people of California, vote YES on this proposition.

The Problem

Our coast has been plundered by haphazard development and land speculators. Beaches formerly open for camping, swimming, fishing and picnicking are closed to the public. Campgrounds along the coast are so overcrowded that thousands of Californians are turned away. Fish are poisoned by sewage and industrial waste dumped into the ocean. Duck and other wildlife habitats are buried under streets and vacation homes for the wealthy. Ocean vistas are walled off behind unsightly high rise apartments, office buildings, and billboards. Land speculators bank their profits, post their "no trespassing" signs and leave the small property owner with the burden of increased taxes to pay for streets, sewers, police and fire protection. The coast continues to shrink.

The Reasons for the Problem

Massive construction projects are often approved solely to benefit corporate landowners. We need a coastal plan, but responsibility is fragmented among 45 cities, 15 counties and dozens of government agencies without the resources to evaluate and prevent developments whose destructive effects may overlap local boundaries.

The Solution?

Your *YES* vote!

Your Yes Vote Will:

(1) Give the people direct participation in planning. No important decisions will be made until commissions hold public hearings and the citizen is heard. Coastal commissions are composed in equal number of locally elected officials and citizens representing the public;

(2) Furnish immediate protection of California's beaches from exploitation by the corporate land grab;

(3) Prevent tax increases resulting from irresponsible developments;

(4) Stimulate growth of the $4.2 billion annual tourist industry and make new jobs;

(5) Stop our beaches from becoming the exclusive playground of the rich;

(6) Bring a runaway construction industry back to the cities where jobs and new homes are needed;

(7) Use the coast to enrich the life of every Californian;

(8) Prevent conflicts of interest. Tough provisions modeled after federal law will keep coastal commissioners from planning for personal profit.

(9) Develop a fair Statewide Plan for balanced development of our coast.

(10) Increase public access to the coast.

The Safeguards

(1) This act will *not* impose a moratorium or prohibit any particular kind of building, but ensures that authorized construction will have no substantial adverse environmental effect;

(2) Homeowners *can* make minor repairs and improvements (up to $7,500) without any more permits than needed now;

(3) The Legislature *may* amend the act if necessary.

Your Yes Vote Enacts A Bill:

(1) Supported by more than 50 *Republican* and *Democratic* state legislators;

(2) Almost identical to legislation killed year after year by lobbyists in Sacramento;

(3) Modeled after the San Francisco Bay Conservation and Development Commission established by the Legislature in 1965, which has operated successfully to plan and manage the San Francisco Bay and its shoreline;

(4) Sponsored by the California Coastal Alliance, a coalition of over 100 civic, labor, professional and conservation organizations.

Vote Yes to Save the Coast

John V. Tunney
United States Senator
Donald L. Grunsky
State Senator
(R — Santa Cruz, Monterey, San Luis Obispo and San Benito Counties)
Bob Moretti
Assemblyman
Speaker — California State Assembly

REBUTTAL TO ARGUMENT IN FAVOR OF PROPOSITION 20

The proponents' Argument for Proposition 20 is a textbook example of circumvention of the facts.

It is filled with such misleading statements as "protection of California's beaches from exploitation by the corporate land grab"; "stop our beaches from becoming the exclusive playground of the rich"; "this act will not impose a moratorium"; "give the people direct participation in planning."

The truth is that the only "land grab" is that planned by the proponents of Proposition 20, who have devolved a scheme for appropriating private property without paying for it.

The truth is that Proposition 20 would make beach lands a haven for the rich who have already developed "exclusive playgrounds." The foremost motivation of the Initiative's elitist proponents is to preclude the enjoyment of coastal areas by retired and working people.

The truth is that Proposition 20 would, as a practical matter, establish a two to four year moratorium on virtually all building in the coastal area, including development for recreational purposes. The result would be a sharp reduction in land values, assessments and local tax collections which would create a severe economic depression in every one of the 15 coastal counties.

The truth is that people would have no direct participation in planning, which would be the sole prerogative of super-State and regional agencies composed of appointed commissioners.

Proposition 20 is discriminatory legislation and should be roundly defeated so that the people's elected representatives can get on with the job of completing sensible environmental and zoning controls over California's coastline.

James S. Lee, President
State Building and Construction
Trades Council of California

George Christopher
Former Mayor of San Francisco

John J. Royal
Executive Secretary Treasurer
Fisherman's & Allied Workers
Union, ILWU

ARGUMENT AGAINST PROPOSITION 20

Proposition 20 on the November 7 ballot represents bad government for all Californians. Proposition 20 is bad because it takes government from the hands of the voters.

In the name of coastal protection, Proposition 20 would impose an appointed, not elected, super-government to control the destinies of almost 3½ million people who live near and over 1 million who work close to our ocean shore.

California's 1,087 mile coastline is not endangered.

The State's official Comprehensive Ocean Area Plan, which has inventoried the total coastal area, shows that 74% of the land is in open space, 65.1% is undeveloped in any way, and 54% is already in public ownership.

Proposition 20 is a power grab — and a land grab — by those who would by-pass the democratic process.

It would substitute for that process the judgment of a vast new bureaucracy and appointive commissioners largely representative of a single purpose point of view.

It is on the ballot because its sponsors have ignored all reasonable efforts by the State, by local government, by labor, by business and civic organizations to develop an orderly land management policy for California through the legislative and regulatory process.

These are the traditional processes and they are working.

A recent State-adopted plan for ocean waste discharges, for example, will cost $770 million — about $5.70 a year for every Californian — but the plan was approved in democratic fashion.

Yet the sponsors of Proposition 20 would lock up California's coastline for at least three years, and probably forever.

The results of Proposition 20 if it should pass include:

• Loss of $25,750,000 in tax revenues annually as values in the coastal zone are reduced and assessments dropped, thus forcing higher taxes on coastal counties, cities and school districts.

• Loss of millions of dollars and thousands of jobs in needed development projects, jobs especially important to racial and economic minorities in the construction industry.

• Delay of needed oceanfront and beach recreational projects because of the measure's disastrous fiscal implications to the State as a whole.

• Loss of local control and local voice in local affairs.

• Threat of increased power shortages and possible brownouts because of delays in construction of new power generating plants.

• Loss of property rights through inverse condemnation without compensation as private land use is denied but properties are not purchased by government.

Even more important if Proposition 20 passes, what's next?

Will the elitists who would grab our coastline for their own purposes then be after our mountains, our lakes and streams, our farmlands? And at what cost?

Nowhere in the planning principles set forth in Proposition 20 are the words "economy" or "economies" used once.

If the people of California want statewide land planning such planning must apply equally to all areas of the State, not just the coast. The federal government, the California Legislature, state and local government plus regulatory agencies are ready to complete the job.

Proposition 20 would halt that effort.

Don't lock up California's coastside.

Vote NO on Proposition 20.

James S. Lee, President
State Building & Construction
Trades Council of California

George Christopher
Former Mayor of San Francisco

John J. Royal
Executive Secretary Treasurer
Fisherman's & Allied Workers
Union, ILWU

REBUTTAL TO ARGUMENT AGAINST PROPOSITION 20

The *real* opponents of the Coastline Initiative — the oil industry, real estate speculators and developers, and the utilities — are primarily concerned with profits, not the public interest. Their arguments are simply *not* true.

• Every government study, every scientific report, every trip to the beach proves that our beaches ARE endangered.

• The public has been denied access to hundreds of miles of beaches and publicly owned tidelands by freeways, private clubs, residential and industrial developments.

• Two-thirds of California's estuaries and many of our beaches have been destroyed.

• Of California's 1072 miles of coast, 659 are privately owned; of the 413 miles publicly owned, only 252 are available for public recreation.

• Proposition 20 represents an open beach and public access policy for Californians now locked out from swimming, beach recreation, surf-fishing and skin diving.

•   The initiative process, the essence of democracy, gives the people this opportunity to enact themselves what unresponsive government has for years refused to do.

• Proposition 20 contains NO prohibition on the construction of power plants. Rather, it offers a sensible plan to determine *where* — not if — new plants may be built.

• *One-half* the membership of the six coastal commissions will be *locally elected officials.*

• The opponents claim revenue and job losses. These scare tactics have *no* basis in fact.

• Many labor unions, including the ILWU, Northern and Southern District Councils, are on record in support of the Coastline Initiative.

Vote YES on Proposition 20.
John V. Tunney
United States Senator
Donald L. Grunsky
State Senator
(R-Santa Cruz, Monterey, San Luis Obispo and San Benito Counties)
Bob Moretti
Assemblyman
Speaker — California State Assembly

SECTION B. THE COMMISSIONS AND THE FINAL PLAN

The commissions created by the Coastal Initiative had responsibility for granting interim permits for coastal development during a planning period. In the first two years, the applications for permits totaled 11,501. Of these, 453 cases or about 5 percent were denied. Most of the denials were appealed to the state commission and about half were granted upon appeal. The very existence of the commissions has, according to some observers, discouraged application for permits by many potential developers.

The commissions were mandated to prepare a "comprehensive enforceable coastal plan for the long range conservation and management of the natural resources of the coastal zone." The plan has developed out of the permit process. Each applicant for a permit raised issues that were incorporated into the final plan. According to State Commission Chairman Melvin Lane, "it is the permit granting function that keeps an agency vital and realistic in the planning arena." The final plan was submitted to the legislature in December 1975. It is supposed to serve as a guide for resolving controversies over coastal land use, and it establishes a state commission charged with seeing that local governments administer coastal land in a fashion consistent with the general plan.

The final plan gives limited responsibility back to the local governments. The plan emphasizes administration above politics by substituting rules and guidelines for political bodies. This faith in the expert administrator is a traditional aspect of the regulatory process and has come to be characteristic of the planning process. Those who put their faith in planning above politics have looked to experts in law, social science, or biological science, and to a variety of other "knowledgeable" people for rational rather than political decisions. Criticism of the reliance on administration is contained in the statement from the Planning and Conservation League. The implications of resolution of problems in line with technical considerations are suggested by the San Diego Supervisors' discussion of the need to expand a coastal power plant. Whatever the outcome, leaving matters to the experts would eliminate the unique opportunity for citizen participation in the planning process that has been afforded by the regional commissions.

The final decision concerning the mechanism for coastal protection will be made by the California legislature. Thus, the effort stimulated by a coalition of citizen groups will culminate in a decision by the body whose inaction led to the initiative in the first place. Citizen action resulted in an electoral mandate and the development of a plan. Both factors are likely to influence the framework within which coastal decision making will be undertaken in the future.

PUTTING THE COMMISSIONS INTO OPERATION

The next segment of Norman Sanders' article provides an introduction to the decisions that gave life to the commissions. His report on the staffing of the commissions is followed by a presentation given by Joseph Bodovitz, the then recently appointed Executive Director of the California Coastal Commission, to a national conference on organizing and managing the coastal zone. Bodovitz raises a number of issues bearing on the process of change in the handling of land. He emphasizes the nature of administration as a professional task and the role of citizen participation in policy making. There is implicit recognition on the part of this "planner" that the planning process will be increasingly dominated by professionals.

Staffing the Commissions

THE NEW TIDE [continued]

Coastal commissions monitor the operation of the act. The 15 coastal counties are divided into six regional districts, each of which has a commission of 12 members. Six of the members are public and six are representatives of local government, elected by local governmental bodies themselves. The public members are appointed as follows: two by the governor, two by the speaker of the Assembly, and two by the Senate Rules Committee. The system looks unwieldy, and it is, but it is an attempt to break

SOURCE: Norman Sanders, "The New Tide of Coastal Legislation," *The Sierra Club Bulletin*, Vol. 58, No. 2 (February 1973).

the hammerlock that industry has had on appointments handed out by the governor alone. In addition to the regional commissions, a state commission exists to oversee the operation, including the actual planning process. The state commission also has 12 members, six public appointees and six delegates elected by the regional commissions.

Coastal Alliance victory celebrations didn't last long after the election. While the citizens were congratulating themselves on a job well done, the "No on 20" group was lining up its appointees to the commissions. Lobbying was intense in the state capital and local government offices. The Standard Oil Company prepared a blacklist of well-known environmentalists who would be unwelcome to them as public members on commissions. They also presented another collection of names more to their liking — for example, university professors who had worked as consultants for the oil companies and utilities.

The Los Angeles City Council set the tone for local government shortly after the election by appointing Councilman Louis Nowell, an outspoken enemy of Proposition 20, to the regional commission. *The Los Angeles Times* responded with an outraged editorial and environmentalists immediately set out to defeat Nowell in the 1973 city elections. The time is passing when local governments can operate in a self-created vacuum.

These "last hurrahs" for the vested interests took place on other parts of the coast. In Santa Barbara County, the lame-duck board of supervisors elected Supervisor Curtis Tunnell to the regional commission. Tunnell, who also opposed the proposition, represents the smallest area of Santa Barbara coastline, and is himself a building contractor. When he was elected to the commission, developers, contractors and representatives of the Southern California Edison Company actually cheered and applauded in the board's meeting room. They normally work behind the scenes, but came out in the open after seeing the handwriting on the wall: The 1973 board of supervisors won't be under their control in Santa Barbara County because the people elected two new representatives on November 7, both environmentally oriented and pledged to support Proposition 20.

California's Proposition 20 campaign built upon itself with a positive feedback effect. As the issue became widely publicized, people started taking more interest in what was happening to their own surroundings. They got involved not only in the Proposition 20 battle, but also in local election issues. This increasing public interest swept environmentalists into a number of county and city offices in many parts of the state. These new, responsible members of local government, backed by the people and armed with legislation such as the Coastal Zone Conservation Act, can do much to halt the rapid deterioration of California's quality of life. . . .

THE COASTAL ZONE: PROBLEMS, PRIORITIES, AND PEOPLE

JOSEPH E. BODOVITZ

As of today, the seven commissions are all fully at work. They are meeting regularly, in some cases as often as one long day a week (from 9 A.M. until after midnight in some instances). The work thus far has been largely processing permit applications and claims of exemption (from those who believe their projects were sufficiently under construction to be completed without a commission permit).

But important as the permit work is, the main responsibility of the commissions is to prepare a plan. And while the planning principles I will suggest below were developed in response to the new California law, I believe they are applicable to at least some extent to coastal zone planning anywhere.

Let me therefore proceed to discuss coastal zone planning:

1. *Decisions, Not Research.* At the outset, there are semantic problems with the word "planning." It means different things to different people. In fact, many kinds of "plans" have already been prepared — by private property owners, by local governments, and by many State and Federal agencies. And many proposals for additional research have been made to assist further planning. But important as further research may be, and good as some of the existing plans on specific topics may be, what is most needed now is a set of comprehensive policy decisions about the future of the coastal zone, in effect, a constitution for the coastline. This is particularly true in the case of a commission with a limited life: obviously, further studies and further decisions will be needed after the commission expires, but equally obviously, the commission can, in even a limited time, set a basic policy direction for the coastal zone. Further research will help solve some problems, but I believe we already know more about the coastal zone than we've thus far been willing to act upon. If, for example, we know that a certain part of the coastal zone has a great potential for landslides and contains active earthquake faults, how much more study do we require before we suggest that such areas are unsuitable for many types of building?

2. *The Public Interest in the Coastal Zone.* One requirement of the Cali-

Source: Text of a talk given by Joseph E. Bodovitz, Executive Director California Coastal Zone Conservation Commission, at the Conference on Organizing and Managing the Coastal Zone, U.S. Naval Academy, Annapolis, Maryland, 13–14 June 1973.

fornia law is that the commissions draw up "a precise, comprehensive definition of the public interest in the coastal zone." There is, of course, no simple definition: it's the competing, conflicting desires of the many "publics" that necessitate planning (i.e., decisions) for the coastal zone. Most of us want a healthy economy *and* a healthy environment — not one or the other — and the public interest consists of both. Defining the goal is not difficult; achieving it is. Most of us want the lights to go on when we turn the switch, but we dislike looking at electric transmission lines, especially if they block the view of the beach; we dislike the air pollution from a fossil-fuel power plant; and we are still uneasy about nuclear power plants. Most of us want the freedom to drive our cars wherever we want to go, but we're dubious about new "superports" to bring us oil and worried about the air and water quality problems of refineries. Most of us want unspoiled beaches, and uncrowded as possible, but we don't know what to do about beach access problems of parking and traffic.

So, it seems to me, we need to assemble the facts we have on these and the many other coastal zone concerns, make the most intelligent guesses we can in areas where the facts aren't as complete as we would like, and then make some decisions. For example, what provision should be made for power plants in the coastal zone? Should they be prohibited? Encouraged? Allowed with strict environmental safeguards? If so, what safeguards? . . . And, perhaps as difficult a question as there is, what is the biological "carrying capacity" of the coastal zone? What is the proper density or intensity of development in the coastal zone? Is there something inherently good about a neighborhood of small homes near the beach, allowing a relatively small number of people to enjoy the pleasures of the ocean, and something inherently bad about a neighborhood of big apartment and condominium buildings, allowing a larger number to live near the ocean?

3. *Change in the Coastal Zone.* If I were asked to suggest two books as indispensable reading for coastal zone planners, one of them would be Alvin Toffler's *Future Shock* (I'll mention the other in a moment). *Future Shock* describes the stresses and disorientations that tend to affect us all because of the rapidity with which our world changes. Obviously, I do not know what was in the minds of the 4.3 million Californians who voted for our State's coastal zone law, but I suspect that one major factor was the rapidity of change. There's the bluff or beach that a short time ago afforded a magnificent ocean view and now has a motel on it. Or the oceanfront area of older, smaller homes and apartments, where people of modest income could live near the water, and where now, seemingly overnight, builders have bid up the price of land, torn down the older homes, and put up larger, more expensive buildings, completely changing the character of the neighborhood, perhaps for the better, perhaps not.

The main point here, however, is not change in the past but change in the future. It's tempting to plan for the coastal zone as we know it now, in part because it's hard enough to assess what's been happening in recent years, much less to try to project what will happen in even another few years. But a plan that's outdated before it's off the presses is going to be of little value, and thus we will have to try to make some predictions about the future. One example should be sufficient on this point: who can yet assess the impact of the energy situation on the coastal zone (or, indeed, on all of American society)? Can anyone doubt that questions of energy will greatly occupy the attention of all coastal zone planners from *now on?*

4. *The Changing Concept of Land.* The second book I'd recommend for coastal zone planners is *The Quiet Revolution in Land Use Control* prepared for the Council on Environmental Quality by two Chicago lawyers, Fred Bosselman and David Callies. This book analyzes some of the innovative land use laws in the nation, to try to see what is being done in areas of great environmental importance. The authors conclude that:

This country is in the midst of a revolution in the way we regulate the use of our land. It is a peaceful revolution, conducted entirely within the law. It is a quiet revolution, and its supporters include both conservatives and liberals. It is a disorganized revolution, with no central cadre of leaders, but it is a revolution nonetheless . . . . The tools of the revolution are new laws taking a wide variety of forms but each sharing a common theme — the need to provide some degree of state or regional participation in the major decisions that affect the use of increasingly limited supply of land.

And, says this report:

If one were to pinpoint any single predominant cause of the quiet revolution it is a subtle but significant change in our very concept of the term "land," a concept that underlies our whole philosophy of land use regulation. "Land" means something quite different to us now than it meant to our grandfather's generation. Its new meaning is hard to define with precision, but it is not hard to illustrate the direction of the change. Basically, we are drawing away from the 19th century idea that land's only function is to enable its owner to make money . . . .

Conservationists describe the changing attitude toward land by saying that land should be considered a *resource* rather than a *commodity.* But while this correctly indicates the direction of the change, it ignores the crucial importance of our constitutional right to own land and to buy and sell it freely. It is essential that land be treated as *both* a resource and a commodity. The right to move throughout the country and buy and sell land in the process is an essential element in the mobility and flexibility our society needs to adjust to the rapid changes of our times. Conservationists who view land only as a resource are ignoring the social and economic impact that would come with any massive restrictions on the free alienability of land. But land speculators who view land only as a commodity are ignoring the growing public realization that our finite supply of land can no longer be dealt with in the freewheeling ways of our frontier heritage.

5. *Permits and Planning.* This may be a matter at present unique to the California law, but combining planning with temporary regulation of development is worth discussing for two reasons: (a) because temporary controls can allow much development to proceed while also insuring that planning options are kept open, and (b) because the plan itself will be better if the same commission members who vote on planning policies are also voting on permit applications. The controversy over a permit proposal can be an excellent education in planning issues for commission members, commission staff, and public alike. For example, one of the many issues before our California commissions now is the appropriate density of housing development in coastal areas. The planners could do their best to make their statistics and presentations lively, but it's hard to imagine that they could have a greater impact than the clash at a commission meeting between the builder with plans for a new development and the neighbors who oppose it.

6. *Policy Planning, One Element at a Time.* The science of ecology has taught us that we should take a comprehensive look at the web of life in the coastal zone, that we should know the ramifications of what we do — the environmental impact of each major proposal. At the same time, however, one of the lessons from much of the land and water planning of recent years is that comprehensive plans with their long summaries and multiple appendices are rarely understood by the public and infrequently adopted by the decision-makers. So, necessity virtually dictates that effective planning be done one element at a time. This approach enables tentative decisions to be developed, subject to further review as additional elements are considered. This was the approach in the successful planning program conducted by the San Francisco Bay Conservation and Development Commission, which considered 25 separate planning elements, from the need to protect marshlands to the need for adequate port facilities. Each topic was studied, with expert consultants contributing to the studies. The goal, however, was not a research report but the assembling of information on which to make decisions. Then the commissioners were asked not to adopt the report of the consultant, but rather to focus on the policy questions, and to adopt findings and policies on each topic.

For example, the *findings* on marshlands emphasized their great productivity, the significance of the loss of valuable marshlands through past diking and filling, and the need to protect the remaining marshland to insure the biological productivity of the Bay. The *policies* on marshlands stated that further filling or diking should be allowed only for purposes providing major public benefits, and only if the same benefits could not be achieved elsewhere without the diking or filling. Moreover, the policies required that all proposed diking and filling projects be evaluated as to their effect on marsh areas, and modified wherever possible to reduce any adverse impact . . . .

7. *Public Involvement.* Another advantage of step-by-step planning is that public involvement is both easier to obtain and more satisfying for all concerned. I recognize that many people believe otherwise, but I think there is limited value to a planning approach in which the experts do their work perhaps not in an ivory tower, such towers being relatively hard to find in our increasingly plastic age, but at least safely screened from the nosy public. Then, with fanfare, the plan is unveiled: a thick book with nice graphics, accompanied by a foot-high pile of back-up studies. At the initial public hearing the first 10 speakers say that they haven't had time to digest the plan, but have gotten indigestion from what they've read thus far. And it's steadily downhill from there on, concluding with hasty efforts to salvage what can be salvaged.

The step-by-step approach, emphasizing decisions on policies, allows everyone — commission members, other governmental agencies, and the public — to deal with one issue at a time (such as, for example, recreation in the coastal zone), try to resolve it, and then go on to the next, recognizing that the policies thus adopted are tentative, subject to further review when all the steps have been completed. The result is more concentration on each issue, more opportunity to hammer out acceptable solutions, and, of great importance, more understanding and support for the solutions thus arrived at.

This whole subject is, as you can see, one of great importance to us because, as I've mentioned, our commissions are temporary. Their plan will be tested in the legislative arena in early 1976. Unless our plan and the proposals in it have substantial public support, the plan can scarcely be successful.

The passage of Proposition 20 does not solve the problems of the California coastal zone. Rather, it provides a mechanism — 7 commissions — by which these problems can be studied, evaluated, and hopefully, made the subject of reasonable recommendations.

THE ENCINA POWER PLANT CONTROVERSY

The next four documents concern interest group and local government consideration of a request for a permit from the California Coastal Commission. They have been included to provide examples of the sort of arguments and positions taken by these groups. The arguments presented by interest groups in this instance have been crucial to the substantive development of a final plan since they indicated the sorts of problems faced in coastal planning during the operation of the commissions. Here, the matter is air quality along the coast. As in all instances, there is a tradeoff between the environmental benefits and other costs. In the case presented here — a request for power plant expansion — the threat is of inadequate sources of power for the region. Opponents of the expansion offer alternatives to power company policies in order to lessen the impact of the "cost" argument for expansion. Such claims are a crucial aspect of environmental politics especially in matters of energy policy. The peak load pricing scheme has come up in the issue of nuclear power plant development and in the plans for new construction of plants in relatively unspoiled areas such as southern Utah, the proposed site of a mammoth coal-powered generating plant to serve southern California.

The selection from local government symbolizes the important interests that these institutions have in the planning process. Traditionally the sole arbiters of the sort of planning that the Coastal Commissions have undertaken, the County Boards of Supervisors represent powerful interests who feel they have been bypassd as a result of the planning mechanism instituted by Proposition 20. Their political clout will again be felt when the legislature of California considers the means for making future planning decisions.

The permit process as set up by the regional commissions is seen by professional planners as a rather amateur operation. Such an assessment reveals their preference for professional standards and guidelines. The power plant case indicates the traditional reliance of regulatory agencies such as the Public Utilities Commission on the information presented to them by the institutions that they are supposed to regulate. That such a situation might ensue with the elimination of the regional commissions is a concern expressed in the debate on the Preliminary Plan in the next section.

In the case of the Encina Power Plant, the permit was approved after going all the way to the State Commission. Some stipulations were made by the city of Carlsbad on the height of the plant's smokestacks.

STATEMENT TO THE CALIFORNIA COASTAL COMMISSION *re* PROPOSED EXPANSION OF THE ENCINA POWER PLANT BY SAN DIEGO GAS AND ELECTRIC COMPANY

LEAGUE OF WOMEN VOTERS OF SAN DIEGO COUNTY

The League of Women Voters of San Diego County based its statement opposing SDG&E's request for a permit to construct Encina Generating Unit 5 on League positions relative to the issues of air quality and need. I believe our statement is in your packet and I refer you to it; we discuss at some length the conservation issues and whether the "need" for the addition has really been fully proved.

One word about air quality: San Diego, as staff points out, is a critical air basin, with a potential because of topography, meteorology, and weather patterns, for worse pollution than the South Coast Air Basin. What has not been said is that the north San Diego coastal area, where the Encina plant is located, has recorded the very worst NOx [nitrous oxide] and particulate readings in the entire San Diego basin. Strong suspicion exists that on our worst smog days, the pollution is entering the county from the North. For this reason, addition of any stationary source emitter in San Diego County should not be located in the north coast area.

The rest of our statement was drawn up by Dr. Alan Schneider, Professor of Engineering Sciences at UCSD. The statement is presented with the full concurrence of the League, and amplifies some of the suggestions in our statement to the regional commission.

SOURCE: Presented to the California Coastal Commission by Pat Sharp on 13 May 1975 in Los Angeles, Calif.

STATEMENT TO CALIFORNIA COASTAL COMMISSION

ALAN M. SCHNEIDER

Peak-load pricing for electricity is a concept that is gaining favor among forward-looking utilities, regulatory agencies, consumer groups, and environmentalists, for it offers benefits to all of these groups. Our own State Public Utilities Commission has shown an interest in the concept, and has asked California electric utilities, starting with Pacific Gas and Electric, to engage in implementation studies. The basic idea behind peak-load pricing is to vary the cost to the consumer of a kilowatt hour of electricity with the time of the day and year, so that the costs are higher during periods of peak demand, and lower during periods, like the middle of the night, when demand is low. The concept is based on the economists' view that pricing should be based on considerations of marginal cost. The marginal cost of producing a unit of electrical energy in off-peak hours is considerably less than during peak hours with respect to both the variable and the fixed costs of the firm.

One of the responses that a consumer can make to a peak-load pricing regimen is to shift his load to an off-peak hour. For example, a householder could put a timer on the electric clothes dryer which would turn it on at 5 A.M., rather than running at 10 A.M. or 5 P.M. as may be the current practice. Over time, the consumers of electricity would be encouraged to acquire energy-efficient capital plant and consumer durables whose loads can be shifted away from peak periods of demand.

The consumers who shift their demand away from the peak hours will change the peak-load requirements for the utility (San Diego Gas and Electric, in this case). Since utility load demand forecasts are geared to peak demand requirements, cutting off peak-load demand will postpone the need for building a new addition to the Encina plant.

If SDG&E were to go to a peak-demand pricing system, with the approval of the PUC, the company would find that they would use their existing plant more efficiently, and would be able to serve a larger total

Source: Text of a statement included with material presented by the League of Women Voters on 13 May 1975 to *California Coastal Commission* in Los Angeles, Calif. Alan M. Schneider, Sc. D., is Professor of Engineering Sciences, Department of Applied Mechanics and Engineering Sciences, University of California at San Diego; Member, Attorney General's Task Force on Pollution, San Diego/Orange Counties; Member, Comprehensive Planning Organization's Technical Resource Panel for Air Quality. (Affiliations for reference only; no official position of the organizations is implied.)

demand without exceeding their peak capacity. This would benefit the company, whose cash position would improve, because their capital funding requirements will have been postponed. It will help the company's stockholders, since sales can be increased without increasing investment. The consumer will benefit; getting more total electricity from the existing plant will ultimately lead to lower prices. The consumer who can shift his load to off-peak hours benefits by lower prices immediately.

The environment will also benefit. SDG&E claims that they will be able to reduce pollution by building Encina 5, because it enables them to use the newer, more efficient boilers more of the time. Precisely the same advantage accrues to the environment *without* building Encina 5, if peak-load pricing is adopted. Adoption of peak-load pricing gives the added advantage of not building any more stacks, or any 400 foot stacks.

Finally, a savings in energy will be realized with peak-load pricing, since a bigger proportion of the total load will be carried by the newer, more efficient plants.

Since everyone stands to gain from peak-load pricing — the company, the consumer, and the environment — it seems reasonable that the permit to enlarge Encina 5 should be denied in favor of this alternate strategy.

LETTER TO THE BOARD OF SUPERVISORS
FROM LEE R. TAYLOR

County of San Diego Board of Supervisors
1600 Pacific Highway, San Diego, California 92101
April 16, 1975

Honorable Board of Supervisors
County of San Diego
Room 335, County Admin. Center
San Diego, California 92101

Gentlemen:

On April 15, 1975, my office submitted Item No. 60 on our regular Agenda relating to the San Diego Coast Regional Commission's decision not to allow the San Diego Gas and Electric Company to build a fifth unit at its power plant complex in Carlsbad. This item was withdrawn at my request.

SOURCE: Reprinted with permission of Lee R. Taylor and the County of San Diego, Calif.

The reason for this withdrawal centered around the recent Attorney General's ruling to not allow a rescheduling of the matter before the San Diego Coast Regional Commission for reconsideration.

As stated in my April 9, 1975, letter to our Board, in my estimation this action by the Coast Commission was ill advised and will have serious adverse impacts on thousands of residents of San Diego County by subjecting them to a real threat of intermittent blackouts in the near future. This decision has been appealed by SDG&E and will be scheduled for consideration before the State Coastal Commission in the near future. The most significant issue at this hearing will again involve the need for the 292 megawatt power plant. The Public Utilities Commission, who in the State of California is charged with the regulation of such matters, after lengthy public hearings concurred with SDG&E that a need does exist for an additional unit if that Company is to maintain its reliability and adequate level of service in the late 1970's. It is inconceivable that the San Diego Coast Regional Commission would entertain the idea that this plant should be built at the Sycamore Canyon site and subsequently oppose the plant at Carlsbad because need was not justified. It is apparent that the use of an existing site with all its existing facilities is far more sensible from a land use standpoint than having a new power plant installation and ancillary fuel oil tanks, power lines, etc., constructed in a new area.

[That] the proposed new unit at Encina with higher efficiency ratings will save 600,000 barrels, or 25 million gallons of oil per year, with a commensurate reduction of total emissions in the San Diego air basin which will provide an obvious improvement of ambient air quality for the City of Carlsbad should also have been a major consideration. These positive aspects are attributed to the high efficiency design of the Encina Unit 5 proposal and in my estimation would far outweigh those negative impacts attributed to increased thermal pollution and the installation of a 400 foot stack to replace four lower stacks currently extant which incidentally is considered necessary to reduce emissions to an acceptable air pollution control standard.

Certainly the City of Carlsbad should have been given consideration in this decision. The proposed new unit which lies in the jurisdictional boundaries of that City is on file as a portion of an approved specific plan which was acted on by that City in 1971.

Additionally, I am also seriously concerned with the potential cost to the County of San Diego and its Cities for backup systems for emergency services such as police, fire, medical (hospitals), and environmental controls (sewage pumping stations, chemical disposal, water filtration), which may result from rolling blackouts.

The seriousness of these potential impacts directly related to this marginal decision (7 "yes", 3 "no"), leads me to recommend to our Board that we take a position in support of SDG&E's appeal to the State Coastal Commision in favor of approval of the Unit 5 expansion of the Encina power plant.

Respectfully submitted,

Lee R. Taylor

Supervisor, 5th District

MINUTES OF THE MEETING OF THE BOARD OF SUPERVISORS AND RECORD OF THE VOTE ON THE MOTION BY LEE TAYLOR, MAY 15, 1975

This being the time set for consideration of the pending matter of Vice Chairman Taylor's recommendation that the Board take a position in support of the San Diego Gas & Electric Company appeal to the State Coastal Commission in favor of approval of the Unit 5 expansion of the Encino Power Plant, Board Order No. 90, May 13, 1975, the matter is now called up.

Representatives of the San Diego Gas & Electric Company, introduced by Art Bishop, orally review, with certain visual aids, the proposed Unit 5 expansion program, particularly the air pollution, environmental and future need issues; and point out that the requested permit is for a five-year period and therefore would be back for review before the Coastal Commission by 1981.

W. Bradley, representing the City of San Marcos, requests that he be recorded as being in favor of the proposed expansion.

Scott Harvey, Construction Industry Coordinating Council, also requests to be recorded in favor of the proposed expansion.

Thomas A. Crandall, Executive Director of the San Diego Coast Regional Commission, reviews the reasons the Commission has denied the requested permit and further amplifies those specific areas which the Commission considers problem areas.

There is discussion relative to the background studies that have been made on the proposal; other site possibilities; air pollution ratings; the proposed height of the tower and other esthetic concerns; savings of fuel oil; development of Agua Hedionda Regional Park; effect on the lagoon and ocean habitat; and whether, in fact, this expansion was really needed to supply energy for the future; and the Board takes the following action:

. . .

On motion of Supervisor Conde, seconded by Supervisor Taylor, the Board takes a position in support of the San Diego Gas & Electric Company appeal to the State Coastal Commission in favor of approval of Unit 5 expansion of the Encina power plant.

Roll call on the foregoing motion results in the following vote: AYES: Supervisors Brown, Conde, and Taylor; NOES: Supervisor Walsh; Absent: Supervisors None; Supervisor Bates is out of the room when the roll is called.

DEVELOPING A FINAL PLAN

The proponents of the initiative set limits on their own action by instituting a procedure by which the legislature would make the ultimate determination of the ongoing operation of the planning mechanism. The following proposal was made in the spring of 1975. It initiated a series of public hearings to consider the final plan to be presented to the state legislature. The testimony on the preliminary plan reveals the concerns about the formulation of the proposal to the legislature. The preliminary plan presented a number of alternatives for the implementation of the comprehensive plan. But with the publication of this document, it became clear that the regional commissions, which had shut local government out of the planning process, would be much less significant. Such a move was considered to be essential if the plan was to gain the approval of the state legislature.

The Preliminary Coastal Plan

Selections from the Commissions' Report, Spring 1975

The Preliminary Coastal Plan has now been published. It is summarized in this report and we seek your views on it. You may send comments in writing, and you may testify at public hearings that will be held this spring and summer . . . .

We particularly seek your views on two things: the Plan itself, with its recommendations for use and protection of the California coast; and the most effective governmental means of carrying out the Coastal Plan.

The Coastal Commissions must adopt their final recommendations this summer and fall, for presentation to the Governor and the Legislature in December 1975. This means that the Commissions must complete their work under a very tight deadline, and we therefore seek your response to the Preliminary Plan as soon as possible.

M. B. Lane
Chairman

A CONSTITUTION FOR THE COAST

No single plan can foresee all the problems or provide all the answers for the future of the California coast. But the Coastal Plan recommends basic rules to govern use and protection of the coastal zone now and in the future, and the Plan will, in its final version, recommend governmental means to enforce its policies and keep them current as circumstances change.

The Plan is, in short, intended to be a constitution for the coast.

The Coastal Plan is designed to achieve two objectives:

1. Protect the California coast as a great natural resource for the benefit of present and future generations.
2. Use the coast to meet human needs, but in a manner that protects the irreplaceable resources of coastal lands and waters.

MAJOR FINDINGS AND RECOMMENDATIONS

The essence of the Plan is that the coast should be treated not as ordinary real estate but as a unique place, where conservation and special kinds of development should have priority. The Plan's foundation is the fact that coastal resources are limited, and that meeting human needs while protecting the coast will require policies such as the following:

Public Use of the Coast

Public access to appropriate coastal areas should be provided. Coastal developments that serve the public — such as campgrounds, resorts, hotels and motels, rental housing, etc. — should have priority over coastal developments that are essentially private, such as typical residential developments.

Wetlands

Coastal marshes and other wetlands, many of which have been filled and diked in past years, should be protected from further destruction and restored where possible.

Agricultural Lands

Coastal lands suitable for agricultural production should be kept in agriculture, and tax policies should be changed to reduce pressures to convert such land to urban development.

Coastal Streams

Free-flowing coastal streams should be protected, because they are necessary for the migratory fish caught by commercial and sport fishermen and because they supply sand for coastal beaches.

Air Quality

Potentially polluting development in critical air quality areas should be allowed only if designed to prevent any significant degradation of coastal air quality.

Energy

The use of increasing amounts of coastal land and water to meet energy needs should be reduced by a vigorous program of energy conservation. Energy installations allowed on the coast must be subject to stringent environmental safeguards.

Transportation

Public transit should receive priority over roadway construction in urban areas, to reduce the need for coastal parking lots and major highway programs, to conserve energy, and to improve coastal air quality.

Hazards to Development

Development should only be permitted in hazardous areas, such as those subject to beach or cliff erosion, landslides, earthquakes, and flooding; if adequate engineering can reduce the hazards to acceptable levels.

Public Recreation

Public recreation should have the highest priority in suitable areas of the coast, and legal rights of the public to have access to publicly owned tidelands should be vigorously enforced. Public use of coastal lands and waters should be consistent with natural resource protection.

Concentrated Development

Where substantial new development would harm coastal resources and restrict public access to the oceanfront, new development should be channeled to the inland parts of coastal cities and to other inland areas. Public investment in roadways, water systems, sewer systems, and other such installations should be designed to concentrate development in existing communities (consistent with their ability to absorb it) and thus to end wasteful, sprawling development along the coast.

Cumulative Impact of Development

In areas where a few developments would not adversely affect coastal resources, but where the cumulative effect of many such developments over several years could be harmful, specific, detailed plans anticipating all such development should be prepared.

Coastal Viewshed and Scenic Areas

Designs for all development should be compatible with scenic areas and not be permitted to degrade areas of high scenic value.

Special Coastal Communities and Neighborhoods

New developments should be consistent with the unique cultural, historical, architectural, and aesthetic qualities of particular coastal communities and neighborhoods.

Highway 1

Highway 1 in rural areas should remain a two-lane highway primarily for recreational travel. A system of budgeting the remaining road capacity should be prepared and the remaining capacity should be allocated so that private residential and commercial development will not limit public recreational travel.

Public Ownership on Shoreline

The long-term goal (possibly 50 years away) of coastal planning and development should be public ownership of a strip of land paralleling the coast, except for ports, urban areas, etc. High priority for public land acquisition should be given to open space on urban waterfronts and to small lots in scattered ownership if their development would impede public access or mar coastal views.

Governmental Actions

The plans and operations of many Federal, State, and local agencies should be reviewed to better protect coastal resources.

CARRYING OUT THE PLAN

Any plan dealing with controversial matters will have lasting value only if it can be enforced. The California Coastal Act, therefore, requires that the Coastal Plan contain "recommendations for the governmental policies and powers required to implement the [plan] including the organization and authority of the governmental agency or agencies which should assume permanent responsibility for its implementation."

There are several ways, some more effective than others, by which the Coastal Plan can be carried out. The Preliminary Plan reaches no conclusions as to which way would be best. But after public hearings this spring, and after further review by the State and Regional Commissions, specific recommendations for carrying out the Coastal Plan will be made in the Commissions' final report to the Governor and the Legislature.

Criteria for Choice

Carrying out the Coastal Plan should involve governmental organizations that will:

- Encourage public participation in decisions affecting the future of the coast.
- Be visible, accessible, and accountable to the public.
- Protect both statewide and local interests in coastal conservation and development.
- Operate with efficiency and economy.
- Deal fairly with the diversity of interests and needs from one end of the state to the other.
- Adapt effectively to changing coastal conditions.

No governmental agency can achieve all these standards to the same degree at the same time. For example, an agency that provides for full public participation in decisions and for thorough hearings will have higher costs and longer processing times than an agency that does not. It is therefore necessary in evaluating governmental options to decide which of these criteria are paramount, and how to achieve a balance among them.

Major Alternatives

The principal ways of carrying out the Coastal Plan are the following:

1. *A Multi-Purpose State Agency.* A new State agency could be created, perhaps with regional divisions or components, not only to carry out the Coastal Plan but also to have major responsibilities in several related areas — perhaps statewide land use planning and regulation, transportation, energy supply and conservation, and control of air and water quality. Whatever the statewide benefits of the possible coordination of such programs, under this alternative coastal protection would not be likely to receive the high priority given it by the people of California with passage of the Coastal Initiative (Proposition 20) in 1972.

2. *A Single Statewide Coastal Agency.* Under this alternative there would be a single, statewide agency. There would be no regional components; without them, it would be difficult for such an agency to fully recognize and deal with the diversity of coastal areas. This alternative would probably require a commission of full-time members, thus excluding local government representation and perhaps reducing public participation.

3. *A State Coastal Agency with Regional Components.* This would be similar to the present State and Regional Coastal Commissions. One variation would be a single State Coastal Commission, with regional as well as statewide representatives, but with regional offices or divisions instead of Regional Commissions.

4. *No Coastal Agency.* Under this alternative, there would be no State coastal agency. Existing State departments (such as the Departments of Transportation, Fish and Game, and Parks and Recreation) would be directed to carry out the Coastal Plan policies within their areas of responsibility and the bulk of the responsibility would rest with local governments. The principal disadvantage of this alternative is that it lacks a comprehensive view of the coast: varying interpretations and applications of Coastal Plan policies could occur, with no agency responsible for insuring uniformity and consistency as the Plan is carried out. There is a further question as to whether this alternative could adequately deal with coastal issues of statewide (and in some cases national) importance, such as protection of agricultural lands, provision of major recreational areas, and siting of major energy facilities.

5. *Plan Implementation Primarily by Local Governments but with a State Coastal Agency.* Under this alternative most Plan policies would be carried out by local governments, but a State coastal agency would be

created (a) to continue the planning work necessary to keep the Coastal Plan up to date as conditions change, (b) to hear appeals from decisions of local governments challenged as being in conflict with the Coastal Plan, and (c) to protect statewide interest in coastal resources. There could be a single State coastal agency under this alternative, or a State agency with regional components. Further, there could be regional components (such as the present Regional Commissions) in existence for a short time, perhaps three years, to review local plans for conformity with the Coastal Plan.

Composition of Coastal Agency

If a State coastal agency is established, how should its members be chosen? Election would provide the greatest degree of public accountability, but running for a position on such an agency could involve high campaigning costs. If appointment is chosen, many points of view can be represented by having several appointing powers. If the coastal agency members serve at the pleasure of their appointing powers, they would be accountable to the elected officials who choose them. Members could serve either full-time or part-time. A full-time agency would allow for technical expertise on the part of its members; a part-time board would continue the tradition of citizen-commissioners, with expertise in staff and outside advisers.

Appeals

Under some of the governmental alternatives, decisions could be appealed to a coastal agency. The appeals system could be essentially as it is under the Coastal Act, or if it were desired to make appeals more difficult, fees or bonds could be required for filing appeals. On the other hand, under the present Coastal Act, the Coastal Commission may decline to hear appeals that raise no substantial issue, and this has worked well to promptly weed out unwarranted appeals. Another alternative is that one or more members of the coastal agency could be permitted to initiate an appeal; under the law governing the State Water Resources Control Board, a majority of that five-member board may, on its own motion, initiate a review of a decision of a Regional Water Quality Control Board.

Inland Boundary

How should the coastal zone be defined for purposes of carrying out the Coastal Plan? There is little doubt that the three-mile water area should be included, but how much land? One alternative is the entire extent of such coastal resources as coastal agricultural lands, or the coastal viewshed; this boundary would require careful mapping, and it would include areas many miles from the shoreline. Another alternative is to establish a readily identifiable, fixed boundary, such as the 1,000 yards in the present Coastal Act; this would include most areas of significant coastal impact, and provision could be made to exclude areas within this line where development would not adversely affect coastal resources.

Restoration

The Coastal Plan is required by law to provide for restoration of presently degraded coastal areas — damaged marshes and other wetlands, deteriorated urban areas, and poorly planned subdivisions and lots where the level of building has not been great and where combining lots for resubdivision would yield better development. Much restoration can be carried out by existing governmental agencies, but this will depend on the priority they give to it; some restoration will require work in several jurisdictions, however, and this could be done either by empowering the coastal regulatory agency to carry out restoration projects, or by establishing a special restoration agency for this purpose. Under any of these alternatives, the coastal regulatory agency could prepare annual recommendations for future projects similar to capital improvement programming by local governments.

Costs

The costs of carrying out the Coastal Plan are of two main types: (a) *administrative* costs (office expenses, salaries of coastal agency members and staff, postage, etc.) necessary to regulate the uses of land and water in accordance with the Coastal Plan and to keep the Plan up to date through further study and hearings; and (b) *acquisition and development* costs of acquiring wetlands, park lands, etc.

The level of administrative costs depends, of course, on the type of agency selected to carry out the Plan and the responsibilities given it. (One preliminary guide is the $2–2.5 million total annual cost of the present State and Regional Coastal Commissions for all their permit and planning work.) Similarly, acquisition and development costs will depend on the amount of land and water proposed for purchase, and the timing of purchases.

Review and evaluation of the Preliminary Plan's acquisition and development proposals will probably suggest some ranges for an annual spending level to be specified in the final Plan.

Sources of Funds

Possible sources of funds for carrying out the Coastal Plan include fees for processing permit applications, Federal grants under the Coastal Zone Management Act of 1972, State tax revenues, and a share of the income from any offshore petroleum production that would be allowed under the policies of the Coastal Plan.

PLANNING AT A TIME OF RAPID CHANGE

In the spring of 1975, as the Coastal Plan is being prepared, Californians are increasingly aware that the postwar era of seemingly endless abundance may be coming to an end. People know that natural resources are limited, that inflation is in part caused by wasteful use of land and other finite resources, that prime agricultural lands needed to feed the world's growing population should not be squandered on development that can be built elsewhere, and that the increasing cost of energy and of raw materials may result in major changes in the lives of Californians.

Moreover, there is increasing recognition that no society can long survive if it dissipates its resources recklessly, and that wasteful use of land and water is bound to be costly in the long run. Although it may be expensive to protect coastal resources, it may be even more expensive not to. The cost will come not only in the health hazards of polluted air and water, not only in the higher food, housing, and transportation costs that result from poor use of land and sprawling development, but also in a diminished overall quality of life. No plan can deal with every possible event that might occur over a period of many years, particularly if the years are ones of rapid change. But the Coastal Plan is designed to be just as useful during a time of scarcity as during a time of abundance: in either case, the careful use of limited coastal resources is essential if the coast is to be protected for future generations.

The following selection is from an interest group newsletter. The organization includes both business and labor interests concerned about the impact of environmentalism on the economy. The organization's name, as well as its careful use of the polling technique, indicates the extent to which ecological concerns have become legitimate. This group advocates an "equitable" solution, rather than attacking the coastal plan, which the group was formed to oppose.

COUNCIL SAMPLES VOTER ATTITUDES ON ENVIRONMENT AND ECONOMY

In January, 1975, the California Council for Environmental and Economic Balance commissioned a poll to determine the attitudes of California voters on a number of major environmental and economic issues. The poll, using representative sampling techniques, was taken statewide in late January and early February by Hugh Schwartz, Public Response Company, Sausalito, California. This issue of *Environment and the Economy* is devoted exclusively to the results of the poll.

Overall, California voters by a margin of better than 3 to 1, placed greater importance on job creation than on environmental protection. This was true regardless of voter residence, age, education, family income or political affiliation.

On specific environmental issues, a clear majority of voters favored increased oil exploration and offshore drilling; the expansion of nuclear power; supported further industrial development in their own community; and expressed a willingness to pay more for environmental protection. In regard to coastal development, however, public attitudes were less clear. Equal numbers of voters either supported further coastline building or indicated their opposition to any more coastal development, with one voter in four having no opinion on the subject.

The balance of this report gives the detailed results of the poll.

JOBS AND THE ENVIRONMENT

All respondents were asked the question "Generally, if you had to choose between creating more jobs and protecting the environment, which would you personally choose?" On a statewide basis 64 percent of the respondents chose "More Jobs," 20 percent chose "Protecting the Environment," and 16 percent chose "Neither" or declined to answer. While regional variations do not appear particularly significant, the preference for jobs was somewhat stronger in Southern than in Northern California. Also, this preference was greater among older voters and labor union members than among younger people and non-union members . . . .

SOURCE: Reprinted from *Environment and the Economy* (March 1975).

PRIORITY FOR JOBS

In another attempt to gauge public sentiment in terms of the often expressed dichotomy between jobs and the environment, all respondents were asked whether they agreed or disagreed with the statement "I think that keeping people working should be given priority over all but the most serious environmental concerns." Statewide 73 percent agreed with this statement. In contrast, only 15 percent disagreed. Among particular groups, persons 30 years of age and under and college graduates tended to be in greater disagreement with the statement than did other groups in the poll . . . .

In addition to these general questions about jobs and the environment, the public was asked its views on some specific issues — oil exploration and offshore drilling; nuclear power; attitudes regarding the California coastline; feelings towards industrial development; and willingness to pay for environmental protection.

OIL EXPLORATION

The poll asked whether the respondents agreed or disagreed with the statement that "We should do anything we can to encourage oil companies to produce gasoline." A clear majority — 61 percent — agreed with the statement, while 23 percent of those polled did not. Among regions, strongest agreement was found in Los Angeles and Orange Counties while somewhat less agreement was found in Northern California. Younger voters and college graduates tended to be in less agreement with the statement than other groups of voters . . . .

To determine attitudes on offshore drilling the poll asked whether voters agreed or disagreed with the statement, "We should encourage oil companies to engage in offshore drilling in areas like the Santa Barbara Channel." Forty-eight percent of the voters said such drilling should occur; 33 percent disagreed; 19 percent were undecided or had no opinion. Regionally, the strongest support for offshore drilling was in Los Angeles and Orange Counties while the greatest opposition was found in the San Francisco Bay Area . . . .

NUCLEAR POWER

The question of whether nuclear power should be relied upon to meet a portion of California's electrical energy needs has received increased public attention in recent years. In an attempt to gauge public attitudes on nuclear power, the poll asked people to state whether they agreed or disagreed with the statement, "I'm against the building of nuclear reactors to provide a new energy source." At present voters seem to support nuclear power expansion by a margin of more than two to one.

Specifically, 25 percent of the voters agreed with the statement. In sharp contrast, 58 percent of those polled disagreed with the statement. Regionally, those in strongest disagreement resided in the Los Angeles–Orange Counties area and in the Sacramento–San Joaquin Valleys area.

Interestingly 58 percent of the persons who placed jobs ahead of environmental protection supported nuclear power, while 57 percent of those who placed the environment before jobs . . . also indicated support for nuclear power. Also, younger voters and the college educated were more in favor of nuclear power than were older voters and people with less education . . . .

COASTLINE

California voters seem to perceive the issue of development somewhat differently along the coast than they do in the state as a whole. The poll asked whether those surveyed agreed or disagreed with the statement, "I think that the State and Regional Coastal Commissions should stop entirely any type of construction along the California Coastline."

Twenty-one percent of the respondents strongly agreed with the statement and another seventeen percent somewhat agreed. In contrast, sixteen percent strongly disagreed and another twenty-one percent disagreed somewhat. The balance — twenty-five percent or one voter in four — neither agreed nor disagreed. Clearly, on a statewide basis those who believe in further coastal development and those who wish no more building are equally divided, with one-fourth of the electorate, at this moment, in neither camp.

Regional variations are particularly interesting. The strongest agreement that there should be no further coastal development was found among voters in the Sacramento–San Joaquin Valleys. Conversely, Los Angeles–Orange Counties voters were more strongly pro-development than those of other regions . . . .

INDUSTRIAL DEVELOPMENT

The poll asked whether people agreed or disagreed with the statement, "To reduce taxes, we need industries in this immediate area." Forty-four percent agreed with the statement; twenty-nine percent disagreed. The balance were undecided . . . . Thus, it appears that among voters who have an opinion the majority favors industrial development, even in their immediate residential area.

PAYING FOR ENVIRONMENTAL PROTECTION

The poll attempted to determine in a general way whether voters would support some increased public expenditures for environmental improvements. Surprisingly, to some, it appears there is public support for modest additional governmental expenditures in this area.

The question was asked do you agree or disagree with the statement "If we need a slight tax increase to preserve the environment, I would go along with the increase." Fifty percent agreed, totally or partially, with the statement; thirty-six percent disagreed, partially or totally. Most in support were persons 30 years of age and under and college graduates. Least in support were people over the age of 50, those with some college education and labor union members . . . .

PROFILE OF THE RESPONDENTS

One-half of those polled were men. Regarding ethnic background, seventy-eight percent were white; twelve percent Spanish surname; eight percent Black; and two percent Asian. Twenty-five percent were union members; seventy-four percent were not (one percent declined to answer.)

Regarding education attainment, eight percent completed grade school or less; twelve percent some high school, seventy-six percent were high school graduates; thirty-one percent completed some college; nineteen percent were college graduates; and four percent did not respond or gave an incomplete answer.

CONCLUSION

Based on the results of this poll, California voters support job creation, oil exploration and offshore drilling, nuclear power and industrial development, while regarding whether the coastline should be further developed opinions appear equally divided.

The Response from the Planning and Conservation League

TESTIMONY OF THE COASTAL PLAN TASK FORCE, PLANNING AND CONSERVATION LEAGUE

The Planning and Conservation League is a citizens lobby which works for sound environmental legislation in Sacramento. We were one of the public interest environmental groups which supported and worked for the passage of Proposition 20 after years of trying to get similar legislation through the state Legislature.

The Task Force is in support of the substantive policies contained in the Preliminary Coastal Plan, and we think these policies, if carried out, would fulfill the mandate of Proposition 20.

For all of its bulk, what we have here are the barest outlines of a Plan. As your Commission has often said, it is a constitution for the coast.

And like the Constitution of our nation, it is what the people charged with interpreting it, say it is.

The vital question, therefore, is: Who is going to interpret this Coastal Constitution as it applies to the countless relevant decisions of state and local government, and what will be their mandate?

As the old, defeated coalition which originally opposed Proposition 20 regroups and gathers its strength, the importance of the question of implementation becomes clear.

PCL believes that if Proposition 20 is allowed to expire without a successor agency which would have the same or a stronger mandate for coastal protection — or if enforcement responsibility reverts solely to local governments, this whole exercise in balanced, comprehensive planning will be lost. The rush to exploit the coast will resume at a pace which will exceed that which originally brought on the citizens initiative to protect the coast.

This is the PCL position:

1. PCL accepts the principle of statewide comprehensive planning. Indeed, this was one of the founding principles of our organization 10 years ago.

2. PCL accepts eventual integration of coastal zone planning and protection with a new statewide system, providing that this does not result in a weakening of standards of protection embodied in the politics of this plan. Under this integration, the coastal commissions might eventually be

SOURCE: Testimony given at the California Coastal Zone Commission Public Hearings on the Preliminary Coastal Zone Plan. Torrance, Calif., 7 May 1975.

transformed into advisory bodies whose function would be to ensure permanent recognition of the basic mandate of Proposition 20: that the coastal zone is special — scenically, recreationally, and economically — and that the coast should have a high priority and a special position among all geographic areas, regardless of how statewide planning is eventually organized.

3. PCL has the strongest possible objection to allowing present coastal zone legislation to expire without a successor agency to proceed with implementation of the Plan, or, in the absence of action on the Plan by the state Legislature, continuation of present permit controls until the Plan is enacted.

We are opposed to making local governments and existing specialized agencies solely responsible for enforcing the Plan, according to their interpretation of it and according to their timetable. We endorse, however, the proposals which were put forward by the South Coast Commission and other regional commissions that local governments and specialized agencies would have primary responsibility for implementation of the Plan, under the supervision of a coastal agency.

Any proposal to give local governments sole authority for enforcing the Plan would be equivalent to returning the coastal zone to the status quo which the electorate of the State decisively rejected when they enacted Proposition 20.

Currently, many self-serving assertions are being made that this is exactly what the people want today. We don't believe it, and we think that another initiative election on the question of strong, statewide coastal protection would be enacted by voters even more decisively today.

4. PCL endorses the continuation of the present state coastal commission with the ultimate enforcement authority for the Coastal Plan until such time as its authority can be integrated into a statewide planning and implementation body which would have at least equal powers and mandate for enforcement of the Coastal Plan.

We think the present state commission has done a good job. On the whole, we think it has been fair to applicants and true to its charge. We think there would have to be a very good reason to tamper with this kind of success. Governing bodies are mainly people and their ideas. The clear and strong mandate of Proposition 20 was helpful. Perhaps the design of the commission and its appointing authorities were helpful. But we see no reason to take chances with different designs and different people, unless there is some compelling possibility for a major advance toward comprehensive statewide planning and environmental protection.

5. PCL endorses the continuation of the present regional coastal commissions with the present permit powers until local city and county plans and codes can be prepared and adopted, by both the regional and state com-

missions. At that time, we think permit powers should revert to local governments, and the regional commissions should be phased out. The State Commission should then be solely responsible for supervising individual local government decisions under the adopted subregional and local plans through a review authority. Citizens would have standing to appeal any local government decision to the State Commission within a reasonable fixed period of time, perhaps 30 days. Commissioners could individually initiate review of local government decisions. The State Commission could control the volume of appeals by applying the test of "substantial issue." The Commission would be authorized to designate hearing officers to deal with the volume of appeals.

We do not think it wise to designate a time certain for the phasing out of the regional commissions. We think local governments would have a valuable incentive to proceed expeditiously with the business of bringing their plans and codes into conformance with the State Coastal Plan if the approval of these plans and ordinances is tied to the end of the individual permit review of the regional commissions.

There is much to be done. Nobody ever said that planning the coastal zone would be easy. Nobody ever said that every competing economic interest would come out a winner when strong land and resource protection controls were put into effect by Proposition 20. As a matter of fact, the two annual reports of your Commission indicate that a very small proportion of permits have been denied. But the few applicants who have been denied, or have had to make concessions in order to get permits, are very unhappy. They would like to think everybody else in the State is just as unhappy. We think they are misleading themselves.

The implementation of Proposition 20 has brought us face to face with the hard choices that have to be made in mediating among intense competing claims on coastal zone resources. Your Commission has no friends among the losers. But it would be a mistake to assume that coastal zone protection has lost all its support among the millions of winners — the general public — whose claim to coastal zone resources had no effective champion until a citizens initiative created your Commission.

> Respectfully submitted,
> Mark Braly
> Chairman, PCL Coastal Plan Task Force

Public Hearing on the Preliminary Plan

The following selection is a summary of statements given by supporters and opponents of the preliminary plan at a public hearing. Although these statements represent only a tiny portion of the thousands of groups and citizens who commented on the preliminary plan, they reveal the way ideas like constitutionalism, freedom, and Marxism enter the debate over policy. They become vehicles for interested parties to present demands, and they are the mode through which interests are potentially translated into influence for persons who wish to build power plants and homes, cut down trees, or enjoy the beaches. The debate is motivated by desires and fears and carried out with reference to those values that have come to constitute the substance of debate over policy in America.

Although these statements fail to depict fully the personal dimensions behind each group or citizen, they show the more generalizable systems of belief through which policy is approached. It was summaries such as these, rather than the actual experience of the debate, that were ultimately transmitted to the policy makers on the state commissions. The fact that these reports seem to be almost caricatures in their superficiality does not alter the fact that much citizen activity is little more than this sort of thing. Indeed, these views were conveyed with substantially greater richness and in greater depth than they would have been had the citizens expressed their preferences in the traditional way, by means of their vote.

Summary of Joint Public Hearing on Preliminary Plan, Eureka, California

Attendance: From North Coast Commission: Benioff, Brown, Grader, Hedrick, May, McClendon, Peterson; from State Commission: Andresen, Fay, Lane, (Peterson).

Audience: Estimated at 600.

Summary: The meeting was relatively evenly divided between supporters and opponents of the Preliminary Plan. However, because of some confusion with the speakers' lists most of the opponents spoke first with the support trailing off into the early hours of Thursday morning. The five-minute time limit was not enforced until late in the meeting.

Groups Appearing: Statewide interest groups included California Citizens for Property Rights, California Manufacturers Association, Shell Oil

SOURCE: Hearing held in Eureka, Calif., 21 May 1975. This summary is an edited version of the full summary, obtained from California Coastal Zone Conservation Commission, 1540 Market St., San Francisco, Calif. 94102.

Company, and the California Building and Construction Trades Council. Local and regional organizations included Assemblyman Barry Keene, Humboldt County Board of Supervisors, City of Eureka, City of Fortuna, Trinity County Board of Supervisors, Citizens for the Coastal Plan, Redwood Region Chapter of the Audubon Society, Straight Arrow, and the North Coast Chapter of the Associated California Loggers.

Individuals: Forty-nine individuals made presentations with twenty-seven supporting the Plan, twenty-one opposed to the Plan, and one relatively neutral.

Tony Zunone, California Citizens for Property Rights: Opposed to the Plan because it is so broad that the structure of government in this country would have to be changed to carry it out, and because Proposition 20 only intended to save the beaches from development. The planning period does not allow enough time for inventorying resources. North Coast has been editorialized out of the Plan because the State staff and Commission has had no dialogue with the public.

Michael E. Conway, California Manufacturers Association: Favors a Plan which would designate only critical resource areas for protection, prevent the successor agency from impeding economic or energy developments that meet environmental criteria, avoid duplication of authority with other public agencies, protect the integrity of local governments, and minimize delays in project approval. Suggests that the Plan be redrafted along these lines and submitted to another public hearing.

R. F. Karshner, Shell Oil Company: Submitted a written statement recommending that the following provisions be in the Coastal Plan: (1) a definition of the public interest in the coastal zone; (2) a clear provision for the location of economic and energy developments when they comply with environmental and land use criteria; (3) no duplication of regulatory authority in acquiring permits for development in the coastal zone. Furthermore, the coastal agency should have no authority over determining whether there is a need for energy facilities.

Peter Fearey, speaking on behalf of James S. Lee, California Building and Construction Trades Council: According to a recent study by the Security Pacific Bank, much of the unemployment in the construction industry is a direct result of the economic confusion resulting from the passage of Proposition 20 and the uncertainties of its implementation. "Ecology is a cloak for the limousine liberals who are blanketing the country in a deathly fog." Labor cannot support the Plan because it is unresponsive to the economic and social needs of the people.

Bill Fisman, speaking on behalf of Assemblyman Barry Keene: Assemblyman Keene has no position on the Coastal Plan and will base his position on the comments from North Coast residents.

Irv Rennor, Humboldt County Board of Supervisors: Objected because informal public meetings were not held prior to the public hearings, and expressed concern over: the lack of a firm implementation recommendation; the lack of a cost estimate for carrying out the Plan; the disparity between the adopted Humboldt County Plan and the Coastal Plan policies; the all-encompassing nature of the Plan; and the conflict between the coastal agency and existing State agencies.

Jack Segal, City of Eureka: Because the Plan deals in generalities and vague concepts, it provides little direction for land use decisions. The Plan would impose requirement on local governments even though these same local governments are ignored in carrying out the Plan. Moreover, the social and economic consequences of the Plan must be delineated.

. . .

Michael Garabedian, Citizens for the Coastal Plan: Submitted a lengthy statement in support of the Plan which largely refutes the claim that the Plan is causing unemployment along the North Coast. Instead, this is the result of long-term trends in the regional economy over which the Coastal Commission has had no control.

Chuck Seldon, Redwood Region Chapter of the Audubon Society: Supports the Plan and notes that none of the critics of the Plan have come up with alternatives that would address the problems any better than the Plan has.

. . .

Skip Richter, North Coast Chapter of the Associated California Loggers: Proposes that the Coastal Commissions be abolished because there are already 21 governmental agencies that can shut down logging, and because the Commissions are taking the power away from local governments.

. . .

Ted Trickelo: Supports the Plan and an extension of the Commissions without elected officials on them so that lagoons, beaches, and marshes of Lake Earl can be protected.

. . .

William Van Fleet: As an architect/planner, he supports the Plan because it gets out in front of future growth and sets up comprehensive means of dealing with it, but he is concerned that access not be provided to fragile areas, and finds the North Coast Plan maps to be inadequate because of their lack of detail. Recommends that the Plan be carried out by an agency similar to the present Commission with all members appointed.

. . .

Katherine Nelson, Bear River: The Plan is impractical and unworkable. The Plan pits the environment against the economy. We can have both if we leave land management to private owners who are the best environmentalists because they must obey the laws of nature . . . .

. . .

Nancy Roloss, Trinidad: Extend the existing structure until a single statewide planning agency which can coordinate State and local land use plans is formed. The Regional Commissions should prepare specific plans and the State Commission should resolve conflicts and hear appeals.

Mr. Deline, Fortuna: The coast is as important as Yosemite and should be protected by extending the existing structure until local governments can develop acceptable plans. The management system should be supported by statewide taxes and land should be acquired for public use at fair market value. Inland resources should be regulated if they affect coast areas. There is economic justification for coastal protection because of all the activities that are dependent on coastal resources.

Gary Roberts, Arcata: Supports the Plan which is a landmark document and recommends that the Commission structure be made permanent.

. . .

Sean Kern: Supports the agricultural protections policies because "there's a fungus amungus in runaway construction." The State must serve the people and not the corporate octupi. "If you don't want to end up in the same boat as southern California, don't jump in the boat." Wanted to know why all the people who opposed the Plan were allowed to speak first.

. . .

E. H. Peterson: Claims that tax dollars are being used to teach people that all the land belongs to all the people, when in reality the land belongs to the people who pay the taxes. Complained that he can't get his land zoned for commercial use because the local government is waiting for the State Coastal Commission to decide what to do about the Eureka freeway.

. . .

Richard Dinbo: The North Coast Region would accept urban sprawl if it would reduce unemployment. There are too many students on welfare and getting food stamps.

Barbara Barratt: Supports the Plan and submitted a detailed series of suggestions for sources of revenue including Federal assistance; tideland oil revenues; property transfer and State income taxes; user fees, and a tax on commercial fishing catch.

. . .

John Armedo, Bayside: Supports the Plan because the North Coast economy is based on resource exploitation and the resources need management for long-term benefits. Respect for property rights also includes property owners respect for their responsibilities in managing the land.

William L. Shapeero: Supports the Plan because local governments have been responsive to local needs when they involve housing and jobs but have not been able to address resource protection which is a public need but is an externality in our present economic system. Countered the argument that the Plan is unconstitutional by pointing out that much of what the Plan advocates has been upheld in courts for years and that the questionable new ideas will not be adopted by the State Legislature unless there is a fair chance they will stand up in court.

. . .

Michael P. Digiler, Arcata: Supports the Plan and is especially concerned about oil spills and sand supply loss. Favors an extension of the present Commissions with some limitation on which cases can be appealed to the State Commission. Permit fees charged of developers should be kept down.

. . .

Elizabeth Smith: All communist invasions begin with land reform. The Commission is a Trojan horse with Marxism inside.

Hillary Packer, Elk River: Would like to live in an area regulated by the Commission because the land around her has been despoiled by developers.

. . .

Terry Woodin, Eureka: Supports the Plan and its agricultural land protection measures and its protection of private property rights which can come only with a well-defined and well-regulated zoning system.

. . .

Mrs. Charles Pedrotti: Opposed to the Plan because the North Coast was beautiful before the establishment of the National Redwood Park (which, she claims, is unneeded) and before the passage of Proposition 20 which caused unemployment in the timber industry. "With all the county laws I do not believe we will have the dense growth of southern California."

Carrying Out the Plan

These following selections are taken from the final plan submitted to the state legislature in December 1975. They indicate the choices made with respect to the way coastal decision making would be carried out if the legislature accepted the plan. With the presentation of the plan, the public policy made by the citizens of California through popular initiative ran its course, and future enforcement would depend on decisions made by the elected representatives in the state legislatures.

Selection from the Final Coastal Plan Submitted to the California Legislature, December 1975

No plan dealing with controversial matters is likely to be self-enforcing. The Coastal Plan thus recommends that the following implementation program be established:

Local Government Responsibilities for the Coast

Because city and county government is accessible and accountable to its constituents, because statewide coastal concerns should be reflected in local planning and regulation, and because Plan implementation should be streamlined to reduce costs and delays, primary responsibilities for carrying out the Coastal Plan should rest with local governments. Within three years of the effective date of State legislation to carry out the Plan, local governments along the coast should be required to bring their General Plans into conformity with the Coastal Plan. Local governments would submit their plans to the Regional and State Coastal Commissions for certification as to conformity with the Coastal Plan. After all the local plans in a region had been certified, the Regional Commission would go out of existence. Local governments would then control coastal conservation and development, subject to a system of limited appeals to the State Commission to insure that approved local plans and thus the Coastal Plan were being followed in day-to-day decisions.

Coastal Resource Management Area

Because the Coastal Plan seeks to provide for the wise use and protection of coastal resources, local plans would be required to conform to the Coastal Plan in an area designated as the coastal resource management area. This area . . . is the area of varying width along the coast containing the coastal waters, wetlands, beaches, bluffs, agricultural lands, and coastal communities and neighborhoods that are the subject of Plan policies. In some cities, the coastal resource management area is *less* wide than the 1,000-yard permit area established in the 1972 Coastal Act (Proposition 20). In rural areas and other areas of undeveloped land, the resource management area may extend to the inland boundary of the coastal zone to include coastal agricultural lands and streams and areas where the cumulative impact of development would limit public access to the coast (e.g., Malibu, Big Sur). As provided by the 1972 Coastal Act, the California coastal zone is the water areas under State jurisdiction, the offshore islands, and land areas inland to the highest elevation of the nearest coastal mountain range, except that in Los Angeles, Orange, and San Diego Counties, the boundary does not extend more than five miles from the mean high tide line.

Permit and Appeals System

To insure that unwise development decisions do not occur while local plans are being brought into conformity with the Coastal Plan, the permit and appeals system specified in the 1972 Coastal Act would remain in effect except that (1) the standards for issuing and denying permits would be compliance with the Coastal Plan, not the 1972 Coastal Act; (2) permits would also be required within the coastal resource management area for the conversion of any prime agricultural land to other uses and the conversion of other agricultural land in parcels of 20 acres or more; (3) anywhere within the coastal zone, a Commission permit would be required for major water, sewer, transportation, or energy developments that could adversely affect coastal resources; and (4) permits would *not* be required where a Regional Commission (or the State Commission, on appeal) determined after public hearing that development of a particular type or in a particular area would not adversely affect coastal resources.

Permits and Appeals After Certification

After a local plan has been certified by the Coastal Commissions as being in conformity with the Coastal Plan, local governments would have primary implementation responsibility, subject to a system of limited appeals to the State Coastal Commission to insure that the approved local plan and the Coastal Plan were being followed in day-to-day conservation and development decisions.

State Coastal Agency

After the Regional Commissions have gone out of existence, a State Coastal Commission with 12 members — one-third appointed by the Governor, one-third by the Speaker of the Assembly, and one-third by the Senate Rules Committee — would have the following responsibilities: (1) carry out the planning and research necessary to keep the Coastal Plan up to date in light of changing conditions; (2) assist local governments in Plan implementation; and (3) through the appeals process, monitor the decisions on proposed coastal conservation and development.

State and Federal Agency Responsibilities

The Plan provides that all State agencies, and all Federal agencies to the extent applicable under Federal law, be required to conduct their activities in full compliance with Coastal Plan policies. The Coastal Commission would seek to insure that California maintains a Coastal Plan complying with the standards of the Federal Coastal Zone Management Act of 1972, thus qualifying the State for Federal funds to help carry out the Plan, and also insuring that Federal agencies would be required to follow the Plan unless an overriding national interest compelled other actions.

Proposed Bond Issue

The Plan proposes that a limited number of key coastal properties be bought by the public, primarily for oceanfront recreation and for the protection of wildlife habitat. Based on assessments by county assessors, the parcels *tentatively* proposed for acquisition have a total market value of about $180 million. Because of inflation, and because some assessments have not been updated recently, estimates may be low with regard to some parcels. On the other hand, the total cost may be reduced by eliminating some parcels from the list (the Commissions are continuing to review the acquisition proposals) and by purchasing easements rather than full title in some cases. The Plan proposes that, after further review of the proposed acquisitions, a bond issue be submitted to the voters of California in 1976 to pay for prompt purchase of coastal properties.

Costs of Carrying Out the Plan and Possible Sources of Funds

Costs of carrying out the Coastal Plan are (1) the cost of land acquisition, not expected to exceed $180 million to $200 million together with some additional operating and maintenance costs to park agencies as new beaches and parks are opened; (2) the cost of Coastal Commission permit and appeals administration, estimated at $1 million to $1.5 million per year; (3) the cost of further Coastal Commission planning to keep the Coastal Plan up to date and to assist local governments in Plan implementation, estimated at $1 million to $1.5 million per year; and (4) the cost to local governments of bringing their plans into conformity with the Coastal Plan, estimated at $600,000 to $800,000 per year for three years.

The Plan proposes that these costs be paid from several possible sources:

• The bond issue cited above;
• Federal acquisition grants from the U.S. Land and Water Conservation Fund;
• Federal planning grants (once California's Coastal Plan has been certified as in compliance with the Federal Coastal Zone Management Act of 1972, Cali-

fornia will be eligible for two-thirds of the planning and administrative costs of carrying out the Plan);
• Taxes on the production and transport of petroleum on and across California coastal waters, because a principal purpose of coastal planning is to provide adequately for needed energy production consistent with environmental protection; and
• Perhaps from added fees on pleasure boats or added taxes on visitor accommodations in coastal areas, in both cases requiring those who benefit most from coastal recreation and amenities to help pay the costs of protecting the coast.

THE LEGAL BASIS FOR STATEWIDE PLANNING

The State of California has legal power to regulate and control land use. This regulation, using such forms as zoning, is part of the inherent power possessed by all States and is commonly called the police power — the power to regulate public and private activity to protect the health, safety, and welfare of the general public.

The California Constitution and other State laws delegate certain police powers, including the power to plan and control land use, to cities and counties in carrying out their local or municipal affairs. The State, however, retains the ability to plan, protect resources, and even control land use in areas or on subjects of greater than local concern.

As one court has said in a case involving the Coastal Commissions, "Where the ecological or environmental impact of land use affect[s] the people of the entire State, they can no longer remain matters of purely local concern." The court added that "the impact of an activity which in times past has been purely local, may under changed circumstances transcend municipal boundaries .... Where the activity, whether municipal or private, is one that can affect persons outside the city, the State is empowered to prohibit or regulate the externalities" [*Ceed v. California Coastal Zone Conservation Commission,* 118 Cal. Rptr, 315 (1975)].

After the plan was submitted to the legislature, the process, which had begun with frustration in that body, threatened to come full circle. The same interests that thwarted legislative efforts four years earlier tried to block the adoption of the final plan. But one major difference was national policy in this area: although it does not mandate state action, the National Coastal Zone Management Act of 1972 provides added financial incentives, a promise of national cooperation in governing federal land along the coast, and a national example to stimulate legislative action in California. Another major difference was the support of Governor Jerry Brown. The early version of the plan died in committee, but the Governor arranged a compromise — which included phasing out the regional commissions — in order to avoid the active opposition of organized labor. On 23 August 1976, the California Senate approved permanent controls on development of the coast.

FURTHER READINGS FOR CHAPTER 6

Callies, David, and Fred Bosselman, *The Quiet Revolution in Land Use Control* (Prepared for the Council on Environmental Quality, Washington, D.C., U.S. Government Printing Office, 1972). A professional view of the changes that have taken place in the legal conception of private ownership of land.

Devine, Donald, *The Political Culture of the United States* (Boston: Little, Brown and Company, 1972). Integrates philosophical and empirical studies to present the nature of American's political beliefs.

Mogulof, Melvin B., *Saving the Coast: California's Experiment in Intergovernmental Land Use Control* (Lexington, Mass.: Lexington Books, 1975). Emphasis on the creation of a new sort of governmental agency through the initiative process.

1 2 3 4 5 6 7 8 9 0